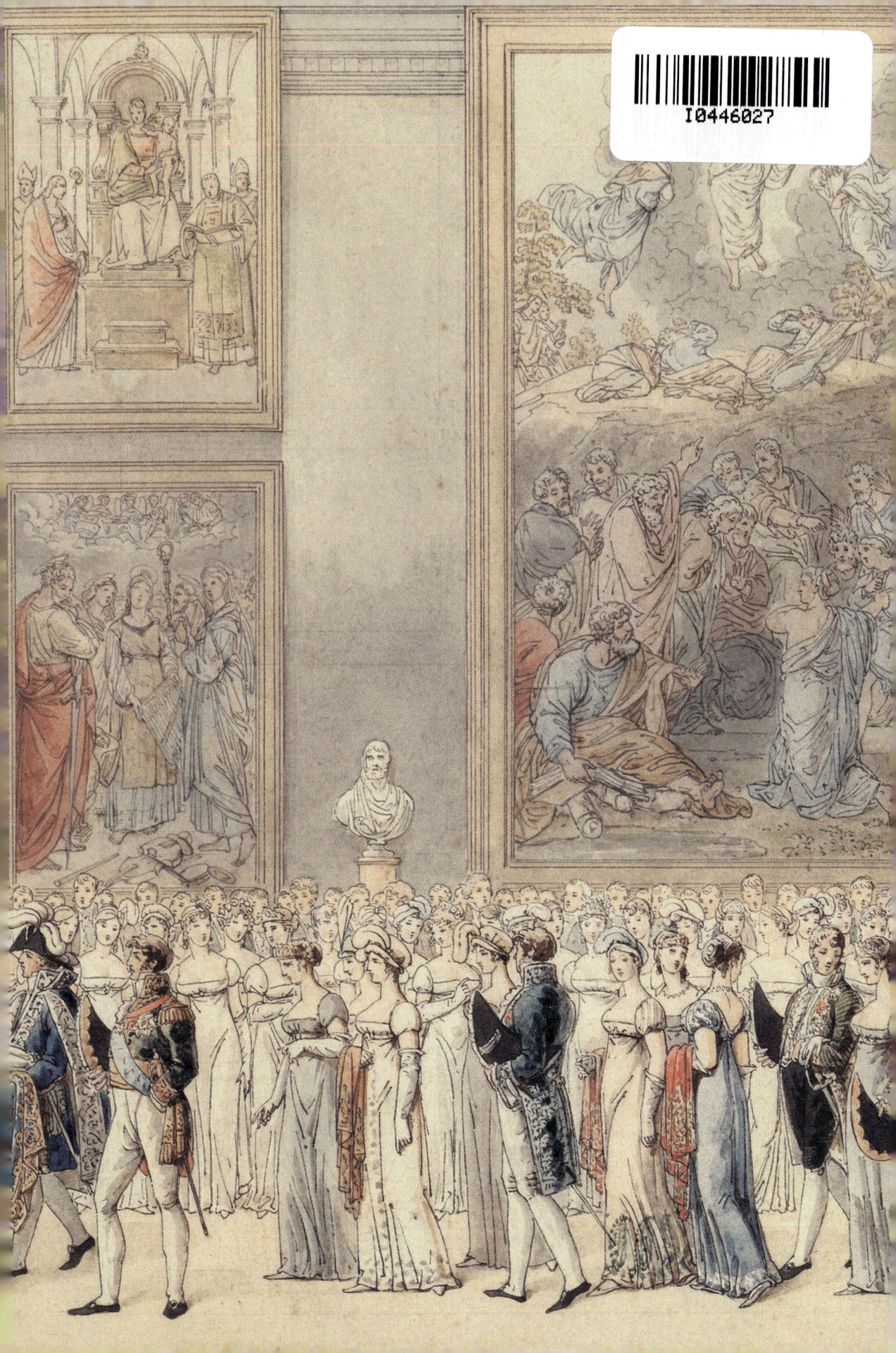

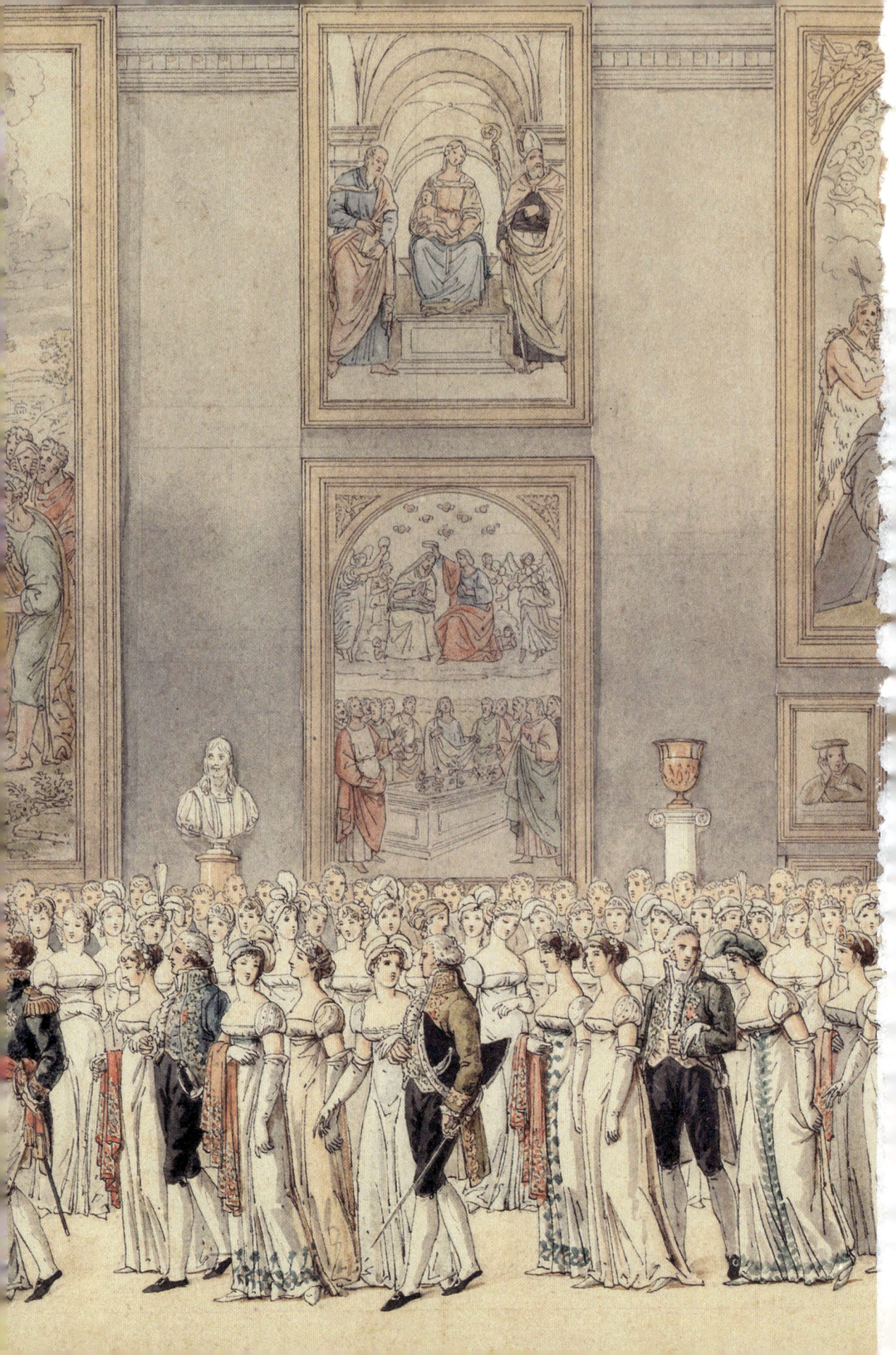

Restoration

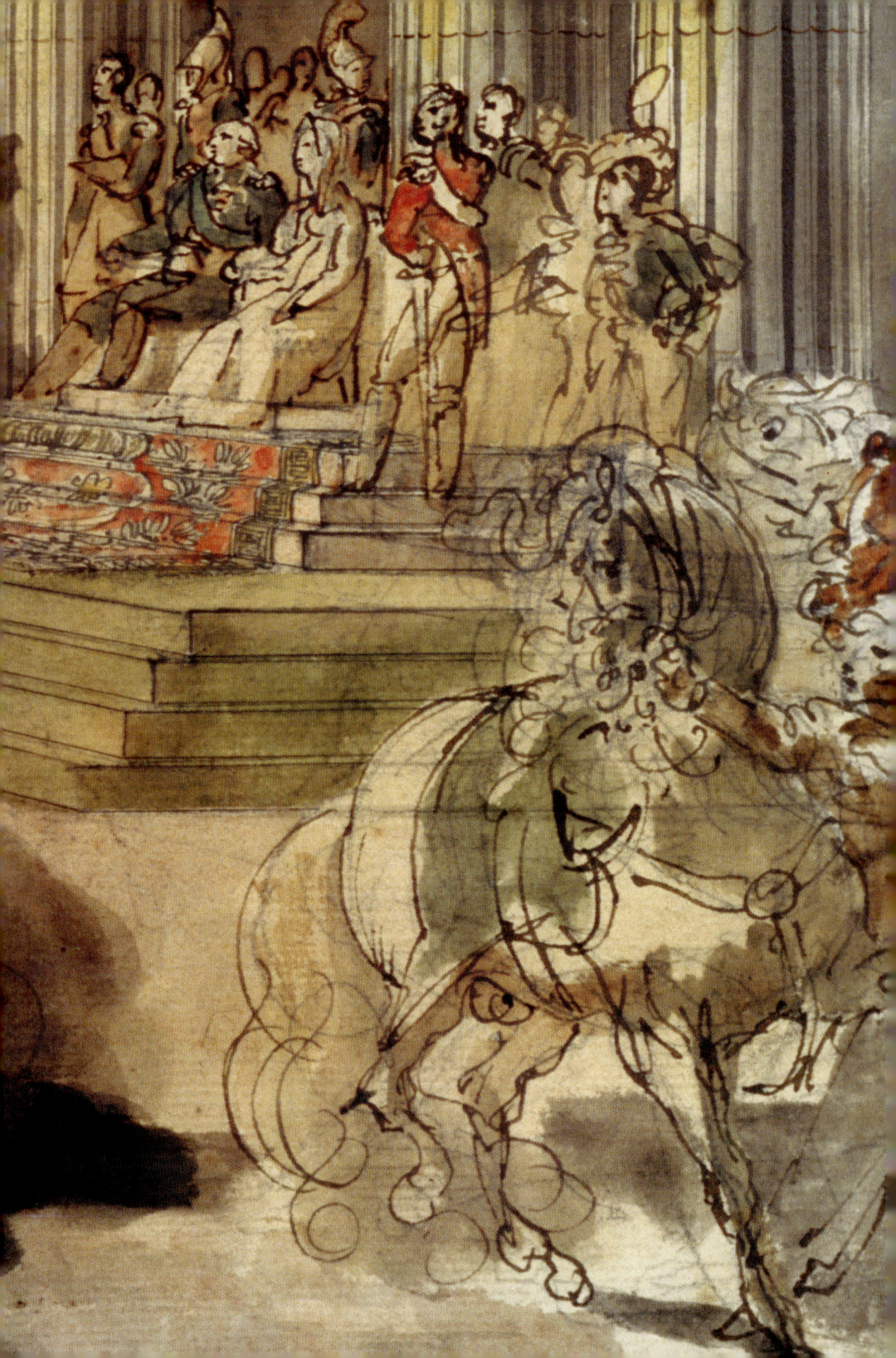

Thomas Crow

Restoration

The Fall of Napoleon
in the Course of European Art,
1812–1820

Princeton University Press
Princeton and Oxford

The A. W. Mellon Lectures in the Fine Arts
National Gallery of Art, Washington
Bollingen Series XXXV: VOL 64

Copyright © 2018 by Board of Trustees, National Gallery of Art, Washington

Requests for permission to reproduce material from this work should be sent to Permissions, Princeton University Press

Published by Princeton University Press, 41 William Street, Princeton, New Jersey 08540

In the United Kingdom: Princeton University Press, 6 Oxford Street, Woodstock, Oxfordshire OX20 1TR

press.princeton.edu

Jacket illustrations: (*front*) Jacques-Louis David, *Bonaparte Crossing the Alps* (detail), c. 1801, oil on canvas, 102 × 87 in. (259 × 221 cm), Châteaux de Malmaison et Bois-Préau, Rueil-Malmaison. © RMN-Grand Palais / Art Resource, NY. Photo by Gérard Blot; (*back*) Théodore Géricault, *African Signaling*, study for *Raft of the Medusa*, 1819, oil on canvas, Musée de Montauban.

Endpapers: Benjamin Zix, *The Wedding Procession of Napoleon and Marie Louise of Austria through the Grande Galerie of the Louvre, April 2, 1810*, 1810, pen and ink with watercolor, 67¾ × 9½ in. (172 × 24 cm), Musée du Louvre, Paris.

Frontispiece: Théodore Géricault, *King Louis XVIII Reviews the Troops at the Champ de Mars*, c. 1814, ink and watercolor (detail), 10⅛ × 14 in. (25.8 × 35.5 cm), Musée du Louvre, Paris.

ISBN 978-0-691-18164-6
Library of Congress Control Number: 2018940957

This is the sixty-fourth volume of the A. W. Mellon Lectures in the Fine Arts, which are delivered annually at the National Gallery of Art, Washington. This volume is based on lectures delivered in 2015. The volumes of lectures constitute Number XXXV in the Bollingen Series, supported by the Bollingen Foundation.

British Library Cataloging-in-Publication Data is available

Designed by Jeff Wincapaw

This book has been composed in Calluna
Printed on acid-free paper. ∞
Printed in China

10 9 8 7 6 5 4 3 2 1

Contents

Introduction

THE ORIGIN OF THESE STUDIES, which examine the experiences of artists at the fall of the French Empire, began in curiosity about Jacques-Louis David's final artistic phase in Brussels, his place of exile from 1816 as a proscribed revolutionary regicide. The work of his final Belgian period has been underestimated when not disparaged for its seeming awkwardness and incongruities, as if his gifts had deserted him. No more than a first level of examination, however, reveals David taking remarkable liberties with the accepted rules of painting in the period—protocols he had done as much as anyone to define—in order to figure the changed circumstances of his existence, while mordantly reflecting on the immense historical processes that had left him to one side.

Looking outward from this one instance of a defining cultural figure displaced to peripheral status, unexpected movements across old boundaries—whether geographical, religious, national, or social—came into focus as transforming the cultural networks of the period. Alongside human actors, art objects were likewise set in motion; the restoration of the works of art transported to Paris by Napoleon Bonaparte's armies made for a drama in itself. Their fate uncertain, the great Vatican antiquities—the *Laocoön*, the *Belvedere Apollo*, the *Belvedere Torso*—loomed large in the pan-European imagination as symbols of all the larger attempts to restore the pre-Napoleonic status quo. Venetian sculptor Antonio Canova assumed the role of roving diplomat pursuing their repatriation. In that capacity, he linked himself to a new set of patrons in England and struck up a close relationship with Thomas Lawrence, their portraitist of choice, who was setting out for the Continent on an unprecedented commission to commemorate the victory of the allies in a mammoth suite of individual portraits.

Key to this part of the inquiry are the pendant portraits that Lawrence painted on arriving in Rome, one of Pope Pius VII and the other of his chief minister, Cardinal Ercole Consalvi. Taken together, these paintings mark an unexpected pinnacle of quality and complexity in Lawrence's capacities as an artist, belying the persistent perception of his output as superficial flattery. The very fact of pope and prelate being portrayed by an English artist at all, in light of the anti-Catholicism deeply engrained in English law and custom, bespeaks a deep unsettling of old orders. These canvases would not have taken their accomplished form—arguably the premier ecclesiastical images of the era—were it not for the rapprochement of an elite British circle, Whig in orientation and close to the prince regent, with a brand of administratively enlightened Catholicism open to foreign and even Protestant allies.

As the Vatican representative in the cross-European negotiations surrounding the Congress of Vienna, Consalvi had won friends in

London, subsequently becoming a central figure within a remarkable colony of expatriate British aristocrats who took up residence in Rome shortly after hostilities were over. Highly consequential in a number of domains—from the return of the Vatican's artistic treasures to the restoration of the old Papal States by Austria under successful British pressure—this Anglo-Italian network represents one visible instance of a larger relational field that emerged from the confusion of interests and affinities that followed Waterloo.

As Consalvi set about transforming the fabric of Rome in line with its function as key meeting ground for the post-Waterloo network of European culture, the large community of foreign artists in the city established their own micronetworks, frequently across confessional boundaries, that paralleled the large, cross-European connections that frame this study. The young J.A.D. Ingres, once a David pupil but by this point a conservatively minded Roman expatriate, greeted the pope's return with a sense of vindication. He sent to Paris a depiction of Pius VII enthroned amid pomp in the Sistine Chapel, a small but dense riposte to the pontiff's symbolic humiliation as depicted in his master's gargantuan, teeming *Coronation of Josephine*.

David and Pius VII, as it happens, had formed a surprising personal bond during the latter's sittings for the *Coronation*, and the artist kept a papal portrait near at hand during his Brussels years. As David's young Belgian followers made their way to Rome, however, their master would doubtless have been dismayed to witness his protégé's attraction, alongside Ingres, to the eccentric piety of the German Nazarene artists. At the same time, Théodore Géricault, the most consequential artist to come of age in this moment, stalked the city virtually unnoticed, drawn as much to raw aspects of plebeian existence as to the monuments he had made his pilgrimage to see— in this an unwitting echo of the distant, disaffected Francisco Goya, a David contemporary likewise fallen from favor. After returning to Paris, the youthful Géricault would transform what was possible in the art of his time. Not only did the profoundly important *Raft of the Medusa* emerge from his labors, he would also anticipate that watershed canvas with three monumental landscapes, grimly enigmatic, dystopic, and off-putting to most observers, but unexpectedly cogent in light of unseen causes. No one in Europe then had any inkling of the titanic eruption in April 1815 from Mount Tambora in the Javanese archipelago, but a great many suffered from the global climate changes engendered by it.

Traveling across the Alps to Rome in the autumn of 1816, returning a year later in the same season, Géricault had ample opportunity to witness and endure the storm-borne privations induced by natural catastrophes across the continent, deepening when not overtaking the pervasive disquiet induced by darkly portentous political events.

His art encompassed manifold facets of the Restoration, condensing and exemplifying the wider currents from which it emerged. Much the same can be said of the five other narrative threads that make up this book: David's art and pedagogy in exile; the vicissitudes of the campaign to restore the art expropriated by the French; Lawrence's painted constellation of Restoration grandees; Ingres's campaign to reconcile religious art with contemporary mentalities; and the brief ascents of youthful stars like the French Antoine Jean-Baptiste Thomas and the Belgian François-Joseph Navez, whose scintillating artistic moments came and went with the political turbulence. The hereditary rulers of European states—abetted by their generals, ministers, and sundry advisors—were united in the conviction that changes effected from the French Revolution of 1789 to the abdication of Napoleon in 1814 had to be rolled back. But artistic change is never so accelerated or unpredictable as when forces gather to stop it, still more when those in authority make a concentrated effort to put things back to some prior, irrecoverable state of affairs.

At certain exceptional moments, the flux of change itself makes an appearance in a work of art. In 1814, Géricault had enlisted in the reconstituted royal guard surrounding the new monarch, Louis XVIII, scion of the restored Bourbon dynasty. That commitment left him some time for making art, which Géricault used to sketch a potential painting of the king reviewing the artist's fellow guardsmen maneuvering on the Champ de Mars from the steps of the national military academy (l'École Militaire) (frontispiece; fig. 2.16). He placed the figure of Louis XVIII, not so obviously obese as he was in life, between the columns at one side, his precise delineation of the seated monarch giving way in the foreground to massed horsemen dissolved in a fluidly indistinct cloud of half-rendered possibilities.

Finished works of art produced in settled circumstances mask the disparate fragments from which they are fashioned. When disruptive events intervene, as they dramatically did around 1814, established formations and expectations break apart and the liberated fragments can be released to go their own way—much as they appear to do on the left side of Géricault's composition. Observing the ways in which these wayward components could be resynthesized into cogent new works is the closest thing we have to capturing change on the wing, and understanding change is the essence of any history worth the name.

Chapter 1

Moscow Burns/ The Pope Comes Home

David, Gros, and Ingres Test Empire's Facade

ANY ACCOUNT OF WHAT HAPPENED to the collective mind of Europe with the towering figure of Napoleon removed will require at its beginning an examination of the emperor as an imaginative construct, so better to gauge the effects of his withdrawal. There are few more resonant examples of this construct—by date, circumstances, and quality—than the 1812 portrait by Jacques-Louis David, *Emperor Napoleon in His Study at the Tuileries* (fig. 1.1) This particular painting would appear a consummate image of the ruler's authority and self-sufficiency. Each of his virtues is represented by a pointed accessory within the picture: an edition of Plutarch's exemplary ancient *Lives* on the floor (fig. 1.1a), candles burned down to their ends (fig. 1.1b), the floor-standing clock reading the predawn hour (fig. 1.1c), the sword belt awaiting his striding forth at dawn to review his troops (fig. 1.1d), all these attributes and more interlocked with the precision of a completed jigsaw puzzle.

At that date Napoleon still brims with confidence in the prospects for his empire. Although executed two years before the official onset of the Restoration in May 1814, David's portrait of the ruler at the height of his powers nonetheless betrays symptoms pointing to the coming collapse. For a start, the time of the painting is out of joint. The emperor appears in his habitual uniform of 1812, adorned with imperial decorations of that same moment. But the task in which he is shown to be immersed, the one that viewers are enjoined to applaud and admire, occurred a good eight years before: the fiction of the portrait is that its subject had worked through the night drafting the Napoleonic Code (promulgated in March 1804), his rationalized, democratized body of law drafted to replace the unequal patchwork of feudal inheritance in every French territory. David includes the word Code on the rolled paper above the hilt of the sword, but that fanciful parchment does not reveal that a sizable commission had completed this body of law years before as a bound volume of over nine hundred pages. What was more, this undeniably colossal achievement occurred before the First Consul Bonaparte had elevated himself to the station of emperor; thus, David tacitly calls attention to that highly contestable self-coronation, contrasting adherence to Republican forms with the currently autocratic condition of empire.

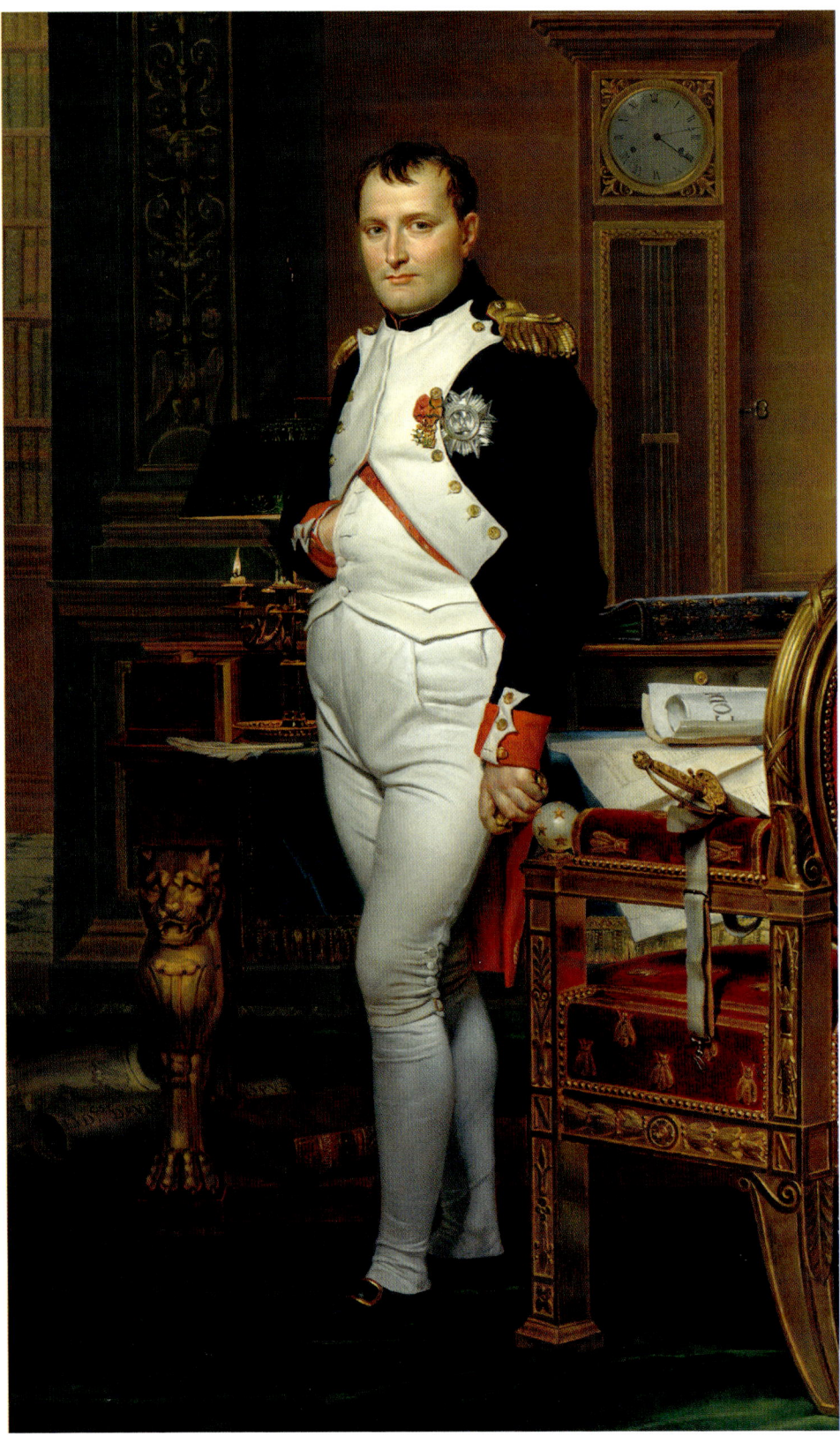

I.I

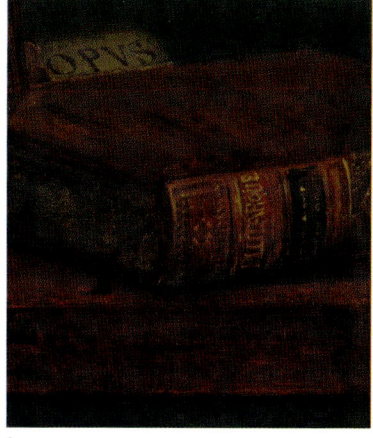
a

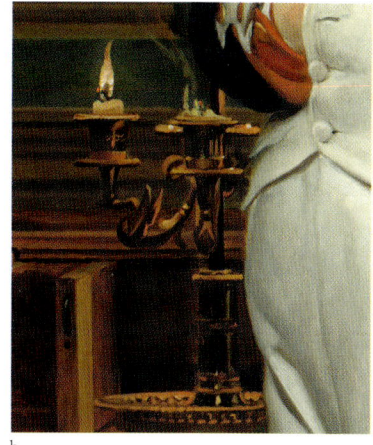
b

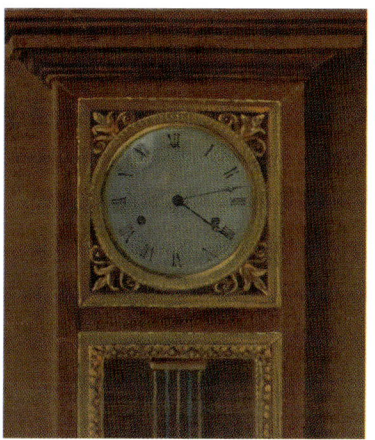
c

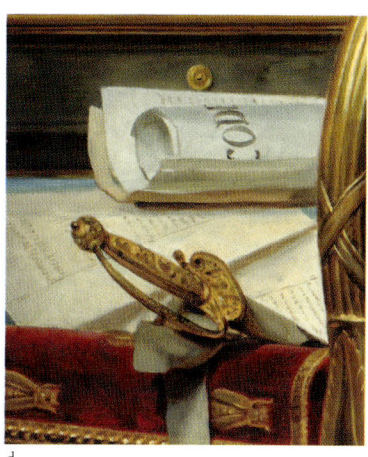
d

I.I. Jacques-Louis David, *The Emperor Napoleon in His Study at the Tuileries*, 1812, oil on canvas, 80¼ × 49¼ in. (203.9 × 125.1 cm), National Gallery of Art, Washington, DC.
a. detail (book on floor)
b. detail (candles)
c. detail (clock)
d. detail (sword belt)

The implications of that discrepancy would not for long have escaped a French audience, which brings up the second point: the portrait was not intended for a French audience. It was going where no wide respect for Republican norms existed, indeed where the opposite was the case. *Napoleon in His Study* did not arise from transactions with the emperor or with any of his agents; it is indeed highly unlikely that the emperor ever posed for it or even saw the completed canvas. The portrait came into existence entirely outside of official channels, a transaction between David and a British nobleman: the Marquis of Douglas, later Duke of Hamilton, the commission conveyed to the artist from Scotland[1] (fig. 1.2). During the period from Douglas's first inquiry in mid-1811 until the emperor's portrait was shipped in November 1812 (to be belatedly delivered to the patron early in 1813), France and Britain were at war, as they had been since the ostensible date of David's scenario.[2]

And not just any state of war. The actual date of the painting in 1812 can only call to mind the invasion of Russia by Napoleon's

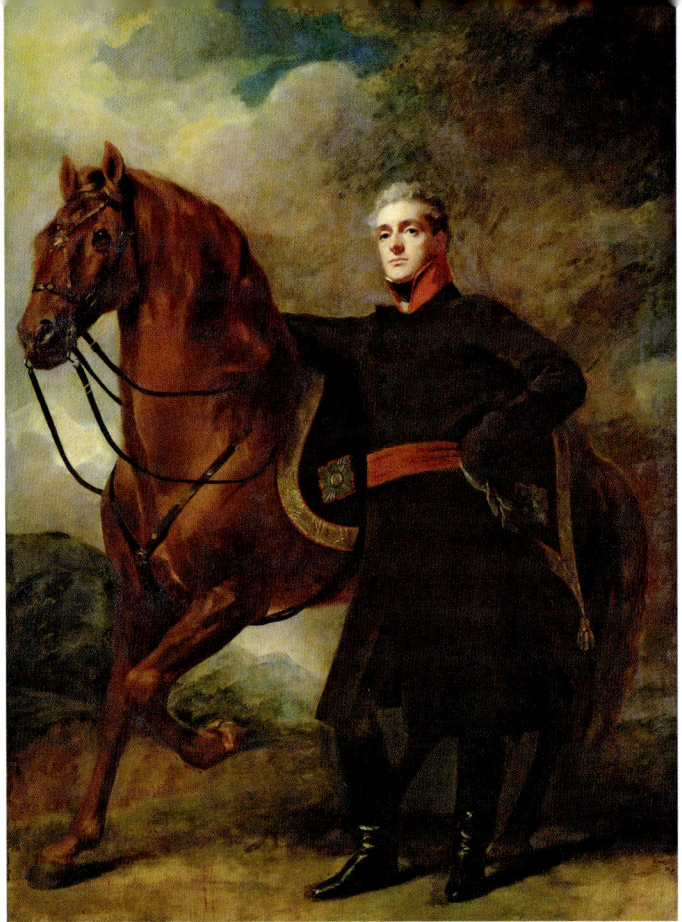

Grand Army. The Russians were in fact ostensible French allies at the time, as were the Prussians and Austrians, through whose territory imperial forces had to pass unmolested along the way. All of these countries were at that point part of Napoleon's "Continental System," and therein lay the source of conflict. The condition of alliance with France was maintaining a trade embargo against Britain, the paramount and enduring enemy. Napoleon led his army to Russia in order to enforce that rule (fig. 1.3). As Russia and Britain had previously been traditional trading partners, the embargo had hit an isolated Russia especially hard. Naturally the Continental System was beginning to leak, and Napoleon wanted it stopped.

These circumstances point up a third, nested contradiction within the work. Not only was Britain the cause of Napoleon's catastrophic attempt to police Russian behavior, but it was also in early 1812 successfully engaging the French on the ground in Spain. Under the command of Arthur Wellesley, the future Duke of Wellington, British-led forces were pushing the French back toward Madrid from a base in Portugal, but the main French army was proceeding far away from the action toward the opposite end of the continent. Absent these pressures and reverses at France's rear in the so-called Peninsular War, the Russian invasion might have had a different outcome.

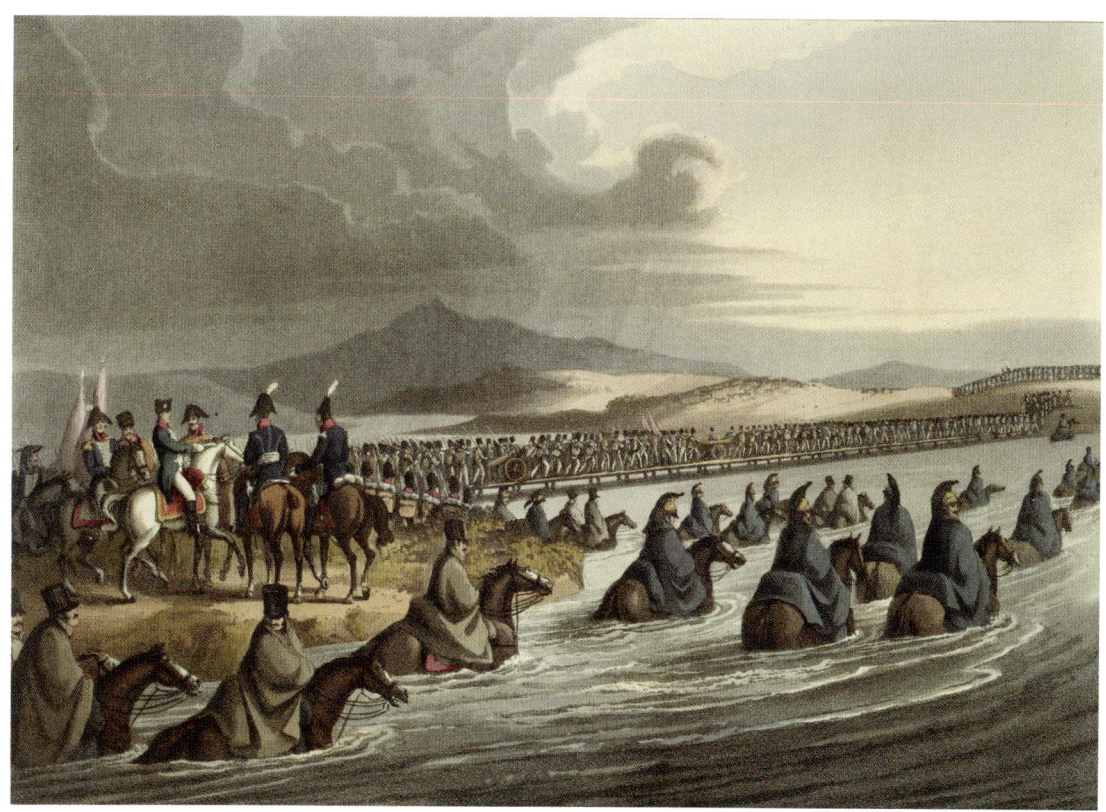

1.3. John Heaviside Clark, engraved by Matthew Dubourg, *The Boasted Crossing of the Nieman, at the Opening of the Campaign of 1812, by N. Bonaparte*, 1816, engraving, The British Library.

Given the appalling losses and profound humiliation visited on French military prestige as Napoleon retreated from enforcement of the anti-British embargo, it might come as some surprise that David was able openly to trade with the enemy over his 1812 portrait of Napoleon. There had been, as might be expected, the granting of exceptions and licenses that made the trade embargo with Britain less than absolute, but nothing so formal entered into David's transaction. There was a powerful sense in which the artist could even have been construed as having appropriated the ruler's image for his own advantage. Such a transfer of symbolic capital gave rise to the urban legend of the period that Napoleon had visited David's studio to demand the painting for himself, then kicked it in when the artist refused.[3]

Fourthly, the fact that a British patron was seeking from David a celebration of a ruler deemed by the great majority of Britons as the virtual Antichrist points to an instability of national loyalties engendered by Napoleon's scrambling the map of Europe. While Lord Douglas had served the British Crown as ambassador to Russia in 1806, he was also very much a Scottish peer, so Scottish in fact that he imagined himself—ignoring the abject Pretender in Rome—the heir to the Stuart dynasty, overthrown in 1688 on account of the Catholic allegiance of James II. And Douglas indeed shared that same confessional commitment and saw himself as the legitimate successor to the current, discredited dynasty; that is, the mad George III and his wastrel heir, the prince regent and future George IV. The Scotsman had, moreover, already been fraternizing with the enemy in Napoleonic Rome around 1804, forging a particular bond with Napoleon's flamboyant sister Pauline, princess Paolina Borghese by marriage.

David's final effort to secure a plausible totem of imperial authority thus intimates, both explicitly and tacitly, the disarray into which the empire was about to collapse. Only by a consummate effort of formal discipline was the artist able to make these seen and unseen fissures cohere into a convincing simulacrum of the man both he and his patron regarded as an incomparable being. The outcome was a sealed, claustrophobic interior packed with abstract, allegorical tokens of what had once seemed a secure and merited European hegemony, recalled by the rolled map that lies at Napoleon's feet. David declared to Douglas, pertaining to their common hero: "any effort of the imagination must always fall short of the reality."[4] As 1812 wore on, of course, reality was precisely the problem. Ways in which to show the majestic, commanding qualities of Napoleon distributed across the wide sphere of combat seemed, as the Grand Army suffered one dispiriting reversal after another, to be drying up.

✳

There was one artist above all who had demonstrated the ability to present the emperor's exploits and virtues within a plausible sampling of the world in which they manifested themselves: that was the David pupil and consummate battle painter, Antoine-Jean Gros. But what could even Gros make of the events of 1812, which were complex and ramified beyond even their military immensity?

While Napoleon's Russian invasion had begun as a trade dispute, it is less often remarked that the expedition took on outsized imperialistic ambition. Included among its ranks were hundreds of seamstresses, embroiderers, musicians, and banquet masters, with imperial scepter and robe packed and ready—hardly the accouterments of a mere police mission. The emperor set himself up in lavish temporary courts along the way, first in Vienna, where he displaced the emperor, his new father-in-law, from his own palace, and then in Dresden, the Saxon capital. It has come to light that French expatriates in Moscow were surreptitiously planning a new coronation, for which the pope would again be summoned to preside.[5] Napoleon appears to have had no less an ambition than to recrown himself Universal Emperor. His happy and successful marriage to the daughter of the Austrian emperor (Josephine having been conveniently divorced), capped by the birth of a legitimately royal son in 1811, made the relatively modest, almost bourgeois character of David's *Napoleon in His Study* seem seriously out of step with that new course of Empire.

In the wake of another mutual decimation at the Battle of Borodino, the French entered Moscow largely unchallenged, next to no Russian troops in evidence. But that same night hidden arsonists sent the city up in flames, denying Napoleon both his material base and his imagined capital in the East. Had Napoleon's plans come to pass for making Moscow his gateway to Asia, Gros would have found himself with an entirely different set of tasks before him. In the end, the carriage transporting the imperial paraphernalia for the new coronation was despoiled by Cossacks, one of whom wrapped himself in the emperor's mantle, while Napoleon's prospective capital burned around them.[6]

Denied any grandiose triumph as a subject, Gros returned to the older theme, close to David's from the year before, of Bonaparte as exemplary public servant bringing the blessings of French humanity to Russians perceived as victims of their own inhumane leadership. Such is the argument of the large presentation drawing, nearly a meter across, that Gros produced in anticipation of a painting that he would never be in a position to complete[7] (fig. 1.4). In Gros's rendering of the night Moscow burned, executed between 1812 and 1813, the emperor assumes an upright pose of stationary command: bareheaded, in similar uniform to David's ensemble of 1812 with sole addition of equestrian boots (fig. 1.4a). The buff ground of the sheet does duty as surrogate for the noxiously illuminated nocturnal atmosphere. As aptly described by the artist's first biographer in 1868: "An immense conflagration lights up the vast scene. An entire city serves to feed these flames reaching up to the clouds, their illumination equal to the day. So storied Moscow celebrates her own funeral."[8]

Attempting to manifest his subject's state of mind in the face of the ruin of his hopes, Gros can do no better than to turn the emperor's left arm in the opposite direction from the leftward turn of his head, seeming to ward off the supplications of the Muscovites variously worshipping or defying his authority. The darker lower right contains the unconverted and doomed. One of a defiant pair of captured arsonists in old Russian dress, their spent torches discarded on the ground, urged forward by imperial guardsmen, points to the sky to invoke the higher power he follows (fig. 1.4b). On the opposite side, the converted rise from darkness, one French soldier even reenacting the Trojan hero Aeneas hoisting his aged father on his back while leading his son out of the burning ruins. A brightly lit, ecstatically relieved woman rushes to embrace the trio (fig. 1.4c). The combination of this female figure with two others in ambiguously frenzied attitudes enacts some ungovernable release of emotion, conveyed by

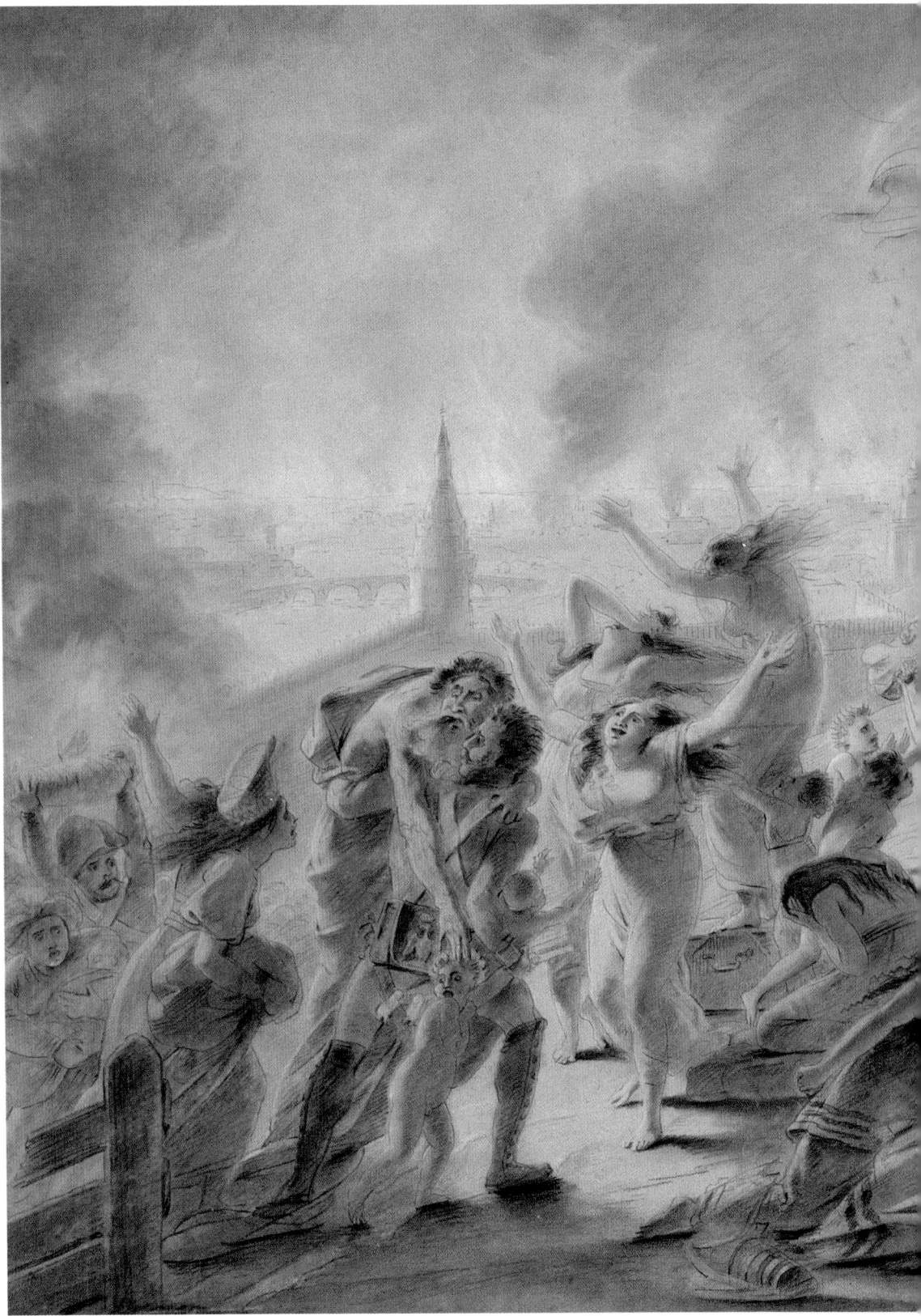

1.4

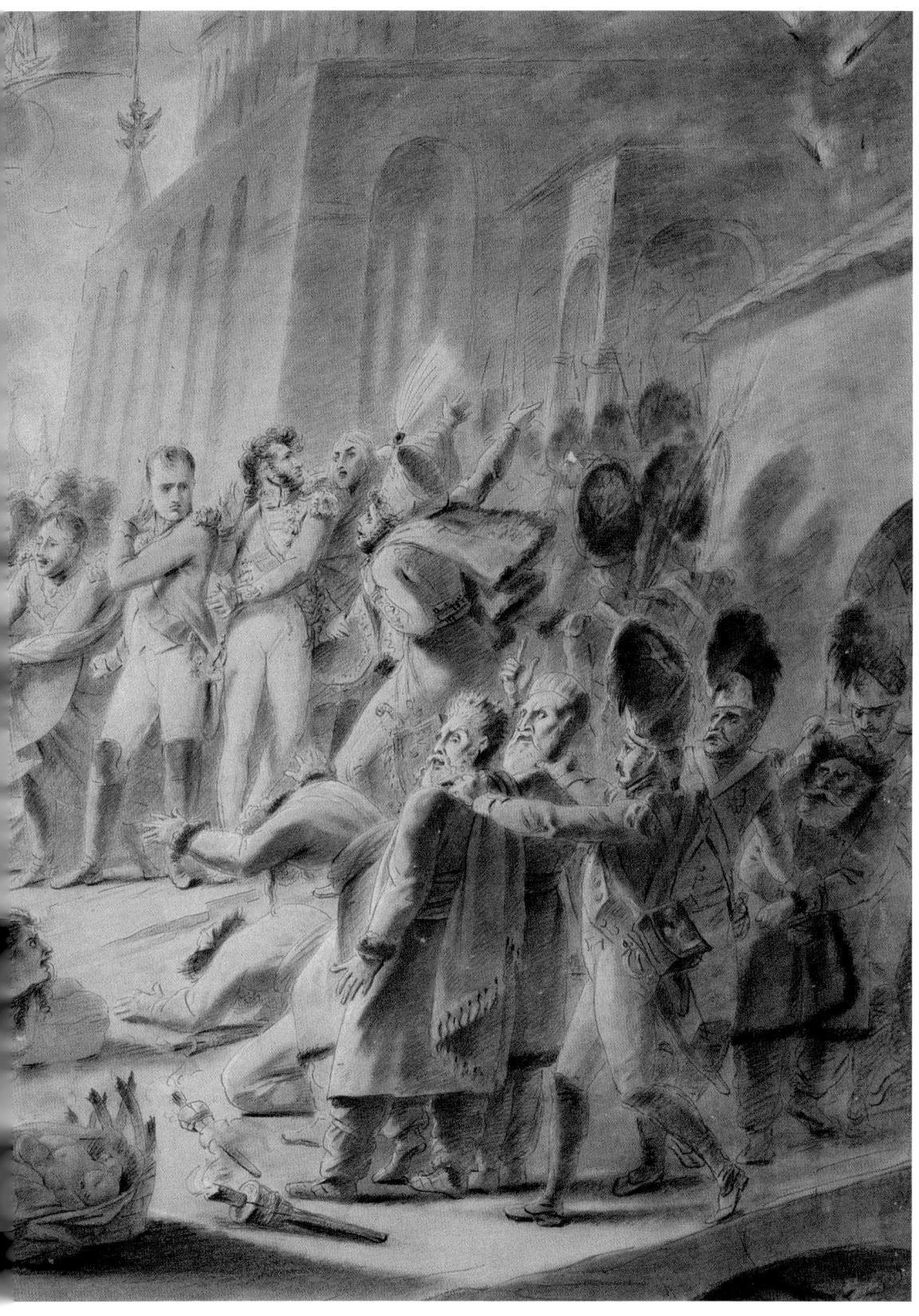

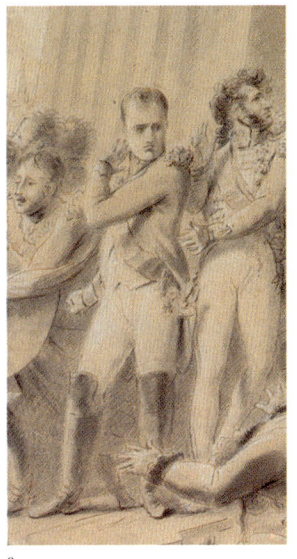

a

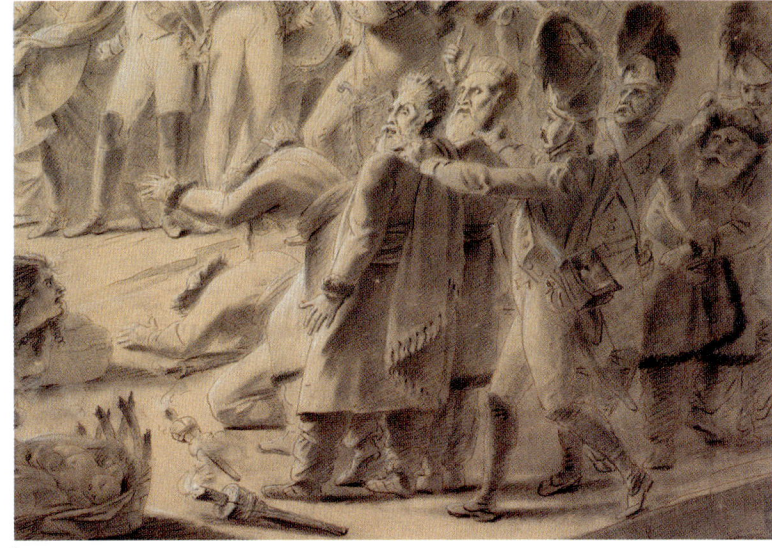

b

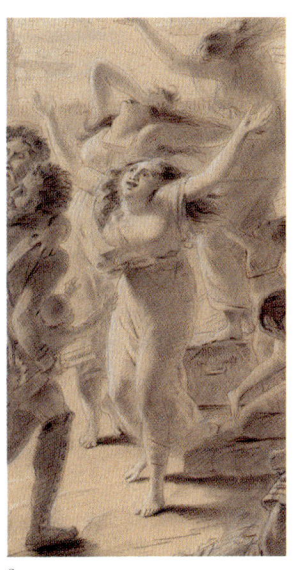

c

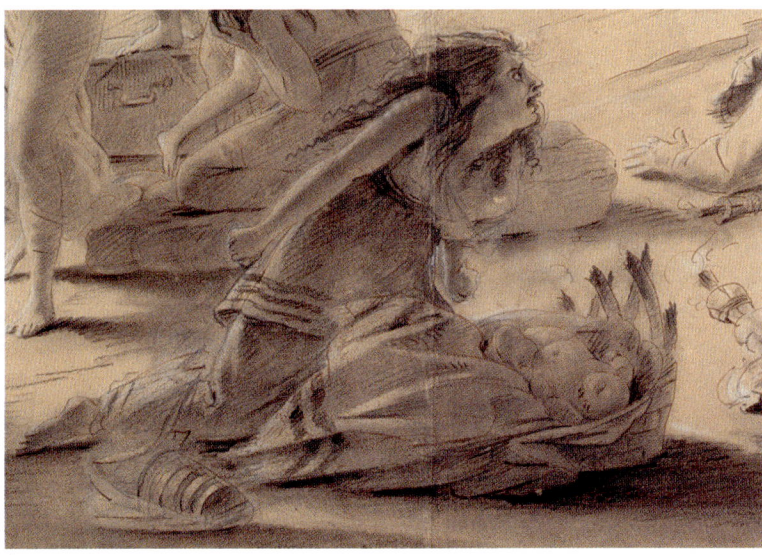

d

1.4. Antoine-Jean Gros, *Napoleon at the Burning of Moscow*, black chalk, ink wash, and gouache highlights on paper, 22½ × 33 in. (57 × 84 cm), Musée du Louvre, Paris.
a. detail (Napoleon)
b. detail (soldiers with arsonist prisoners)
c. detail (women in panic)
d. detail (woman with child in cradle)

Gros in a rivetingly expressive rhythm of flailing limbs and hurtling postures, a match for anything in this vein by Fuseli or Goya.

On a downward arc comes the tragic contrast: an agonized woman, kneeling not in homage but in exhausted despair over the broken cradle of her dead baby on the ground (fig. 1.4d). Surrogates to either side of the emperor take the active parts of offering succor or sounding the alarm about the overwhelming extent of the fires. But what is left for Napoleon actually to do? He makes a fist with his right hand, while gesturing over his shoulder at the utterly obvious conflagration, as he appears narrowly preoccupied by confronting the captive miscreants with their crimes, something that lowers rather than enhances any air of majesty.

In light of these expediencies, it might appear easy enough to condescend toward poor Gros, stuck in a historical dead end—as he was. But the actual event was more at odds than usual with Gros's powers of redemptive vision: most of the starving French troops having been engaged in looting and rapine, Napoleon himself making a quick exit from the Kremlin gate to the safety of a nearby country house. But that pathetic reading of Gros's effort would be too easy; one cannot fail to credit the technical brilliance of the Moscow drawing, its interplay of broad tonal passages establishing its architecture of lights and darks against a fine, economical use of defining contours, touched with judiciously applied white highlights.

And is it necessarily the case that the internally conflicted pose and expression of his Napoleon, so impinged on by more dynamic forces unleashed all around him, represents a failure of resources or imagination? Place that isolated figure against another hero, this one from the classical rather than modern repertoire, who also appears pressed by surrounding forces into an internally conflicted passivity. This was David's rendering of the first Brutus, founder of the Roman Republic, turning his back to the procession bearing the headless bodies of his two sons (fig. 1.5). The pair had been drawn into a conspiracy to restore the old monarchy, thus subject to certain execution under the law put into place by their own father. Taking in the entire tableau—the sensation of the 1789 Salon exhibition in the Louvre—their mother and sisters react in ways that span the emotional spectrum, while their aged nurse hides her face in what reads as the

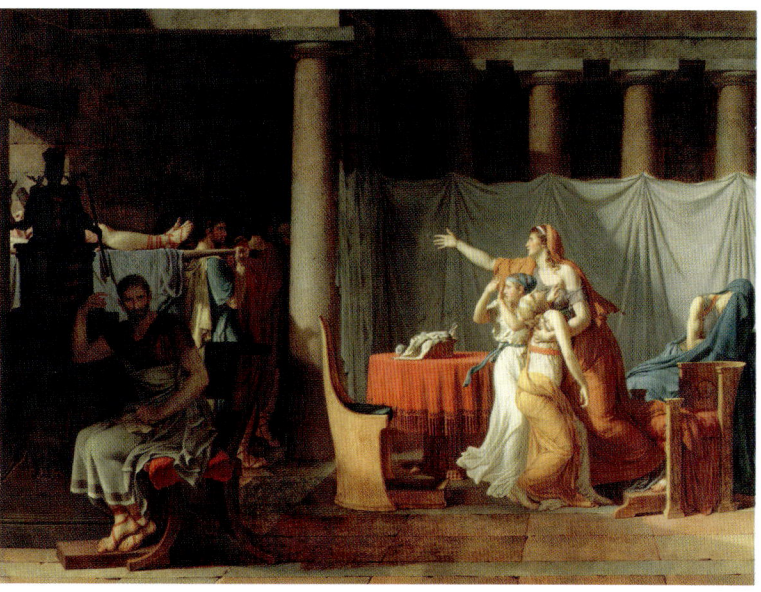

1.5. Jacques-Louis David, *The Lictors Bringing to Brutus the Bodies of His Sons*, oil on canvas, 127 × 166 in. (323 × 422 cm), 1789, Musée du Louvre, Paris.

most profound mourning. The self-canceling forces of duty and grief render the expression of Brutus likewise one of agonized indecision and ambiguity.

Nearly a quarter century stands between these two figures of stymied heroism. But the *Brutus* was not only a defining moment in David's career; its making coincided with the very first years in the master's studio for the young Gros, whose close friends were assisting David with major portions of the composition.[9] In moving from David's Napoleon portrait to consideration of Gros's Napoleon in Moscow, it is vital to consider the close emotional bond that existed between the two artists, and the deep and lasting imprint made on Gros by an exemplary tragic work like the *Brutus*. For all of the success he had enjoyed as far and away the most accomplished panegyrist to Napoleonic victories, that role turned him decisively away from facing the flawed and tragic dimensions of heroism. Even amid the overwhelming and futile carnage following the 1807 Battle of Eylau in northern Prussia, Gros's renowned painting of the event from the following year has Napoleon playing a purely salvific part, his presence a benediction that transfixes even enemies like the blond braided Lithuanian at the emperor's stirrup (fig. 1.6). While Gros agonized that requirements for documentary veracity and rapid execution had compromised the rigor of his art, it was the suppression of any flaw in his

1.6. Antoine-Jean Gros, *Napoleon on the Battlefield of Eylau, 9 February 1807*, 1808, oil on canvas, 205⅛ × 308⅝ in. (521 × 784 cm), Musée du Louvre, Paris.

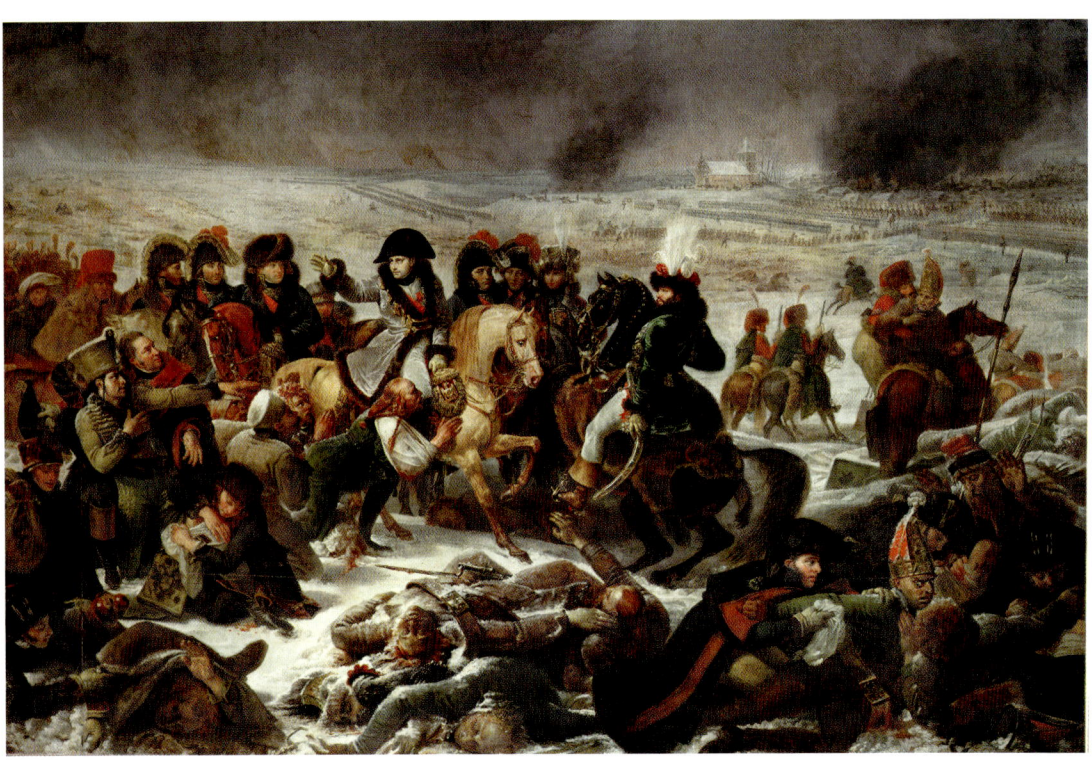

hero that had most distanced such efforts from the tragic standard of history painting as a calling.[10] In this light, Napoleon, tied in knots on the steps of the Kremlin, the flawed hero, promised the redemption of Gros's whole Napoleonic itinerary as an artist, irredeemable imperial failure securing the very thing that he could never have hoped to find in imperial success.

But the recovered tragedy turned back on Gros himself, as the onrushing Restoration of the monarchy meant that no venue or possibility of patronage existed for the tragic vision Gros had only just recovered for large-scale history painting—which left his conception for *Napoleon at the Burning of Moscow* as out of place and time as the portrayal of the ruler by his former master David had been the year before. But it would be a mistake even to imagine Gros's drawing as falling short of some prospective realization in oil on canvas. The greatest part of what makes the drawing exceptional, most notably its fluid and excitable expressivity of line, would not have survived the transition. As the empire unraveled and shortly collapsed entirely, grand artistic projects could never come to realization. For a history of the art of the period, that means finding prime material in incomplete fragments: studies, sketches, and proposals. Gros's *Burning of Moscow* demonstrates just how compelling and revealing such works can be, how much more immediate in their communication than the glaciated surfaces of finished canvases. Not for the last time in this study, a consummately achieved work, fully absorbing and absorbed in its complex circumstances, presents itself in the guise of partial or preliminary outline.

✳

Much the same can be said of the painting with which this chapter concludes. The life of its author, J.A.D. Ingres, had been closely bound to the two principal artists adduced so far. He belonged to the next cohort of pupils to enter David's studio after its first wave, that is, the one to which Gros belonged. He won his Grand Prix de Rome in 1801, but military turmoil in Italy delayed his taking up residence at the French Academy in Rome until the latter part of 1806. He then stayed on after his three-year fellowship period expired, which made him an artist out of place, still a Roman expatriate in 1814, the year in which he completed *Pope Pius VII in the Sistine Chapel*, or more simply, *The Interior of the Sistine Chapel*[11] (fig. 1.7).

Hardly larger than Gros's drawing of Moscow burning, Ingres's painting offers a lapidary, jewel-like intimacy and precision of detail, almost like a tempera panel from the fifteenth century. But the physical size of a painting is something different from its sense of scale. As with the recollection of David's *Brutus* in the Gros drawing, Ingres

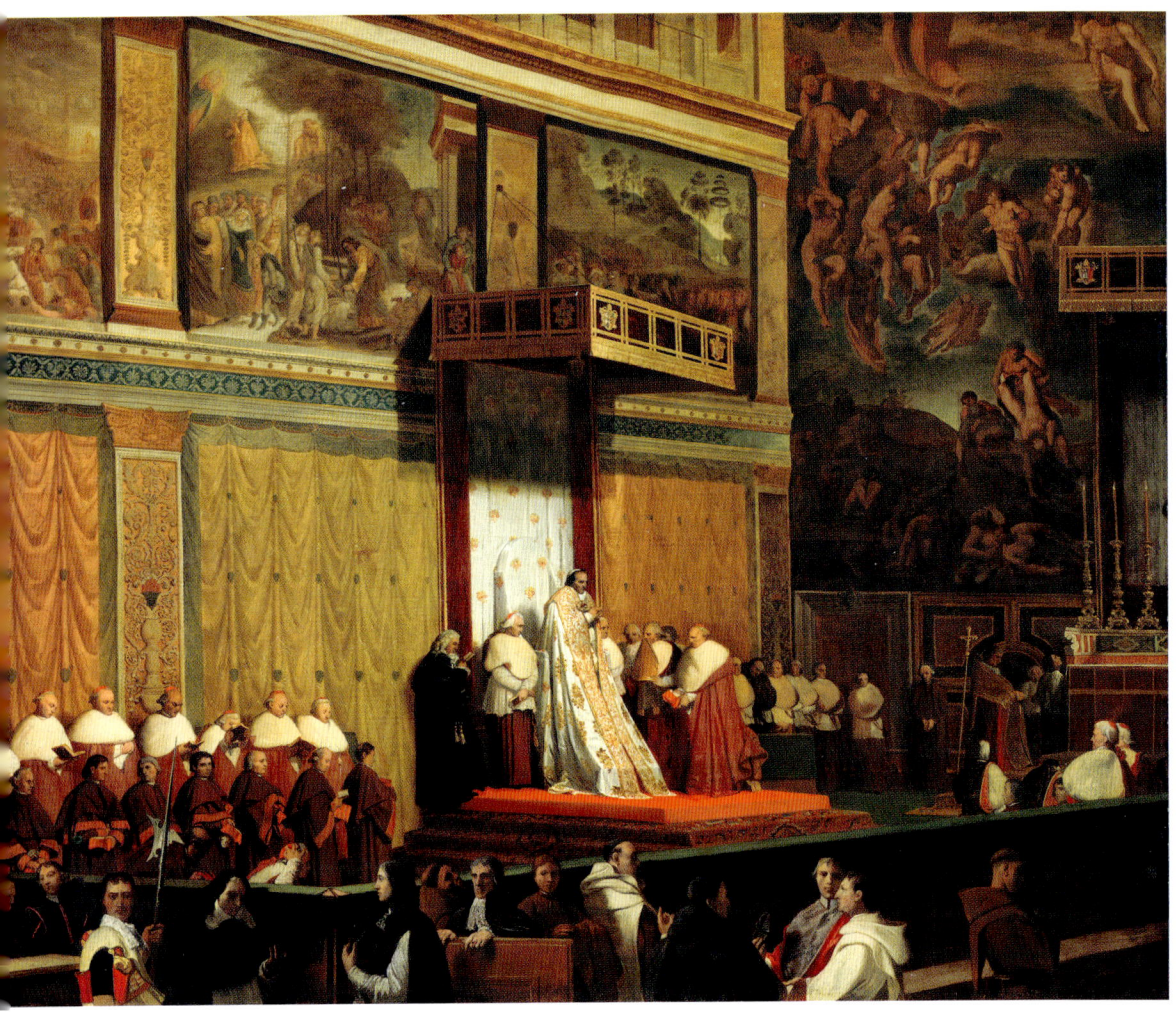

1.7. Jean-Auguste-Dominique Ingres, *Pope Pius VII in the Sistine Chapel*, 1814, oil on canvas, 29⁵⁄₁₆ × 36½ in. (74.5 × 92.7 cm), National Gallery of Art, Washington, DC.

was implicitly inviting comparison with an earlier, landmark painting of immensely greater physical size—namely, David's 1808 *Coronation of Josephine*, in which Pope Pius VII assumes a passive seated position behind the imperial couple (fig. 1.8). Where Gros's work offered an honorific allusion to David, Ingres's represented a reproach and rejoinder.

In forcibly summoning the physically frail pope to Paris for his investiture as emperor in 1804, Napoleon had been seeking to place his own coronation in the ancient line of Holy Roman emperors. The coronation concluded, Pius VII returned to Rome but found himself at dramatic odds with Napoleon when France annexed the Papal States in 1808. Pius VII retaliated by no less a step than excommunicating the French emperor, following which a zealous younger officer, seeking to imitate the emperor's lightning improvisations, retaliated by kidnapping the pope. Although the move had taken Napoleon by surprise, it played into his ambition to make Paris the capital of Europe

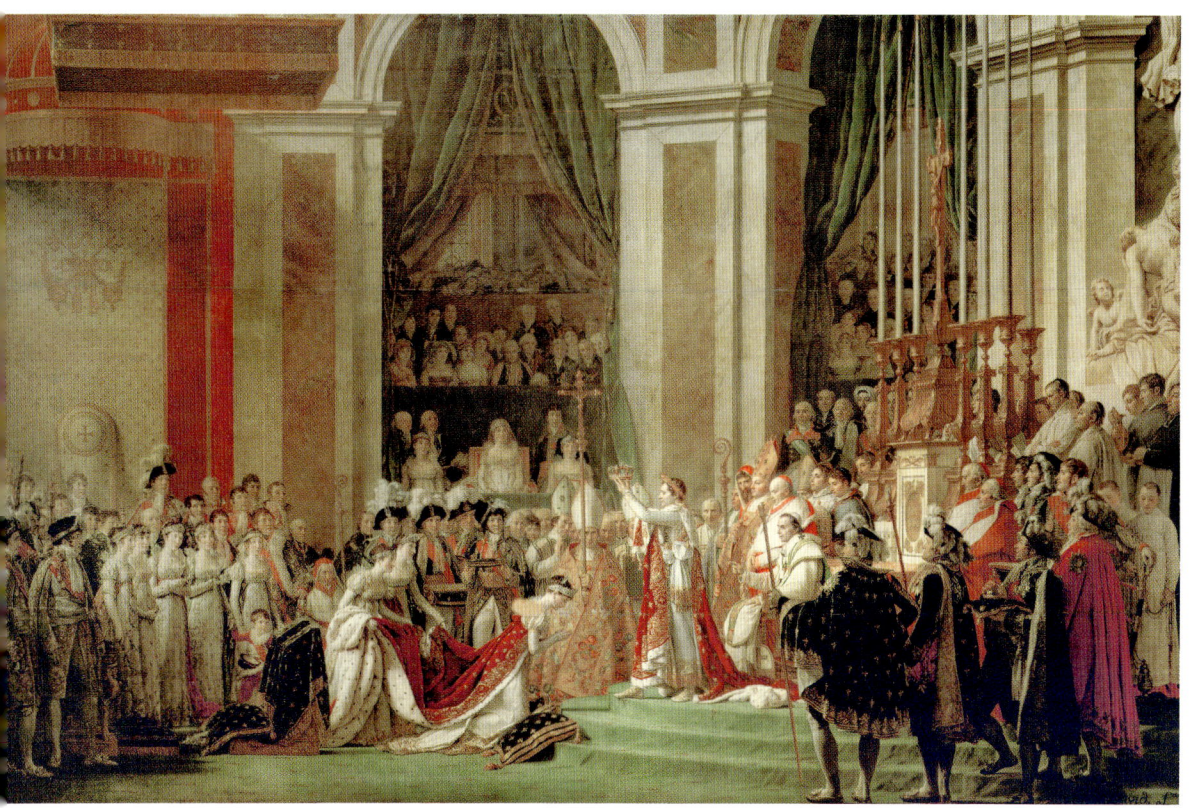

1.8. Jacques-Louis David, *The Coronation of Josephine (Le Sacre de Napoléon)*, 1806–7, oil on canvas, 244½ × 385½ in. (621 × 979 cm), Musée du Louvre, Paris.

in every respect, including hegemony over the Faith. Thus Pius VII spent the latter years of the empire incarcerated just outside of Paris at the château de Fontainebleau. In reaction to David's memorializing the pope as ineffectual and subservient to the emperor, Ingres offers a riposte in which Pius VII is restored to his rightful position of majesty and deference, rivaling David's *Coronation* in ritual gravity, grand space, and crowds of onlookers, narratively enlarged and augmented by the abundant personages present in the famous frescoed decoration of the room.

The patron for the work was Charles Marcotte d'Argenteuil, a close friend to Ingres as well as a professional supporter. The two had first become acquainted in 1810 after Marcotte arrived in Rome as an imperial administrator for water and forests in Italy. Seeking to have his portrait painted as a gift for his mother—understandable in light of his long postings abroad—he settled on Ingres after consulting friends conversant with the local French art community. That employment led to a close personal bond, which continued after the administrator was posted to the Low Countries in 1812, then back to Paris two years later. In their correspondence, Marcotte recalled drawings of the subject he had seen in the artist's studio and imagined a painting worked up from them—a paradoxical Roman souvenir of an event that he had never been able to witness, which in *Pius VII in the Sistine Chapel* Ingres proved more than pleased to supply. The interval between the commission and the public exhibition of the painting in the Paris Salon of 1814 crossed from the waning days of Empire to the aftermath of Napoleon's first fall from power, the pope back in Rome and Louis XVIII presiding over the first Restoration Salon. As the Louvre exhibition also included Ingres's 1810 portrait of Marcotte, the patron appeared personally to assert ownership over the *Pius VII*, along with all of its enhanced, post-Napoleonic implications of restored papal sovereignty.

Caution would nonetheless be in order concerning ascription to Marcotte of precise political convictions or satisfactions, however congruent with the ethos of the Bourbon Restoration this public statement may have appeared. There is no surviving indication that Marcotte ever wavered in his fealty as an imperial servant. It is the case, however, that his family, with whom he lived in Paris both before and after his late marriage of 1828, was intensely pious. Their house contained a private chapel, and all of his siblings, two male and two female, carried Marie among their other given names; the family celebrated the saint's days—not the birthdays—of its members.[12] In adjusting the size of his painting to his patron's domestic circumstances in Paris, Ingres would have been aware of their receptive ethos of Catholic piety, which permitted if not encouraged his own contrarian attitude toward both the apostate Empire and its servant David.

In 1812, Pius VII still a captive, and the outcome still in the balance between Napoleon and the powers of the Old Order, Ingres the traditionalist had seized the opportunity to correct history. Unable to observe his subjects as he painted, Ingres's was a wholly imaginary act of restoration (when viewing the painting now, some imagination is required to envision its initial state, as the whole foreground rank of figures was added decades later).[13] For his central vignette, Ingres relied on a drawing from 1809 (fig. 1.9), the one recalled by Marcotte, which recorded the enthroned pope and the papal secretary of state, Cardinal Consalvi, immediately to his right. Consalvi and the other cardinals had likewise been sequestered in Paris, so Ingres enjoyed no opportunities to observe them either. Needing to be on guard against attempting too close a set of likenesses, Ingres emphasized instead the miniaturized scale of his doll-like figures, along with touches of humor, such as the near-sightedness of the small, portly cardinal. His pope's face became an expressionless mask, the body made imposingly tall in the manner of a carnival mummer by his long gown trailing over the base of his throne.

Ingres confessed to Marcotte that he chose to dress the pope in white "for the effect of my picture, having no other way to draw the light to him," but nonetheless feels that he remembers seeing "all the

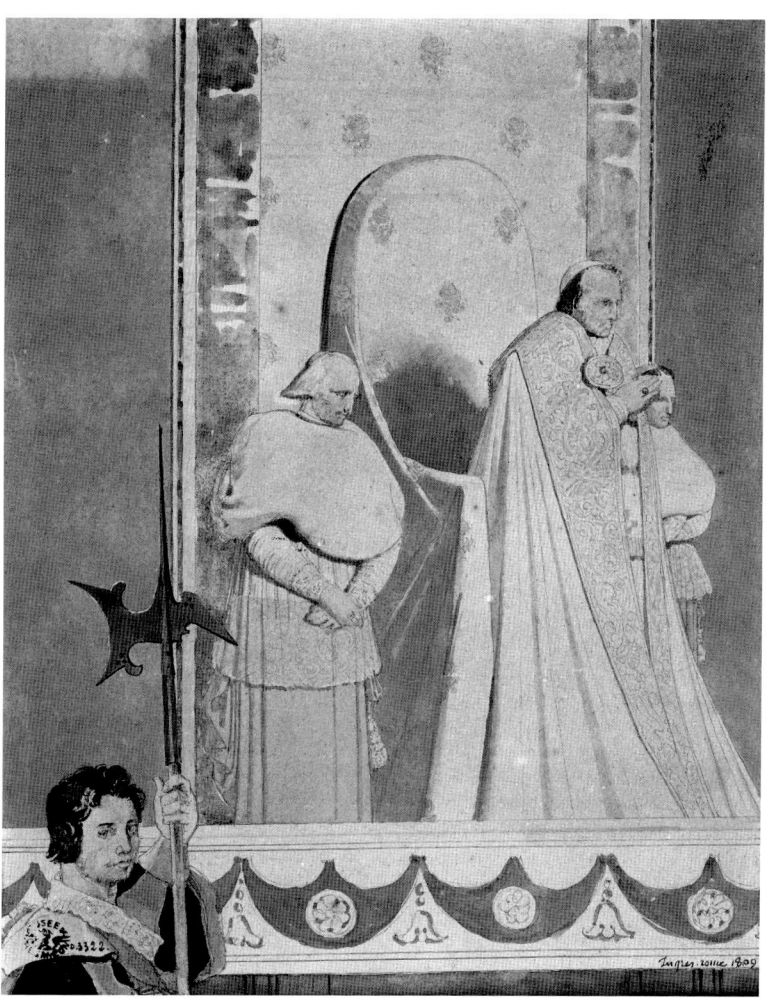

1.9. Jean-Auguste-Dominique Ingres, *Pope Pius VII and the Cardinal Consalvi at Prayer in the Sistine Chapel*, 1809, graphite, ink, and wash on paper, 9⅞ × 7⅞ in. (25 × 20.1 cm), Musée des Beaux-Arts et d'Archéologie, Besançon.

dais and himself dressed in that color."[14] He included a large segment of the baleful lower left section of Michelangelo's *Last Judgment*, the company of the damned serving as both a Dante-esque commentary on the pope's enemies and a warning to any that might emerge in the future—at least in the artist's private imagination. (That feature of the painting helps explain why the walls appear to meet at a wider, obtuse angle; correct perspective would have entailed too much distorted foreshortening for both that message and Ingres's consummate miniaturization of the fresco's commanding scale to be adequately legible.)

By an uncanny irony of history, the letter that Ingres wrote to Marcotte proudly announcing the completion of *Pius VII in the Sistine Chapel* coincided almost to the day with the pope's physical return from Paris to Rome on May 24, 1814. But his painting remained an imaginary act of restoration. And memory can indeed be a greater resource for art than observed reality. Recalling the ceremonies of

Holy Week before the pope's forced abduction from Rome, Ingres had written: "There is nothing more impressive than all the ceremonies presided over by the Pope, that good and venerable man, and all the cardinals. I cannot begin to tell you how beautiful it is, simple and rich at the same time."[15] The music-loving novelist Stendhal, writing in 1817 after all the requisite personnel had been reassembled, painted a different word picture of the same ceremony, though adding a back-handed compliment to the artist:[16]

> I have just returned [he set down in his journal] from the famous Sistine Chapel after hearing Papal Mass, for which I had managed to secure myself the best place available on the right just behind the Cardinal Consalvi; and I may now claim to have heard the celebrated *castrati* of the Sistine choir … Never did I, in all my days endure so demonic a caterwauling. This was the most excruciating cacophony I have encountered these last ten years. [Though] I found delight and compensation in the manly beauty of Michelangelo's ceiling and *Last Judgment*; … *Cf.* the excellent painting by M. Ingres.

※

1812: *Napoleon in His Study*. 1813: *The Burning of Moscow*. 1814: *Pius VII in the Sistine Chapel*. This sequence of works takes us year by year from the beginning of the end to the actual end of Empire—or rather the first of two endings, in that Napoleon will have his encore, the brief but climactic "One Hundred Days" in 1815. Ingres painted an intended triumph of the old order restored before it happened and in the absence of its central subject, absences papered over by quasi-medieval elaboration of heraldic, lapidary embellishment. All three artists found themselves revisiting pregnant moments from their earlier lives to fill in the abysses opening before them. Gros's *Burning of Moscow* amplified and multiplied the most extreme vehemence of expression in his existing repertoire as compensation for the irrecoverable loss of the core component in his art's internal economy—the commanding leader and victory itself. David's construct of Napoleon in 1812 manifests the strain in the unrelenting control exerted over every pictorial element, the tightness of their mutual adjustments leaving no suggestion of free play or any opening beyond its airless confines: the price paid by the artist in order to block contrary information pressing in from the world beyond.

Of the three works, the two paintings propose an invariant, unchanging reality unaffected by contingent events: for David, one in which Napoleon always rules; for Ingres, one in which he never ruled. Gros's improvisatory drawing, by contrast, had the capacity to immerse itself in vertiginous historical change. The root of the word "analysis" is "a breaking up, a loosening, releasing." In order to understand the complex unity of an artistic talent, the interpreter cannot break it up or loosen its moorings at will, but certain moments in history accomplish that task by proxy, allowing one to assess the ways in which the fragments are subsequently reassembled in the effort to recover a coherent identity. For diagnostic purposes, not all periods in art history are created equal: works generated during exceptional moments of upheaval can reveal more about how art comes together from heterogeneous ingredients by dint of the exceptional exertions required to hold them together or, conversely, the failure of such efforts when contradiction becomes too great to be contained inside any settled form.

The two artists addressed in the chapter to follow, the elderly Francisco Goya and the neophyte Théodore Géricault, both arrived at artistic templates that broke the bonds of humanistic precedent, dislodging even the primacy of the human as an adequate vehicle for expressing the violent uncertainties of the coming moment.

At the Service of Kings, Madrid and Paris, 1814

Aging Goya and Upstart Géricault
Face Their Restorations

THE OPENING OF THE CONGRESS OF VIENNA in 1814—as admiringly rendered by a German-Austrian former pupil of Jacques-Louis David named Johann Peter Krafft (fig. 2.1)—began an intensified cycle of pageantry by which the traditional powers of Europe offered themselves as victorious agents of peace and reconciliation. But the terrors and atrocities of the warfare just past (and soon to return) could not so easily be put aside in the minds of Europe's most salient artists. Under this heading comes a Restoration work of art so indelibly familiar and so thoroughly examined that one feels some trepidation in presenting it: Francisco Goya's *The Third of May 1808* (fig. 2.2), painted far from Vienna in a place where past wounds remained raw. Its dramatic clarity and moral force speak and have spoken so directly to countless viewers that the first task of the interpreter is not to get in the way of that empathetic connection. At the same time, it is crucial for the present inquiry to understand the status of this painting as a primary artifact of the wider European Restoration, without which it would never have come into existence.

2.1. Johann Peter Krafft, *Entry of Austrian Emperor Francis I into Vienna after the Peace of Paris, 16 June 1814*, 1828, encaustic, 147⅝ × 253⅛ in. (375 × 643 cm), Schloss Schönbrunn, Vienna.

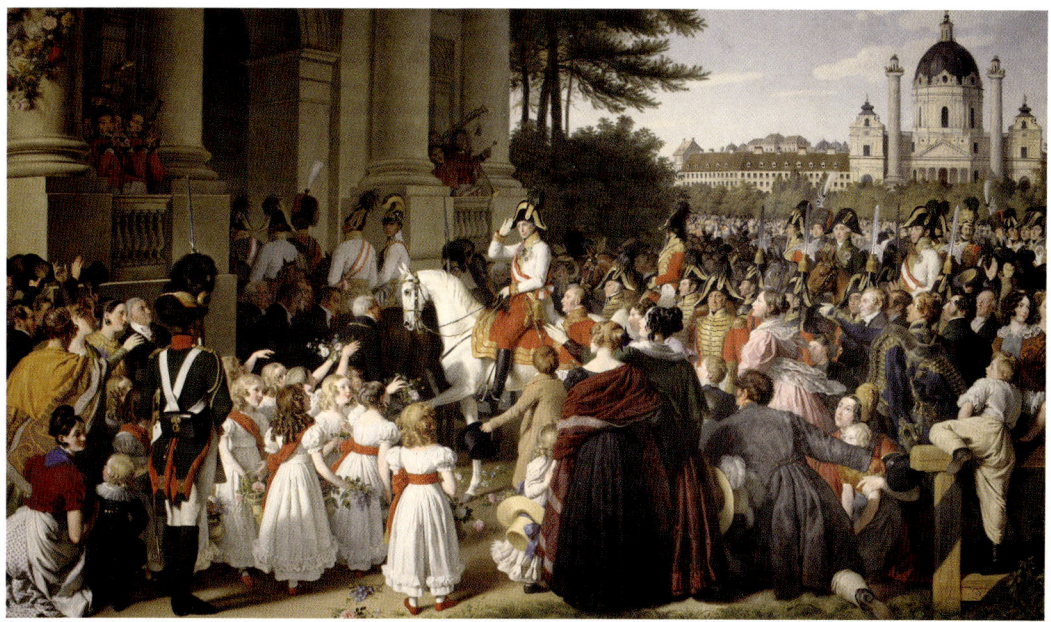

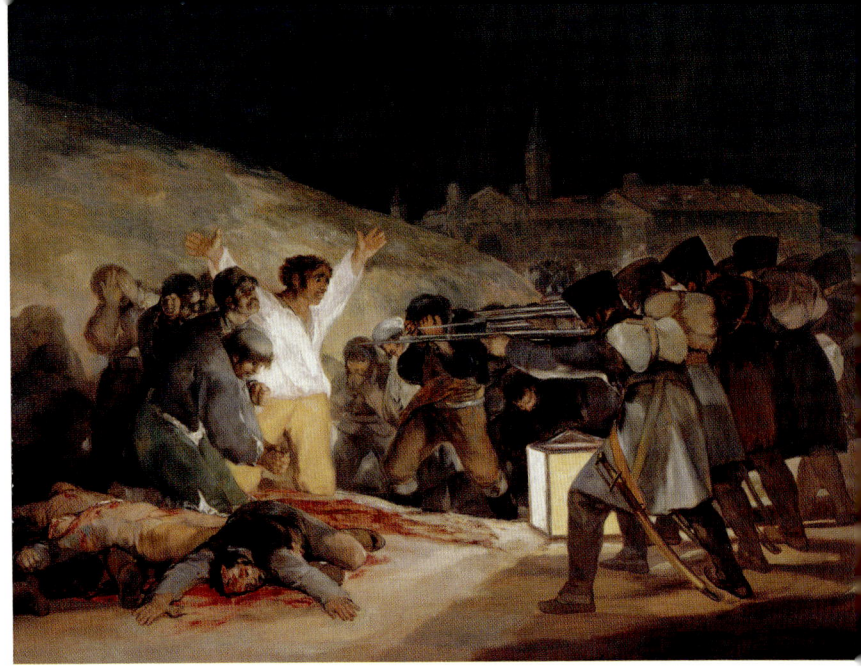

2.2. Francisco Goya, *The Third of May 1808 in Madrid*, 1814, oil on canvas, 105½ × 136⅝ in. (268 × 347 cm), Museo Nacional del Prado, Madrid.

On May 2, 1808, crowds at the Puerta del Sol near the Royal Palace in central Madrid had spotted Crown Prince Ferdinand being transported away. He was aiming to join the rest of the Spanish royal family, sequestered in Bayonne across the French border, where the French emperor was bestowing the Spanish Crown on his brother Joseph Bonaparte. A riotous uprising broke out in an effort to prevent the prince's escape, an uprising soon suppressed without quarter by mounted French Guard under Joachim Murat. In the dark early hours of the next morning, the captured rebels were executed: the event from which Goya took his subject, infusing it with every analogy to Calvary and the martyrdom of Christ.

Goya worked on the canvas during the first half of 1814. By February 24, he had proposed to the liberal provisional government an "ardent desire" to memorialize "the glorious insurrection against the Tyrant of Europe." To this end, the state provided him with materials and a substantial monthly stipend until the work was completed.[1] He responded to one-half of this charge with the *Third of May*, a painting unlike any he had ever painted before on such a scale; nor would he ever do one like it again. For that reason alone, it can be taken as the product of a special, unrepeated set of circumstances.

In the literature on the artist, it is common to juxtapose the painting with certain sheets in the print series much later titled *The Disasters of War*, which Goya in these years was keeping almost entirely private. These etchings were Goya's way of recording the struggles for control of Spain between the 1808 Madrid uprising and the restoration in 1814 of the exiled monarch, Ferdinand VII: a morass of butchery and continually confused lines of battle involving remnants of the French-Spanish regular army, the British with their Portuguese

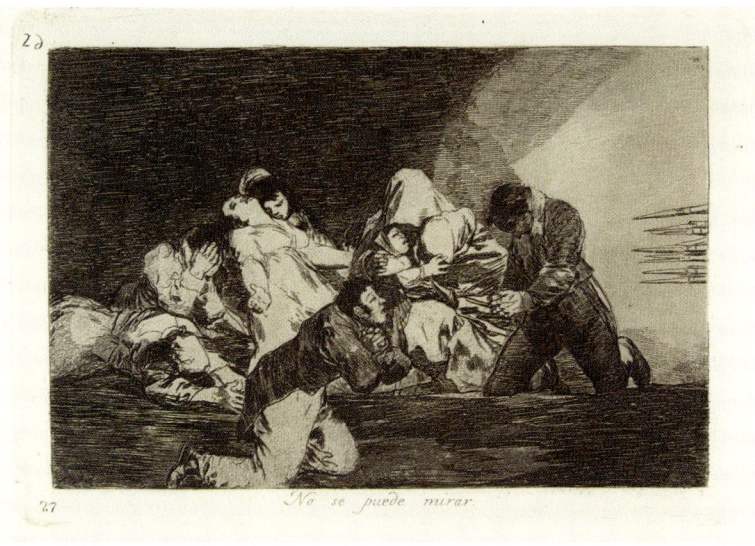

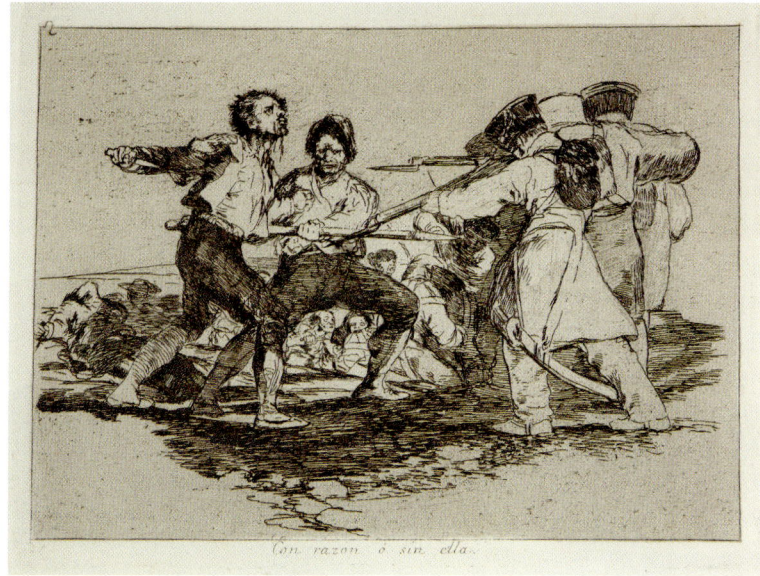

2.3. Francisco Goya, *One Cannot Look (No se puede mirar)*, plate 26 from *"The Disasters of War" (Los Desastres de la Guerra)*, 1810–20, etching, burnished lavis, drypoint, and burin. Plate: 5¹¹⁄₁₆ × 8¼ in. (14.5 × 21 cm), Purchase, Rogers Fund and Jacob H. Schiff Bequest, 1922, Metropolitan Museum of Art, New York.

2.4. Francisco Goya, *With or without Reason (Con razón e sin ella)*, plate 2 from *"The Disasters of War" (Los Desastres de la Guerra)*, 1814–15, etching, burnished lavis, drypoint, and burin, 6⅞ × 8¼ in. (15 × 20.9 cm), Museo Nacional del Prado, Madrid.

allies, and the irregular peasant bands that gave the world the term *guerrilla*. The most cognate of these impressions separate out the meanings, often contradictory ones, that the great painting holds in suspension. *One Cannot Look* (fig. 2.3) reduces the mechanical uniformity of the French occupiers to nothing but rifle barrels and bayonets; so, by compensation, the Spanish of all types become entirely victims, all traces of resistance removed. Conversely, in *With or without Reason* (fig. 2.4), the French, in a semblance of battlefield formation, remain faceless killers, but find themselves in equal danger from the simple but terrifying weapons of their frenzied intended victims. It is difficult to tell which of the two bestialized guerrillas is holding the lance,

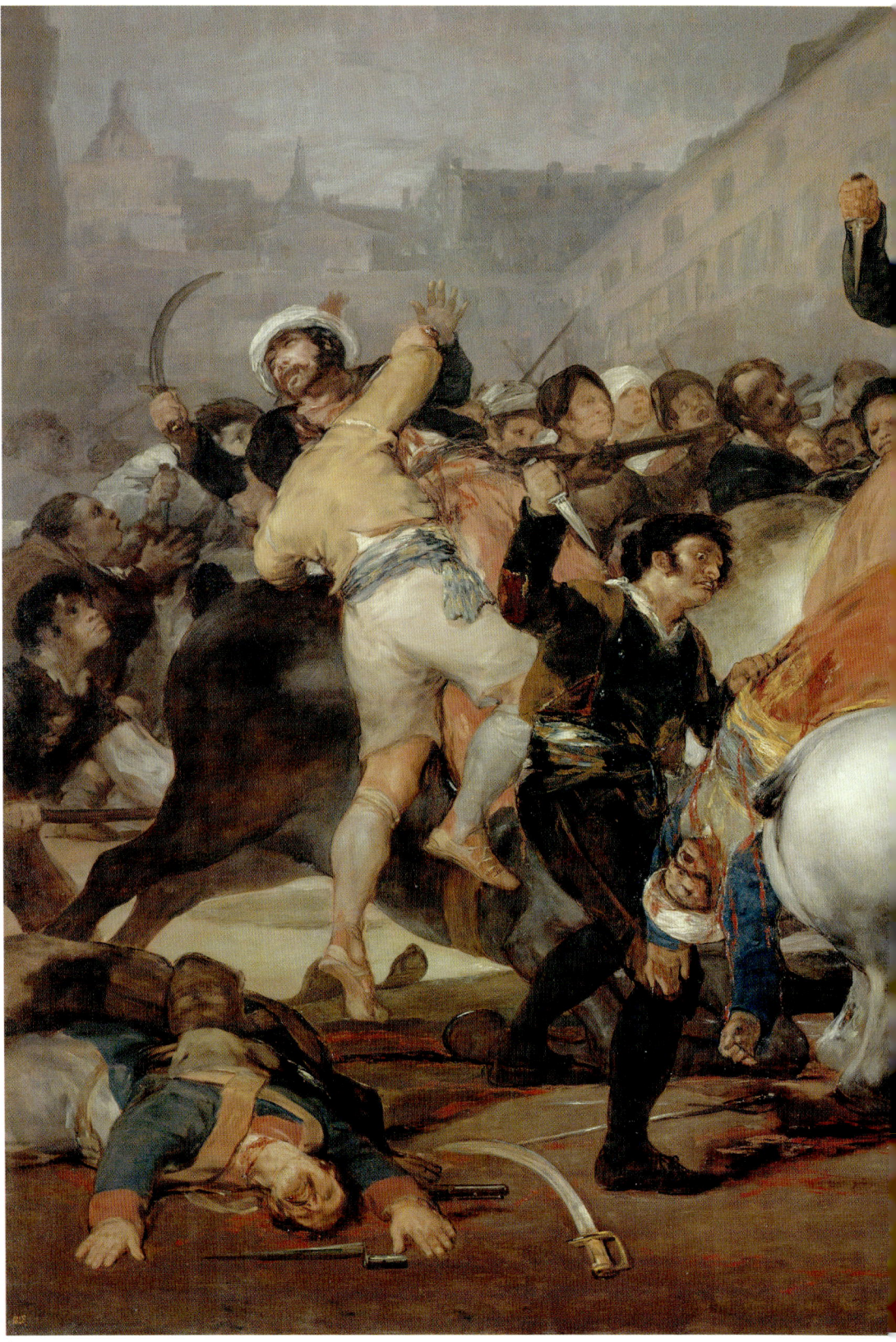

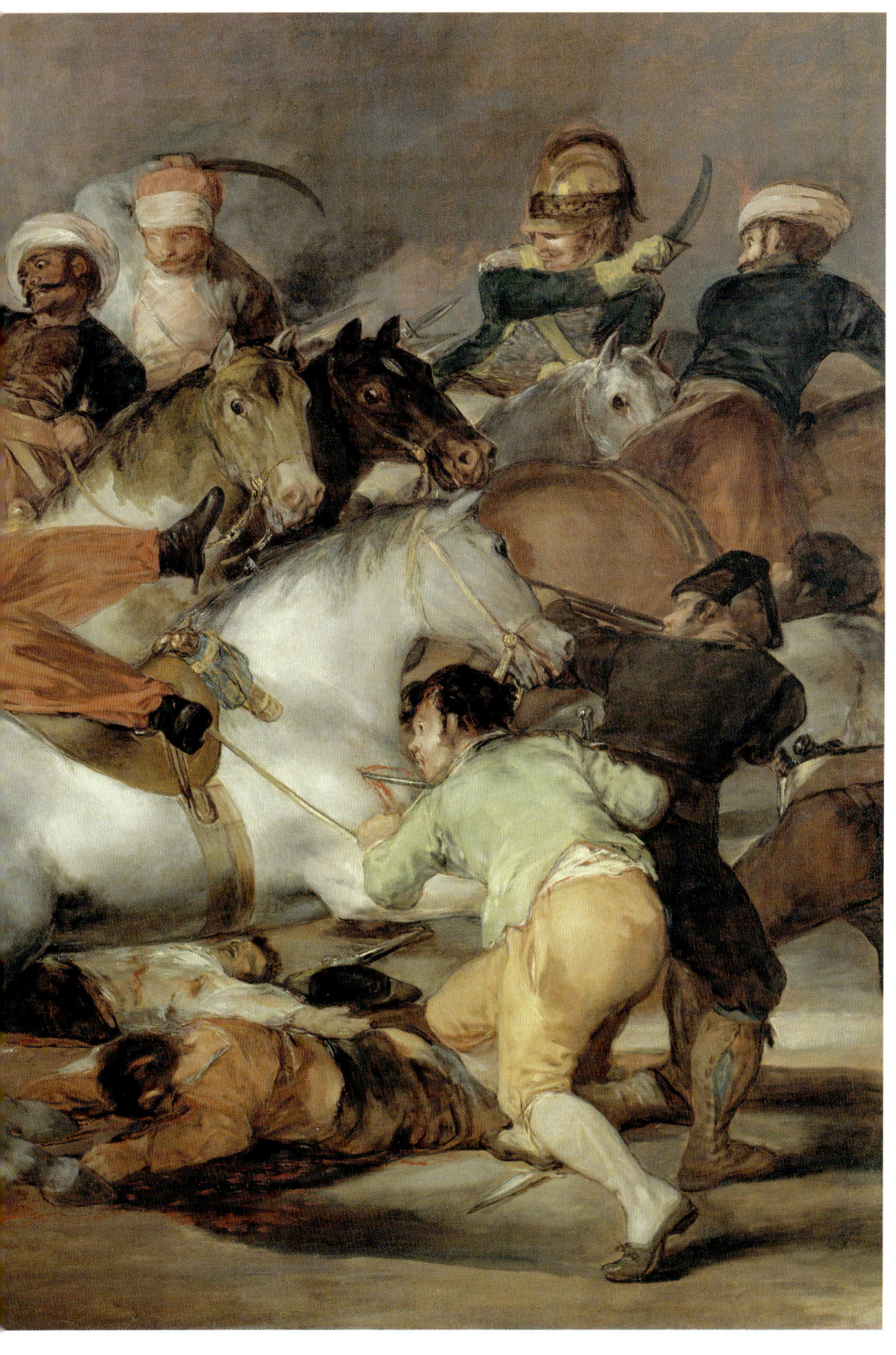

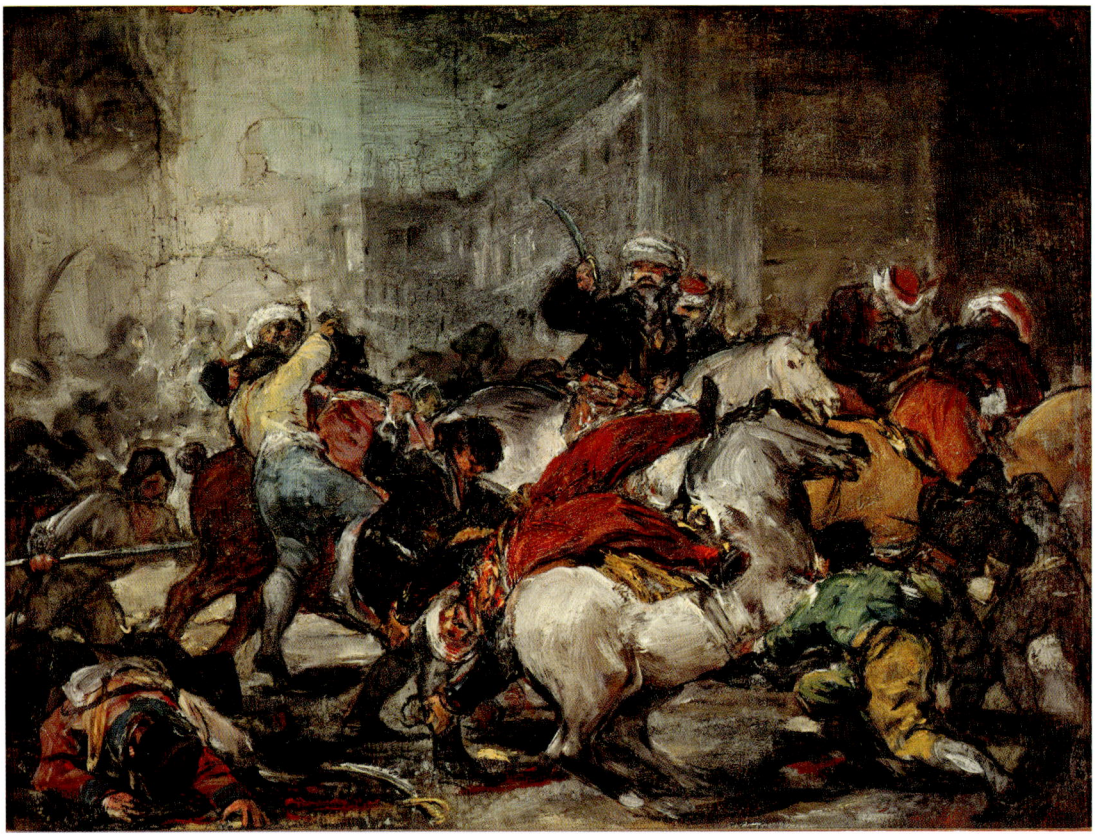

(previous spread)

2.5. Francisco Goya, *The Second of May 1808 in Madrid*, 1814, oil on canvas, 105¾ × 136⅞ in. (268.5 × 347.5 cm), Museo Nacional del Prado, Madrid.

2.6. Francisco Goya, *The Second of May 1808 in Madrid*, 1814, study, oil on paper mounted on board, 9⅝ × 12¾ in. (24.5 × 32.5 cm), Museo Goya, Zaragoza.

about to strike home regardless of the consequences to its maddened wielders, the dagger set to inflict secondary damage.

That dagger signals an implicit passage to the other half of the commission that Goya had been granted to welcome the returned royal regime in 1814: his lesser known rendition of the uprising at the Puerta del Sol, *The Second of May 1808* (fig. 2.5). In this scene the weapon has struck home more than once into the body of the French cavalryman being dragged from his horse, while the consternated French rider above holds his in ineffective suspension. The victim of that assault wears striking red pantaloons, which create a dynamic crimson smear tracing his descent and focusing the whole of a composition otherwise teetering on the edge of incoherence. Those pantaloons, along with turban and ornate cummerbund, mark the victim—along with several of his barely upright comrades—as a Mameluke: successors to the Egyptian warriors recruited during Bonaparte's expedition to the Middle East back at the turn of the century. When the French departed, a good number of their Mameluke auxiliaries came with them to form a permanent corps of Napoleon's army. As the Second of May uprising had no leader, no evident organization, and no heartening outcome, it was the exotic appearance of the Mamelukes, with

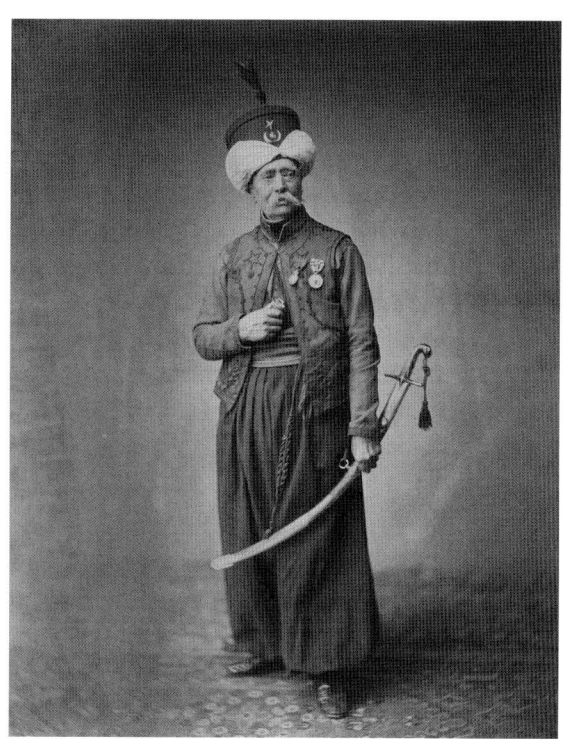

their tie to Islam, that gave Goya the center he otherwise lacked (he can be seen searching in the oil sketch of the subject [fig. 2.6] for that emphatically descending red arc, which provided the complementary analogue to the forked white smock of his central victim among the May 3 martyrs). The six years of terrible warfare sparked by the Second of May revolt were thus retrospectively mapped onto the struggle of the *Reconquista*, the painful, centuries-long winning back of the Iberian Peninsula from Moorish domination: a Holy War in short, in which "the Tyrant of Europe" played the part of the Antichrist.

If one enters more deeply into the circumstances of 1814, the significance of these Mamelukes becomes even more resonant. The ranks of original Egyptian recruits had been deeply eroded, especially by the grinding war of attrition in Spain. For some time, their numbers had been replenished by recruits of other ethnicities: sub-Saharan Africans and Frenchman could increasingly be found in that distinctive middle-eastern costume. By the year of defeat in 1813 and 1814, French recruits dominated these companies (one of the last surviving French Mamelukes, François Ducel, lived long enough to be photographed in costume [fig. 2.7]).[2] With the abdication of Napoleon, Mamelukes in royalist southern France became targets of vigilante lynchings on account of their close association with the departed ruler in the popular mind. For both the French and the Spanish who had accepted the imperial order in its day, isolating the Oriental as carrier of the bad old Bonapartism, offered one way to displace any inconvenient history of complicity.

Even in the absence of the least contemporaneous commentary on the pair, the vividly hued *Second of May* can be taken as the turbulent premise for the somber suspended violence in the elegiac *Third of May*. But the neatness of the former's religious, ethnic, and ideological divisions nonetheless proved insufficient for Goya's effort to contain the details of the Puerta del Sol mayhem into one coherent message or effect. Neither official approval nor disapproval of either painting was ever recorded; in fact, there is no record of their existence at all until they turned up in a Prado storeroom inventory in 1834; for all of the importance to posterity of *The Third of May*, these paintings seem not to have figured one way or the other when Goya was put through a "purification" trial—on grounds of French collaboration and the immorality of the *Naked Maja* (fig. 2.8)—by the restored Inquisition later in 1814.[3] Despite his record of work for Joseph Bonaparte and that bygone erotic provocation, he passed. But it is safe to say, nonetheless, that Goya's efforts, via his great pair of publicly scaled canvases, to paint his way out of political difficulty amid the turbulence of 1814, left his primary audience unmoved and unconvinced: yet another instance of Restoration works of art—even the greatest— launched but never arriving at their intended destination. Although he evidently aimed in both paintings to please official sensibilities and moderate the worst excesses of the crowd violence, could he ever

2.8. Francisco Goya, *Naked Maja*, 1797–1800, oil on canvas, 38⅝ × 75¼ in. (98 × 191 cm), Museo Nacional del Prado, Madrid.

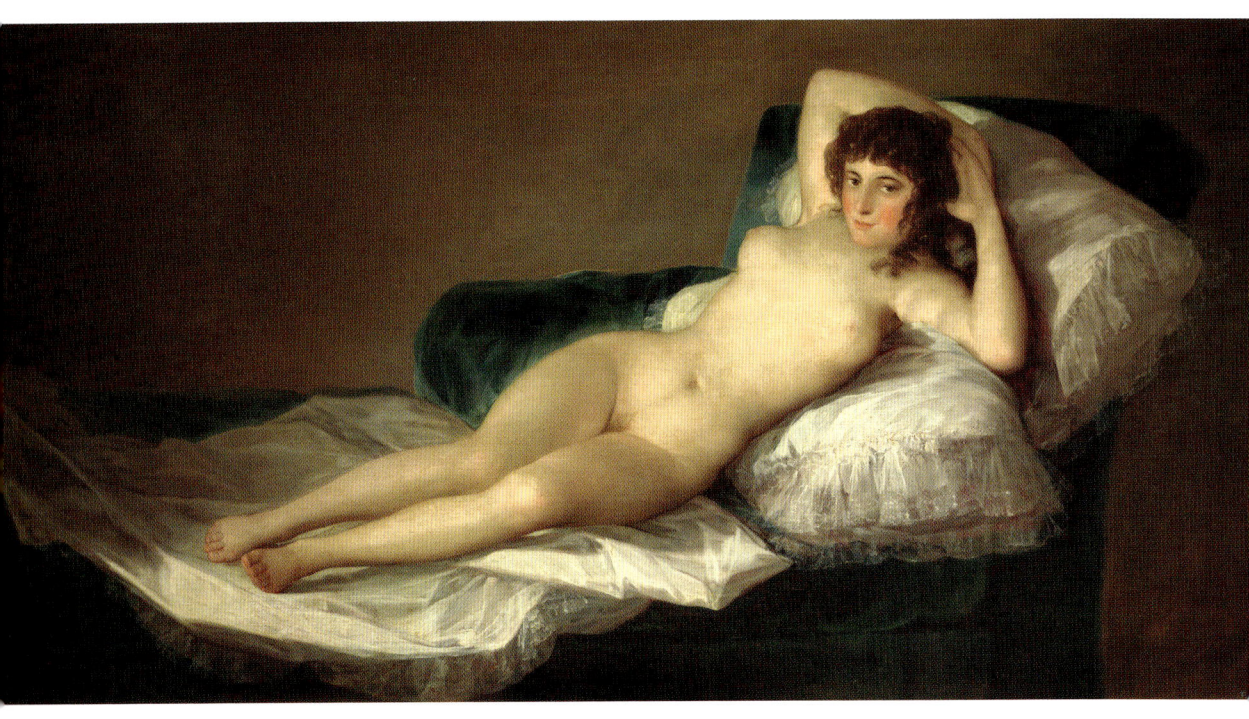

entirely expunge from his art a measure of the complexities he faced? The dead French officer placed in the lower left-hand corner of the *Second of May* appears no less pathetic than the corpses found at the foot of the descending arc of firing-squad victims in *The Third*. Both manifest the terrible finality of death via Goya's astonishing ability to render blood in painted pigment in such a way that actual dried gore appears to be adhering to the canvas: an uncanny, wrenching effect of profane transubstantiation.

Besides this crossing of the membrane between representation and actual substance, the *Second of May* engenders the crossing of another divide: the one that divides human from animal. The urchin in the pale green jacket at the lower right does the Madrileño cause no credit by furtively inserting his narrow blade into the shoulder of the horse carrying the unfortunate Mameluke: as it has yet drawn little blood, that thrust marks the instantaneous moment of the painting. The incipient faltering of the horse in turn provides perhaps the most pathetic moment in the painting (what viewer would want to identify with the cruelty of such an act or such an assailant?). And the expressions that connect most sympathetically with those of the viewer belong to the three horses above. The resignation, regret, and reproach conveyed in those stoic gazes, lovingly rendered by the artist, manifest some dimension of his thought for which no human vehicle could be found to serve.

When Goya first secured official support for the work that became the *Second of May* and *Third of May* canvases, he was appealing to a liberal Spanish government, which had outlasted the French puppet regime of Joseph Bonaparte by retreating under British protection to the southern port of Cádiz. This rump state had promulgated the constitution of 1812, imposing new electoral rights, freedom of the press, land reform, abolition of the Inquisition, among other checks on the monarchy, the church, and the old aristocracy. The new King Ferdinand VII, whose restoration had been secured by the British victory over France in the struggle for the Iberian Peninsula, obtained his release from French captivity by agreeing to abide by the restraints on absolutism contained in the 1812 document. One month after Goya had made his request, however, Ferdinand had already abrogated the constitution. Taking a roundabout route back to Madrid, his reactionary supporters were able to turn out larger and larger crowds at each stop on the itinerary, culminating with an entry into the capital at the beginning of May 1814, attended by a frenzied popular mob whipped up to acclaim his rule—a sixth anniversary equivalent to the one that Goya was attempting to paint in *The Second of May 1808*. Nor could the artist escape the obligation to paint the newly minted, miscreant king (but yet again employing a quizzically expressive horse as background relief) (fig. 2.9).

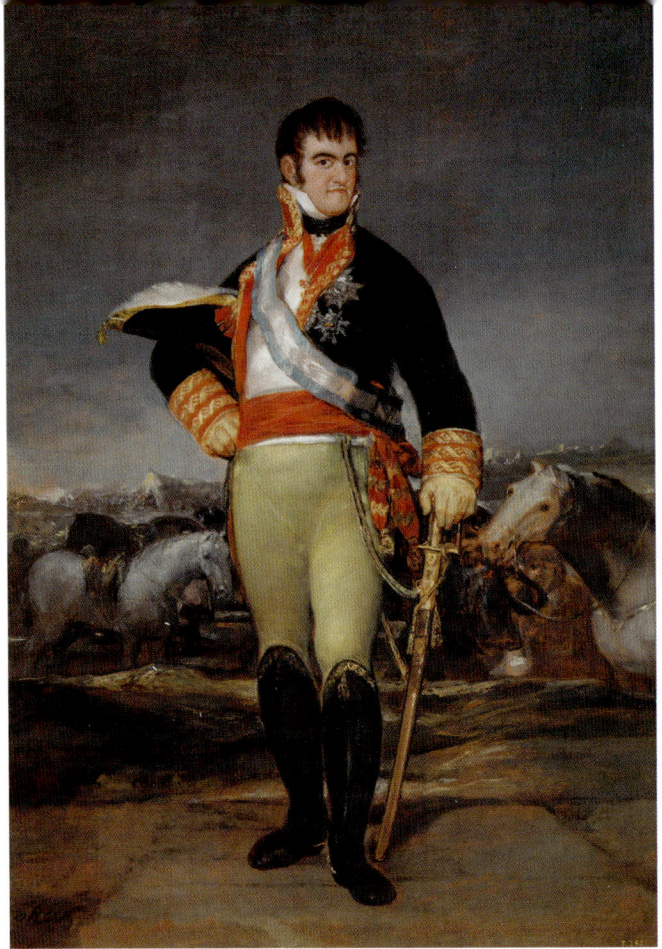

2.9. Francisco Goya, *Ferdinand VII at an Encampment*, after 1815, oil on canvas, 81½ × 55⅛ in. (207 × 140 cm), Museo Nacional del Prado, Madrid.

✳

A canvas by Louis-Philippe Crépin, titled *Allegory of the Return of the Bourbons on April 24, 1814: Louis XVIII Raising France from Its Ruins* (fig. 2.10), can stand as an example of truly servile art marking the restored monarchy after Napoleon's first fall from power in early April 1814. The setting is the gritty port of Calais, depicted in the stage-like backdrop, but that fact interferes not at all with the sumptuous grandeur of the setting. All is brittle artifice in every feature of the imagined scene. The artist already dresses the new French king, just off the boat, in his coronation robe and crown. Like David's Napoleon in the great *Coronation* canvas of 1808, Louis XVIII has risen from his throne and turns his attention to a kneeling female figure, but a bare-breasted, apparently dazed and confused personification of France, her rich gown embroidered with gold fleurs-de-lis, substitutes for the flesh-and-blood Josephine. The cast of Bourbon family members stiffly look on: the younger brother and future Charles X with his sons form a rank across the center; the Duchess of Angoulême—daughter of Louis XVI and niece to the restored king—poses prettily on the left. But Crépin's pantomime reveals nothing of actual royal

Chapter 2

agenda. Proceeding from Calais, Louis XVIII entered Paris on May 3, nearly coinciding with the entry of Ferdinand VII into Madrid. And just like the Spanish monarch, he abrogated the restraining constitution to which he had agreed to adhere as a condition of his restoration, abolishing the entire bicameral legislature in the bargain. In both countries, absolutism was back, though the French case lacked most of the gratuitous cruelty and caustic mockery of liberal beliefs exhibited by the odious Ferdinand, whose vindictively arbitrary rule Goya was forced to negotiate.

At that juncture, Goya was sixty-eight years old and had witnessed virtually every enormity one life could encompass. Looking past the opportunistic Crépin, the artist who commands attention in the aftermath of the French king's return is one who had yet to see much of life, the twenty-one-year-old Théodore Géricault (fig. 2.11). Almost as soon as Napoleon's first 1814 abdication had been made public, the young artist enlisted in the King's Musketeers, a corps replete with ultraroyalist recruits. It has been difficult for most observers to

2.10. Louis-Philippe Crépin, *Allegory of the Return of the Bourbons on April 24, 1814: Louis XVIII Raising France from Its Ruins*, 1814, oil on canvas, 18⅛ × 21⅞ in. (46 × 55.5 cm), Châteaux de Versailles et de Trianon, Versailles.

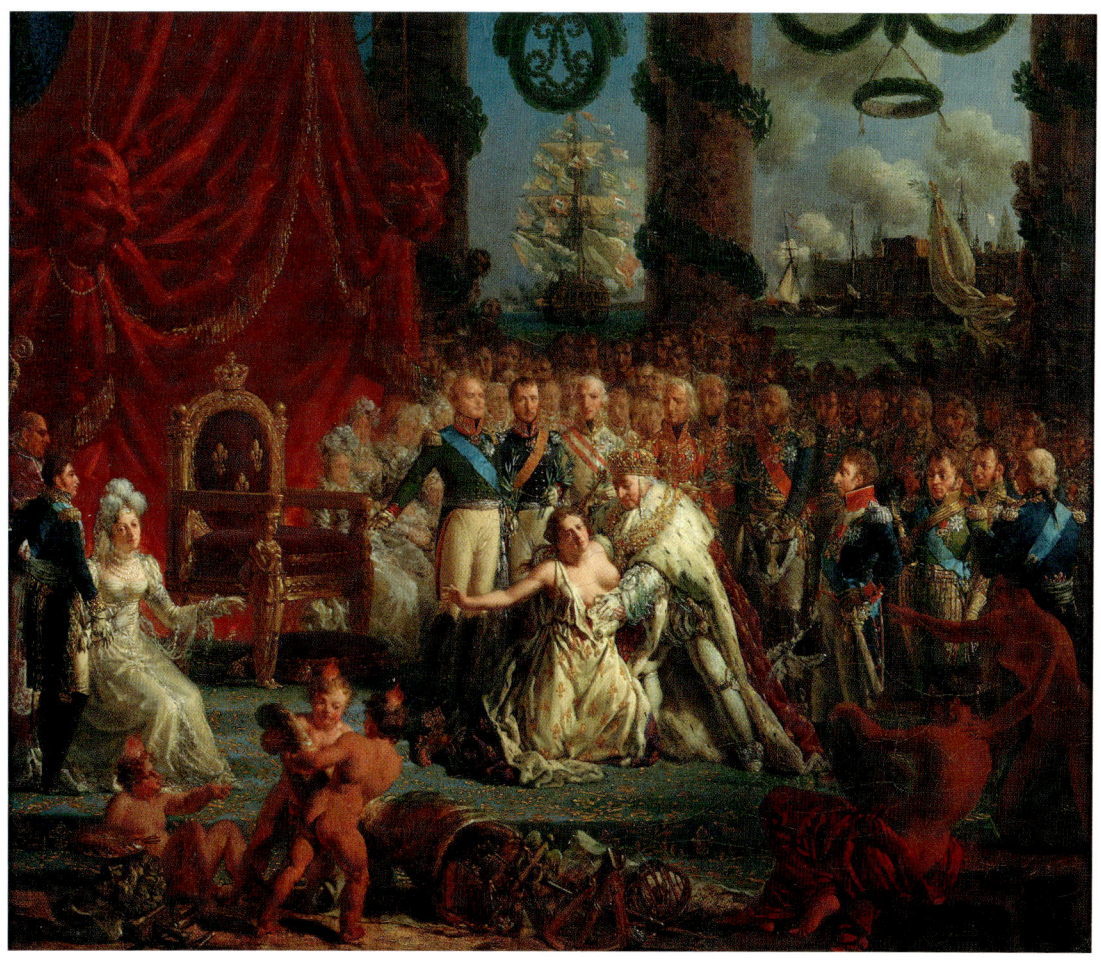

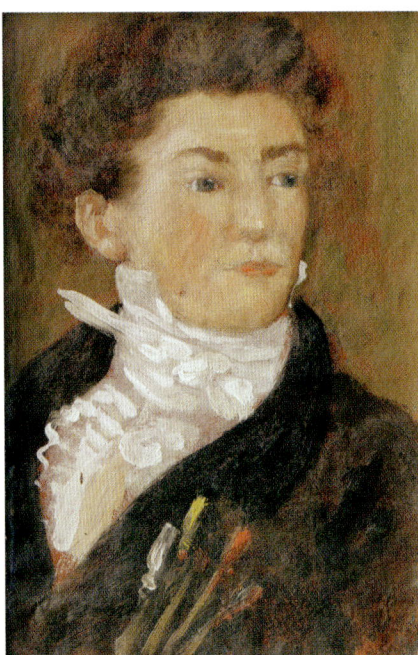

2.11. Théodore Géricault, *Self-portrait in Youth*, oil on paper, 8¼ × 5½ in. (21 × 14 cm), private collection, Paris.

reconcile the evidently democratic sympathies present in Géricault's later art with this active embrace of the Bourbon Restoration as a cause, especially when so many Parisians remained ambivalent or antagonistic toward the returning Bourbons. But no less a Napoleonic exemplar than Louis-Alexandre Berthier, Napoleon's long-serving chief of staff, took up a command in the new royal guard, while the majority of the Imperial Marshals likewise declared their loyalty to the restored monarch. The ambiguities of 1814 lay in blurring lines between old warring factions: not just conservative royalists, but a significant number of liberals and republicans welcomed Louis XVIII as a man of peace.[4] Napoleon's desperate levies of new men and supplies, as he maneuvered to survive in 1813, had broken the unspoken compact with too many French subjects who had, until 1812, been his loyal if long-suffering adherents.

In that light, Géricault's enlistment can be understood under an essentially patriotic heading, with the possibility that it entailed a measure of compensation for his avoidance of action and commitment in the past (when his family paid one Claude Petit to take his place in the military call-up), as well as providing a camaraderie missing from the solitary artistic life. He was thus effectively in uniform himself as he prepared his entry for the first Restoration Salon of 1814: *The Wounded Cuirassier Leaving the Field of Battle* (fig. 2.12). Patently appropriate as an allegory of the reverses suffered by the Grand Army since its retreat from Moscow, the dismounted heavy cavalryman nurses a wound that leaves him far from the fray.[5]

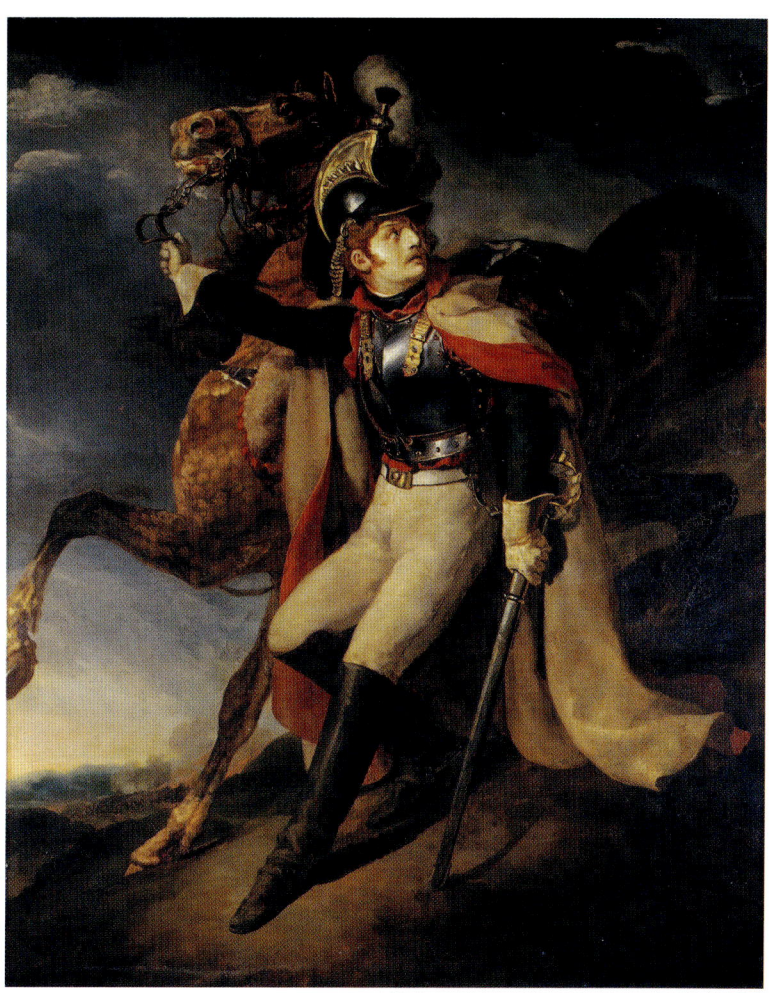

2.12. Théodore Géricault, *The Wounded Cuirassier Leaving the Field of Battle*, 1814, oil on canvas, 137⅜ × 104¾ in. (349 × 266 cm), Musée du Louvre, Paris.

Because the previous Salon exhibition of 1812 had been declared null and void by the returned regime, Géricault was free to rehang his entry from that last of the Napoleonic exhibitions, the *Charging Chasseur*, or light cavalryman of the Imperial Guard (fig. 2.13), thereby enlisting the *Cuirassier* into a pointed diptych of advance and retreat, the highs of victory and the lows of defeat. The symmetries are striking: the canvases are almost exactly the same height; the two cavalrymen direct their equivocal expressions in opposite directions—all this amid artful contrasts like the fire of battle flaring vividly beneath the charging horse while in its pendant only glowing distantly beneath the forelegs of the restively retreating mount. Géricault creates contrast within symmetry to most telling effect in the heads of the two horses. Both are made to face each other, and both are joined, Janus-like, to the faces of their riders. In the charging *chasseur*, a mimetically ambiguous splash of red, melding with the streaming strands of mane, makes for a clear vector between man and animal. The equivocation

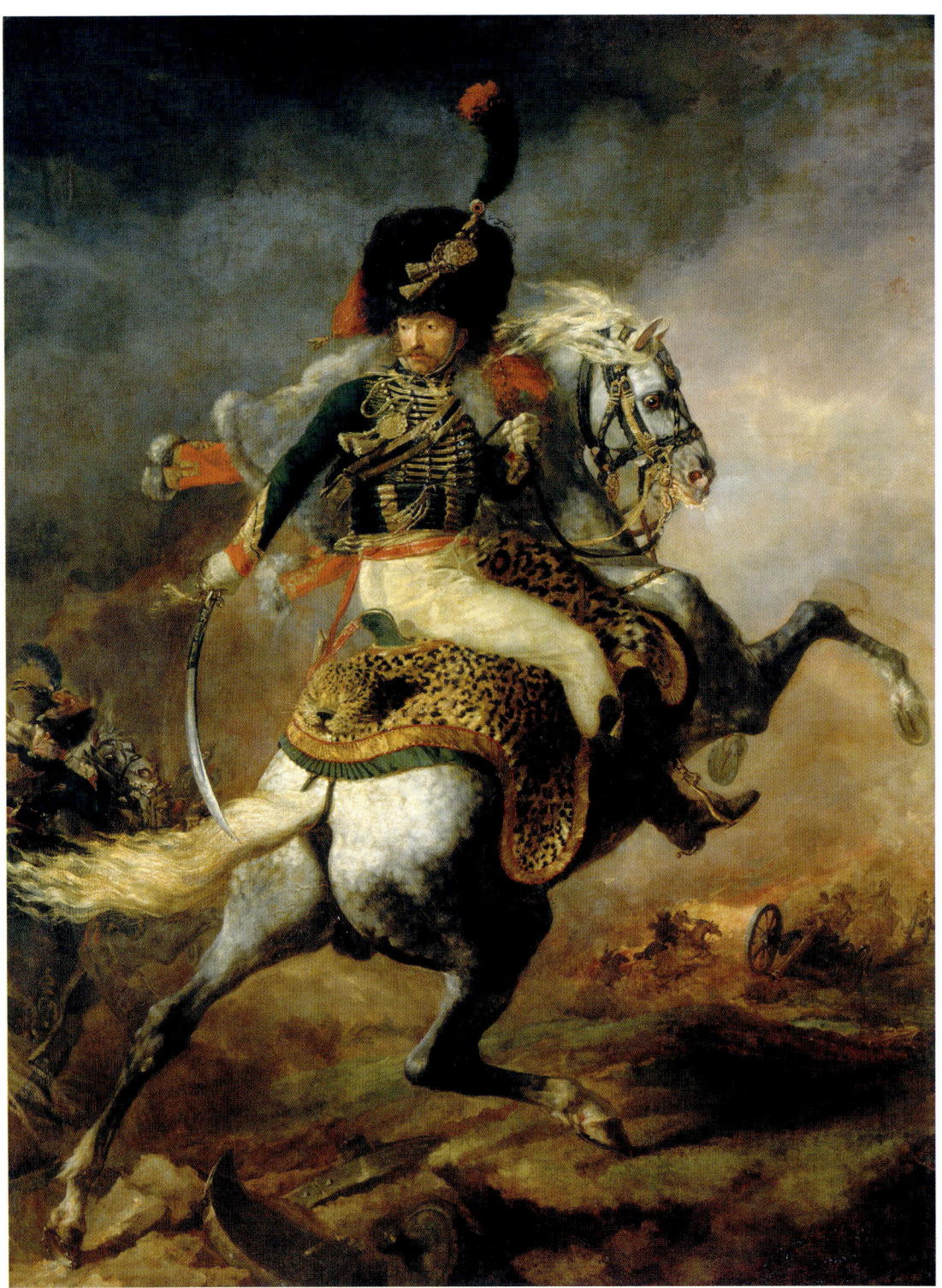

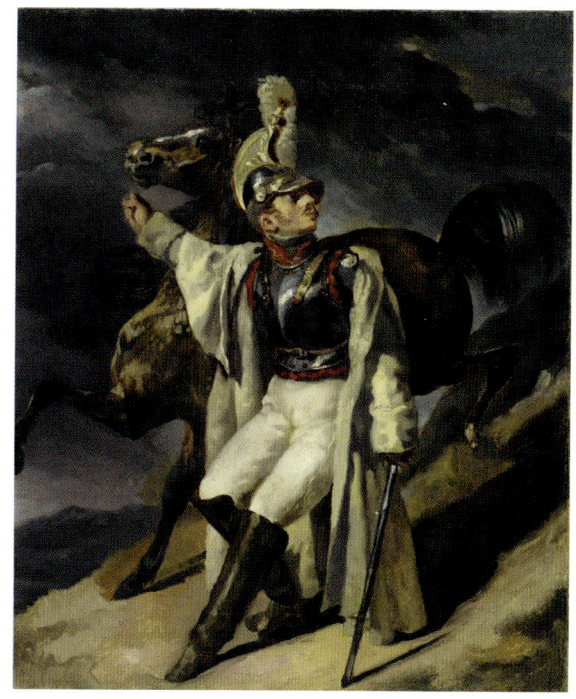

2.13. Théodore Géricault, *The Charging Chasseur of the Guard*, 1812, oil on canvas, 137⅜ × 104¾ in. (349 × 266 cm), Musée du Louvre, Paris.

2.14. Théodore Géricault, *The Wounded Cuirassier*, 1814, oil study on canvas, 21¾ × 18⅛ in. (55.2 × 46 cm), Brooklyn Museum, New York.

of the man's expression is answered by the excitement in the horse, its ornately decorated bridle bestowing on the animal a military rank of its own. If the foam flecks in its gaping mouth hint at frenzy, that excess would balance the impassivity of the human subject. In the new companion picture, the askew helmet, with its gilded crest and plume, makes for an almost literal hinge between the human countenance, eye rolling wildly, and the horse's head, where the animal's wide eye reveals either panic or some superior, all-seeing point of view. There is an infernal hint to the red note in its orifices, the wide nostril and outline of the ear. Place the final version of the *Wounded Cuirassier* next to the very advanced oil study that preceded it (fig. 2.14), then gauge how much Géricualt has amplified each salient trait of the animal so as to intensify this transferred expressivity, even enlisting the complicated rhythms of the bit and reins around the mouth into a galvanic overall effect.

The unknowing parallel with Goya at the identical moment in Madrid lies in Géricualt's and Goya's common transfer of affect from the human vessel to the animal as double or surrogate. As the charge of meaning and feeling becomes too great for human subjects convincingly to convey, that load distributes itself over any other likely vehicles in the vicinity. Géricault, as is often observed, was a passionate horseman as much as a tireless student of the horse in his drawing and painting. But he leaves much of that knowledge aside in these two paintings, as the horses' bodies are to a great extent obscured,

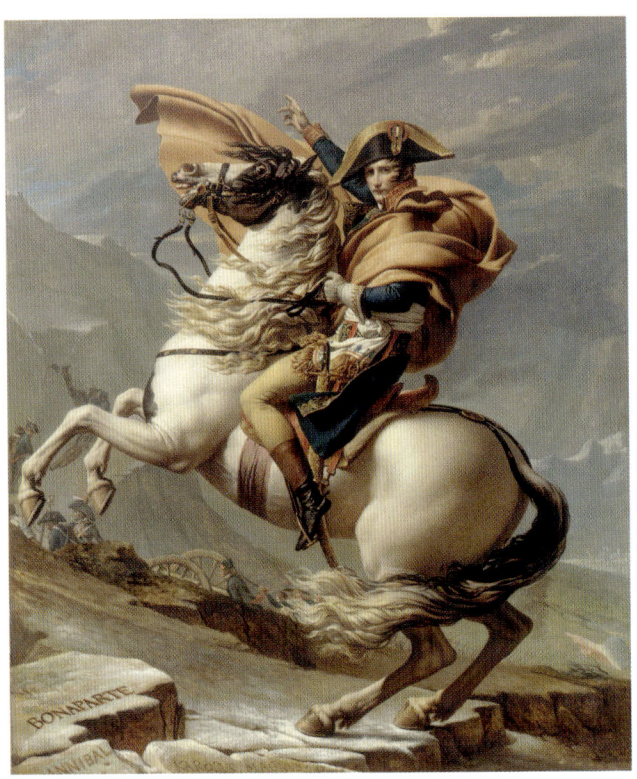

2.15. Jacques-Louis David, *Bonaparte Crossing the Alps*, c. 1801, oil on canvas, 102 × 87 in. (259 × 221 cm), Châteaux de Malmaison et Bois-Préau, Rueil-Malmaison.

and what we are able to see is anatomically distorted or implausible: virtually all of his attention is lavished on the heads, that is, where the closest correspondences to human expressions are to be found.

Among all the other things that these two famous paintings accomplish, their pairing conjures a new variety of hybrid being quite apart from the standard equestrian portrait, the purpose of which invariably is to extrapolate mastery over the animal into a general mastery over people and events—as David had so indelibly accomplished in his *Bonaparte Crossing the Alps* (fig. 2.15) back at the turn of the new century, an eon in the past by the reckoning of 1814. A variant on the retreating cuirassier appears in the 1814 sheet instanced at the very outset of this book, *King Louis XVIII Reviews the Troops at the Champ de Mars* (fig. 2.16), a projected royal tribute by Géricault not far in apparent intent from the appalling canvas by the servile Crépin. The efficient rendering of the architecture of the French military academy (l'École Militaire), with the fainter dome of Louis XIV's Invalides in the distance, was the work of a specialist collaborator.[6] The mass of cavalry contains comparably careful draftsmanship by Géricault, but large portions of that description are lost by his later imposition of nearly opaque swaths of dark brown ink, as he seems to be trying and failing to lend some coherence as a three-dimensional mass to his turbulent collection of officers reining in their mounts. Compared to

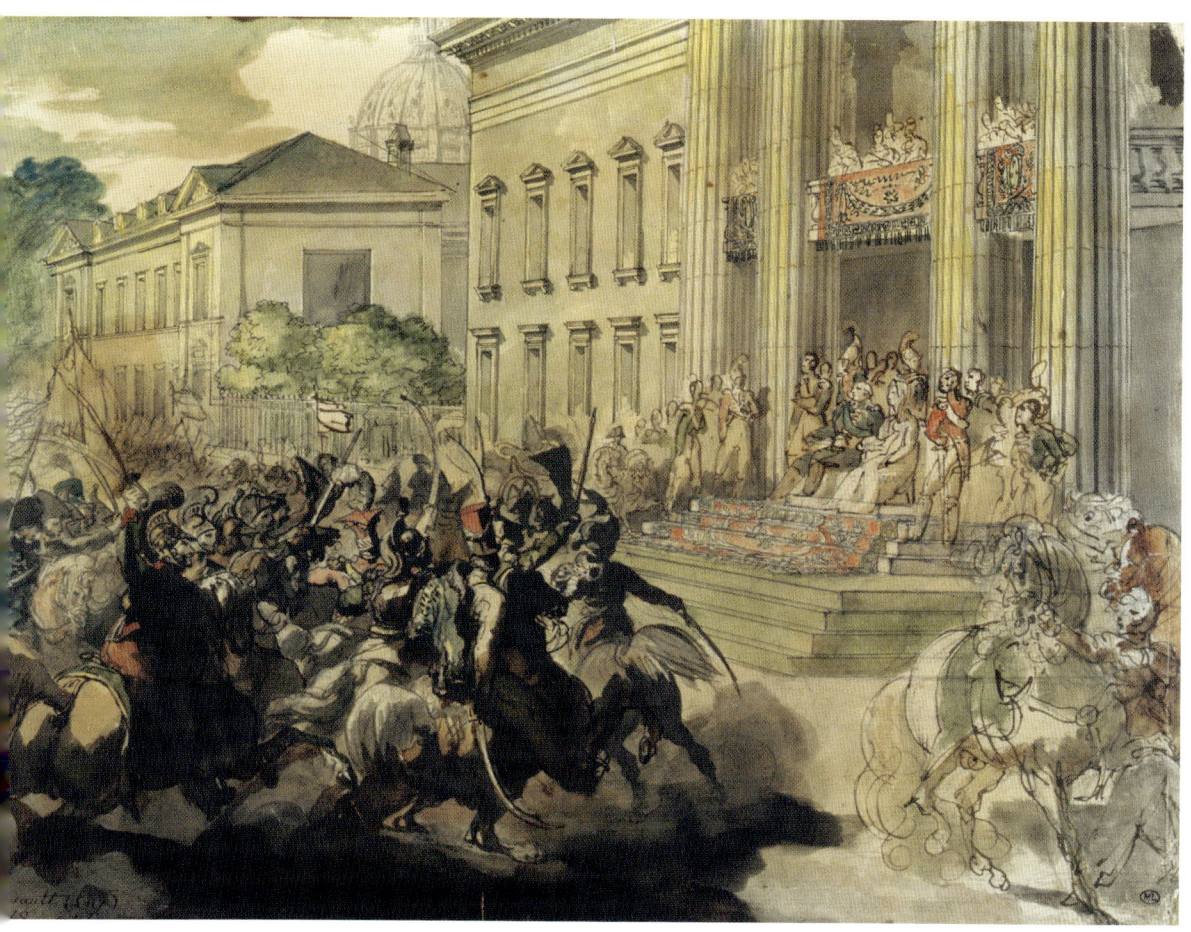

2.16. Théodore Géricault, *King Louis XVIII Reviews the Troops at the Champ de Mars*, c. 1814, ink and watercolor, 10⅛ × 14 in. (25.8 × 35.5 cm), Musée du Louvre, Paris.

that animated but ruined passage (along with the blandly perfunctory treatment of the obese king), the young equerry among the riderless mounts in the lower left corner stands apart as the one passage on the sheet executed with conviction, even as Géricault still experiments with different postures and attitudes for the figure.

That vignette of horse and dismounted rider also reveals how far away Géricault remained at this point from being able to fulfil the defining brief for a painter of the first rank: the interlocking articulation of multiple figures in a way that defined a dramatically significant event. For all the monumental scale of his Salon entries, he had limited himself to single equestrian figures. Their pendant display in 1814 opportunistically cobbled together the scale and multiple figures of a true historical tableau but without structural integration beyond these contingent circumstances. An artist of his talent and vision could not summon that higher capacity without finding a distinctive subject worthy of both, and this discovery would come only after he makes his decisive journey to Rome in 1816. As will become abundantly evident in the following chapter, he was able to discover his guiding themes without abandoning the hybrid human animal subjectivity to which he had resorted between 1812 and 1814; indeed, he would ramify and intensify that commitment under the stimuli of the sights he encountered in the Roman streets and piazzas of Carnival season.

*

In order to grasp the possibilities and pitfalls Géricault faced as he strove to master the history painter's brief, it may be illuminating to observe just how past-master Jacques-Louis David put his own skills to the test at roughly this same historical moment, as he fashioned his last new project of the Napoleonic era. The constituent materials for David's ultimate Napoleonic exercise came from a repertoire of the kind that Géricault would be seeking to create for himself on his Roman journey—though one vastly larger than the young artist could hope to approach: a remarkable set of albums grouping roughly related drawings made mainly during his sojourns in Rome, their origins stretching back four decades, carefully cut and glued into uniform pages.[7] His subject, *Alexander, Apelles, and Campaspe* (fig. 2.17), traditionally served as an exemplification of the creative process,

2.17. Jacques-Louis David, *Alexander, Apelles, and Campaspe*, 1813, pen and wash on paper, 11 × 15¼ in. (28.1 × 38.8 cm), private collection.

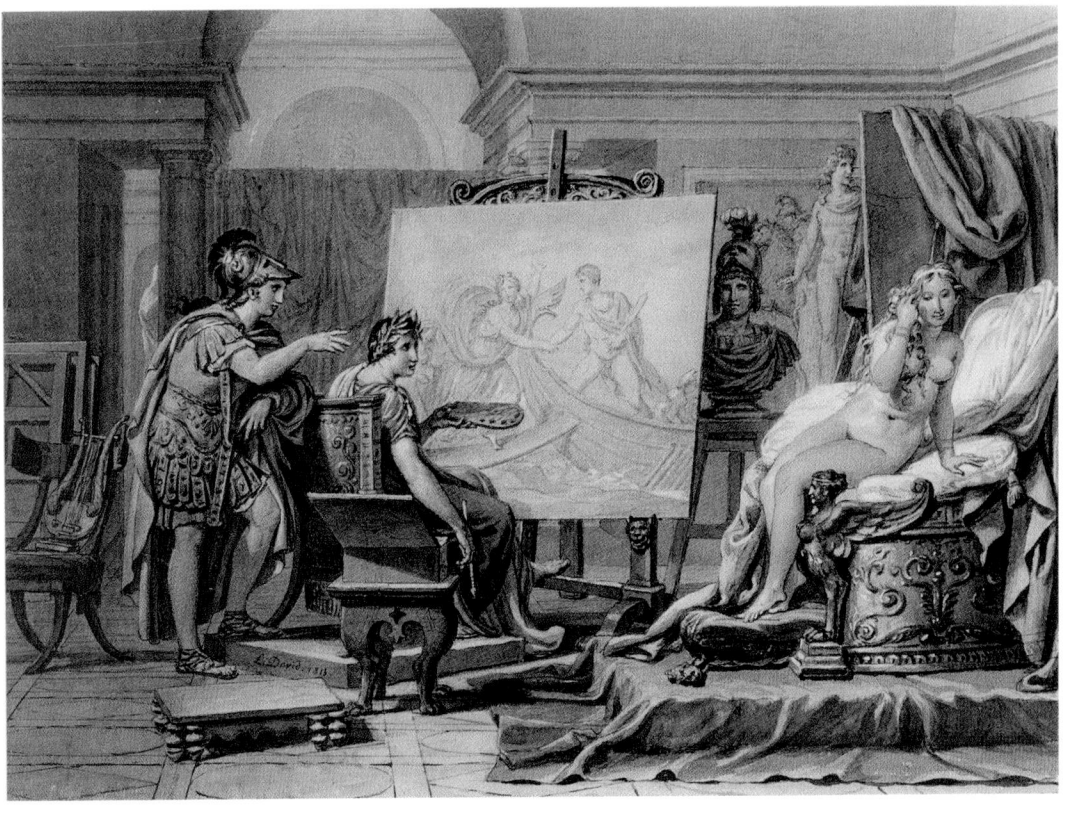

while doing double duty as meditation on the relation between artist and absolute ruler, the latter taken both as patron and as portrait subject. David used the exercise in such a way that each of those two artistic faces of rulership reinforced and intensified the other, the most completely realized outcome a densely populated presentation drawing likely completed in 1813.[8] In sifting through his albums with this *Alexander, Apelles, and Campaspe* in view, one can imaginatively reverse-engineer the scanning, filtering, selecting, and synthesizing of motifs that generated its composition.

The Roman author Pliny relates the legend that Apelles, reputedly the greatest painter of the ancient world, fell in love with Alexander's concubine Campaspe as he painted the portrait commissioned by the emperor of his beloved.[9] In the tradition of noble magnanimity, Alexander not only tolerates this servant's impertinent infatuation but also surrenders his concubine to the possession of Apelles. In David's version of the tale, this action may be occurring as we watch, expressed and effected by Alexander's gesture toward her, followed by the parallel gaze of the artist. The transactional character of the scene gains salience by the absence of any portrait on the artist's easel, for which David substitutes another motif entirely. In 1780, he had copied at the top of one album sheet (fig. 2.18) an ancient relief sculpture in Venice depicting the departure of Iphigenia and Orestes from the Black Sea outpost of Tauris—a contemporary theme from the operas of Christoph Willibald Gluck as much as from ancient art and drama—which he transcribed to the incomplete panel ostensibly by Apelles. The discrepancy might be rationalized by supposing that the artist has been using Campaspe as a model for the royal princess Iphigenia and that she has modestly retreated and turned away on Alexander's entrance into the studio.

A scene from the Trojan-War cycle carried the cachet of the intellectual history painter over and above the potentially servile connotations of portraiture. The fact that the depicted subject betokens the murders and parricide that haunted the House of Atreus further signals some disturbance to the straightforward gallantry recounted by Pliny. But the arrangement of the room remains that of a portrait sitting, though the only evident portrait subject is Alexander rather than his lover. A bust from the Giustiniani collection in Rome, thought at the time to represent Alexander, entered David's albums in the form of drawings in both upper corners of another sheet (fig. 2.19). Eminently useful prototypes for heroic narrative, this twin motif appears twice in David's *Alexander, Apelles* drawing, once as the basis for the active personage of Alexander leaning over the painter's shoulder and a second time as a portrait bust positioned behind the canvas, the principal human likeness in the scene.

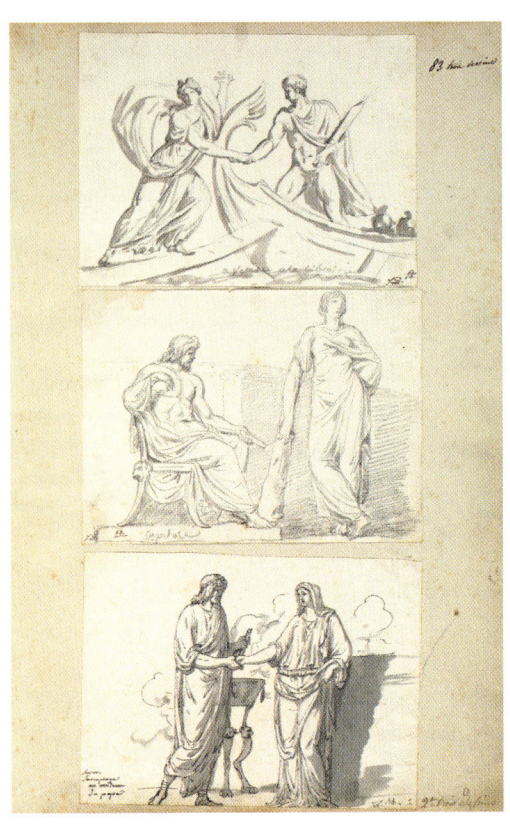

2.18. Jacques-Louis David, *Album 11*, 1775–1785, pencil, charcoal, ink, and wash, 20½ × 13⅝ in. (52 × 34.7 cm), Getty Research Institute, Los Angeles.

2.19. Jacques-Louis David, album drawing, 1775–1785, 6 × 8½ in. (15.2 × 21.6 cm), *Album factice, No. 8*, Department of Drawings and Prints, Pierpont Morgan Library, New York.

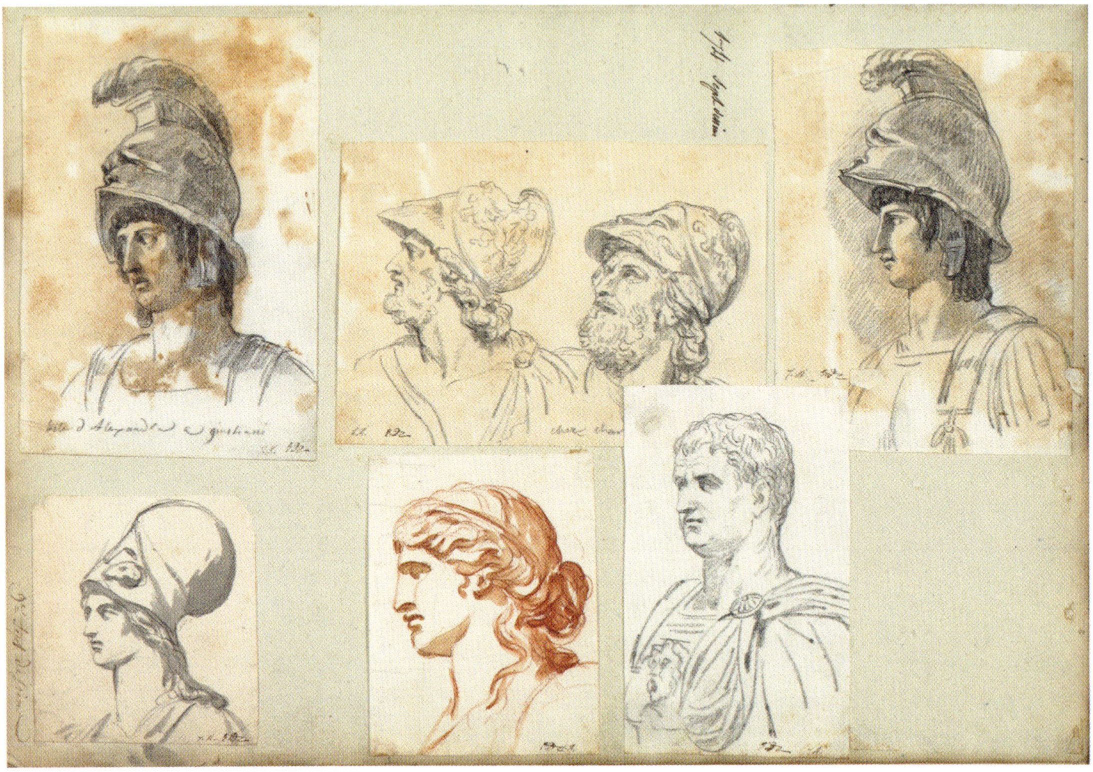

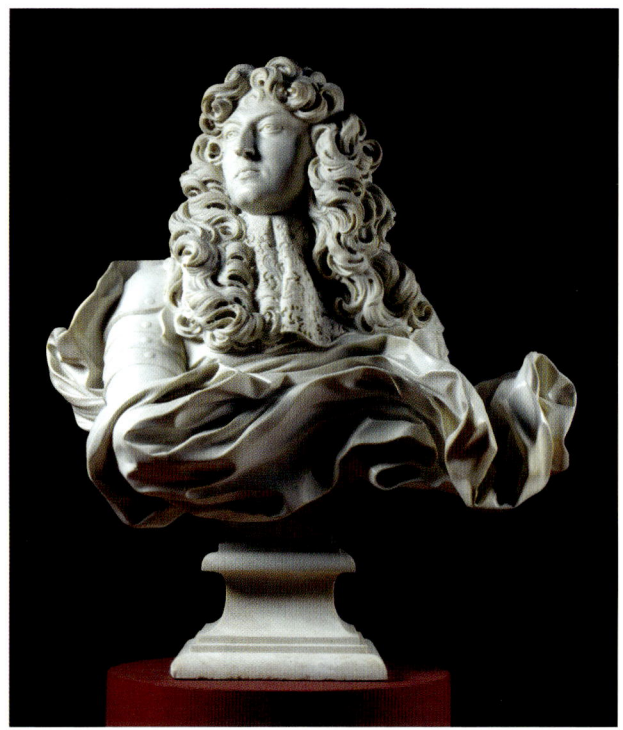

2.20. Gian Lorenzo Bernini, *Louis XIV, King of France and Navarre*, 1665, marble, 41⅜ × 38¼ × 15 in. (105 × 97 × 38 cm), Châteaux de Versailles et de Trianon, Versailles.

David thus shifts this inherited episode of portraiture from one subject, Campaspe, to another, Alexander. The theme of royal portrait as transaction had a well-known precedent in French art history, dating from the visit of Gian Lorenzo Bernini from his native Rome to Paris in 1665, both to offer his design for the new east front of the Louvre and to sculpt a bust of the young king, Louis XIV (fig. 2.20). Just as Alexander does not pose in David's drawing, the French king never properly sat for the Italian artist either: Bernini was only permitted to observe his subject in the midst of other activities. On the first such occasion, patron and artist shared a brief exchange: "I am stealing," Bernini said, when Louis happened to look at him. "Yes," replied the king, "but it is only to give back." To which Bernini responded: "But to give back less than I have stolen."[10] Bernini's reply makes a courtly compliment with ceremonial humility ("I am no better than a thief"), acknowledging that the artist's representation is always less than majesty of the king's physical presence, which the artist has stolen for his own endeavor. But it also contains an insolent claim, in that the artist asserts that the remainder of what he has taken is his to keep, that he has come out the better in the exchange.

The legend of Alexander and Apelles makes the terms of this commonplace concrete, with the surplus, personified in the figure of Campaspe, accruing to the artist. The story of Bernini and Louis XIV being known to any French artist as learned as was David, the modern import of Pliny's story is signaled by the palette in the left hand of Apelles, an anachronistic attribute, unknown in antiquity, of a present-day practitioner rather than an ancient Greek one. The first painting considered in this book was likewise a ruler portrait, *Napoleon in His Study*, David's last major likeness of the emperor, completed in the previous year (see fig. 1:1). In fashioning that painting for his foreign client, the artist was effectively stealing the likeness of the emperor—who regularly likened himself to Alexander—for his own highly profitable endeavor via the sale of the painting to the Scottish Lord Douglas. No Campaspe, but a thousand guineas from the buyer came into his hands. And Napoleon appears in the painting just as David wished, as a circumspect ruler removed from the grandiose pomp with which the Russian campaign had commenced.

Where *Napoleon in His Study* exhibits something close to a compulsive overcontrol in its tightly interlocking almost airless composition, the drawing of *Alexander, Apelles, and Campaspe*—composed as Napoleon desperately maneuvered in the field with the forces of the allies slowly closing in—appears at an opposite pole from that quality. Likewise, replete with multiple attributes and symbols (lyre, chair, cuirass, sphinx, *Belvedere Apollo*) (figs. 2.21–23) traceable to his personal catalog of studies, the drawing exerts only provisional control over them, tending to excessive accumulation rather than parsimonious

2.21. Jacques-Louis David, *Three Lyres*, gray wash and black chalk, 4⅜ × 6⅛ in. (11.2 × 15.4 cm), Musée du Louvre, Paris.

2.22. Jacques-Louis David, album drawings, formerly Lodewijk Houthakker collection, Amsterdam (top left and right, bottom right); Rijksmuseum, Amsterdam (bottom left, 8⅜ × 6 in. [21.2 × 15.3 cm]).

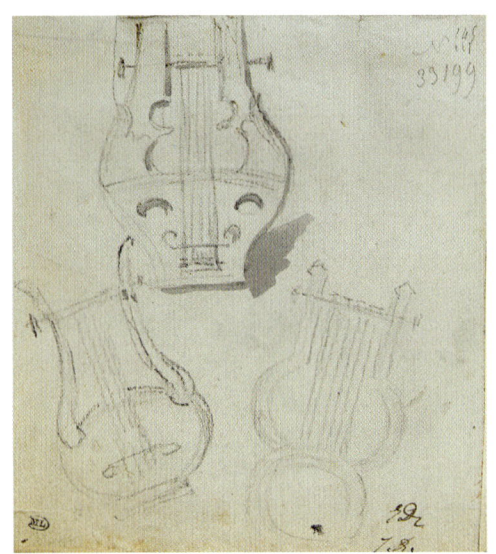

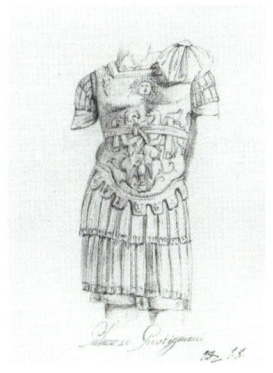

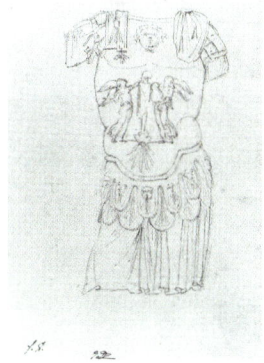

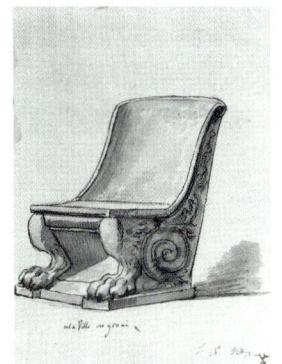

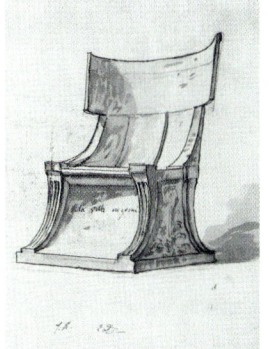

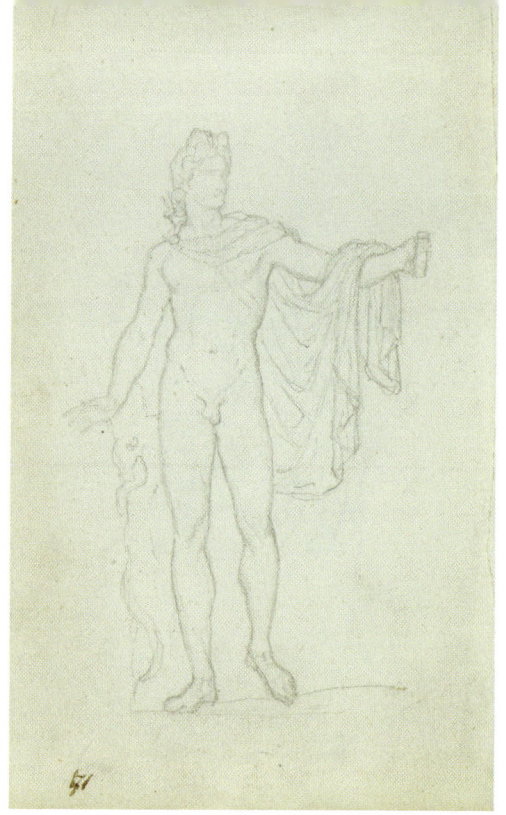

regulation of meaning. David left his album sources incompletely synthesized, lending his crowded composition the character of a jumbled antiquities storeroom. The scattered elements just minimally cohere into a subject that would forcefully have entered the mind of the artist when Napoleon had asked why he should pose for David when Alexander had never posed for Apelles.[11] David adapts the well-known tale from Pliny in order to contradict that confident assertion. At the same time, the counterfactual nature of the artist's claim betrays itself in a rendition of the classical Greek world as a catalog of incompletely synthesized artifacts.

When David subsequently attempted to translate the drawing of *Alexander, Apelles, and Campaspe* into such an integrated and plausible scene, the resulting painting (fig. 2.24)—never exactly dated or finished—sacrificed much of the liveliness and variety of its graphic predecessor, but finds its way to new and intriguing ambiguities of its own.[12] The vicissitudes of David's removal to Brussels (to be explored in chapter 5) were such that he had left behind the laboriously compiled albums of drawings from which his crowded conception of *Alexander, Apelles, and Campaspe* had arisen. Where he had been able to marshal the drawings from his youthful self to animate the lively, be-laureled Apelles of the drawing, translation into painting dragged on into the altered life of his exile. Rethinking the subject in the absence of his stored repertoire of Roman motifs, he replaced the anachronistic palette featured in the drawing with pots of color and

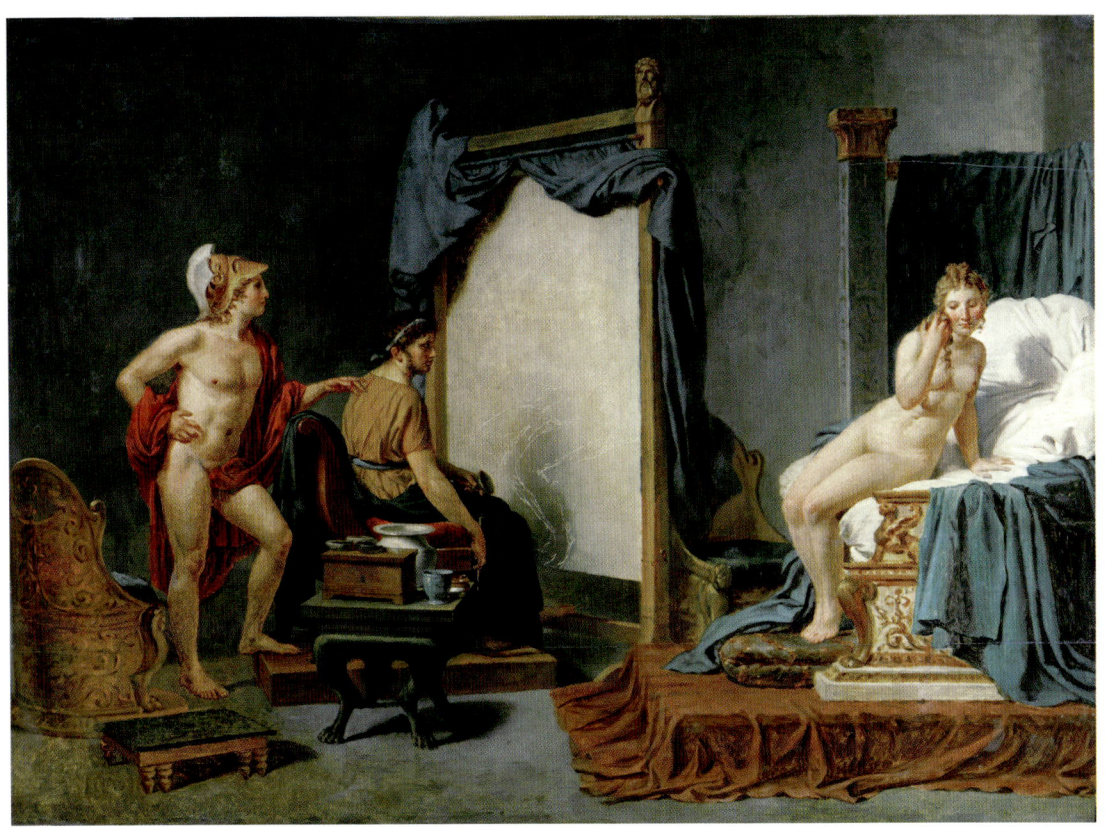

2.24. Jacques-Louis David, *The Painter Apelles, Alexander the Great, and Campaspe*, after 1813, oil on panel, 38 × 53½ in. (96.5 × 136 cm), Palais des Beaux-Arts, Lille (with 2 details a–b).

a small stove, true to the encaustic (melted wax) practice in ancient Greece (David's rendering of them an example of the underestimated vividness and delicacy he could bring to still life, fig. 2.24b). In more salient respects as well, he brought his conception of the scene closer to the ancient sources. The task at hand is once again the painting of a portrait: an actual outline of Campaspe appears on the panel, the legs of that figure matching those of the model as she poses to the far right (fig. 2.24a). In the panel's upper register, however, there also appears a less evolved sketch of Alexander himself reaching an arm around his concubine. This addition justifies the nudity of the ruler, who has taken a break from posing on the bed in order to inspect the painter's progress and point out some particular with the gesture that rests delicately on the shoulder of the latter. That byplay conflates the two positions of ruler as ideal patron and ruler as ideal model, positions that David had before kept separate. Although unauthorized by the Plinian anecdote, Alexander, leaving his position beside Campaspe on the bed to engage with the artist in such an intimate way, could enact that moment of the gift, the ruler acquiescing in the painter's "theft."

But the painter displays no trace of elation or inflation vis-à-vis his imperial patron. The slumped, downcast attitude of the second Apelles instead bears witness to some unsurprising sense of depletion

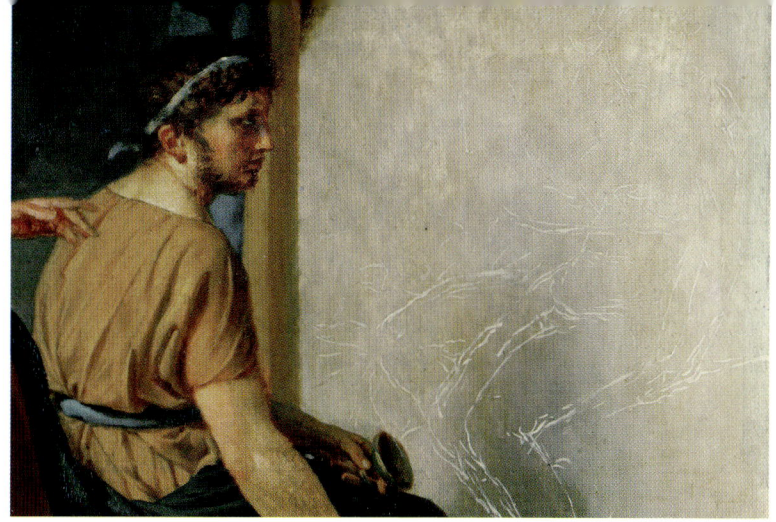

a

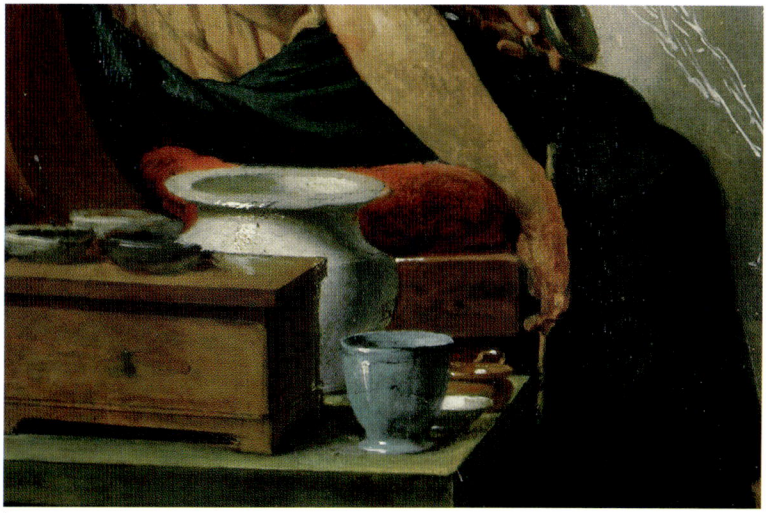

b

arising from displacement and loss, which far outweighed any relative gain that David may have enjoyed in his late transaction with Napoleon. His evacuated stock of motifs and ideas on paper weighed on him to the extent that he henceforth made it his business to rebuild that foundation from his own memory and imagination to serve the remarkably altered and energized last decade of his life and career. David's example in this regard manifests a more general pattern of the period whereby art was being perpetually unmade, then to be remade from the fragments and shards of the previous unmaking. The disintegration of the empire as a cultural platform and network hastened this process of unmaking; what will follow in the chapters to come will be an examination of the official attempts to restore the stable forms and meanings that predated the onset of revolution in France. But nothing, as stated at the outset of this book, seems to accelerate innovation and unpredictable change more than does the effort to reverse it.

Chapter 3

Waterloo Sunset, 1815–17

Napoleon Returns, David Crosses
Borders, and Géricault Wanders
Plebeian Rome with Thomas

IN THE LATE AUTUMN OF 1814, the prodigious young Théodore Géricault, just twenty-three years old, could count himself both a mounted royal guardsman and the author of two monumental paintings in the annual Salon exhibition at the Louvre. His pairing of the older *The Charging Chasseur*, first shown in 1812, with the new *Wounded Cuirassier* (see figs. 2.12–13) set up resonant contrasts apposite to that year of Napoleon's abdication and return of the Bourbon dynasty: the light cavalryman versus the heavy, troubled defiance versus resigned surrender, each horse bearing opposed loads of emotion suppressed in the faces of the riders. A small *Trumpeter of the Hussars* from this moment in his career recalled (fig. 3.1), with enhanced technical command, his triumphs just past along with his current military reality.

Thoughts of further artistic pursuits on his part, however, were eclipsed in February 1815, when news reached Paris of Bonaparte's escape from captivity on the Mediterranean island of Elba. The once and future emperor had landed with a small force near Antibes on the south coast and immediately began making his way up the valley of the Rhône. He succeeded in converting to his cause all the ostensibly royalist troops and commanders sent out to block him. The king's brother, le comte d'Artois, sent out to confront him, simply abandoned the field at Lyons.

Having cashiered so many able officers, Louis XVIII—despite the flourish of his personal cavalry—found himself with neither effective defenses nor the personal courage required to rally support in the royalist west of the country. As Bonaparte was preparing to enter Paris from Fontainebleau, Géricault's company found itself summoned in the night to accompany their just-restored king on a furtive flight across the Netherlandish border, aiming for ignominious exile in Ghent (an event the unfortunate Antoine-Jean Gros was later enjoined to celebrate in a crowded and perfunctory composition as if it were some exemplum of virtue and command [fig. 3.2]). Not long after departing the Tuileries Palace, however, the king's nocturnal column, dogged by lancers loyal to Bonaparte, disintegrated in an incessant downpour. Géricault found himself among those riders hastily dismissed from service and effectively abandoned to their fates, while the monarch struggled on with only a tiny entourage.

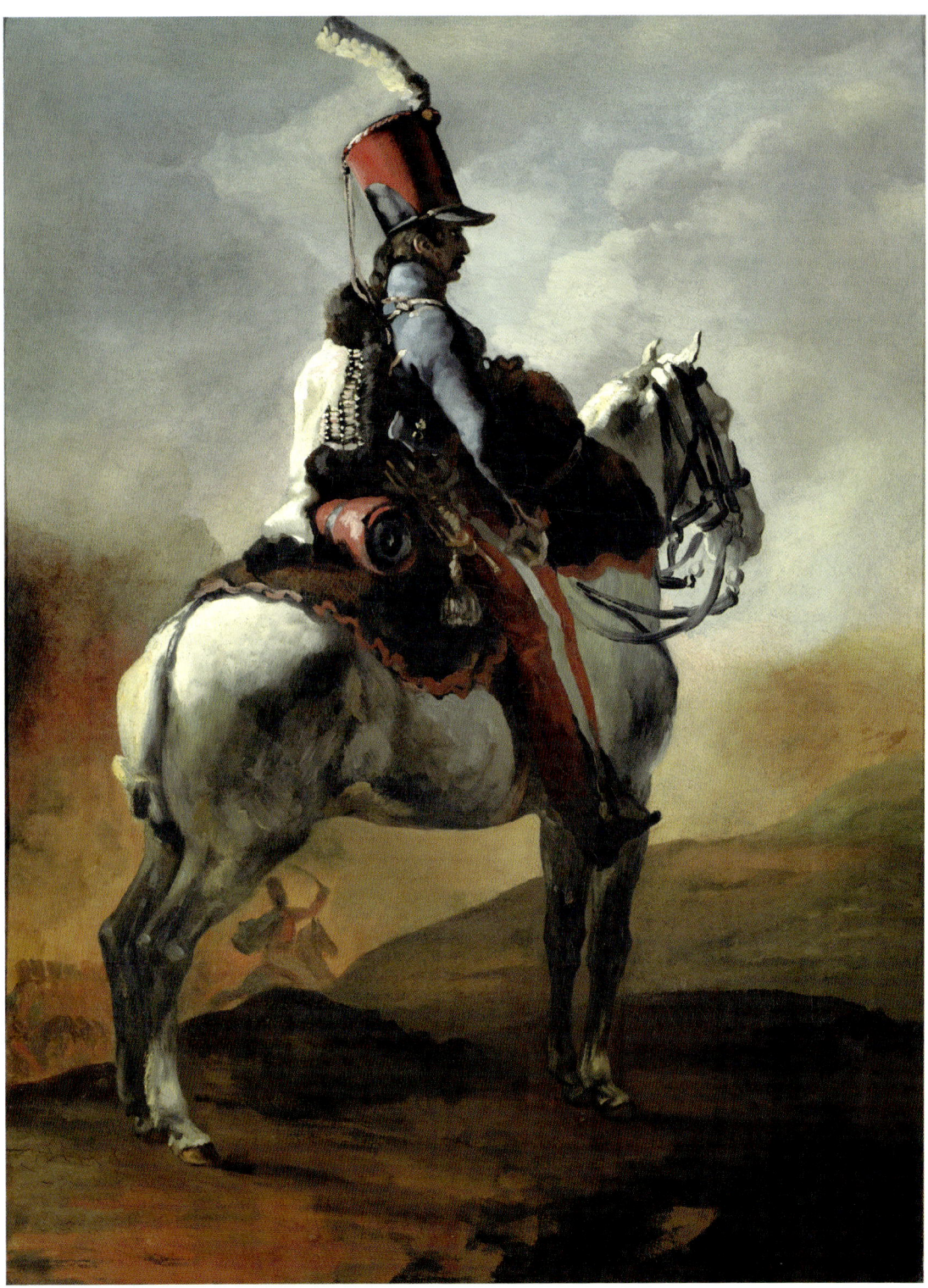

3.1. Théodore Géricault, *Trumpeter of the Hussars*, c. 1815, oil on canvas, 37¹³⁄₁₆ × 28¼ in. (96 × 71.8 cm), Clark Art Institute, Williamstown, MA.

Discarding the sodden ruins of their splendid uniforms and tack, each of the suddenly former guardsmen made his own way in shabby civilian dress; for his part, Géricault assumed the disguise of a teamster.[1] Caution was necessary, as Bonaparte had forbidden any members of the royal companies from residing in or near Paris. Fearing retribution should he reveal himself there, Géricault made himself exceedingly scarce, perhaps hiding out with family in Normandy or simply going to ground in his studio in the rue des Martyrs. No one seems to know where he kept himself over the next three months. When Louis XVIII, now the pawn of the Duke of Wellington, returned at the end of June 1815 in the wake of Napoleon's final defeat at Waterloo, Géricault stayed clear of any renewed military service.

The king, no longer the acclaimed harbinger of peace he had been in the first Restoration, promptly unleashed a harsh return to arbitrary, authoritarian rule in the second Restoration, the royal family and entourage determined to efface as many of the changes wrought by revolution and empire as they could possibly accomplish. While Géricault's record in the Royal Guard meant that he had nothing personally to fear, the same did not apply to Jacques-Louis David, who had not only served and celebrated Napoleon but had also in his days as a revolutionary deputy voted for the execution of Louis XVI, older brother of the current ruler.

3.2. Antoine-Jean Gros, *The Departure of Louis XVIII from the Tuileries on the Night of 20 March 1815*, 1817, oil on canvas, 159½ × 206¾ in. (405 × 525 cm), Châteaux de Versailles et de Trianon, Versailles.

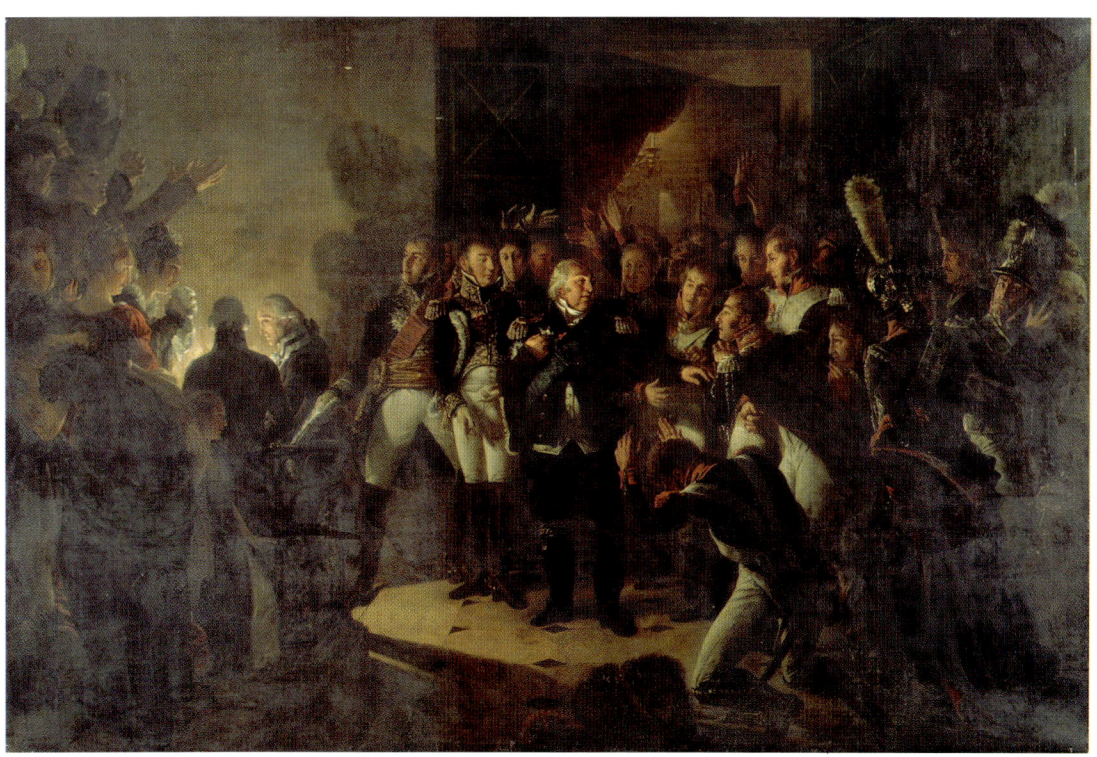

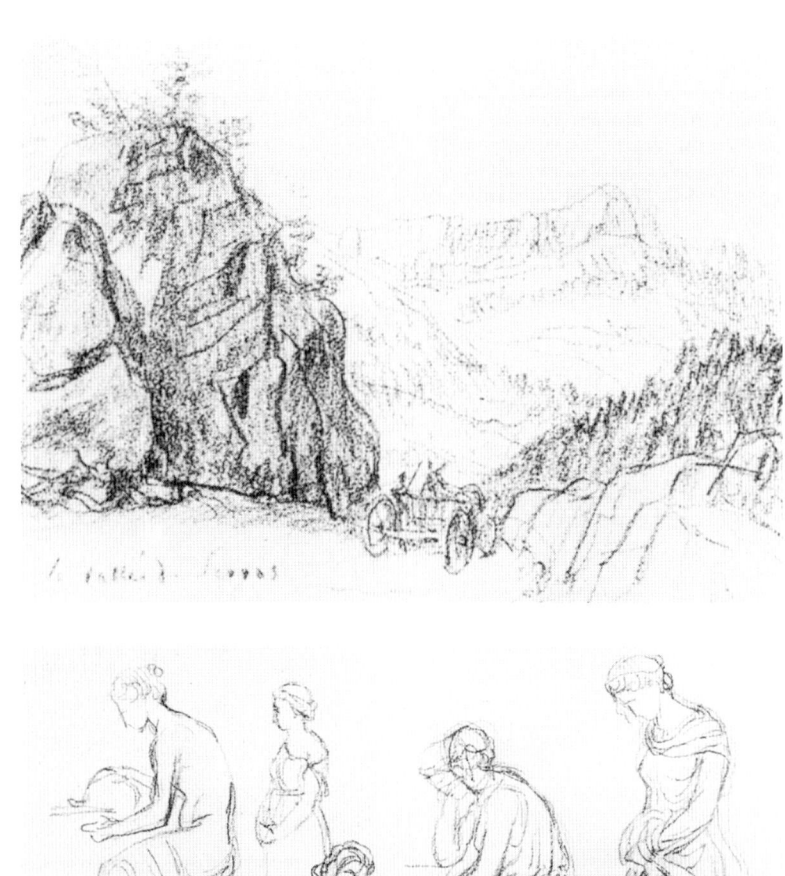

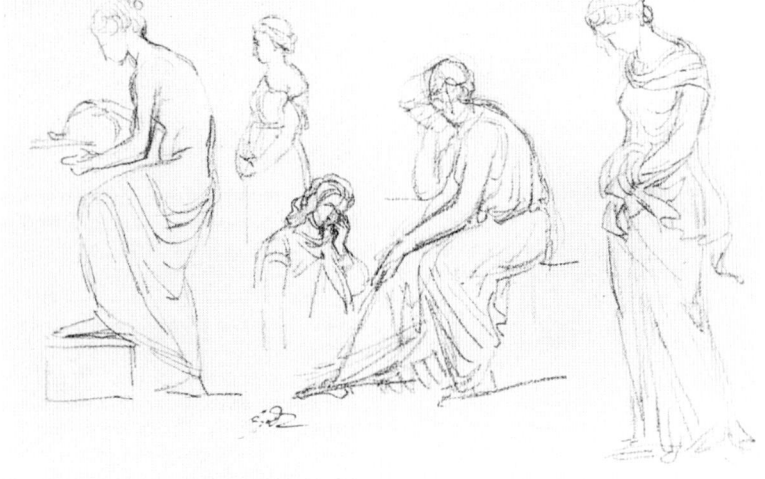

Within days of the news from Waterloo reaching Paris, David made a request for a passport that would allow his crossing the border into Switzerland. Under the circumstances, it is difficult to credit David's explanation that his apparent flight would be no more than a "voyage pittoresque," long in the planning, but he made good on that promise by augmenting in the course of his travels the stock of drawings discussed in the previous chapter.[2] Accompanied only by a servant named Geoffroy, he crossed the border on the road to Lausanne, then circled the lake to Geneva and back across the modern French border to the villages of the valley of Chamonix below Mont Blanc (during these travels, David had kept up a clandestine correspondence with his wife under the name "M. and Mme Geoffroy"). Along the route, he stopped to record the inarguably picturesque vistas (fig. 3.3),[3] but continued to have the classics on his mind, producing alongside the landscapes a succession of improvised studies with human figures. Few possess any self-evident subject, but all point simultaneously to his own past and to some future, unexampled repertoire of classical themes.[4]

One sheet (fig. 3.4), for example, promises but does not quite deliver a ritual procession of maidens toward some suggested sacrifice; David's thoughts were sufficiently developed, whatever the intended theme, that he began to experiment by turning the central seated figure from a melancholy profile to a downward regard in the direction of the viewer. More worked out but still elusive in its narrative (fig. 3.5) is a languishing young male lover, accompanied by a melancholy cupid, about to be ministered some potion (poison?) by a hovering female nurse. Other pages present looser arrays of figures, the most intriguing of which (fig. 3.6) includes a denser, overlapping group on the right-hand side with an ominously resonant legend in David's hand: "these condemned ones adorned with flowers." One exceptional sheet (fig. 3.7) offers a recognizable mythic motif, Leda ravished by Zeus in the guise of a swan, which David displaces to a landscape akin to the Alpine valleys through which he was then traveling (fig. 3.8).

As explored in the previous chapter, a young student in Rome is typically keen to gather from the city's artistic riches a repertoire of possible types, poses, gestures, and expressions, later to be recombined as needed into narratives that would serve the artist over the span of his career. With the drawings from his hasty Alpine sojourn, David appears to have renewed a parallel process late in life, but one

3.5. Jacques-Louis David, *Seated Male Supported by a Veiled Woman Extending a Vial, a Cupid Crying,* album drawing, 1815, black chalk on paper, private collection.

3.6. Jacques-Louis David, *Condemned Women Adorned with Flowers*, album drawing, 1815, black chalk on paper, private collection.

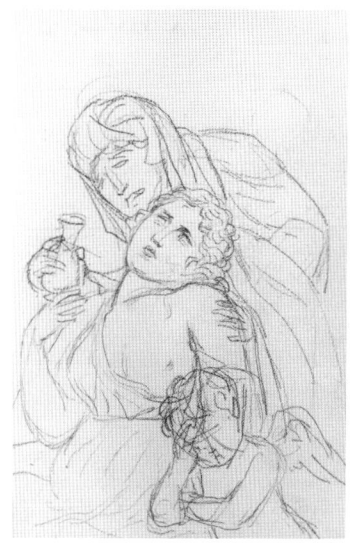

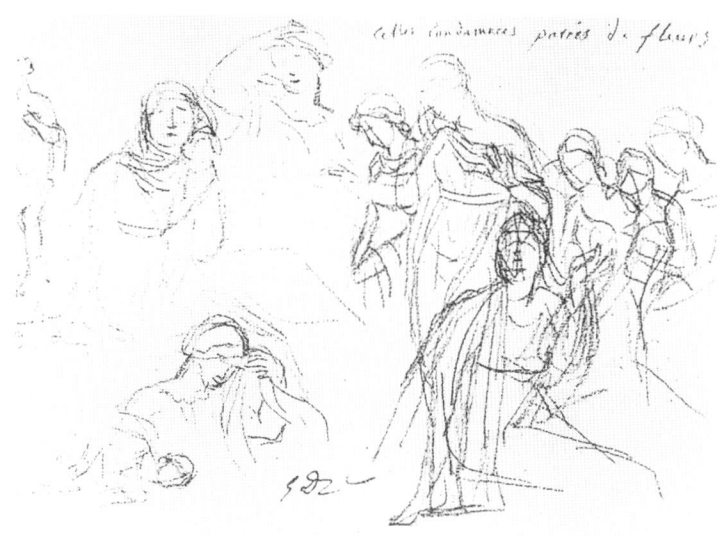

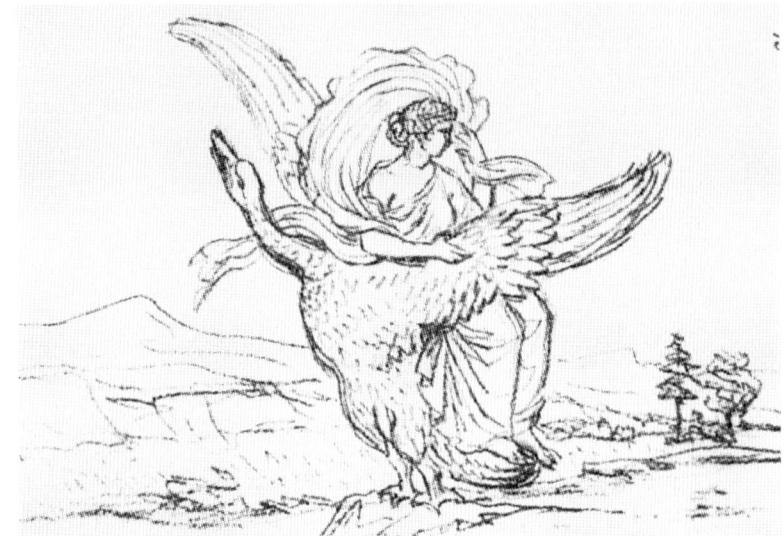

3.7. Jacques-Louis David, *Leda and the Swan before a Mountainous Landscape*, album drawing, 1815, black chalk on paper, private collection.

3.8. Jacques-Louis David, *Vallée de Servos*, album drawing, 1815, black chalk on paper, 1815, private collection.

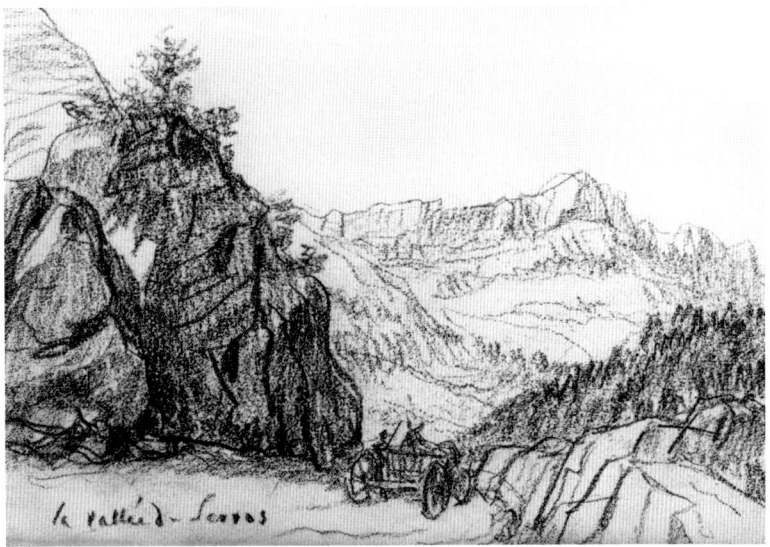

that relied on his own reserves of memory and imagination, freely reassembling known narrative groupings into new situations and stories outside of an inherited repertoire of themes dictated by the classical texts. How far he might have gone with these exercises cannot be known, as word reached him in early August, while circling back to Geneva, that the fears behind his first panicked flight had not been borne out by events, and that it appeared safe for him to return to Paris. But he remained wary nonetheless. Thanks to the favorable intervention of an Austrian diplomat, his passport was finally delivered at Besançon, but so eager was he to escape his military custody that he set out for home under the cover of darkness at three o'clock the next morning.[5]

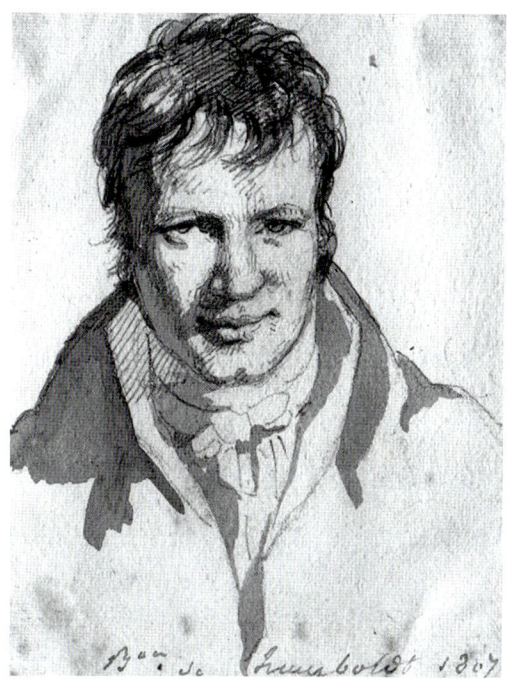

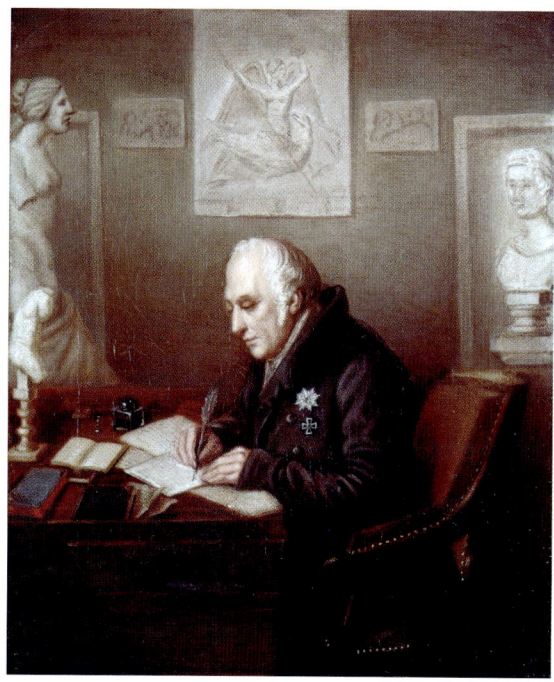

3.9. Frédéric Cristophe de Houdetot, *Portrait of Alexander von Humboldt*, 1807, graphite and wash, Library of the Conseil d'Etat, Paris.

3.10. Anonymous, *Wilhelm von Humboldt in His Study at the Tegel Castle*, c. 1830, oil on canvas, 14 × 11¾ in. (35.5 × 30 cm), Goethe House and Museum, Frankfurt am Main.

Once reinstalled in Paris, he kept to a quiet life for the remainder of 1815, as the policy of the restored monarchy toward those who played prominent roles in the revolution and empire gradually took shape. In mid-January 1816, the ambiguity came to end: all regicides— that is, those deputies who had voted for the death of Louis XVI— were to be permanently banished from France. David's request to the authorities that he be allowed passage to Switzerland or to Italy was denied. So, just eleven days later, he and his wife arrived in their final, permanent home near the center of Brussels, about which much more will be said in chapter 5.

David and his family, however, were not the only ones anticipating this outcome and considering their options. Soon after settling into their new home, David received a written entreaty from Alexander von Humboldt (fig. 3.9), the celebrated naturalist and explorer of Latin America. The letter conveyed a message from his brother, Wilhelm (fig. 3.10), leader of the Prussian delegation to the Congress of Vienna, where the victorious allies had been hammering out the post-Napoleonic settlement for Europe. The Humboldts were proposing that David immigrate to Prussia, where he would be appointed court painter to King Friedrich Wilhelm and oversee, in parallel with Wilhelm's renowned educational initiatives, "the establishment of a new Museum and the advancements of studies in all branches of the arts and drawing."[6]

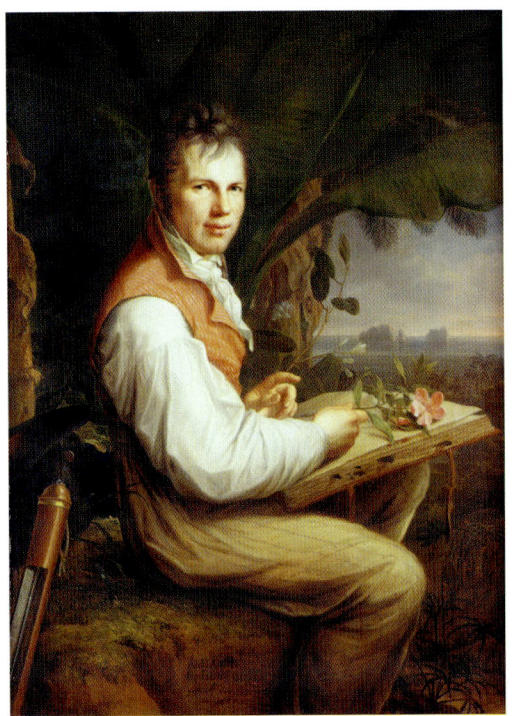

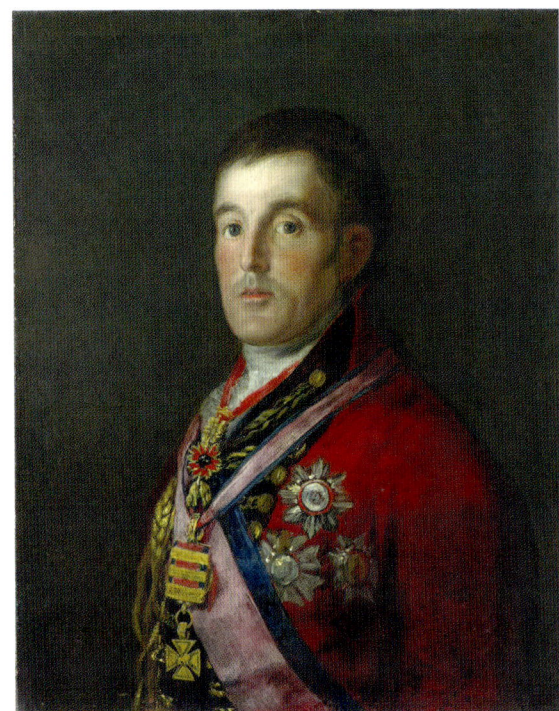

3.11. Georg Weitsch, *Portrait of Alexander von Humboldt*, 1806, oil on canvas, 49⅝ × 36⅜ in. (126 × 92.5 cm), Nationalgalerie, Staatliche Museen, Berlin.

3.12. Francisco Goya, *Portrait of the Duke of Wellington*, 1812–14, oil on mahogany, 25⅜ × 20⅝ in. (64.3 × 52.4 cm), National Gallery, London.

The brothers Humboldt can be said to have led Europe intellectually, Wilhelm being an eminent linguist and architect of the Prussian educational system, a worldwide model, which included his founding the University of Berlin. Alexander, mostly resident in Paris since returning in 1804 from his expeditions in the Americas (fig. 3.11), had received acclaim akin to the reception accorded Charles Lindbergh after his trans-Atlantic flight in the early twentieth century. Thereafter he dedicated himself to publishing the first comprehensive scientific accounts of South American geology, zoology, and botany—volumes avidly consumed, if not always read and understood, by a broad educated public across Europe. Their entreaty to David points to the ways in which culture was coming to be conceived on a European rather than parochially national scale. It also demonstrates the ways that artistic matters frequently confounded the divisions and fault lines of political affairs. In this case, the Prussians had been the most punitive in their attitudes and behavior toward the French, the most vociferous in expressions of emerging German nationalism, the architects of the final coalition that brought down Napoleon in 1814, as well as providing the fiercest auxiliaries to Wellington in the allied victory at Waterloo.

The latter aspect of Prussia loomed larger in David's mind, steeling him against further inducements after he refused the Humboldts' initial offer. The undeterred Prussian Chancellor Hardenberg made

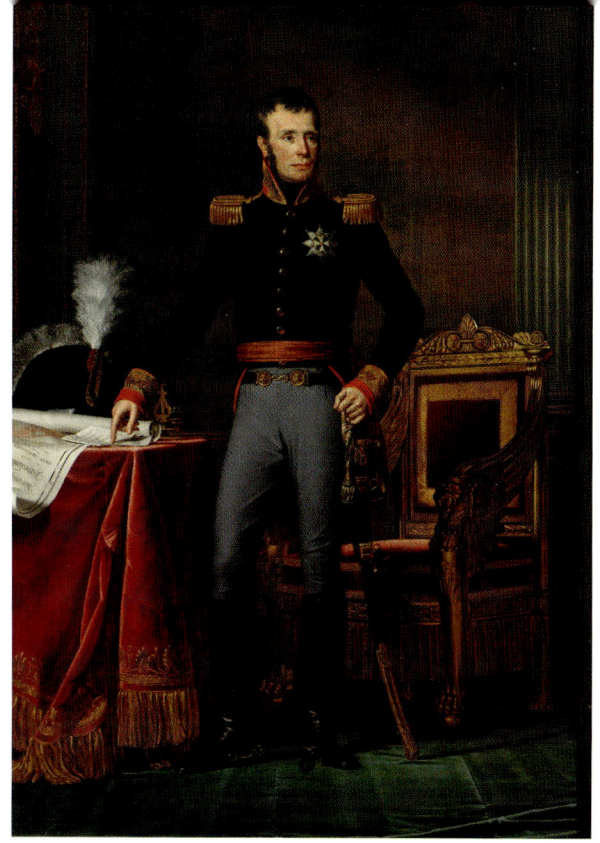

3.13. Joseph Paelinck, *Portrait of William I, King of the United Netherlands*, 1817, oil on canvas, 88 × 69 in. (223.5 × 175.3 cm), Museum of the Rhode Island School of Design, Providence.

it again, while the Prussian ambassador to the Netherlands promised that the artist's promised ministerial status would reopen the borders of France to him.[7] David nonetheless held firm, stating forthrightly to one correspondent: "I do not want to use my brush to recall the reverses and misfortunes of my country." When an intermediary conveyed an offer to paint the Duke of Wellington (as Goya just had done [fig. 3.12]), he replied: "I have not waited seventy years to defile my brush. I would rather cut off my hand than paint an Englishman."[8] Either the experience of defeat had reversed the easygoing commerce that David had enjoyed with Lord Douglas over the commissioning of *Napoleon in His Study* (see fig. 1.1) or, as is likely, he drew a hard and fast distinction between celebrating a French subject, whoever the client might be, and doing the same for an enemy sitter.

The Davids' arrival at their new Brussels address preceded by only a few months the unification of present-day Belgium with the Dutch provinces under a newly created Kingdom of the Netherlands—this larger polity fashioned by the allies as a further, post-Waterloo bulwark against traditional French designs on that territory. Despite these geopolitical origins, however, its newly entitled monarch, William I, former Prince of Orange, showed himself hospitable to French Restoration exiles—generosity for which David publicly praised him (David's Belgian pupil, Joseph Paelinck, painted the new ruler of the Netherlands in the year after the master's exile [fig. 3.13]).[9]

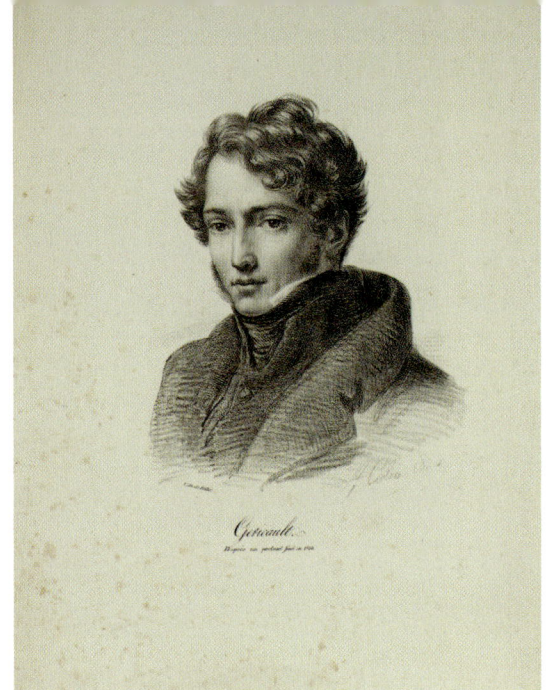

3.14. Alexandre Colin, *Portrait of Géricault*, lithograph on cream wove paper, image: 7⅞ in × 5⅝ in. (20 × 14.3 cm); sheet 13¾ × 9⁹⁄₁₆ in. (34.9 × 24.2 cm), Portland Art Museum, Portland, Oregon.

That lenient policy meant that David could enjoy the company of friends among the fellow exiles, along with his extended family and a small but talented circle of Belgian pupils. He would henceforth refuse to entertain any idea of returning to France, even when the tirelessly loyal Antoine-Jean Gros would make it a genuine option.

✳

In this present account, 1816 emerges as the year of wandering for both the anxious, threatened David at the age of sixty-six and the discarded, rudderless Théodore Géricault (fig. 3.14) at age twenty-five. Belatedly setting his sights on the journey to Rome lately denied to the older artist, Géricault enrolled in the competition for the Grand Prix, the annual winner of which was accorded a three-year residence in the French Academy in Rome. Since Napoleon's conquest of the city, that institution had been enviably located in the Villa Medici on the Pincian Hill, next to the French church of Trinità dei Monti and backing onto the Borghese Gardens—as seen in the middle ground of an 1809 cityscape by François-Marius Granet (fig. 3.15). The competition of 1816, commencing in March, was the first to be held since the final abdication of Napoleon the previous summer. As such, it carried the burden of reasserting continuity with the prerevolutionary past. The subject chosen for the final production, *Oenone Refusing Aid to the Wounded Paris*, came from the saga of the Trojan War, but from an esoteric, non-Homeric source.[10] In its account of the city's fall, the mortally wounded Paris must turn for aid to his spurned first wife, the nymph Oenone of Mount Ida, which she indignantly refuses. The

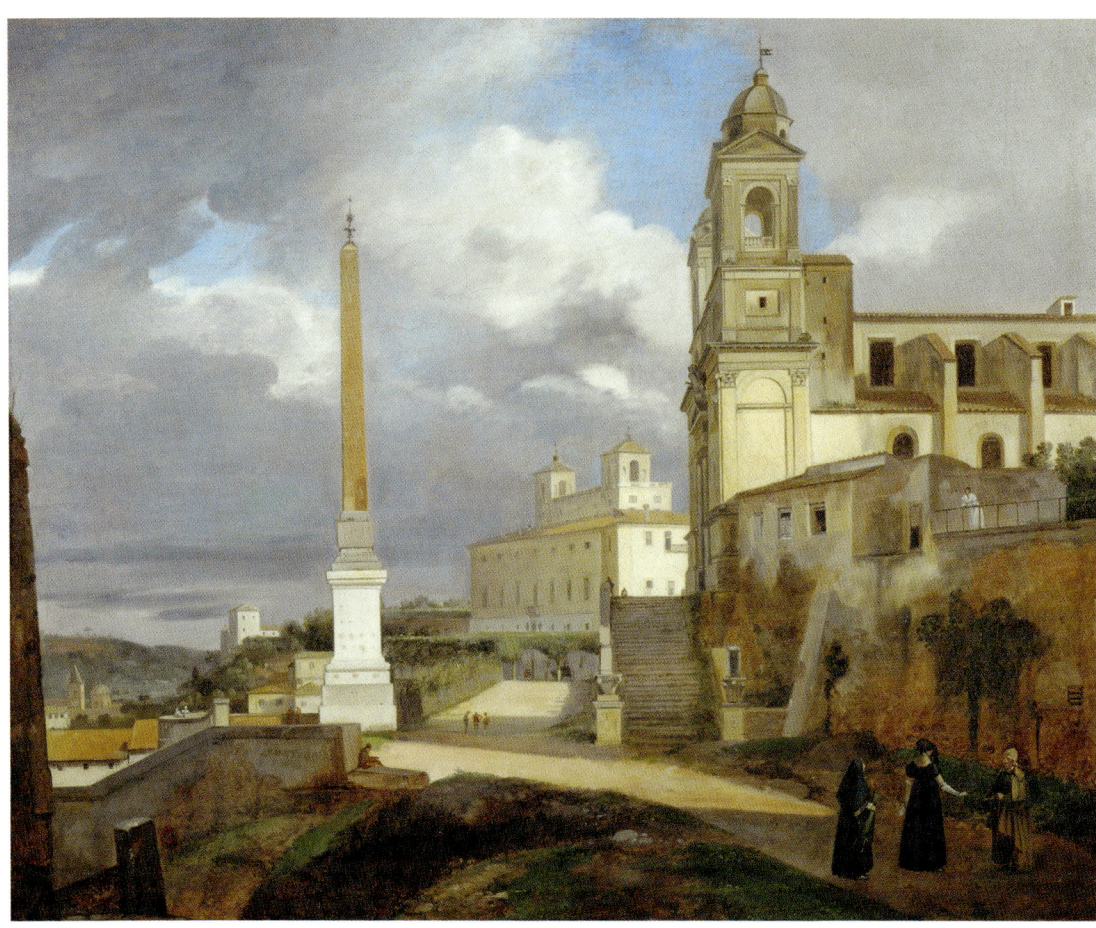

3.15. François-Marius Granet, *Trinità dei Monti and the Villa Medici, Rome*, 1808, oil on canvas, 19¼ × 24⅜ in. (49 × 62 cm), Musée du Louvre, Paris.

main actor in the scene, wearing the Phrygian cap that symbolized both Troy and French republican radicals, thus fatally suffers punishment for past betrayals.

In the eyes of posterity, Géricault was far and away the best-known and most gifted entrant in the competition, but the victor was Antoine Jean-Baptiste Thomas (fig. 3.16), a student of David's perennial competitors François-André Vincent (then in his last months of life) and Pierre-Narcisse Guérin. In realistic terms, Géricault would never have been permitted to win—not without an influential senior sponsor and a record of dutiful observance of the training protocols, neither of which he possessed. He was duly eliminated in an early round, well before the finalists entered their solitary chambers to produce their finished paintings in seventy-one days. But the proudly wayward young artist and soldier had staked his claim to possessing all he needed to prevail in the competition, despite minimal vetting and mentorship. That attitude would be consistent with Géricault going on to shadow the successful contestants with his own studies for the final subject. The most accomplished of these (fig. 3.17) throws down the gauntlet to Thomas, who had ostentatiously turned the largely covered body of Oenone away from both the viewer and her estranged spouse, who dominates the foreground. Géricault pushed the torso of Paris to the edge of the composition in favor of a proudly erect and defiant female protagonist. As he had been eliminated at the stage of drawing from the live model, the nudity of the figure asserts the autodidact's achievements as being commensurable with any of his peers.

In September 1816, Géricault made good on that defiant stance by taking himself off to Rome on his own account, something the wealth of his family permitted him to do. At the moment of his departure, other family considerations—a clandestine love affair with a woman who was his aunt by marriage—doubtless roiled his emotions more than had professional disappointment.[11] He thus arrived in Rome—by

3.16. Antoine Jean-Baptiste Thomas, *Oenone Refusing Aid to Paris, Wounded at the Siege of Troy*, 1816, oil on canvas, 44⅞ × 57½ in. (114 × 146 cm), École nationale supérieure des Beaux-Arts, Paris.

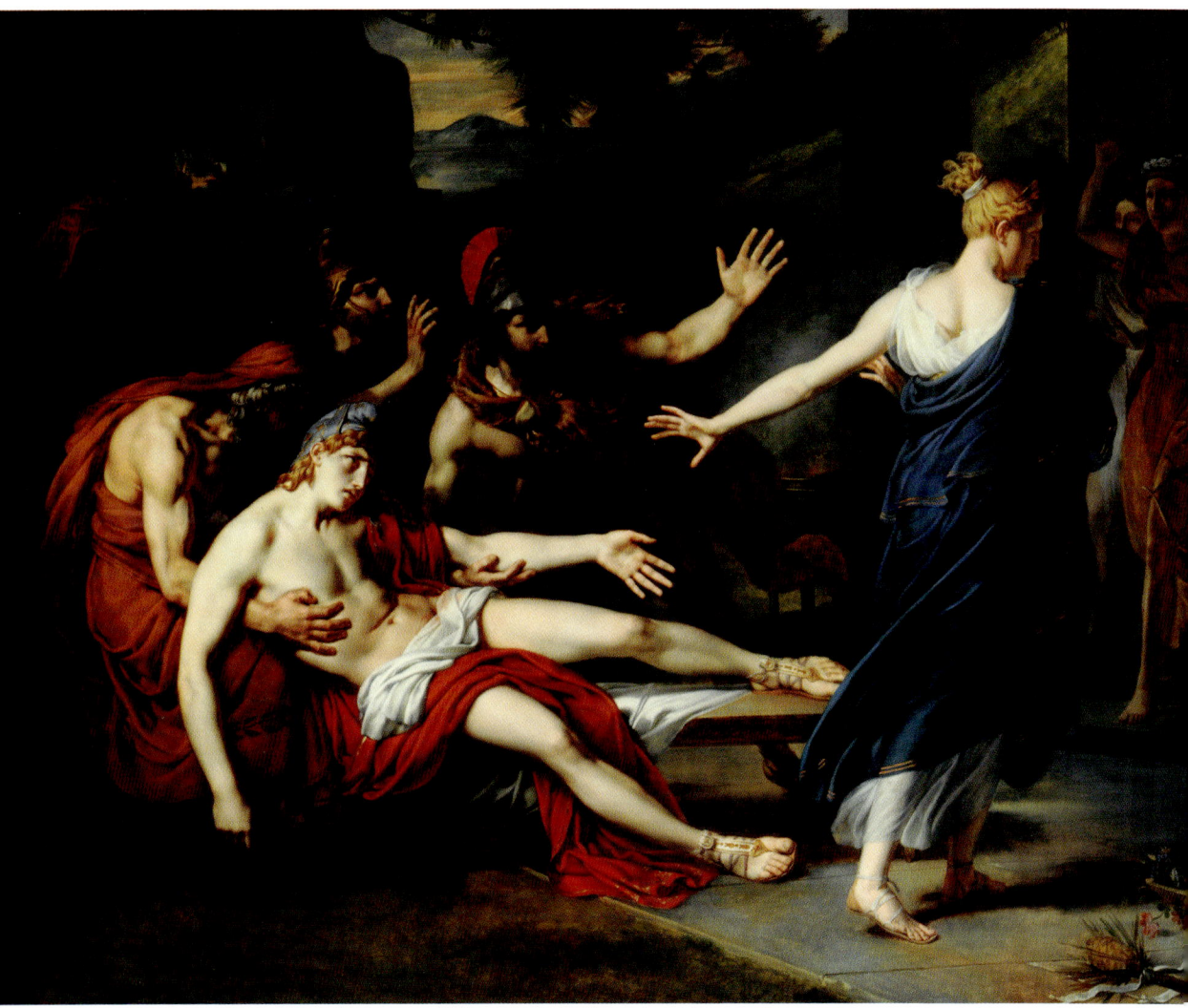

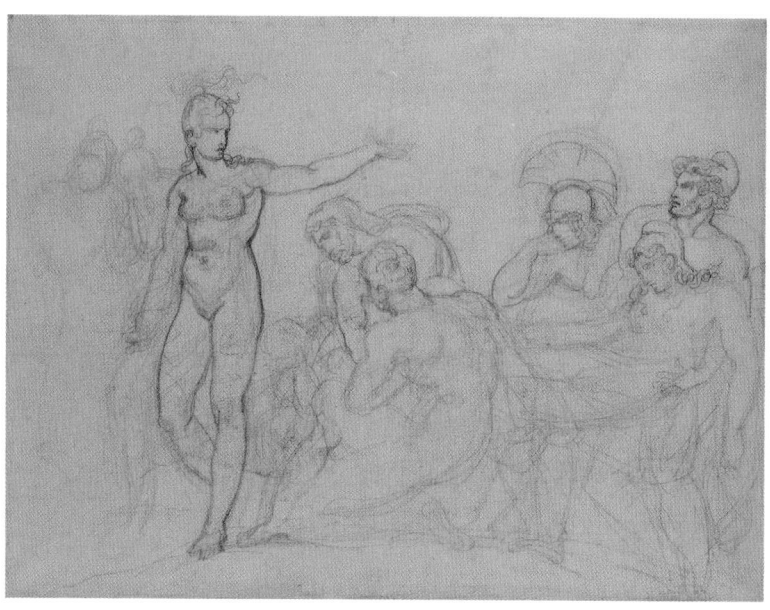

way of Florence—in an unsettled mental state, answering to no one, bearing a reputation for headstrong impetuosity and independence. To dwell on these qualities, however, tends unhelpfully to isolate the artist from his contemporaries, chiefly the same Thomas who had bested him for the Grand Prix. Residual bad feeling from the Rome Prize competition might have been expected to distance the young artists from each other, but the opposite appears to have been the case. One can indeed reasonably ask: Who, between the outsider Géricault and the groomed insider Thomas, was more likely to have followed a regimen of dutiful study when both found themselves in Rome that autumn? And who, between them, was more likely to be the disobedient scoffer at academic norms?

Although Géricault, as will become evident, claimed a considerable degree of independence for himself, the more wayward one turns out to have been Thomas, though the nature of his disobedience differed greatly from that displayed by the far more famous rebels of past decades like Jean-Germain Drouais and Anne-Louis Girodet, who chafed against the supervision of the Academy in order to pursue what each believed to be a deeper and truer commitment to the ideals of antiquity.[12] While Thomas fulfilled the customary obligation of any Rome prizewinner by painting a heroic male nude—the *envoi*—to be judged in Paris by the professors of the Academy, he only finished his *Dead Greek Warrior* (fig. 3.18) in 1819, shortly before returning to Paris.[13] Over the previous two years he had largely directed his energies toward documenting in studies on paper his walking itineraries around Rome. Nothing at all unusual in that, but Thomas barely registered the antique remains, stately altarpieces, and Campagna

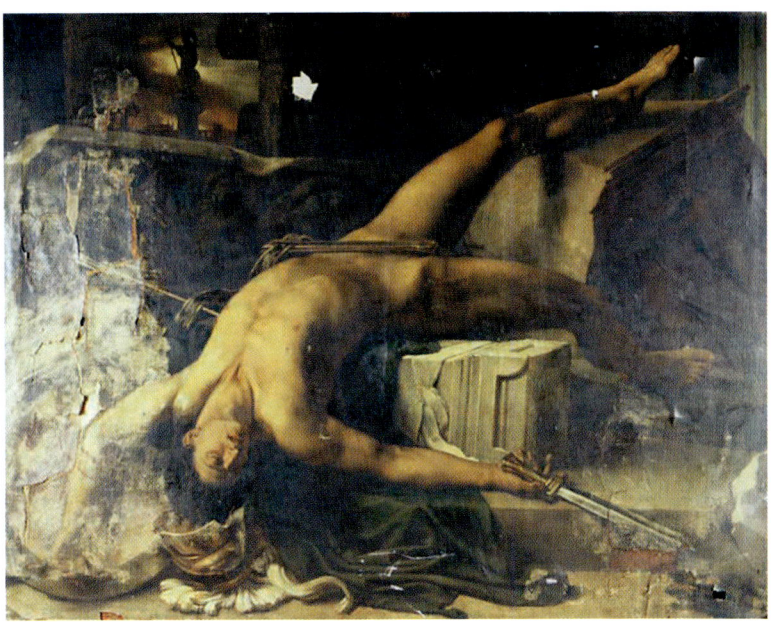

landscapes that preoccupied his peers and predecessors in their bulging sketchbooks. The number and observational immediacy of these studies have virtually no counterpart in the annals of young French artists in the city.

One telling example presents itself as a simple vignette (fig. 3.19) of two women of fashionable appearance speaking to each other from separate upper-story windows. The deft economy of description in the contrast between the illuminated figure and the shadowed one—the confident characterization of both setting and human life in a minimal number of touches to the paper—need no belaboring. The sheet is one of many that transform a moment in Roman street life into a fully realized artistic statement, however slight the artist's touch or the dimensions of a given sheet. But Thomas by no means relied on the inherent charm of miniaturization. Another sheet (fig. 3.20) captures the entire sweep of a crowded bullfight in the Corea Amphitheater, an imposing arena installed inside the ruin of the Mausoleum of Augustus. Named for the Portuguese marchese who had constructed this scaled-down Coliseum, the venue had since 1802 had been owned and administered by the Vatican treasury (the Camera Apostolica). Ecclesiastical oversight had not tempered the violence of its various spectacles. The resemblance to the ancient Roman amphitheater went beyond appearance, the menu of entertainments including wild animal hunts and a brand of bullfighting more akin to animal baiting than any stately Spanish *corrida*, fireworks concluding every day's events.[14]

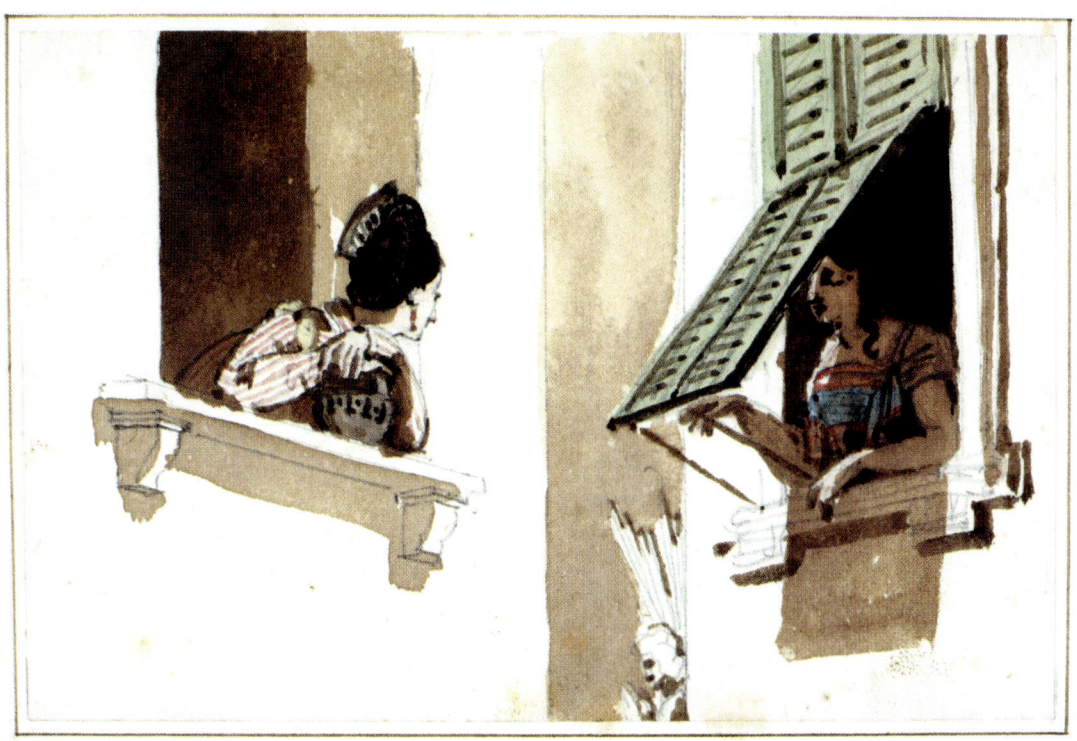

3.19. Antoine Jean-Baptiste Thomas, *Roman Women Conversing from Their Windows*, 1818, watercolor on paper, 2⅞ × 4½ in. (7.3 × 11.4 cm), Museo di Roma.

(following spread)
3.20. Antoine Jean-Baptiste Thomas, *Bullfighting in the Corea Amphitheater*, August 1817, ink and watercolor on paper, 8½ × 11¼ in. (21. 5 × 28.5 cm), Museo di Roma.

In the lower left of Thomas's large sheet, the bull enters the ring confronted by a whole range of goading torments. Among his individual studies (fig. 3.21), he recorded the bulls tossing dummies and dogs, the latter event the subject of a dynamic vignette in which pools of dark wash establish the dark mass of the beleaguered bull set against the precise canine anatomy. Where the human actors were concerned, Thomas granted them a grace in movement that can only be called balletic (fig. 3.22), once again with no sign of artistic hesitation or need for second thoughts—the execution with brush and pen the counterpart to the practiced bullfighters' movements. Steps away from the Corea Amphitheater, in the vast, ornate Milanese church of San Carlo al Corso (interior by Pietro da Cortona), Thomas recorded the analogous movements of a sermonizing priest, bridging popular sport and popular piety on the feast day of the Virgin's birth. This rare record of popular preaching style includes a series of close shots, like a sequence of proto-animation, and wider ones that take in the massed spectators below the platform (figs. 3.23–27). The figure of the sacrificed Christ, wielded by the preacher like a dramatic prop, possesses the same scale and presence as the living actor, while hooded confraternity members, both standing at the rear of the platform and forming a torch-bearing phalanx before it, appear more like statuary.

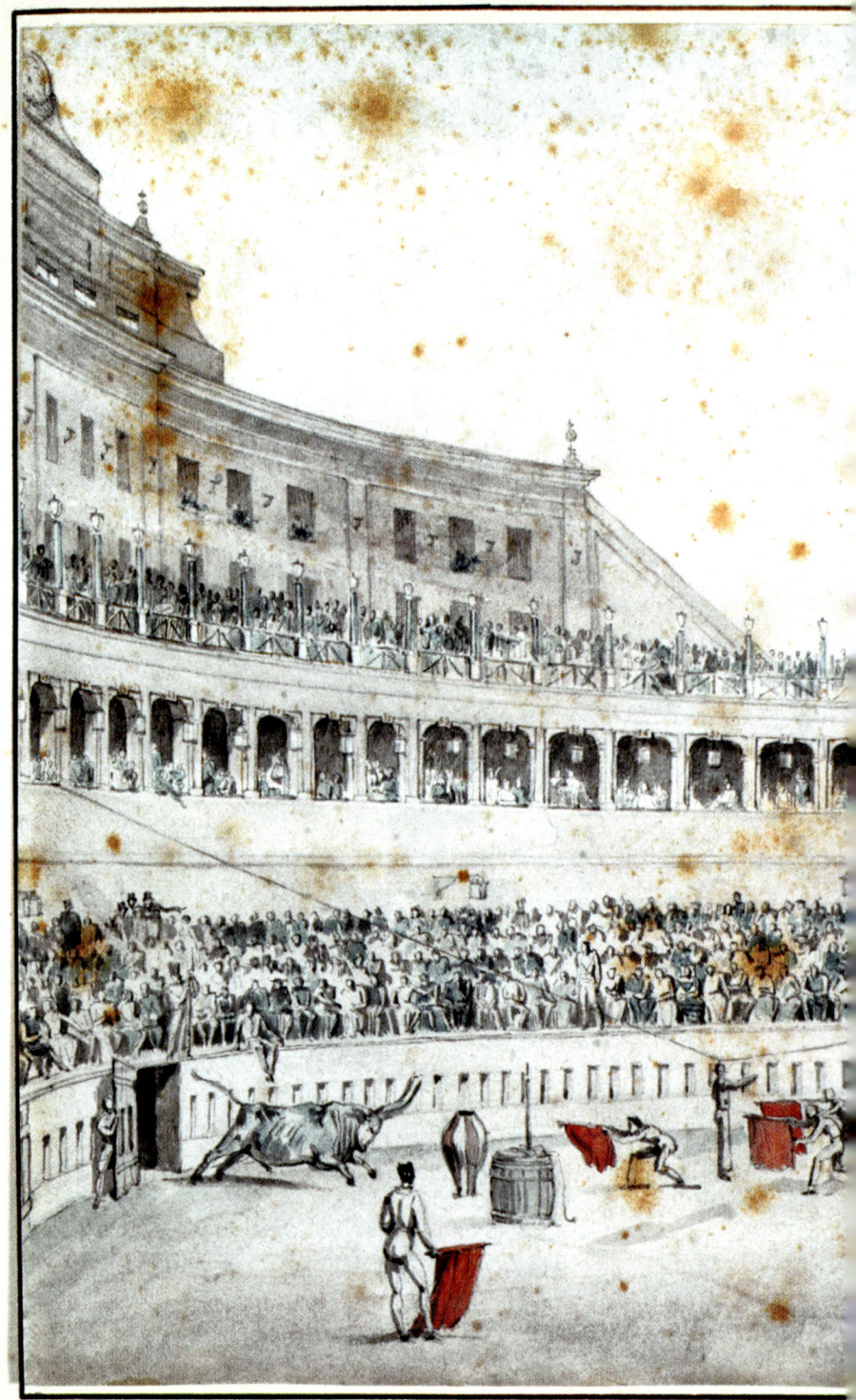

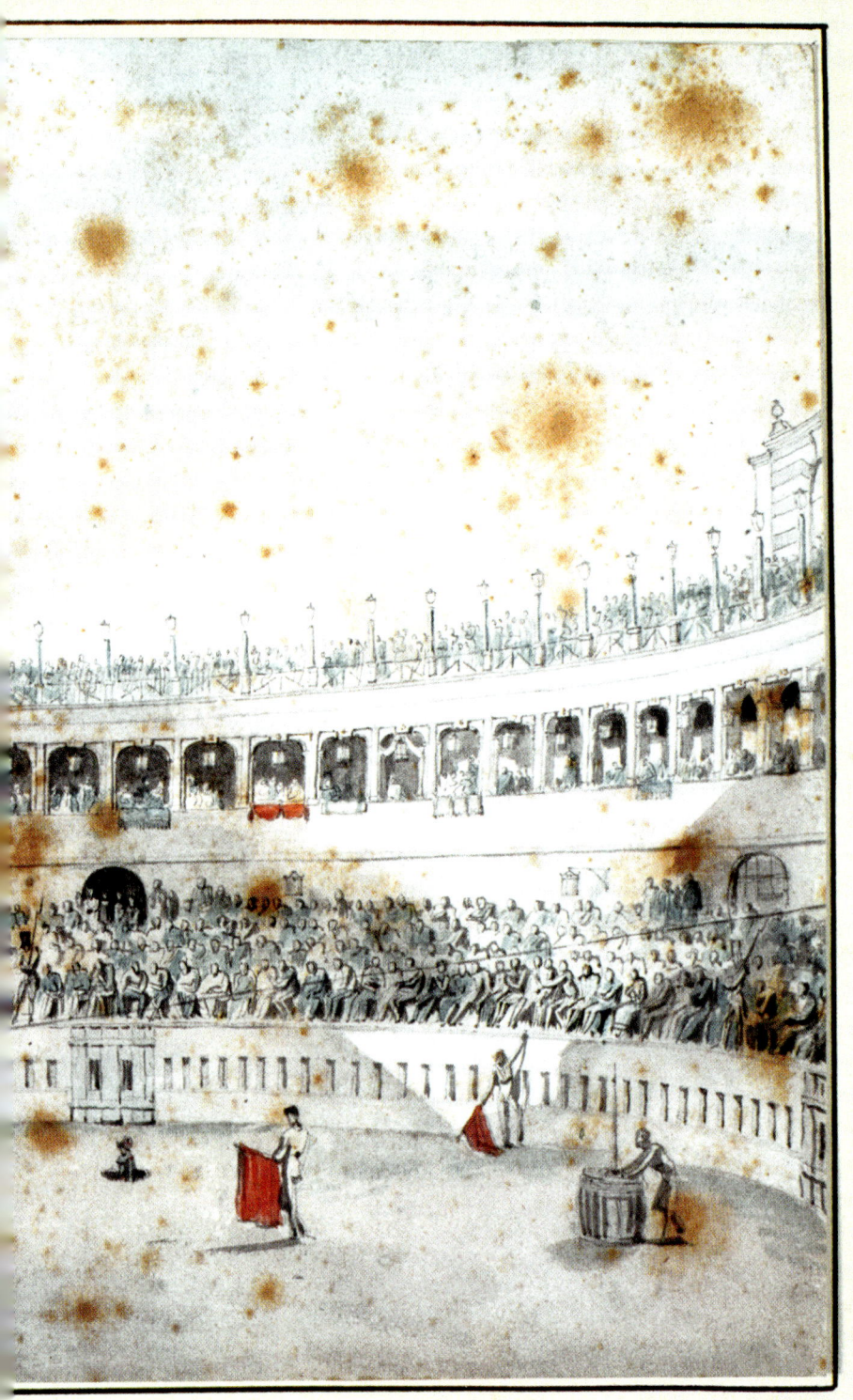

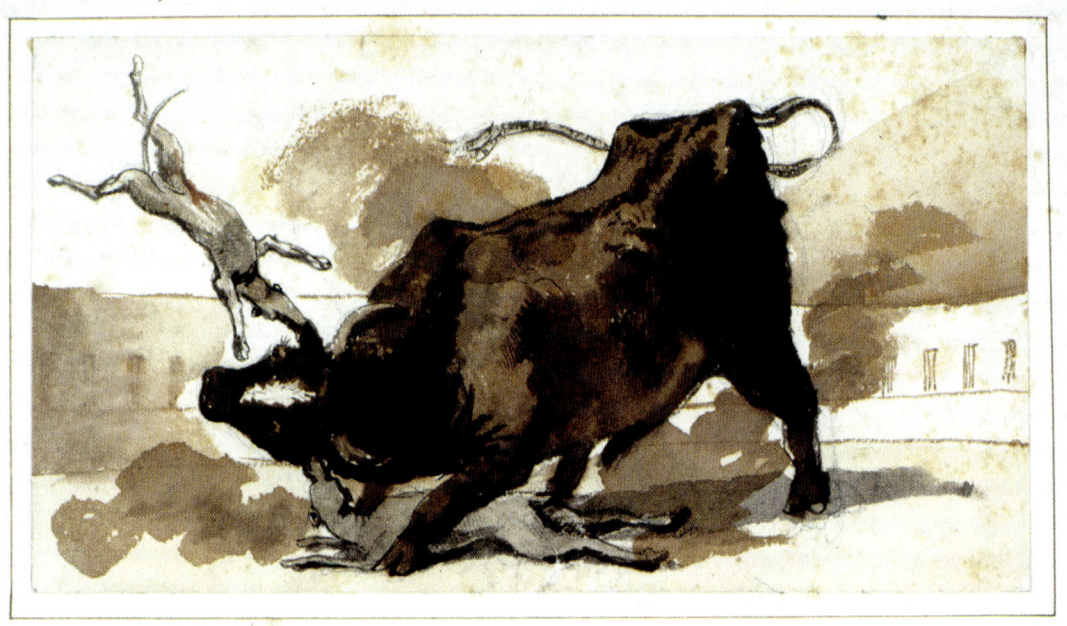

3.21

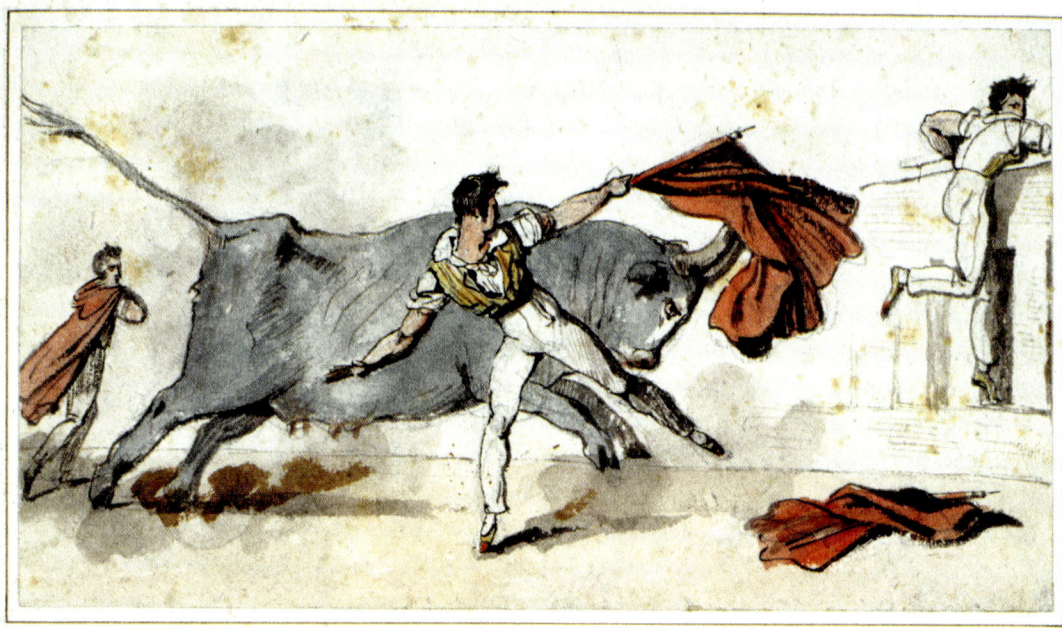

3.22

3.21. Antoine Jean-Baptiste Thomas, *Bull and Dogs in the Corea Amphitheater*, August 1817, ink and watercolor on paper, 3 × 5½ in. (7.6 × 14.1 cm), Museo di Roma.

3.22. Antoine Jean-Baptiste Thomas, *Bullfighting in the Corea Amphitheater*, August 1817, ink and watercolor on paper (detail), 3⅛ × 5⅔ in. (7.8 × 14.4 cm), Museo di Roma.

3.23. Antoine Jean-Baptiste Thomas, *Priest Speaking to a Child during a Sermon*, September 1817, ink and watercolor on paper, 3⅖ × 2⅜ in. (8.6 × 6.7 cm), Museo di Roma.

3.24. Antoine Jean-Baptiste Thomas, *Priest Addressing Crucifix during a Sermon*, September 1817, ink and watercolor on paper, 3½ × 2¾ in. (8.9 × 6.9 cm), Museo di Roma.

3.25. Antoine Jean-Baptiste Thomas, *Priest Showing the Cross to the Faithful during a Sermon*, September 1917, ink and watercolor on paper, 4⅜ × 2⅜ in. (11.1 × 6.1 cm), Museo di Roma.

3.26. Antoine Jean-Baptiste Thomas, *Preacher Embracing the Cross*, September 1817, ink and watercolor on paper, 4⅞ × 2⅞ in. (12.4 × 7.4 cm), Museo di Roma.

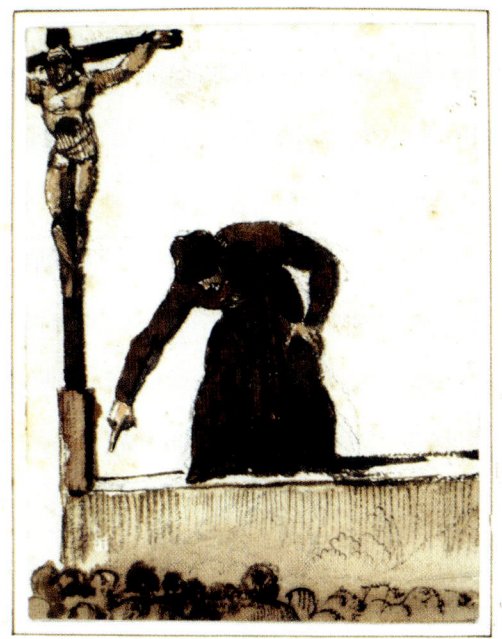

3.23

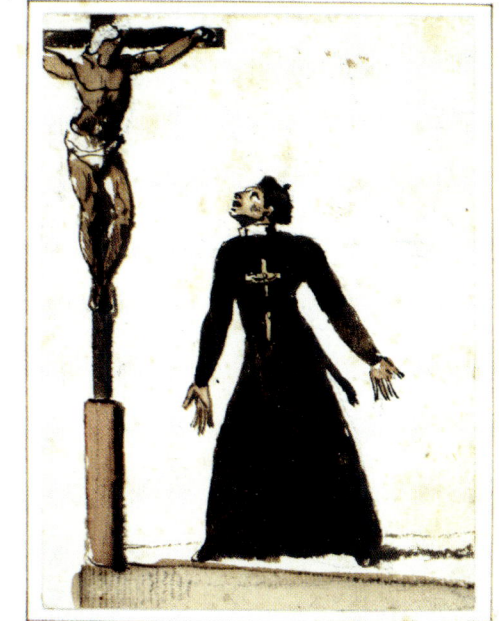

3.24

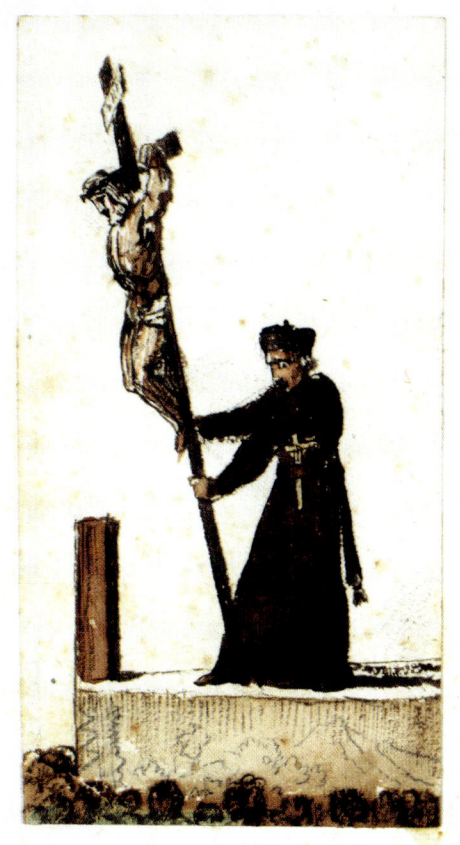

3.25

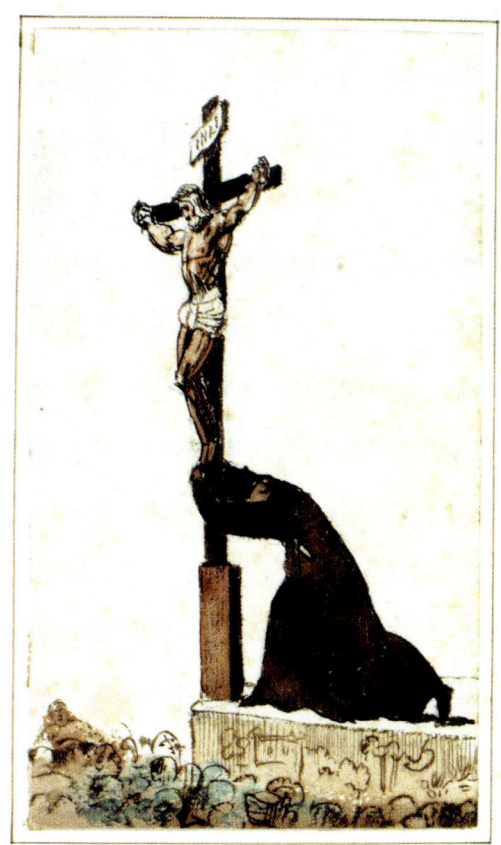

3.26

3.27. Antoine Jean-Baptiste Thomas, *Priest Showing to the Faithful the Image of the Madonna Supported by Hooded Brothers*, 1817, ink and watercolor on paper, 3½ × 5⅛ in. (8.8 × 13.1 cm), Museo di Roma.

3.28. Antoine Jean-Baptiste Thomas, *A Confraternity Goes to Pick Up a Corpse with the Castel Sant'Angelo in the Background*, 1817, ink and watercolor on paper, 3⅜ × 8 in. (8.6 × 20.2 cm), Museo di Roma.

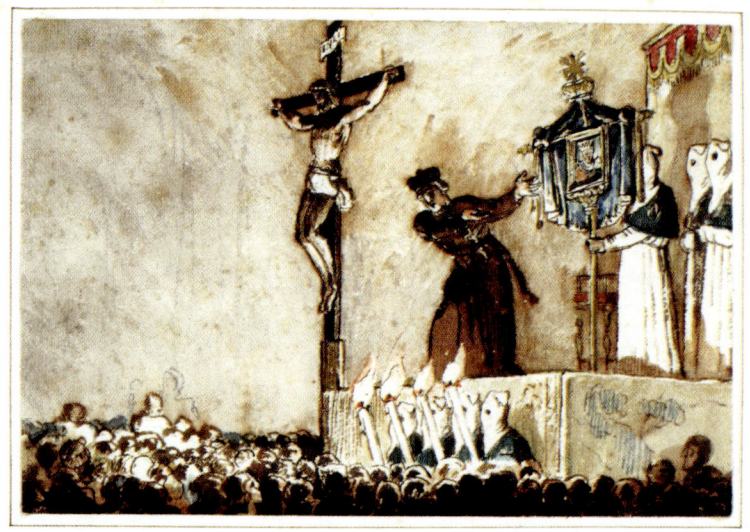

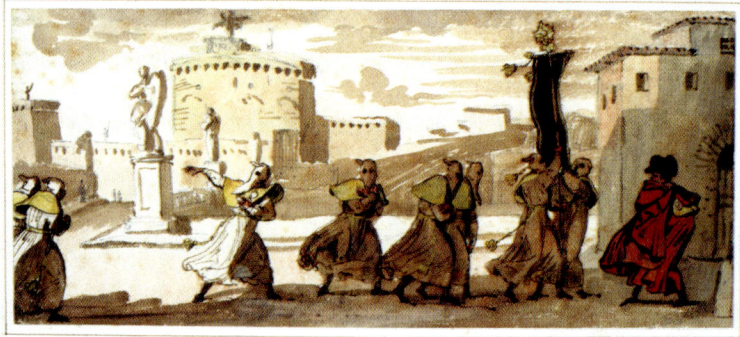

Thomas chronicled the continual rounds of religious processions by similarly disguised penitents bearing sanctified standards through the city's streets. In one study (fig. 3.28), a group hurries past the prison of the Castel Sant'Angelo, confronted by a profane figure in exaggerated Carnival costume. The route was the one along which prisoners condemned to death were carried on the first day of Carnival from that same prison to the headsman's scaffold in the Piazza del Popolo (fig. 3.29). Called the *Somaro* after the donkey on which the prisoner was propped, this custom provided both entertainment value and a caution against excess in the revels to come (capital punishment being rare in Rome, the condemned of the year were saved for this occasion). Confraternity members in hooded robes played their part, one group dedicated to the Agonizzanti di Gesù e Maria accompanied the prisoner to his fate; another, the Confraternity of Misericordia, bore the corpse away. The latter group drew the attention of Thomas in a series of studies; he also left a precise rendering of another scaffold (fig. 3.30) just down the Corso from the Piazza del Popolo, erected for

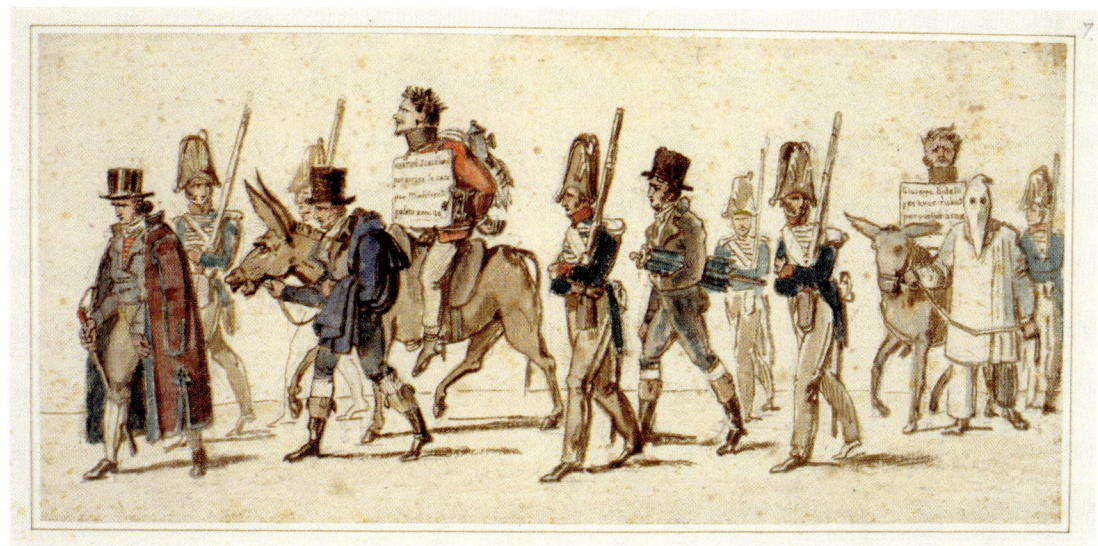

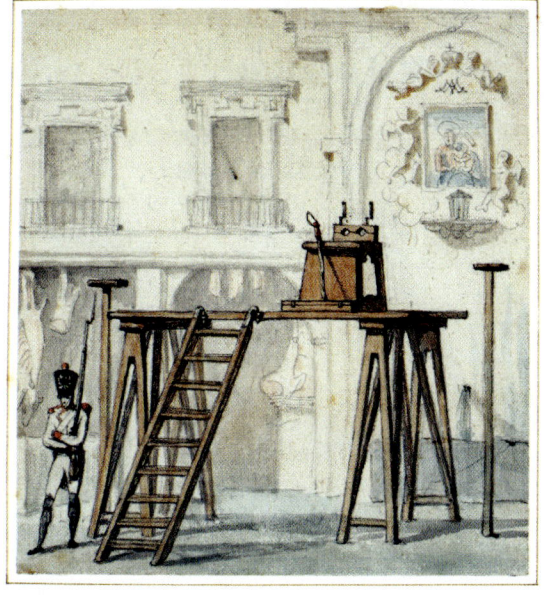

3.29. Antoine Jean-Baptiste Thomas, *"The Donkey" (Prisoner Led to Execution),* 1817, ink and watercolor on paper, 4½ × 9¾ in. (11.4 × 24.8 cm), Museo di Roma.

3.30. Antoine Jean-Baptiste Thomas, *The Scaffold,* 1817, ink and watercolor on paper, 4⅛ × 3⅞ in. (10.6 × 9.9 cm), Museo di Roma.

the lashing of lesser offenders (in front of the same church of San Carlo where he recorded the episode of histrionic sermonizing).

The culmination of Carnival season arrived with the night of the Moccoletti, the celebrants each bearing lighted candles in mock mourning for the death of Carnival (fig. 3.31). The game was to keep one's own candle lit while blowing out as many others as one could, and Thomas devoted a large sheet to a bravura rendering of the chaotic play of bodies, lights, and shadows that ensued. These examples form no more than a sample of Thomas's fecundity and seemingly endless inventiveness in graphic observation. After his premature

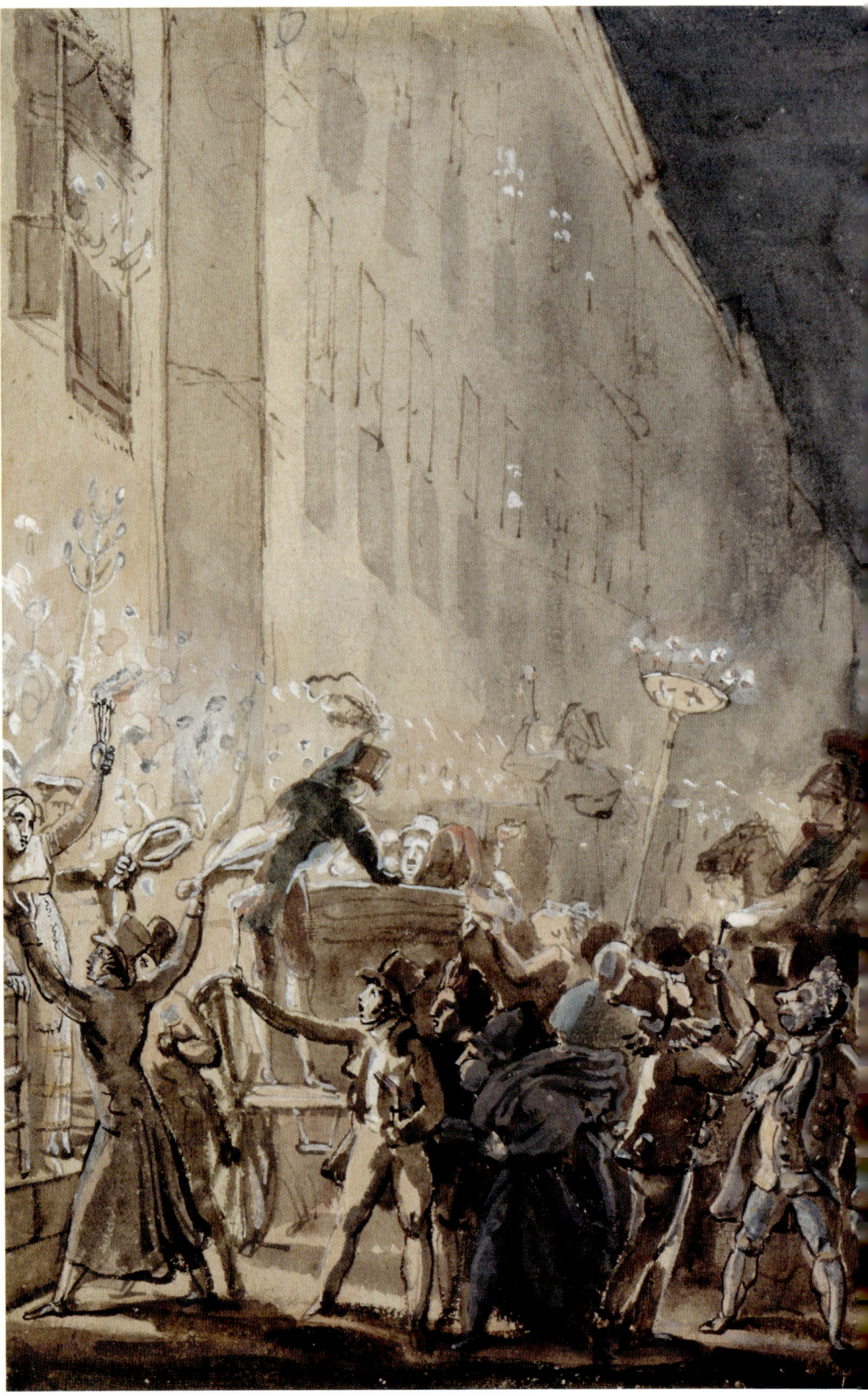

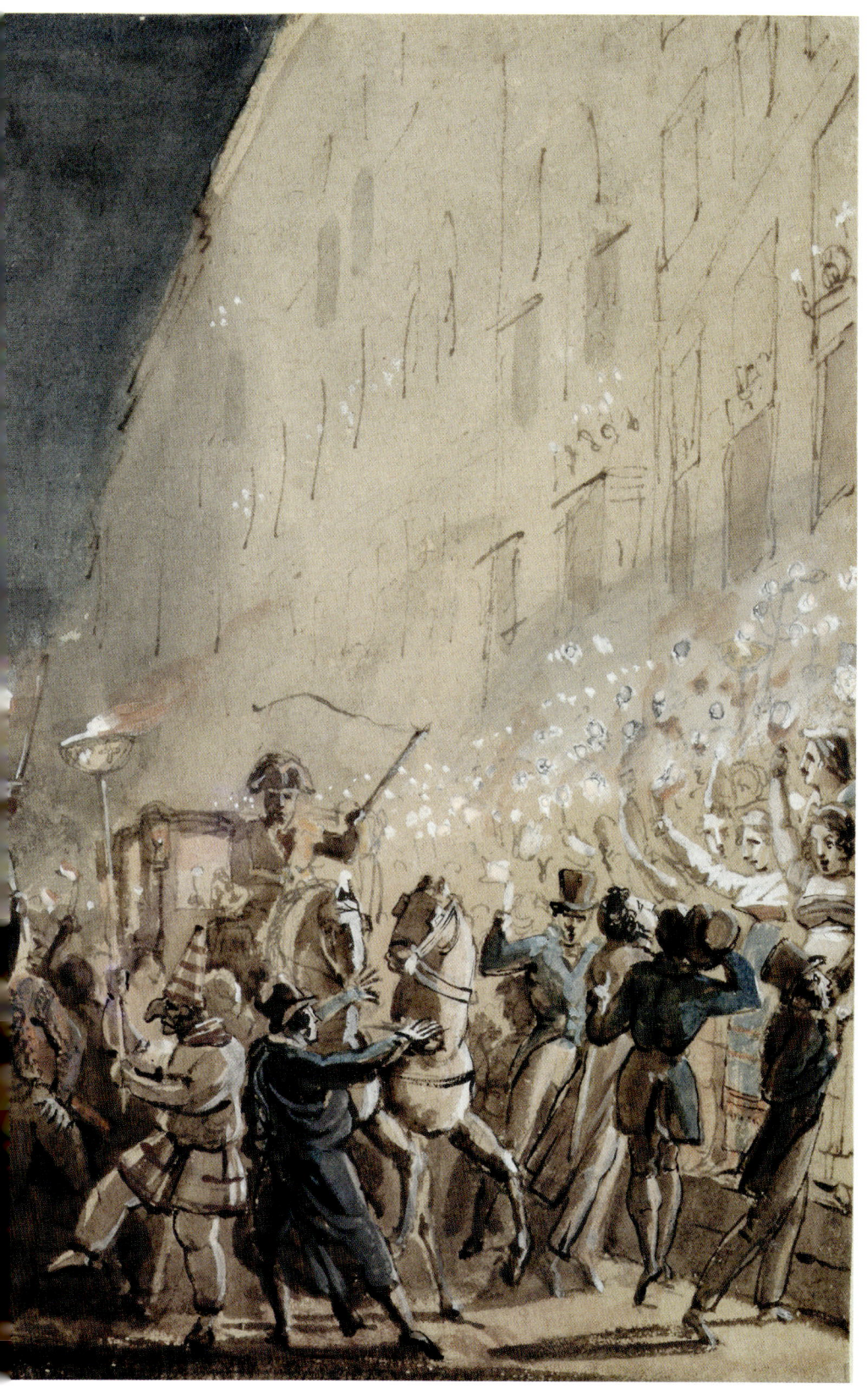

(previous spread)

3.31. Antoine Jean-Baptiste Thomas, *Festival of the "Moccoletti" in the Last Week of Carnival*, 1817, ink, watercolor, and gouache on paper, 8⅜ × 11¼ in. (21.4 × 28.6 cm), Museo di Roma, 1817.

3.32. Antoine Jean-Baptiste Thomas, "Blessing of the 'Bambino' at the Basilica of Our Lady of Ara Coeli on the Capitoline Hill," plate 1, 8½ × 13⅛ in. (21.6 × 33.3 cm), *Un an à Rome et dans ses environs: Recueil de dessins lithographiés, représentant les costumes, les usages et les cérémonies civiles et religieuses des états romains, et généralement tout ce qu'on y voit de remarquable pendant le cours d'une année* (Paris: Firmin Didot, 1823).

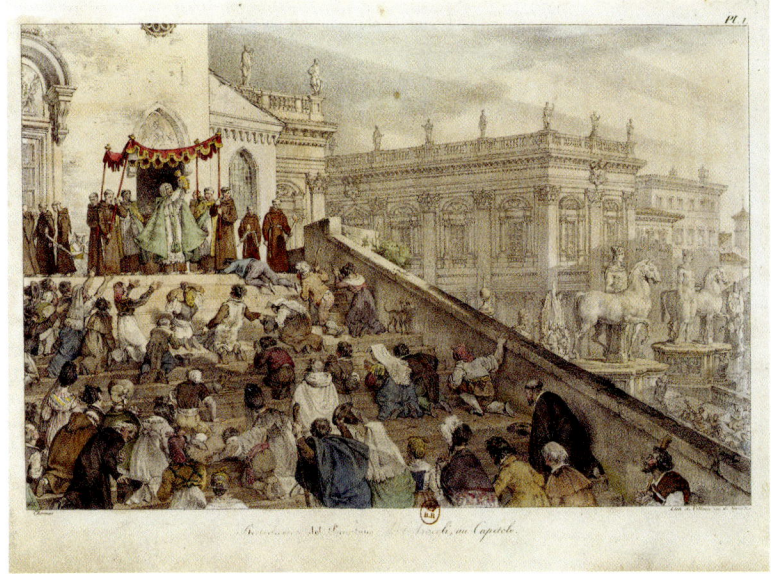

return to Paris, he would exploit his cache of streetwise studies by publishing in 1823, with the assistance of lithographer François de Villain, an album of prints, accompanied by his own well-informed commentary (fig. 3.32): *One year in Rome and its surroundings: Collection of lithographic drawings representing the dress, the customs, and the civil and religious ceremonies of the Roman estates and generally all the remarkable things one sees there over the course of a year.*[15] The success of this enterprise was such that a year later Thomas could purchase, while still a young artist, a house in the upscale quartier d'Antin (though he died in apparent penury only a decade later, just nine years after Géricault's own early demise).

✳

The pattern of Thomas's Roman activity strongly suggests that he had in mind the commercial possibility of a print series—so at odds with the disinterestedness enjoined by the Academy—at or near the start of his stay in the city. In that light, his lack of application to the artistic monuments of Rome seems understandable. In Géricault's output from the same period, by contrast, there exist ample numbers of studies that suggest an apprentice artist obediently applying himself to the mastery of inherited norms. One sheet (fig. 3.33), for example, features in its upper register three views of the Belvedere Torso at varying angles, that fragment being one of the chief glories of the Vatican antiquities collection and a perennial touchstone for artists of mature masculine strength. In the register below appear three parallel views of a contrastingly youthful torso after the

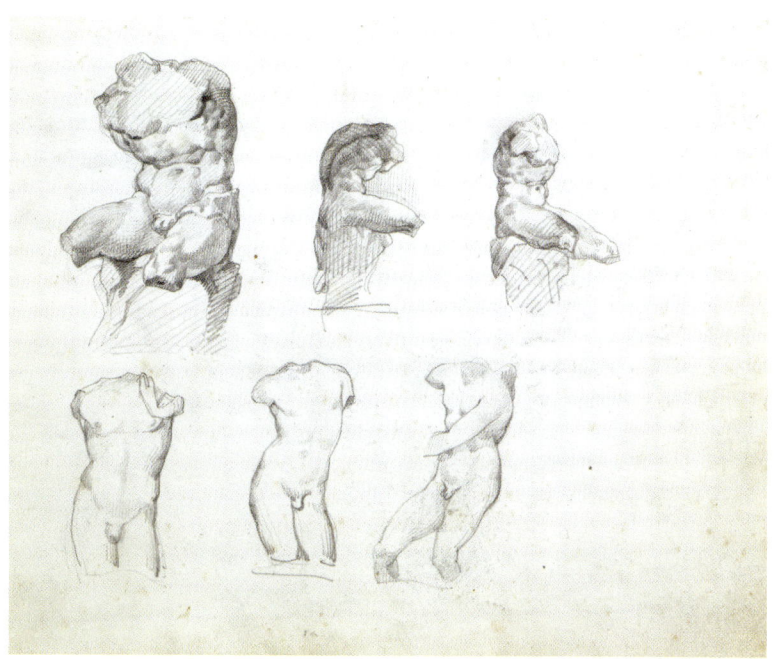

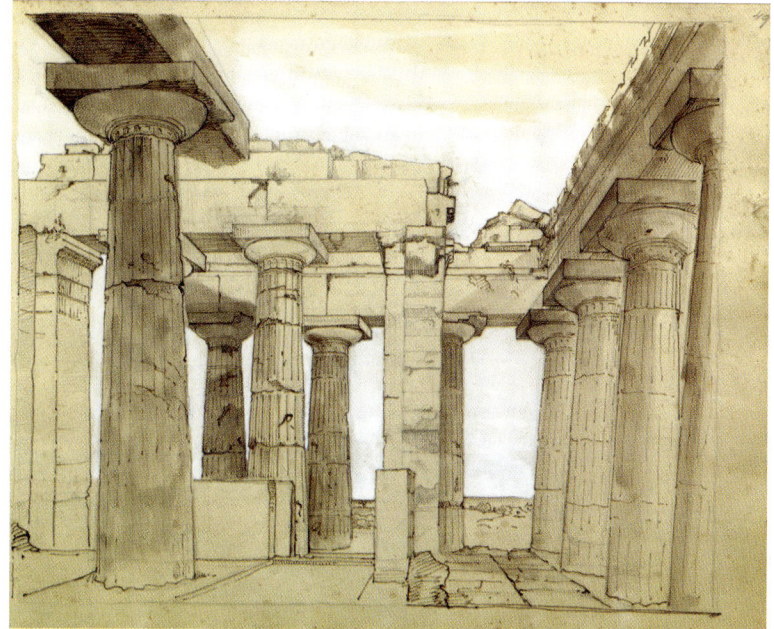

3.33. Théodore Géricault, ***Belvedere Torso*** et al., 1816–17, carnet d'études, sheet 3, 8⅜ × 10⅝ in. (21.1 × 27 cm [sheet]), Kunsthaus, Zurich.

3.34. Théodore Géricault, *Ruins of Paestum*, 1817, carnet d'études, sheet 49, 7¾ × 9⅝ in. (19.7 × 24.5 cm [image]), Kunsthaus, Zurich.

antique. This systematic cataloging of impressions would typically be undertaken as a resource for future multifigure narrative tableaux. Traveling south, Géricault recorded the Greek ruins at Paestum (fig. 3.34) with similarly careful rigor, and, while in Naples on that excursion, the equine-mad young artist meticulously rendered three views of Donatello's monumental bronze horse's head, centerpiece of the royal Museo Borbonico (fig. 3.35).

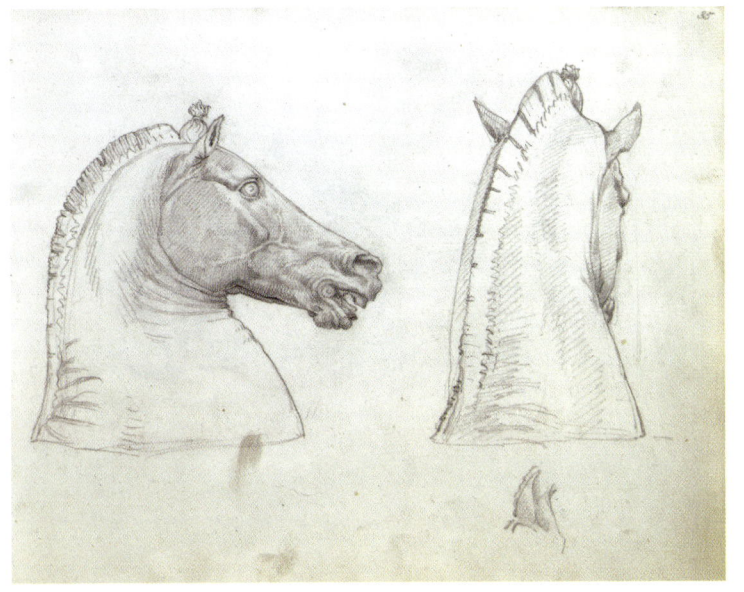
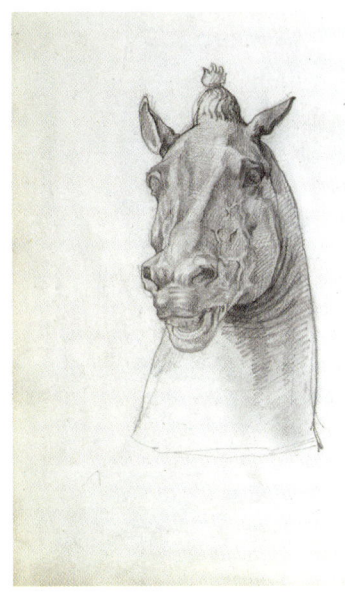

3.35. Théodore Géricault, studies of Donatello, bronze horse's head in Naples, 1817, carnet d'études, sheet 35 (left), 8⅜ × 10⅝ in. (21.1 cm × 27 cm [sheet]), and sheet 34 (right), 10⅝ × 8⅜ in. (27 × 21.1 cm [sheet]), Kunsthaus, Zurich.

This paradoxical distinction between the two artists was nonetheless a long way from absolute. Beyond the discipline entailed in copying the great monuments, Géricault seconded the example of Thomas with studies of his own—scores of them—depicting some of the same street scenes and events. The parallelism can be so strong that one readily envisions them working in tandem, at least on occasion. Géricault pursued a similar fascination with popular religious processions (figs. 3.36–37), following one as far as the distant Sanctuary of Our Lady of Divine Love where a medieval fresco of the Madonna was credited with miracles; in his study, impassioned pilgrims press themselves against the entrance to the overflowing church interior, watched by impassive horsemen in popular costume. This pilgrimage took its adherents far to the south of the city walls, but the pattern of overlap between the two artists focused itself on one limited area of Rome: that northern portion of Rome inside the Aurelian Wall in the vicinity of the Piazza del Popolo. Thomas judged that the sight (fig. 3.38) of mounted herdsmen from the surrounding *campagna* driving their unruly herd into the same piazza through its famous gate would intrigue his future Parisian readers, especially with an improvised *corrida* on horseback as the errant steers are goaded back into line. And Géricault took on the same subject (fig. 3.39), lending its human and animal actors a monumentality that defies the relatively small dimensions of the sheet. Especially striking is the compressed power of the white bull or steer, head lowered, on the right-hand side, despite our glimpsing only a fraction of the hurtling animal.

Whether this is a bull intended for the Corea Amphitheater or a steer meant for delivery to the butchers would be a matter of fine

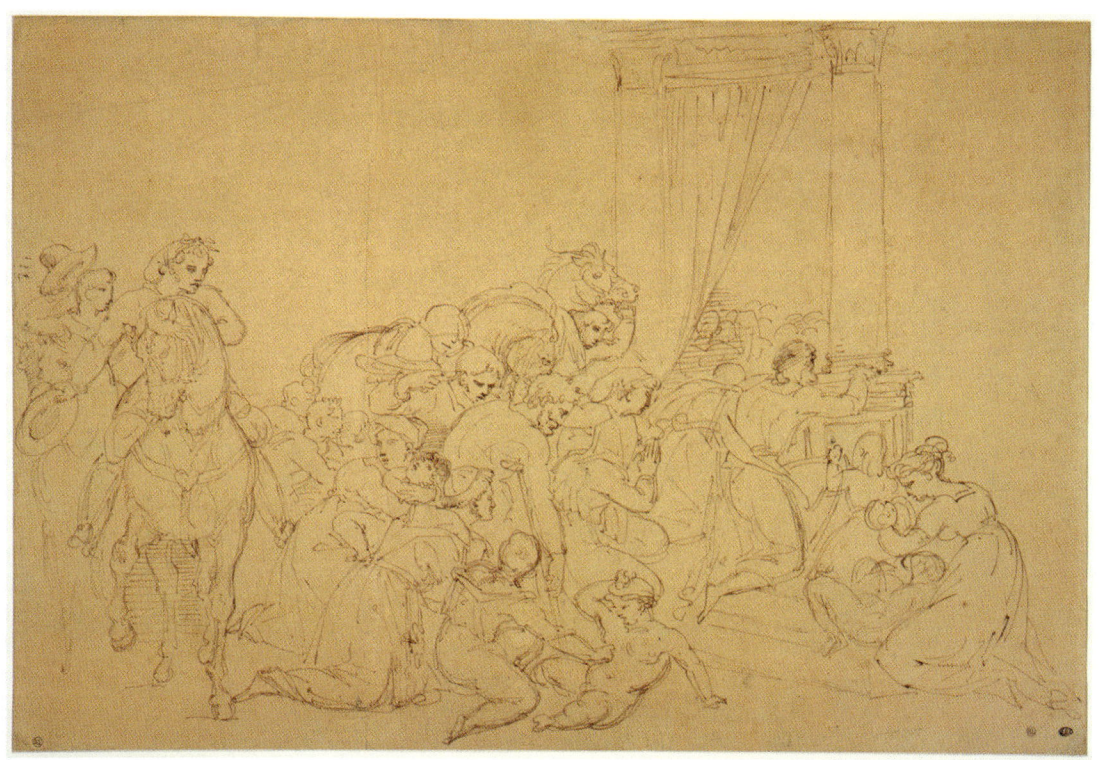

3.36. Théodore Géricault, *Prayer to the Madonna: Pilgrimage to the Sanctuary of Our Lady of Divine Love*, ca. 1817, graphite and brown ink on paper, 10⅜ × 15⅝ in. (26.5 × 39.8 cm), École des Beaux-Arts, Paris.

3.37. Antoine Jean-Baptiste Thomas, "Return of the Procession," plate 30, 8½ × 12⅞ in. (21.6 × 32.7 cm), *Un an à Rome*, 1823.

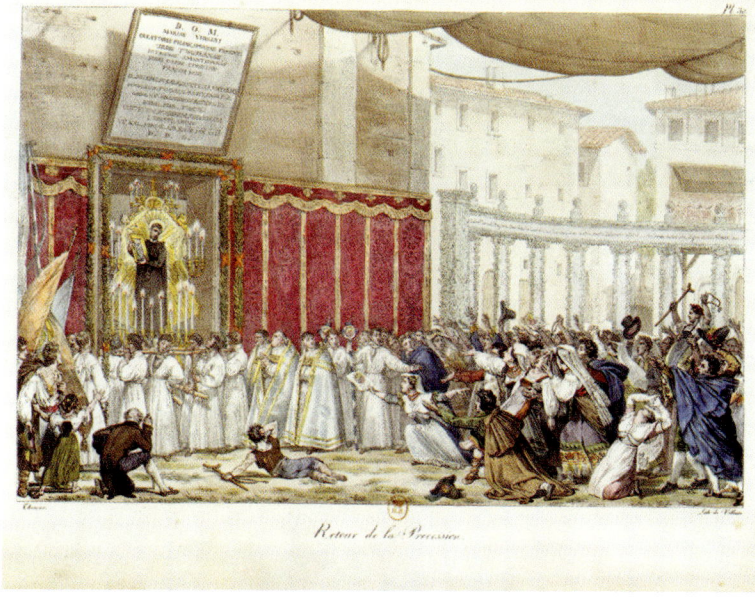

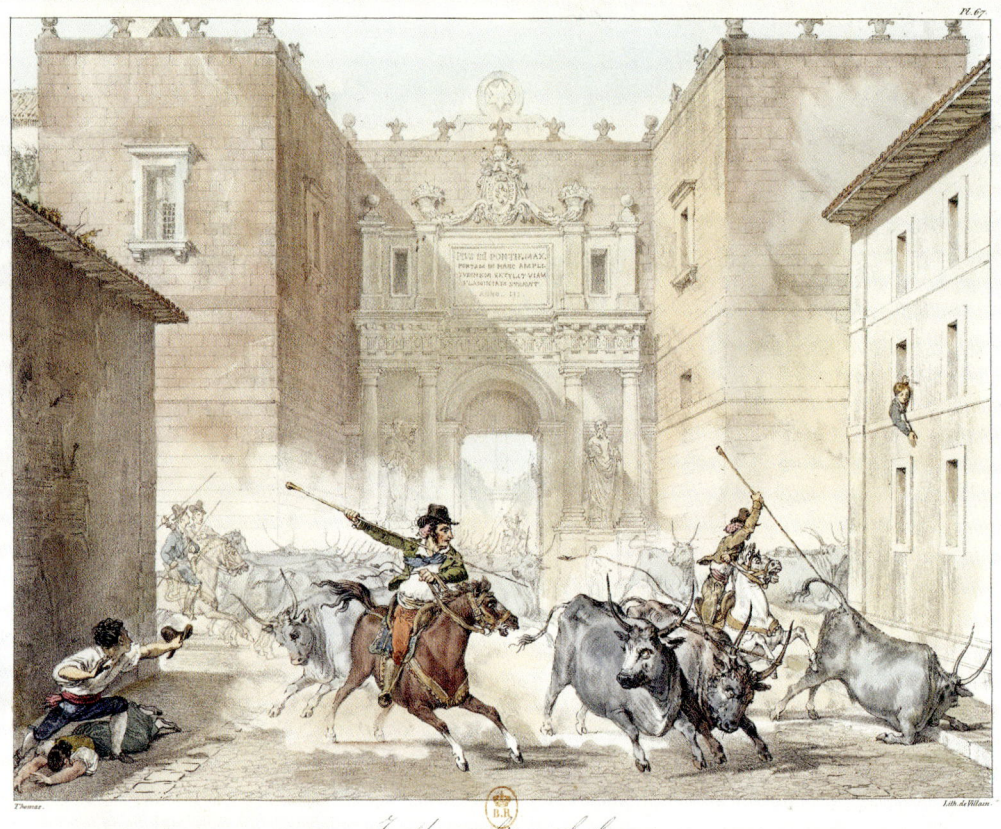

Pl. 67

Jour de marché aux bœufs

3.38. Antoine Jean-Baptiste Thomas, "Day of the Cattle Market," plate 67, 8⅛ × 10½ in. (20.5 × 26.5 cm), *Un an à Rome*, 1823.

3.39. Théodore Géricault, *Roman Herdsmen*, 1816–17, black chalk, brown wash and white gouache on brown wove paper, 8¼ × 11⅛ in. (20.9 × 28.1 cm), Harvard Art Museums/Fogg Museum, Bequest of Grenville L. Winthrop, 1943, Cambridge, MA.

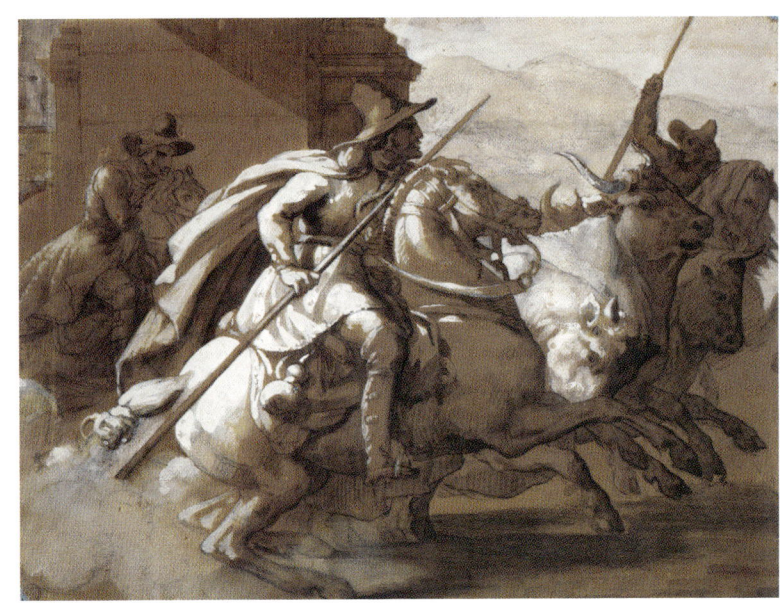

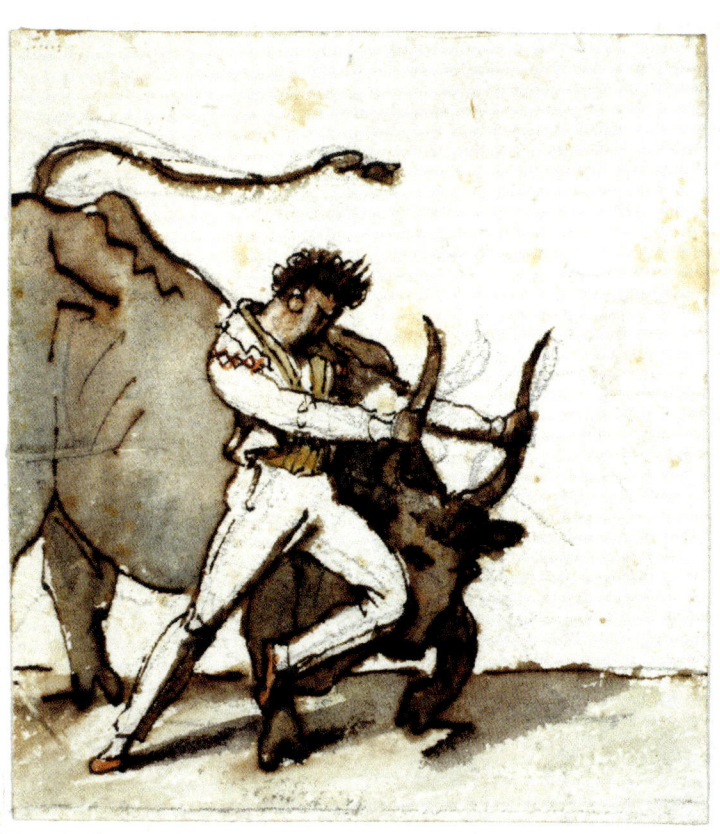

distinction as the cattle markets, slaughtering done on the spot, had a nearby, ritualized counterpart in the bullfights staged in the Mausoleum of Augustus. Were it a bull for the arena, the herdsmen might well be landed aristocrats in the same broad hats as their hirelings, driving their fighting stock through the same Piazza del Popolo. Géricault's body of work on the theme favors both interpretations. It was part of the show for bolder performers in the arena to make a display of wrestling a bull to the ground by the horns. Thomas made a drawing (fig. 3.40) that isolates such a feat, the resolute bull tamer's elegantly planted right leg seeming hardly substantial enough to anchor the exertion of his upper body. The tiny size of Thomas's vignette belies the strength of the composition, bright costume played against the bull's darkened mass, tail and tips of the horns making a dynamically inflected rhythm with the black flying hair of the human profile.

Like his colleague Thomas, Géricault possessed an exceptional ability to capture quick and lively animation in humans and animals. But he also aimed to incorporate the lessons of enduring monuments without sacrificing the intensity and vivacity of lived time, an ambition that yielded one especially powerful contour drawing (fig. 3.41) of a powerful male athlete likewise forcing a bull into submission. That central motif plainly channels ancient representations

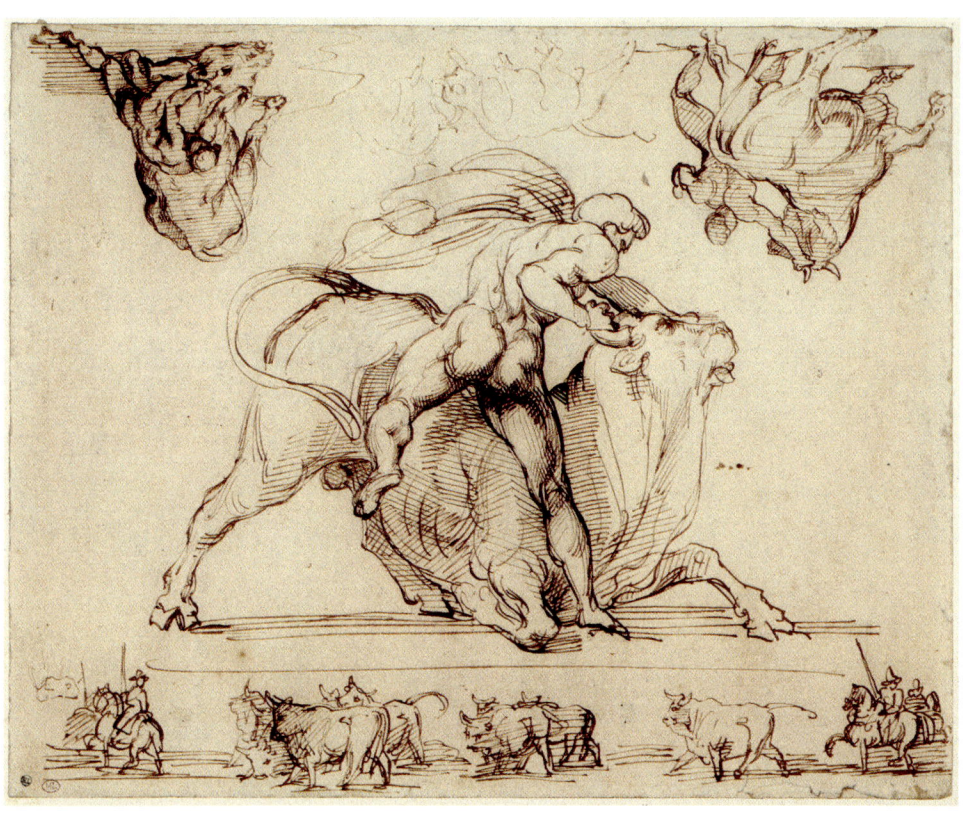

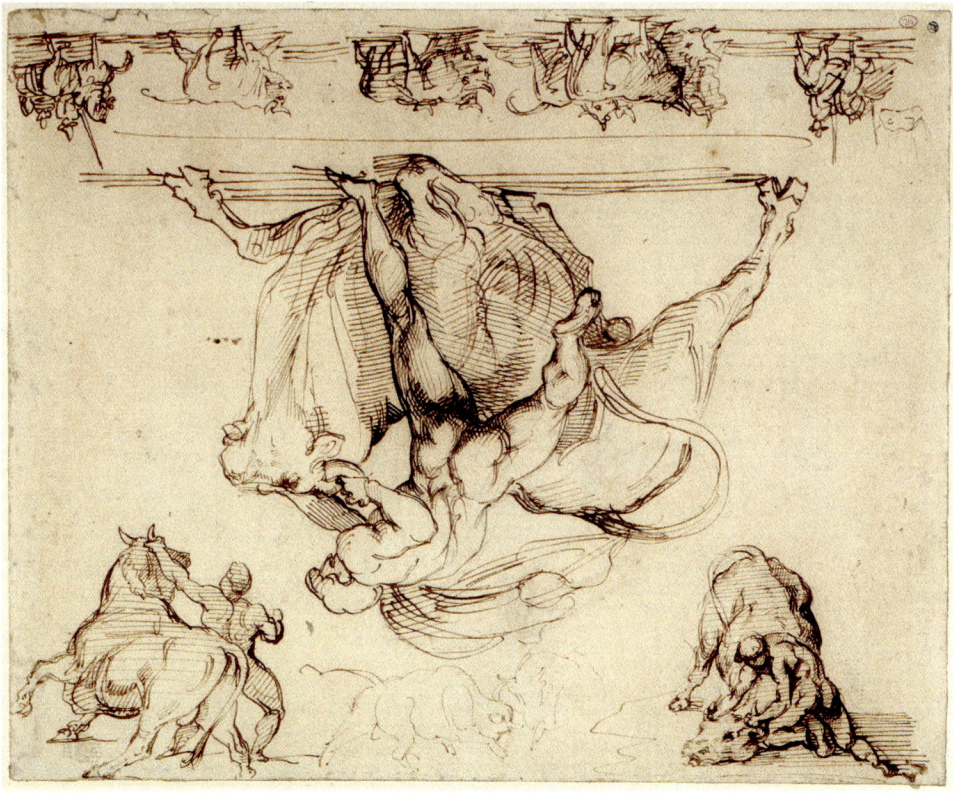

3.41. Théodore Géricault, *Naked Man Slaying a Bull; Herd of Oxen and Roman Herdsmen*, 1817, pen and brown ink, 9½ x 11¾ in. (24 × 30 cm), Musée du Louvre, Paris.

3.41a. Théodore Géricault, *Naked Man Slaying a Bull*, 1817 (upside down).

of the Persian cult deity Mithras slaying a bull, a sacrificial effigy-type imported to Rome by soldiers returning from the eastern empire—and just as importantly the dominant, beast-subduing son of Antiope in the "Farnese Bull," the Hellenistic/Roman sculpture group the artist encountered on his trip to Naples. Nudity and the sweeping cloak place Géricault's figure firmly within the Hellenistic classical idiom, apparently far from the contemporary reportage of Thomas, but observed contemporary life is fully as evident in the sheet as a whole, which manages to overlay antiquity with the animal torments of both the market abattoirs and the bullfighting arena.

Comprehending all this, however, requires treating the sheet as no study or exercise but instead as a consummated representational instrument, in no way preliminary to anything else but fully realized and sufficient in itself. And its internal system of transformations asks that the viewer engage with the sheet physically rather than just visually. Turning it upside down (fig. 3.41a) brings into focus two vignettes that turn the great central man-animal emblem into the middle point in a temporal sequence: to the right the athlete—unencumbered by cape—first seizes the horn of the beast; to the left, he pins its head to the earth. Despite the 180-degree reversal in orientation, there is a strongly composed arc that launches itself from the bull's turn of the head at the lower left through the large central motif—the tamer now suspended like a falling rebel angel—then descending like the defeated animal to the ground in the lower right. Between these anchoring poles, at bottom center, there appears a purely animal combat between two bulls in distinctly and intentionally fainter lines. That passage links the bolder vignettes to either side into a complete cycle whereby the human conquest begins and ends in an animal drive for domination.

The various aspects of the human tamer represent a single personage throughout, whose nudity, in combination with a placeless background, renders the whole dynamic abstract and apparently timeless—at least until one turns the sheet back to the original orientation of the central group. Below the dominant motif of heroic combat, a miniaturized procession proceeds from right to left: calm, even stately, compared to the agonistic struggles above. Contemporary riders identified by the same pikes and hats seen in the gouache drawing (see 3.39) take the lead and the rear of their orderly herd. The coordination between this lower band and the forms above is subtle and comprehensive, sealing a kind of circular pact between ancient and modern prototypes. No exercise in provisional improvisation, Géricault enlists an impression of casually disposed marginalia or afterthoughts in order to generate a precisely engineered, diagrammatic composition in which conceptual relationships, as conveyed by these correspondences, supersede unities of time and place, even the direction of gravity, that is, the normal scene-setting of a fictional picture. Had he respected those unities, there is little likelihood that he could have integrated the present with the past in anything like as compelling a form. The pathos of Géricault's unmoored status under the confused and contradictory circumstances of the Restoration meant that it remained all but invisible and its ingenious internal strategies of orientation, placement, and juxtaposition fated to go unrecognized.

✳

Géricault augmented this unseen triumph with an astonishing pictorial account of the final destination for the cattle in the butcher's yards around the Corea Amphitheater: another consummate drawing in which the ancient and the modern merge almost completely (fig. 3.42). He essentially repeated the vignette of subduing the bull, but its male nudity of sweating exertion comes accompanied by contemporary details of hairstyle, moustache, and frothing dogs. The human subjects in the drawing invite little in the way of subjective identification, as they turn in profile intent on their variously murderous tasks. Much as in Goya's *Second of May*, discussed in chapter 2, any intersubjective connection with the work devolves onto the animals, all of whom in some way face and lock eyes with an implied spectator. Victimhood overrides species identity as the key to Géricault's bond with his subjects.

3.42. Théodore Géricault, *The Cattle Market*, 1817, brown ink on yellow paper, 11⅜ × 19⅝ in. (28.8 × 50 cm), Musée Gustave Moreau, Paris.

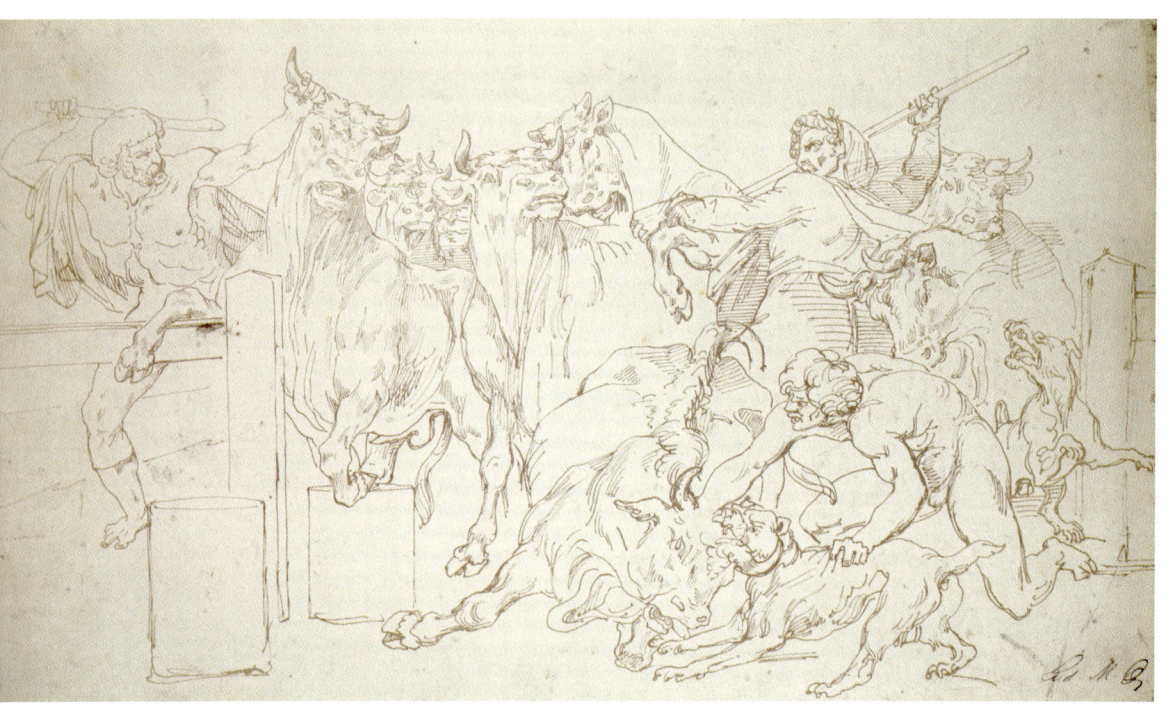

The very year that Géricault and Thomas spent together in Rome was chronicled by the formidable English writer Charlotte Anne Eaton (née Waldie) over three volumes published in 1820 under the title *Rome, in the Nineteenth Century*, containing, as the title page states, "Remarks on the fine arts, on the state of society, the religious ceremonies, manners, and customs, on the modern Romans." In her letter on the Roman Carnival season, she illuminates the renderings by Thomas of the rituals surrounding capital punishment: "its amusements are uniformly ushered in by a public execution. If any criminals are destined to condign punishment, they are reserved for this occasion; and I suppose it never happened that some head was not laid on the block at this festive period. Three were guillotined this year. It is done with a view to restrain the people, by the immediate terrors of the example, from the commission of crime, to which the license of the season may be supposed to lead."[16] The scaffold on which public executions took place, as noted above, could likewise be found in the same Piazza del Popolo through which cattle and fighting bulls were driven. For his part, Géricault made direct analogies between the humanly subjectivized cattle of his slaughter drawing and the parallel putting to death of human beings.

In one drawing (fig. 3.43)—out of a half dozen known that record his stark impressions of the headsman's block—Géricault placed the executioner at an apparently indifferent remove from the sinister-appearing figures in robes and hoods bundling the blindfolded victim toward his fate, members of the confraternity charged, as noted above, with accompanying and putatively comforting condemned men in their final moments.[17] As Eaton relates: "A number of penitents attended these unhappy criminals to the scaffold, as well as the pious brotherhood, who make this their peculiar duty; and both before and after the execution, they begged alms to say masses for their souls, to which hundreds, even of the very poorest of the people, contributed their mite."[18] She relays gossip that some of the most licentious of the maskers hid under these pious getups, hoping to expiate the sins of Carnival they had yet to commit. In this sheet, these characters take on an infernal appearance, forcing the uncooperative criminal backward up the steps. Perhaps the best-known sheet of the series suppresses the hooded penitents, aiming to capture the brutal moment when all consolation vanishes with the life of the victim. Maintaining the consistency of heavily inked line appears to have prevented sufficient characterization of the features on the severed head; so Géricault supplied a second head, rotated and rendered in greater detail, underscoring the contrast between nuanced subjectivity in dead victim and the lack of any such quality in his live killer (fig. 3.44). Much as in his drawing of the classical bull tamer, Géricault used the appearance of a draftsman's marginalia or afterthought to generate a considered new kind of discursive composition (could the

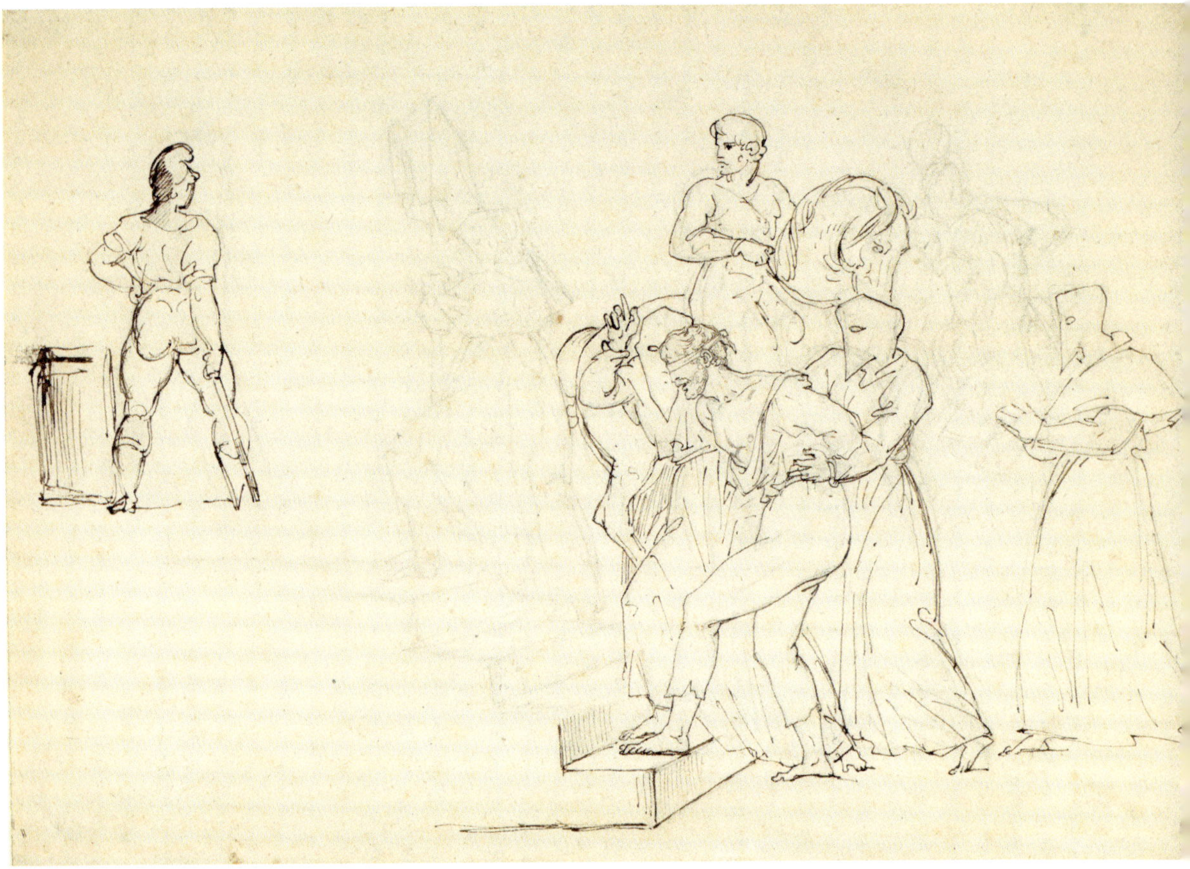

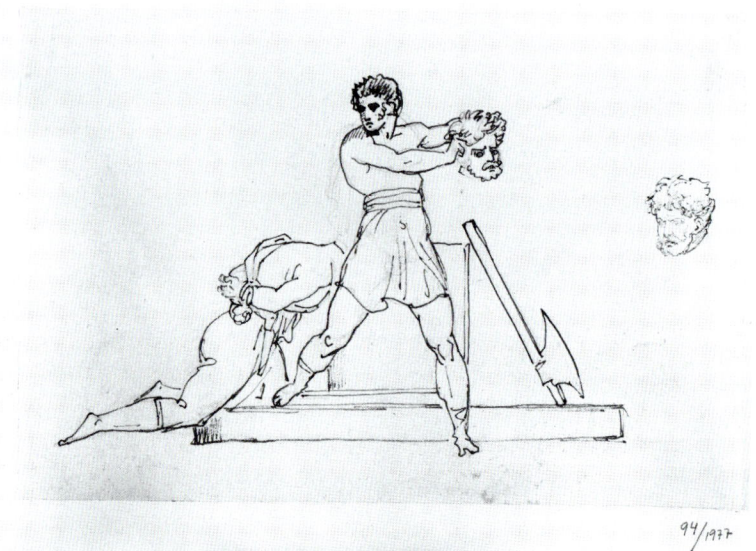

3.43. Théodore Géricault, *Condemned Man Being Led to the Scaffold*, pen, brown ink, and graphite on paper, 10¼ × 15 in. (25.9 × 38.2 cm), Fitzwilliam Museum, Cambridge.

3.44. Théodore Géricault, *Execution in Italy*, 1817, ink on paper, 6⅛ × 9⅜ in. (15.5 × 23.9 cm), National Museum, Stockholm.

position of the second head be more exactly placed on the sheet?) in which conceptual relationships supersede the unities of time and place.

✳

While Géricault accumulated scores of drawings on a wide variety of subjects over the course of his stay in Rome, there exists this core devoted to this specific quarter of the city, one centered on animals and humans undergoing physical duress and death—with an empathetic emphasis on the non-human. The same can be said of his companion Thomas, who may have done even greater justice to the phenomenon of the Roman calendar that brought these themes to a head in the most spectacular fashion: the races of the riderless horses. These were contests of ancient origin that took place daily during the final eight days of Carnival—the same period when full masking was typically permitted by papal authorities. Thomas devoted a number of studies to the event, so proximate to the location of the cattle market and bull fights. In his panoramic overview (fig. 3.45) of the impending start (the *Mossa*) in the Piazza del Popolo, the expanse of sky and hills in light washes contrast with the human density at the center of the piazza; their impassive distances emphasize its place at the margin of Rome's urban fabric (the sweep of landscape also bringing home the proximity of farms and pastures to the city gate). In a close-up view of the starting line (fig. 3.46)—traditionally the greatest focus of spectator interest—the handlers struggle to keep their frenzied charges in line; in another (fig. 3.47) the released horses appear in full flight down the Corso past costumed revelers in front of the Palazzo de Carolis-Simonetti, charging toward the great curtain suspended outside the Palazzo San Marco, at which point more handlers would lunge from the sidelines to bring the animals under control (fig. 3.48).

To understand just how the horses were induced to make the run from the starting line in the Piazza del Popolo, and why it was so perilous to corral them at the end, one can turn back to Charlotte Anne Eaton: "[The horses'] impetuosity in the race ... is not so much owing to their natural spirit, as to the agony of the goads or balls, covered with sharp spikes of metal, suspended from their backs, which, at every motion, fall heavily on the same spot, making large raw gory circles over their bodies, horrible to behold. Sometimes six or eight of these goads are beating their bleeding sides at once, and as if this were not torment enough, fire is likewise applied to them, so that the poor animals, furious under these tortures, often cannot be restrained by the force of eight or ten men, from leaping the cords which confine them at the entrance of the Corso."[19]

Such a subject might have been invented for Géricault. More than any other Roman custom, the event shifted agency as far as possible

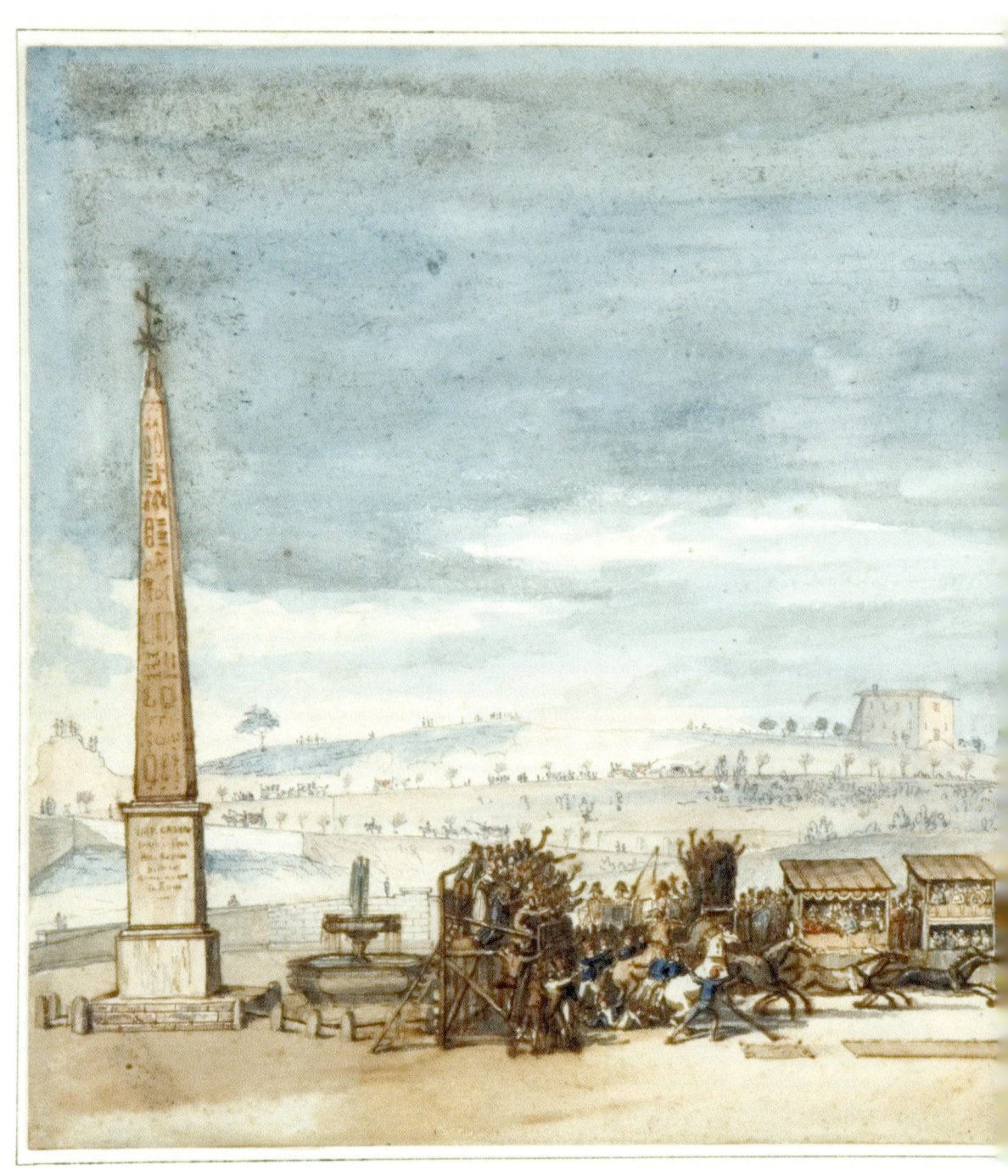

3.45. Antoine Jean-Baptiste Thomas,
*"La Mossa," Start of the Barbary
Racehorses in the Piazza del Popolo*,
February 1817, ink and watercolor on
paper, Museo di Roma.

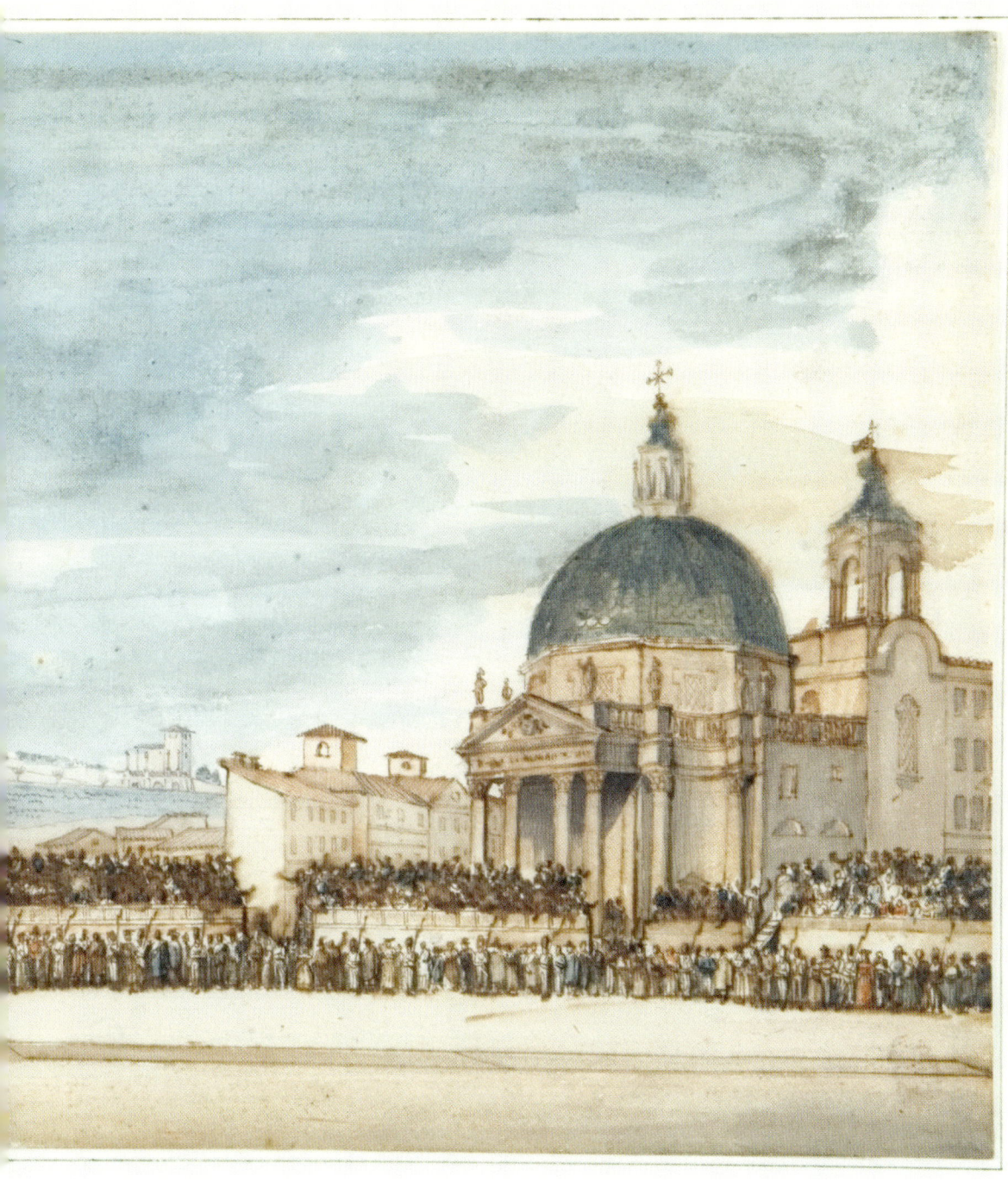

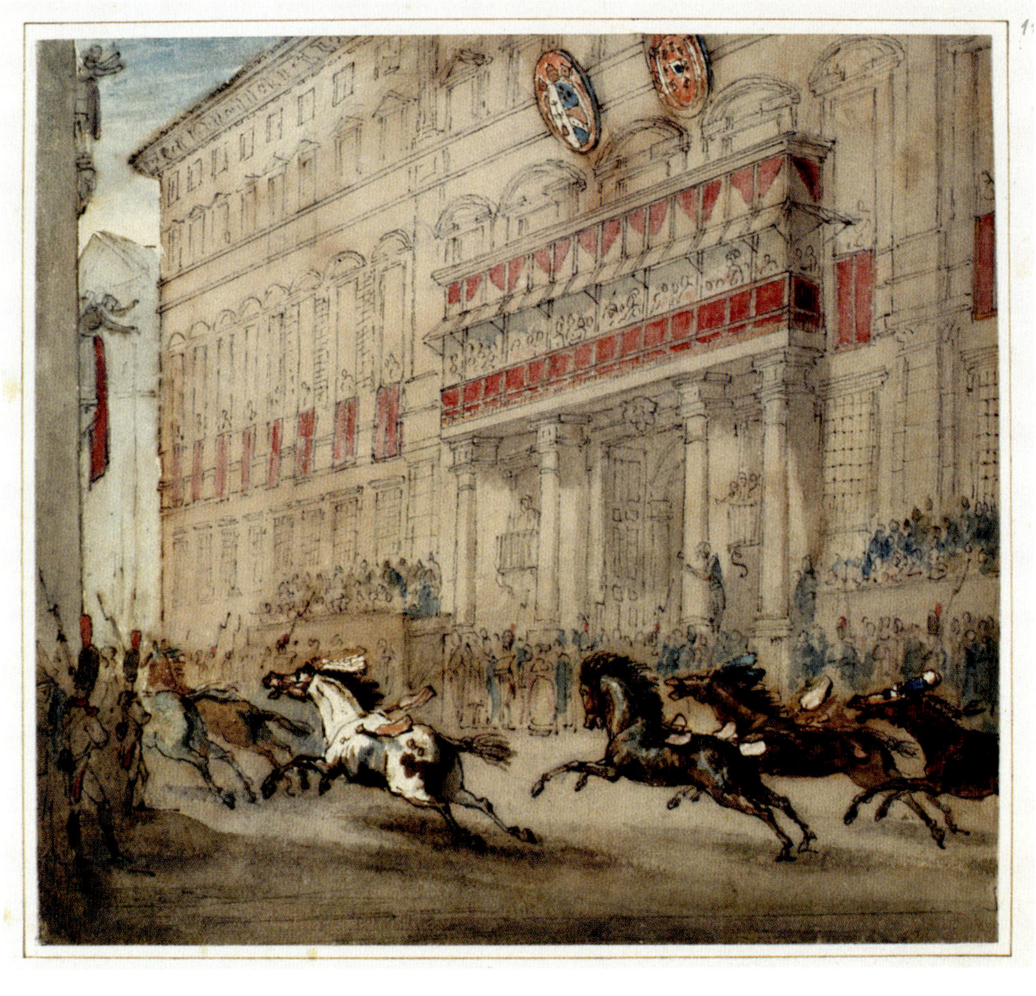

3.46. Antoine Jean-Baptiste Thomas, *"La Mossa," Start of the Barbary Racehorses in the Piazza del Popolo*, February 1817, ink and watercolor on paper, Museo di Roma.

3.47. Antoine Jean-Baptiste Thomas, *"La Mossa," Race of the Barbary Racehorses down the Via del Corso Passing the De Carolis-Simonetti Palace*, February 1817, ink and watercolor on paper, Museo di Roma.

(facing page)
3.48. Antoine Jean-Baptiste Thomas, "The Recovery of the Barbary Racehorses, plate 11 (detail), *Un an à Rome*, 1823.

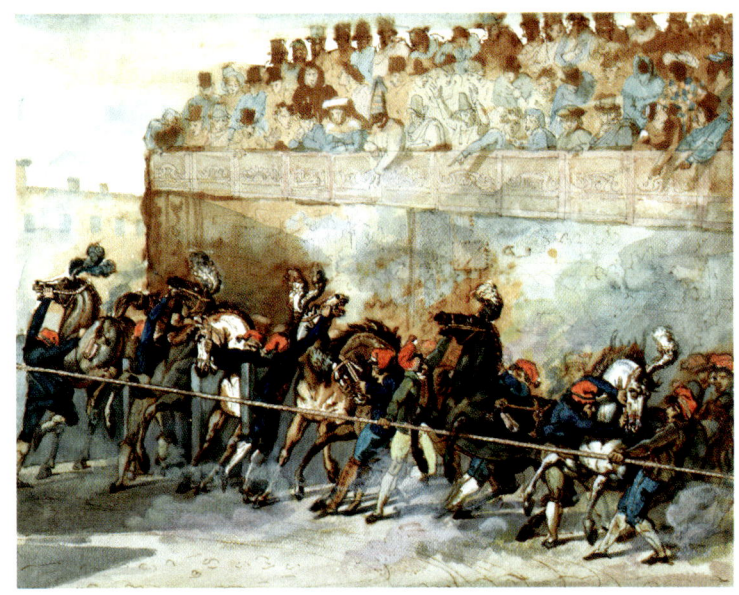

Pl. II

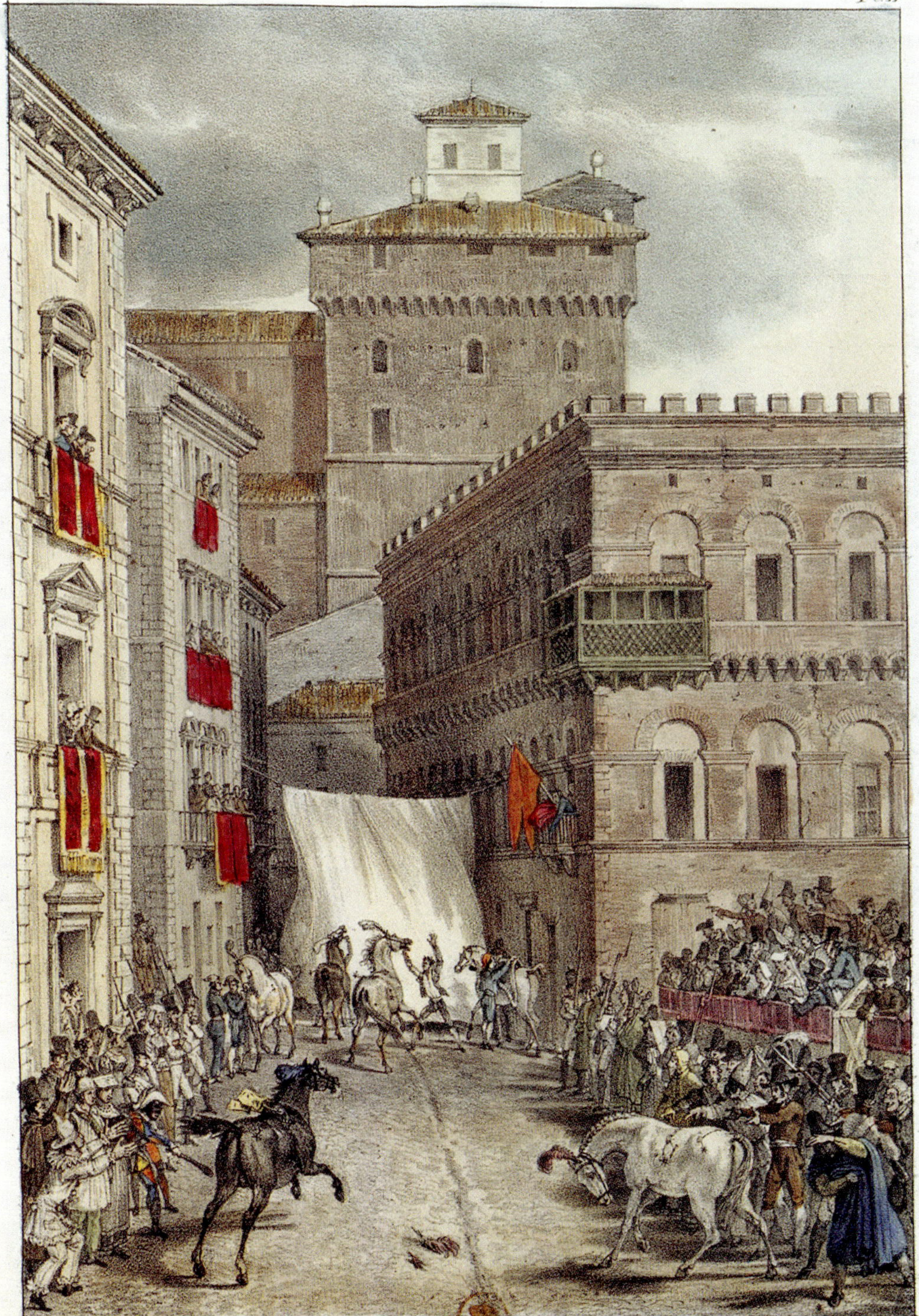

Thomas

Lith. de Villain

La ripresa de' barberi.

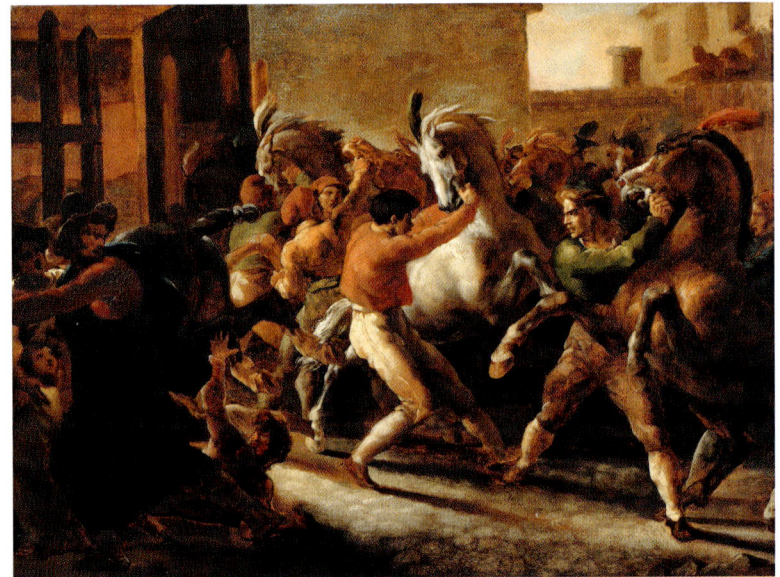

3.49. Théodore Géricault, *Race of Riderless Horses in Rome*, 1817, oil on paper, 17¾ × 23⅝ in. (45.1 × 60 cm), Palais des Beaux-Arts, Lille.

3.50. Antoine Jean-Baptiste Thomas, "The Riderless Race-horses Ready to Start," plate 10, 8½ × 13 in. (21.6 × 33 cm), *Un an à Rome*, 1823.

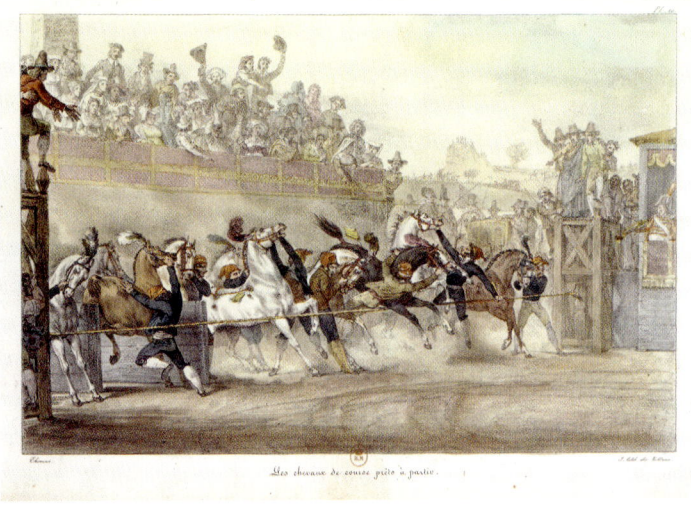

toward the animal and away from human mastery; it entailed a trial by pain and the not uncommon fatality of animal and human. Of his numerous studies on the subject, one (fig. 3.49) comes close to capturing the mayhem evoked by Eaton and the vividness captured by Thomas, but it nonetheless lacks a key, repellant detail that Thomas included in his otherwise milder lithograph (fig. 3.50) rendering of the start: the goads along the flanks of the horses that spurred them to run, supplemented by barbs in their festively ornamented headgear. The best known and probably most admired of Géricault's oil studies (fig. 3.51) cannot find the pain; indeed, he suppressed in it almost any hint of the agonizing duress the horses suffered. The stately order of the study comes at the expense of the intensity, the call of the wild

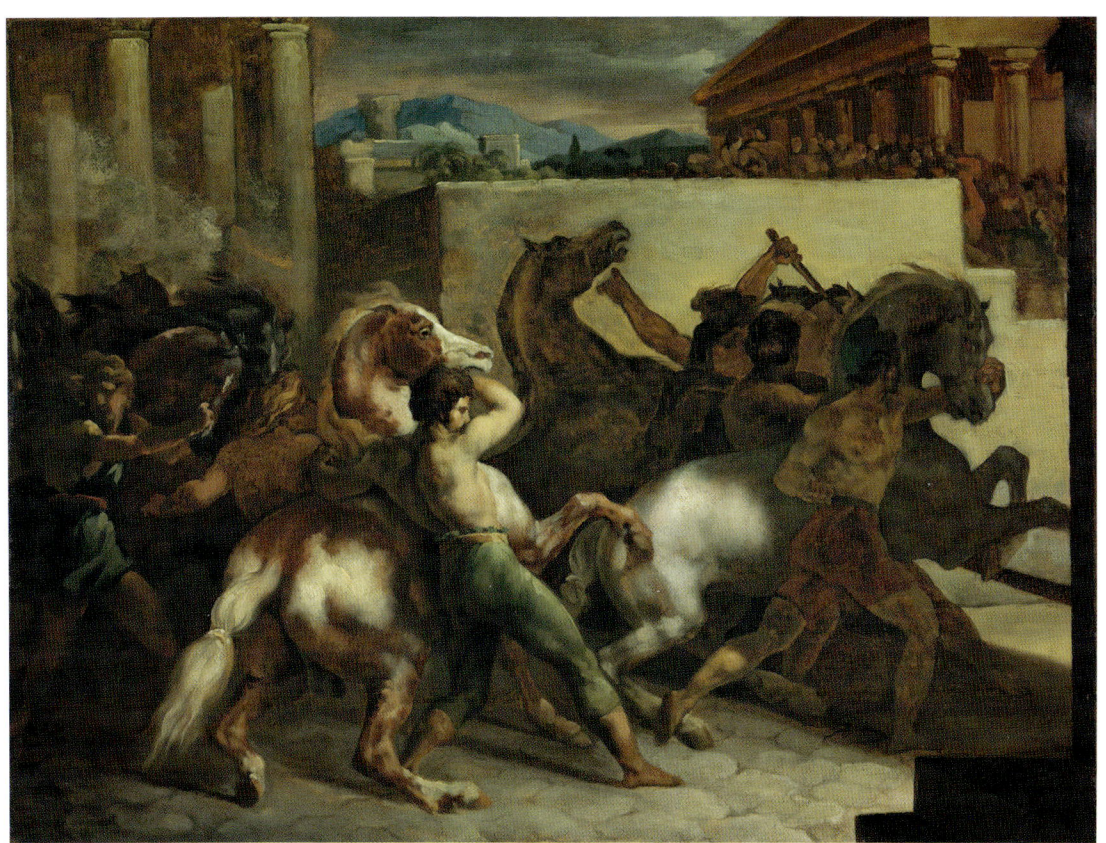

that had drawn him to this Carnival complex of suffering and death around the Piazza del Popolo.

The dark thread running through this discussion—as in the one beginning with the mayhem of Goya's *Disasters of War* and paintings of the Second and Third of May—has been the responsibility for any artist aspiring toward greatness to confront the catastrophic levels of violence and endemic cruelty visited on Europe by the onset of total warfare. No profundity would be possible without that recognition. And such memories, overwhelming the capacities of painting to convey human pain, required other channels, which for Goya and Géricault alike entailed a displacement of feeling and identification from the human to the animal. The riderless horses of the Corso, Géricault decided, was the one Roman subject that might have engendered a great painting. But none ever issued from his myriad sketches and studies devoted to the ritual, neither in Rome nor on his return to Paris in the autumn of 1817. The following two years, however, would witness the young artist's triumphant reckoning in oil on monumental canvas with the immensity of inherited pain and loss, raising a new humanity out of bestialized ordeals and thereby transforming for his generation what a painting could be and could accomplish.

Chapter 4

The Religion of Ancient Art from London to Paris to Rome, 1815–19

Canova and Lawrence
Replenish Papal Splendor

THE PREVIOUS CHAPTER treated three out of many artists set in motion after the drastic events of 1815, the final capitulation of Napoleon and his transportation to the lonely south Atlantic. At the turn of 1816, the aging Jacques-Louis David accepted permanent exile in Brussels; later in the same year, the young Théodore Géricault absconded, out of mixed personal compulsion and aesthetic attraction, from Paris to Rome. Antoine Jean-Baptiste Thomas took the same route, at first on the standard academic itinerary but soon to deviate in response to the new condition of Rome as a European open city.

Cardinal Ercole Consalvi (fig. 4.1), secretary of state to Pope Pius VII and highest executive authority in the Church, had personally experienced his share of displacement during the war years.[1] In 1809, as noted above, the pope had excommunicated Napoleon and then found himself seized in turn, to be held in French captivity for the next five years. Consalvi followed his kidnapped master to Paris, where both were confined until shortly before the emperor's first abdication in 1814. While the pope returned to Rome in triumph, it fell to Consalvi secretly to scheme on behalf of Vatican interests at the Congress of Vienna among the other statesmen of the Old Order. There the cardinal enjoyed a status comparable to other lions of the Restoration like Metternich, Castlereagh, and Talleyrand. Among the great and pressing issues of territory and dynastic ambitions, questions of art and its disposition claimed some significant share of attention as well. In January 1815, Consalvi wrote to the clerical governor of Rome concerning an issue at an intersection between the fraught international diplomacy of the day and the cardinal's ambitious plans for cultural renewal in the papal capital after the era of French occupation.[2] In question was the *Barberini Faun* (fig. 4.2), one storied piece of ancient sculpture not requisitioned by Napoleon Bonaparte for export to France in 1796. The crown prince of Bavaria, future Ludwig I, had recently bought it from the Barberini family for transport to his capital in Munich, but Consalvi insisted on "the advantages of retaining the statue of the Faun, which I believe is one of the very few, if not the only statue of great importance left in Rome." The Musée Royal

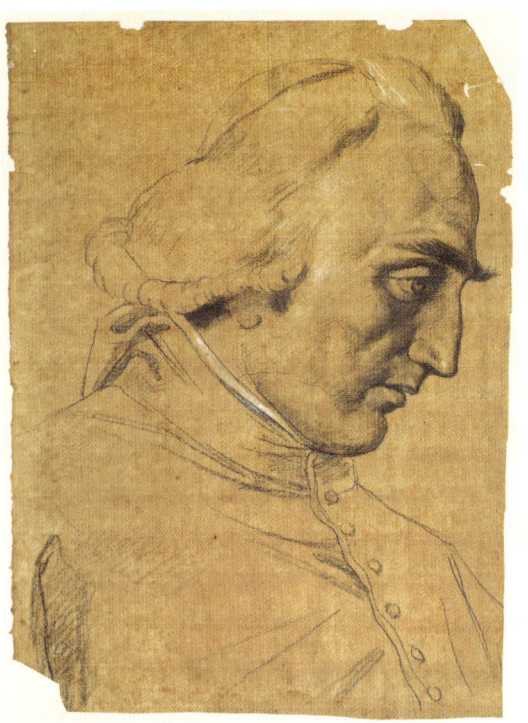

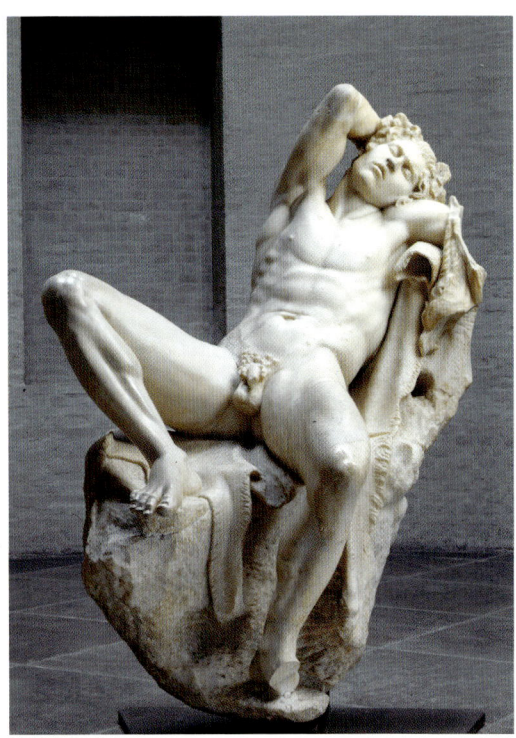

4.1. Jean-Auguste-Dominique Ingres, *Profile Portrait of the Cardinal Consalvi*, 1814, graphite on paper, Musée Ingres, Montauban.

4.2. *Barberini Faun*, 220 BCE, Staatliche Antikensammlungen und Glyptothek, Munich.

in Paris (just lately the Musée Napoléon), he implies, retained most of the others.

At this juncture, there can be no doubt that the cardinal's concern about Rome's once unparalleled stock of antiquities would have been acute. While any foreign art student could have testified that there remained countless valuable antiquities in Rome, enough to sustain a lifetime of copying, the relative absence of popular and well-known items was certainly hurting the image of the city, particularly as a tourist destination. Having met with the young Ludwig in Vienna, Consalvi reported that the prince "has accepted that he cannot obtain permission to export the Faun." In this instance as classicists and visitors to Munich will know, the cardinal nonetheless came up short in his effort to refuse Ludwig the nineteenth-century equivalent of an export license for the Faun—the Bavarian prince being the brother of the Austrian empress, whom Consalvi could not afford to alienate. Nor had the principle of restoring all the requisitioned art to their places of origin even yet come to the fore in the negotiations among the allies. In the first treaty of Paris after Napoleon's 1814 abdication, French retention of all the artworks taken from Italy—statuary, paintings, medals, gems, and manuscripts—had gone uncontested. The pope and Consalvi made their pleas, but they met with reluctance to undermine the precarious legitimacy of Louis XVIII, and the Russian czar flatly opposed any such demands.[3]

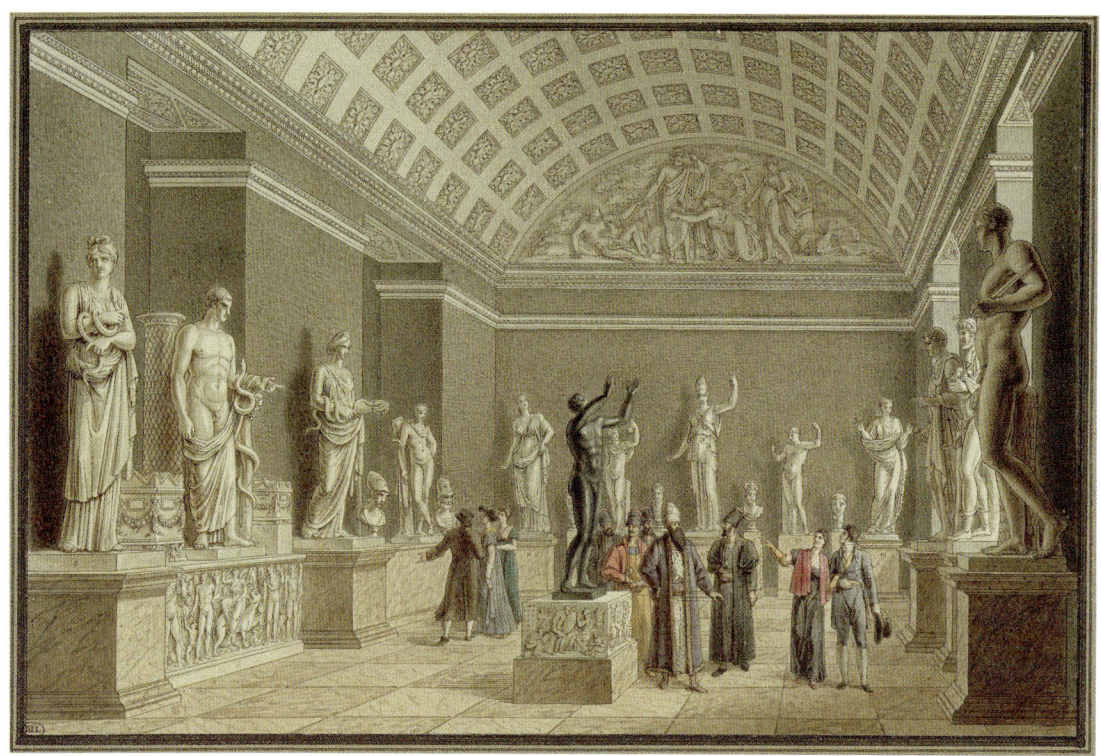

4.3. Attributed to Charles Normand, *Foreign Visitors in the Louvre Museum*, early 19th c., engraving with watercolor, pen and gray ink, and gray wash, 6¾ × 10¼ in. (17 × 26 cm), Musée du Louvre, Paris.

Napoleon's escape from Elba early in 1815 and subsequent return to power in France for the fabled One Hundred Days—with the horrendous further losses incurred by allied armies during the Waterloo campaign—made the victors far less accommodating to French sensibilities than before. Sensing his opportunity, Cardinal Consalvi renewed his efforts with greater energy within weeks of Wellington's Waterloo victory. A charter from the Roman Senate dispatched the sculptor Antonio Canova to Paris as Vatican representative with the brief that he make a blanket claim for "restitution of all the ancient works of art and paintings" taken by the French.

Possession of the pope's antiquities lay at the symbolic core of Napoleon's unprecedentedly comprehensive presentation of ancient and modern art offered in the Louvre by the Musée Napoléon (fig. 4.3).[4] Their presence signaled what Napoleon envisioned as an eventual removal of the seat of Christendom to the French capital, so his dominion would encompass worldly and spiritual realms alike. The *Laocoön* group (fig. 4.4), which had been paramount in the collections of the Vatican since its 1506 excavation in a vineyard near Santa Maria Maggiore, served as the cornerstone of the museum collection that Bonaparte had been imagining years before its full imperial realization: the artist Hubert Robert fittingly placed it squarely at the vanishing point when he painted the interior of the Louvre in 1802 (fig. 4.5). Antiquities of equal renown competed for the attention of visitors:

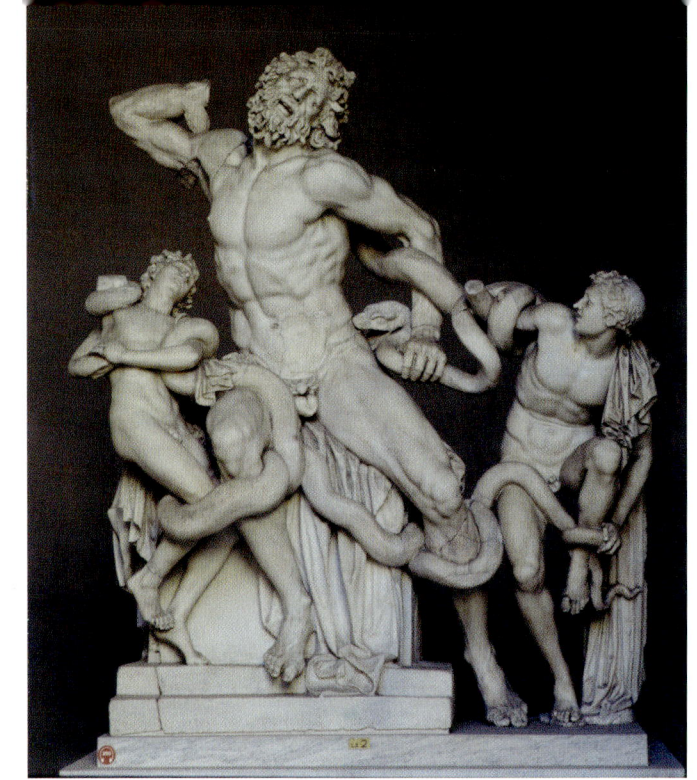

4.4. *The Laocoön Group*, Museo Pio Clementino, Vatican Museums, Vatican State.

4.5. Hubert Robert, *The Salle des Saisons at the Louvre*, c. 1802–3, oil on canvas, 14⅝ × 18⅛ in. (37 × 46 cm), Musée du Louvre, Paris.

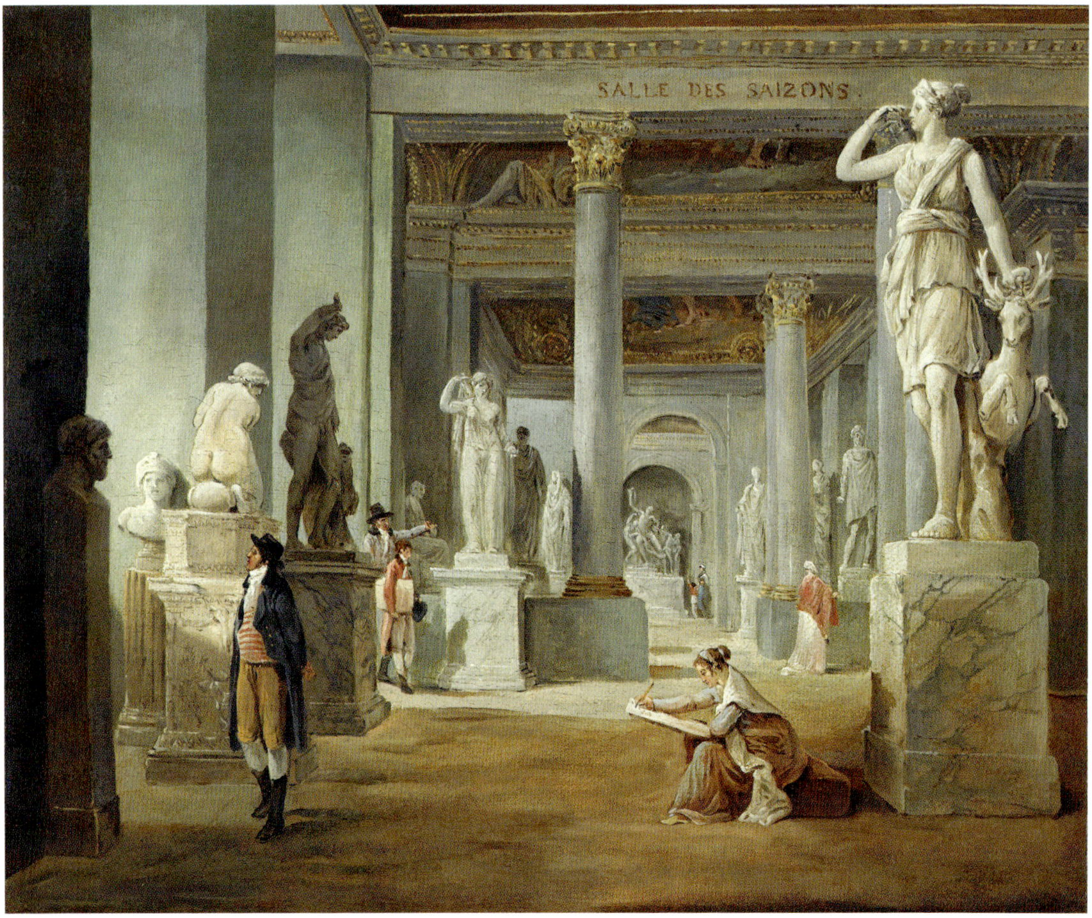

4.6. Apollonios of Athens, *The Belvedere Torso*, 1st century BC, marble, H: 159 cm, Museo Pio Clementino, Vatican Museums, Vatican State.

4.7. Attributed to Leochares, *Belvedere Apollo*, c. 120–40. Roman copy of Greek bronze original of c. 350–25 BC, c. 120–40, marble, Vatican Museums, Rome.

4.8. Anonymous, *"Eh bien, Messieurs ! - deux millions !", Napoleon declares while pointing out the Belvedere Apollo to a group of people gathered in the gallery of antiquities of the Louvre,* c. 1804, aquatint, 6⅜ × 8¼ in. (16.3 × 20.9 cm), Cabinet des Estampes, Bibliothèque Nationale, Paris.

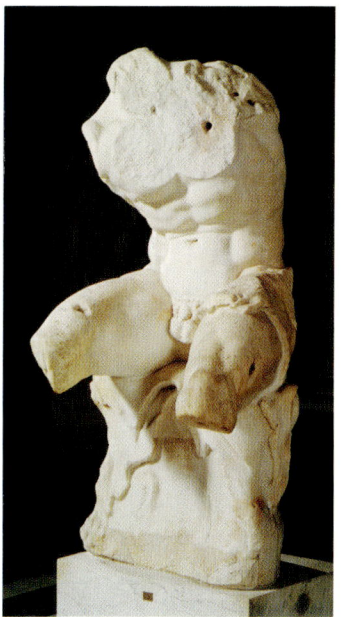

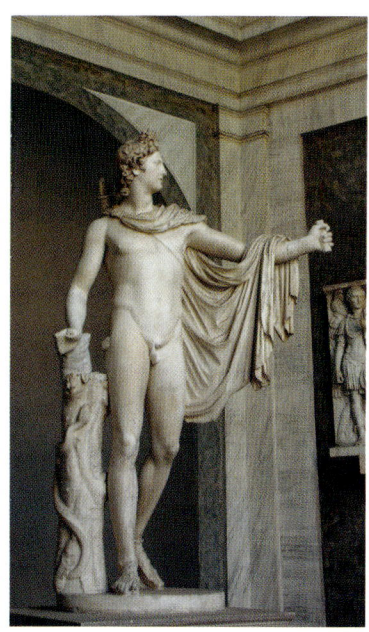

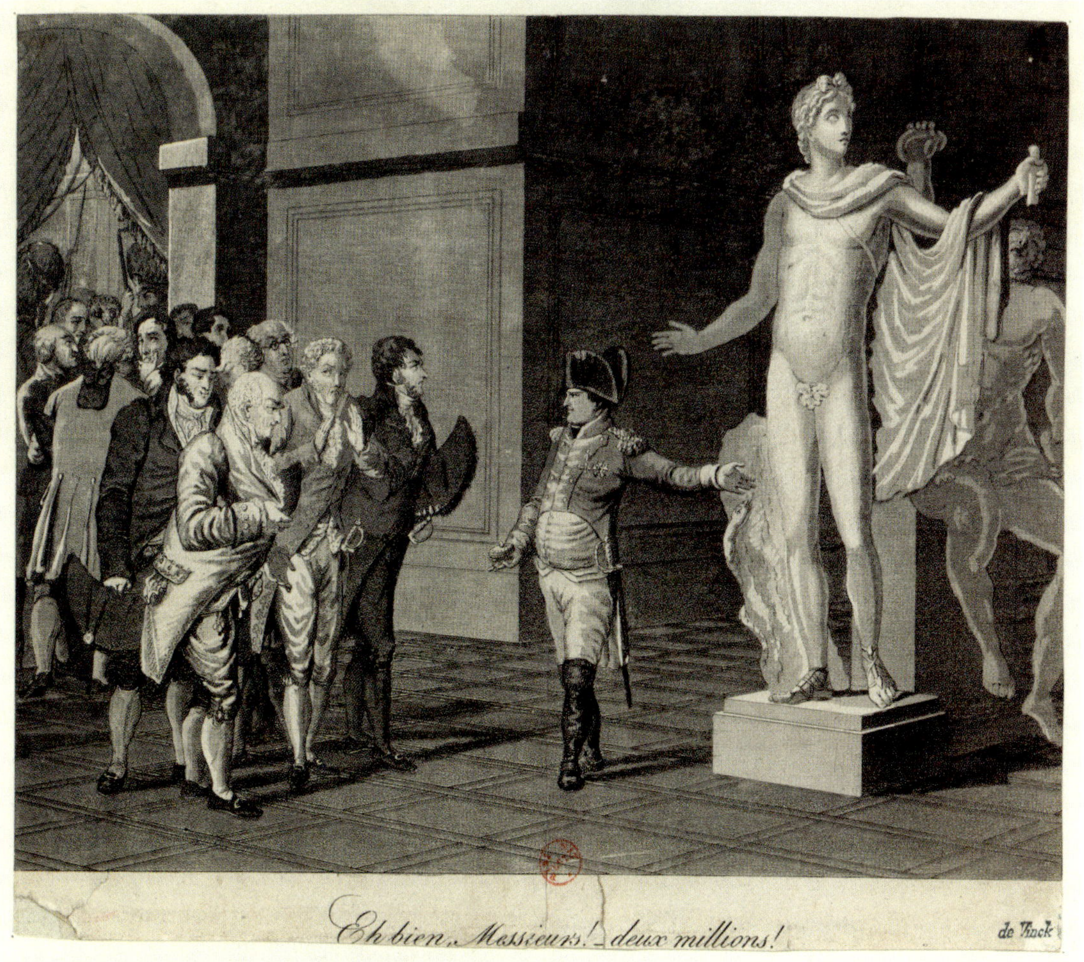

Eh bien.. Messieurs! deux millions!

de Thack

preeminently the battered *Belvedere Torso* (fig. 4.6) and *Belvedere Apollo* (fig. 4.7) (which an anonymous print records as a special Napoleonic prize [fig. 4.8]), both so named for the Vatican courtyard where both had formerly been installed in honor.

Just how central the Musée Napoléon had become in the consolidation and projection of Empire can be gauged by Napoleon's commandeering the museum as the setting for his second marriage in 1810, the dynastic match with Archduchess Marie Louise, daughter of the Austrian emperor. In his official rendering of the 1810 wedding (fig. 4.9), painter Georges Rouget feebly attempted an update of Jacques-Louis David's great *Coronation* (see fig. 1.8), but registered in the process an important symbolic shift. The ceremony occurred in what was, by use and tradition, an artistic domain: the Salon Carré of the Louvre, the double-height chamber where the great Salon exhibitions of contemporary painting took place every two years. The

4.9. Georges Rouget, *The Religious Marriage of Napoleon I and Marie-Louise Celebrated in the Salon Carré at the Louvre, on 2 April 1810*, 1836, oil on canvas, 148 ⅜ × 198 ⅞ in. (377 × 505 cm), Châteaux de Versailles et de Trianon, Versailles.

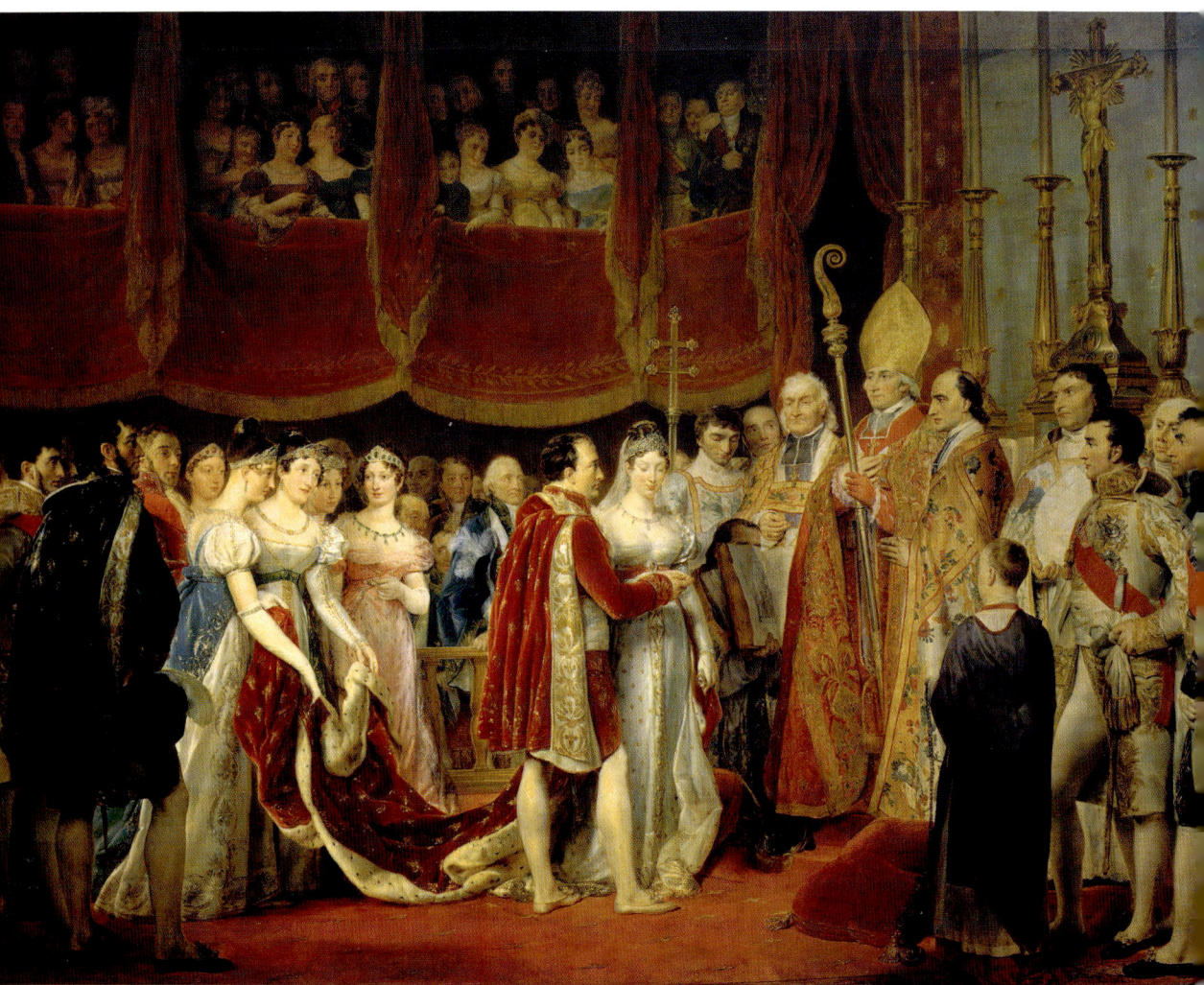

chamber had been temporarily stripped in order to accommodate viewing tribunes over an improvised "chapel" for the ceremony, the ritual that cemented in the mind and ambitions of the emperor his claims to equality with ruling dynasties of Europe.

Following their prior proxy marriage in Vienna, the itinerary of the new empress led her to the Louvre, where the wedding party processed the length of the Grande Galerie beneath a wealth of paintings from Italy, Flanders, and France.[5] Benjamin Zix, the Alsatian artist who served as official graphic artist to the court, memorialized the occasion with an immense, scroll-like commemorative drawing (fig. 4.10), which recorded the entire passage of the party beneath the great Raphael canvases and the rest of the works on the walls. Zix also produced a print (fig. 4.11) depicting the couple and entourage exiting the Grande Galerie, on their way to the improvised chapel set up in the Salon Carré. So much was the event imbued with the aura of art that, on the evidence of another drawing by Zix (fig. 4.12), the event was not complete until the imperial couple and entourage had viewed the *Laocoön* by torchlight.[6]

The sacredness conferred on the museum by imperial ceremony thus made its dismantling far more than a matter of title to property; both the collection and its display went to the heart of state authority and legitimacy. The issue split the famous brothers, Wilhelm and Alexander von Humboldt, whose solicitations to David figured in the last chapter. Prussian delegate Wilhelm was bound to promote repatriation, while the naturalist and explorer Alexander called the Musée Napoléon the great solace of his long Parisian residence and its potential dismantling an act of "iconoclasm."[7] Much as today, questions were raised as to the public accessibility and conservation of repatriated objects. The English portrait painter Thomas Lawrence said at the time to the Scottish miniaturist Andrew Robertson: "every artist must lament the breaking up of a collection in a place so central to Europe where everything was laid open to the public with a degree of liberality unknown elsewhere."[8]

✳

Thomas Lawrence will emerge as the main protagonist in the latter part of this chapter. His high regard for the achievement of Napoleon and his museum director Vivant Denon, if shared at all by his British patrons, did not deter them from successfully advancing the cause of restitution. Decisive in this was the resolve of the Duke of Wellington, hardened over the losses sustained in subduing Napoleon a second time at Waterloo. In September 1815, he wrote to Castlereagh at the Vienna talks, arguing that to retain Napoleon's cultural spoils in the Louvre "must necessarily have the effect of keeping up the

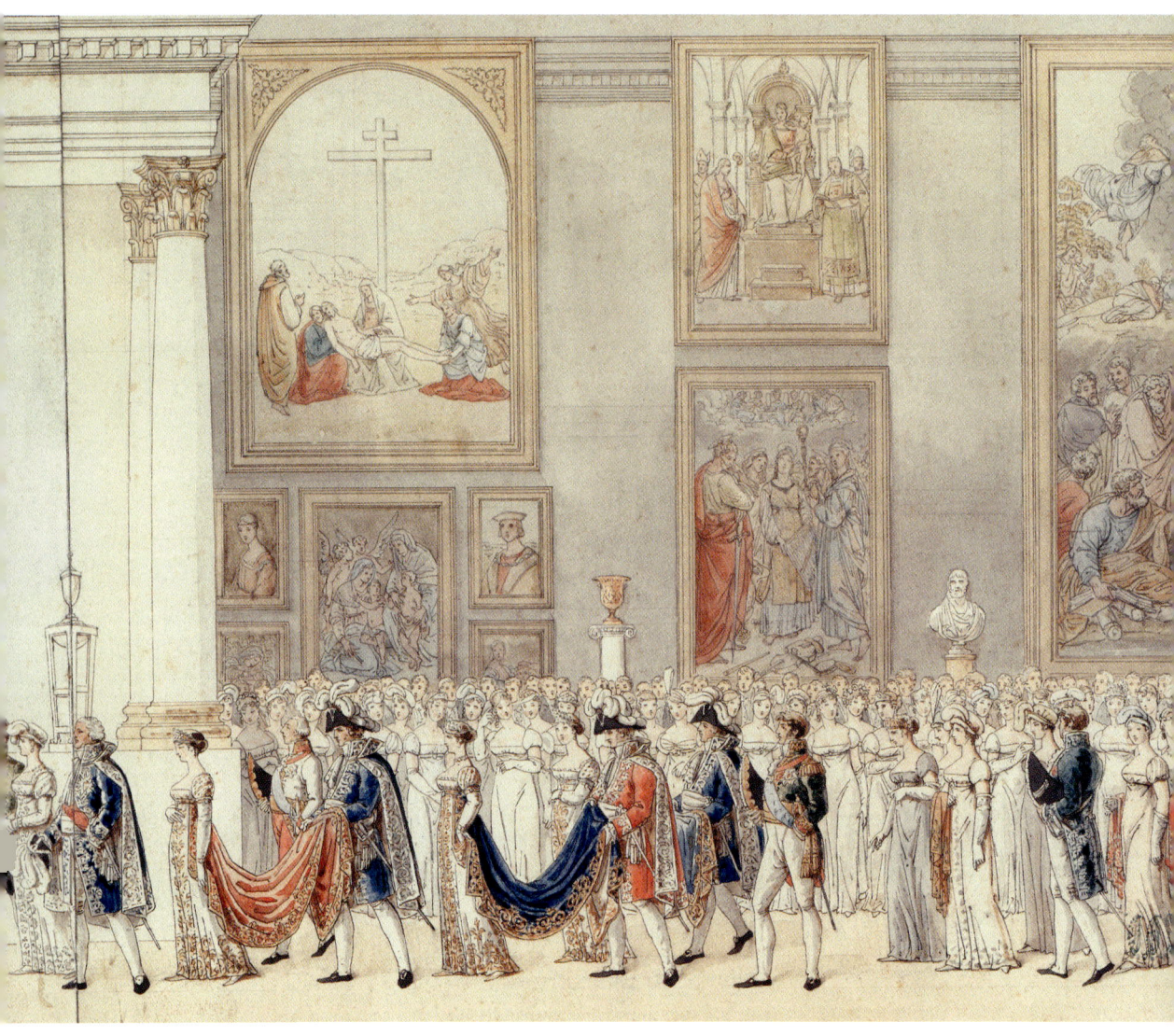

4.10. Benjamin Zix, *The Wedding Procession of Napoleon and Marie Louise of Austria through the Grande Galerie of the Louvre, April 2, 1810*, 1810, pen and ink with watercolor, 67¾ × 9½ in. (172 × 24 cm), Musée du Louvre, Paris.

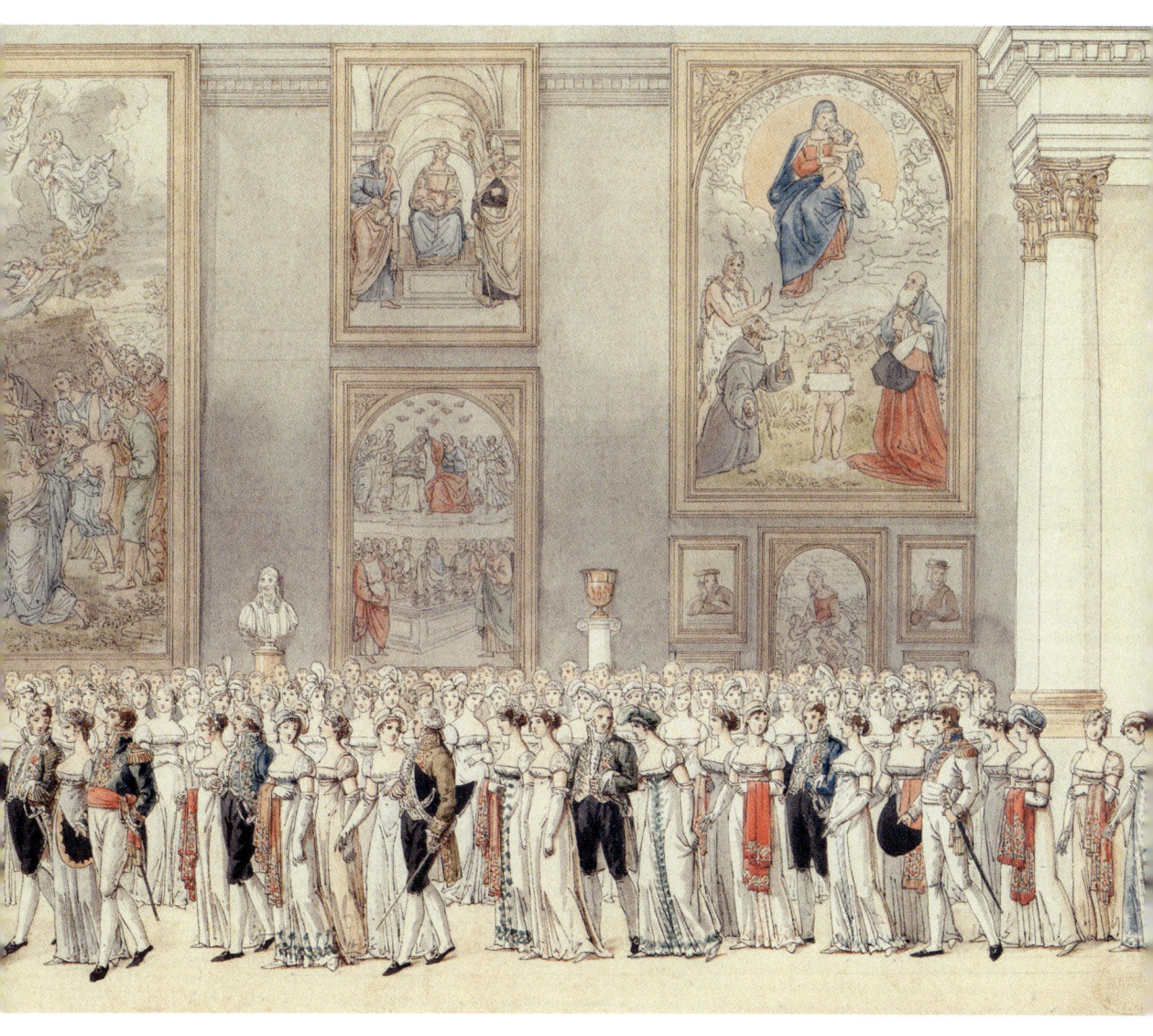

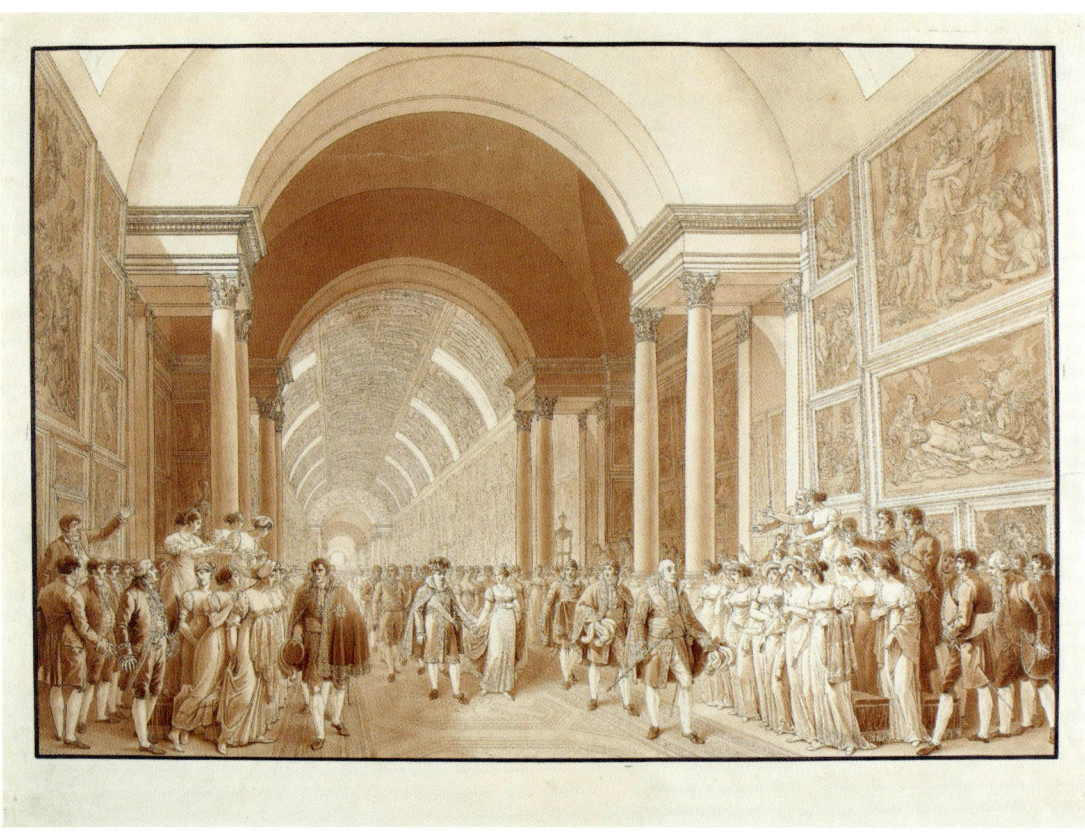

4.11. Benjamin Zix, *The Wedding Procession of Napoleon and Marie Louise through the Grand Galerie of the Louvre, April 2, 1810*, pen and gray ink, brown wash, 15¾ × 23⅝ in. (40 × 60 cm), Musée du Louvre, Paris.

remembrance of their former conquests, and of cherishing the military spirit and the vanity of the Nation."[9] English supporters extending up the level of the prince regent (soon George IV), emboldened by the precedent of Prussian troops removing German-sourced paintings without waiting for permission, proved decisive for Canova's mission. The allies conceded the requests over the art from the pope and cardinal, along with most of their territorial demands. But making good on the agreement proved no easy matter. The danger of crowd violence became so acute that Wellington began regular reviews of allied troops as a conspicuous show of strength.

As a papal agent in Paris, Canova carried no adverse reputation for hostility to France or the Bonaparte family. His commissioned portrait of Pauline Bonaparte as the reclining nude Venus (1805–8) had been just one instance of his willingness to accommodate the requirements of the French occupiers. His standing portrait of the emperor himself in the naked guise of Mars the Peacemaker—if less finely judged than the classicized rendition of his sister—bore far greater significance in advancing the claims of Paris to unchallenged preeminence as a European capital. Canova's statue of the emperor (fig. 4.13) had been intended to greet visitors on entrance the to the Musée Napoléon—its counterpart in implied prestige no less than the *Laocoön* itself.

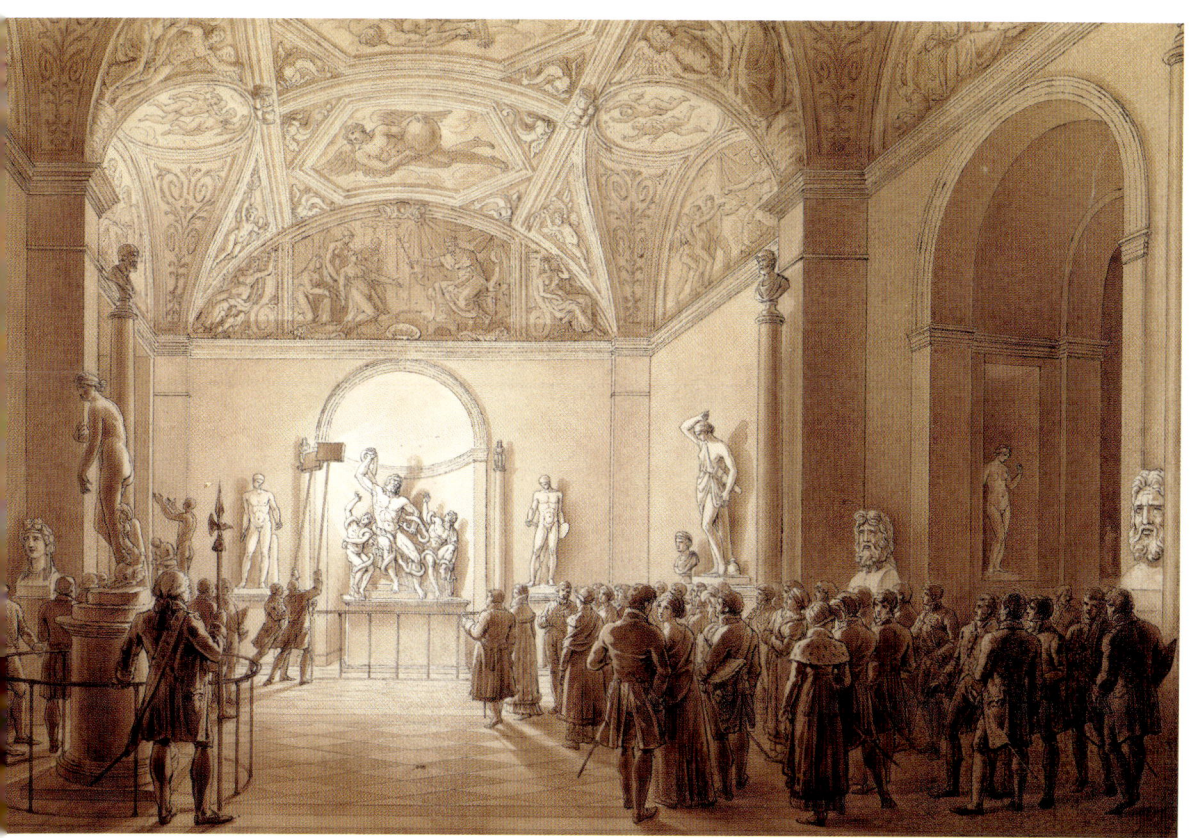

When Bonaparte as first consul had earlier summoned Canova to Paris in 1803, he was among other things rehearsing the demand of Louis XIV that Bernini journey to Paris (addressed for other reasons in chapter 2) where the artist had likewise sculpted a portrait of the ruler. Notwithstanding the emperor's well-remarked discomfort with the blatancy of his oversized nude representation, the celebrated sculptor would have seemed an ideal ambassador. But the sculptor found sympathy in short supply on arriving in the French capital at the end of August 1815. One anonymous print (fig. 4.14) depicts the grief of a generic French artist—palette and easel cast down—as the *Laocoön* and *Apollo* exit the portal of the Louvre. French hostility to Canova's mission was such as to render him perpetually anxious, fear-ridden and miserable, longing for the process to be over. Another British artist, Richard Reinagle, describes Canova being lambasted by bread pellets on a visit to the study room of the French Academy, where his French counterpart, the great sculptor Jean-Antoine Houdon, refused to speak to him.[10] "He was one day," related painter Thomas Phillips, "afraid to go to his lodgings there for fear of being murdered and that one day one of the French *artists* said in his hearing that he should like to stick a dagger in him."[11] Robertson paid a call on the illustrious Napoleonic battle painter Antoine-Jean Gros, reporting afterward: "I

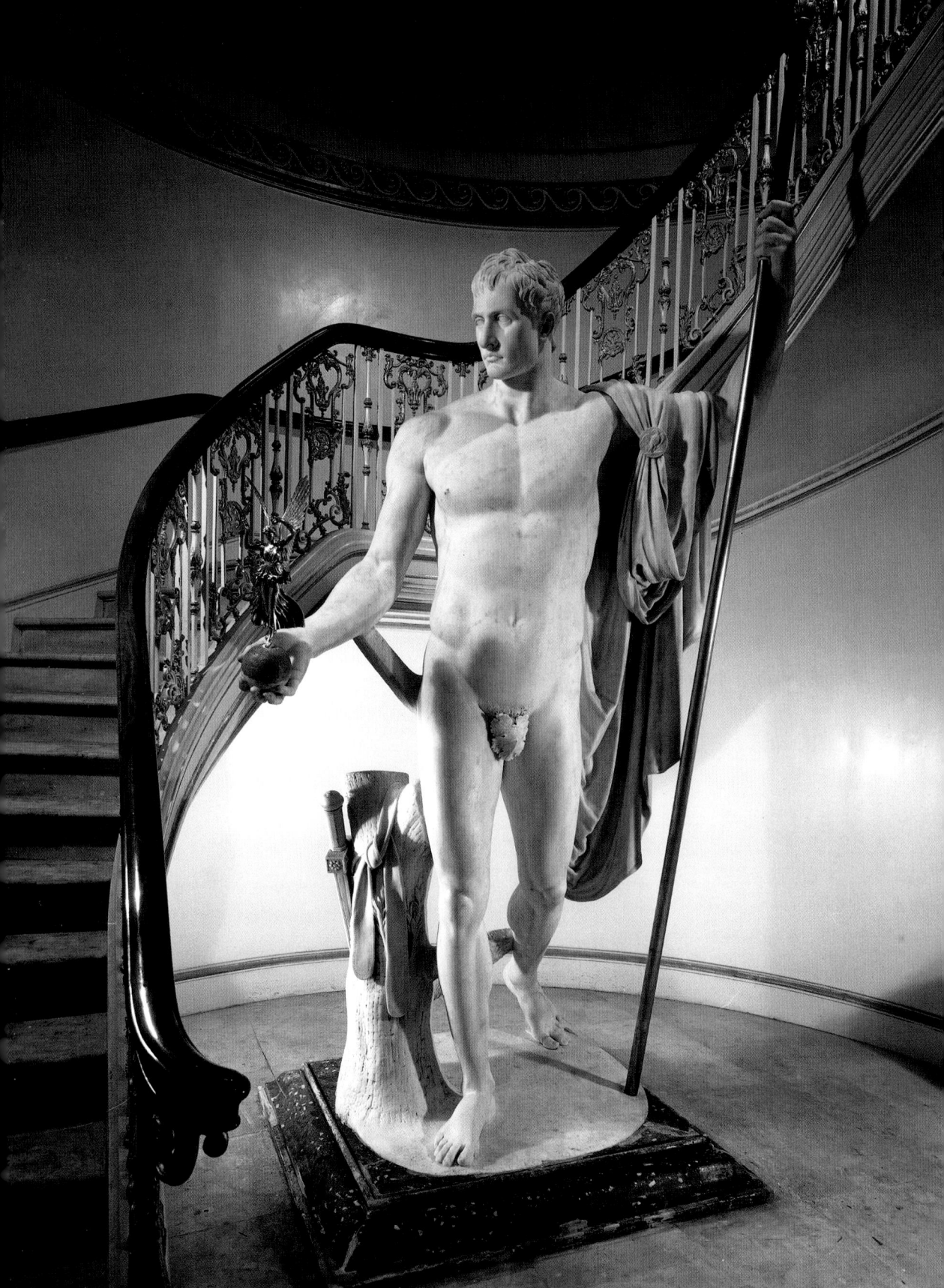

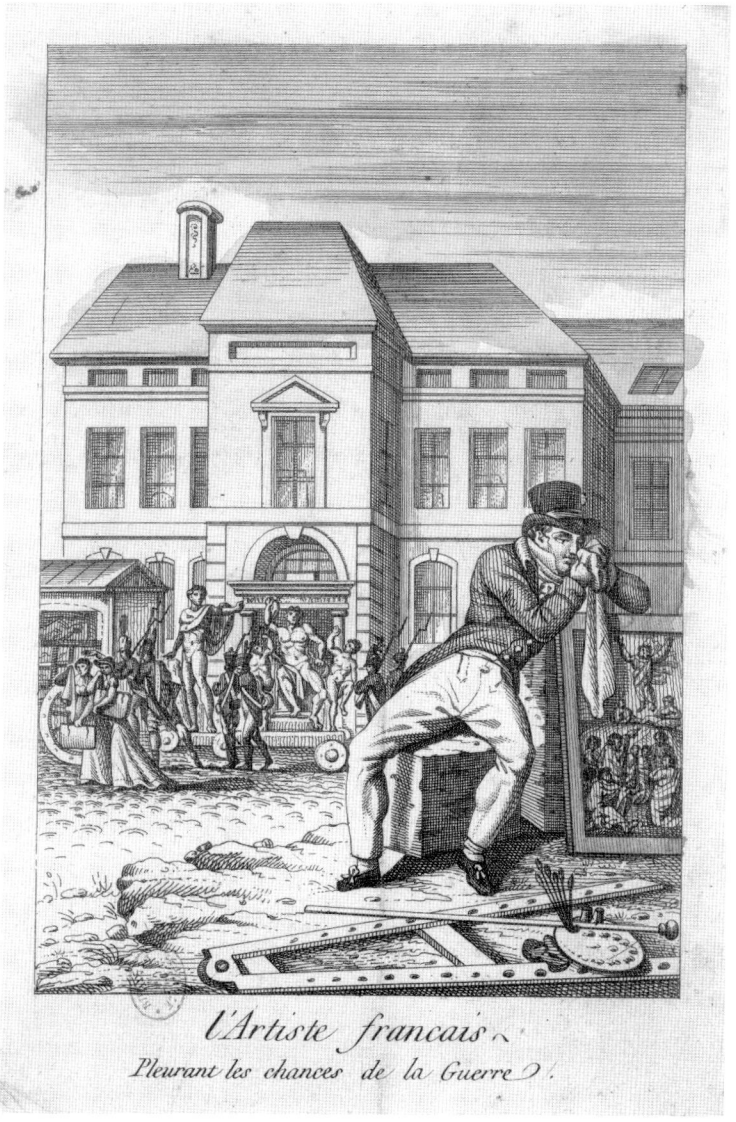

l'Artiste francais

Pleurant les chances de la Guerre

have never seen a volcano—but after this interview, I can conceive an eruption of Vesuvius."[12]

Thomas Lawrence may well have regretted on some level the dismantling of the collections in the former Musée Napoléon when both he and Canova were witnessing the event, but that opinion appears to have been his only recorded difference with official British positions. Since May 1814, just after Napoleon's first abdication, Lawrence's personal and artistic interests lay firmly aligned with state policy. In that month, three continental sovereigns—the Russian and Austrian emperors with the Prussian king—paid a visit to London in their temporary triumph, each attended by his respective field marshal.[13] Lady Anne Barnard, a writer and society figure, wrote to both the prince

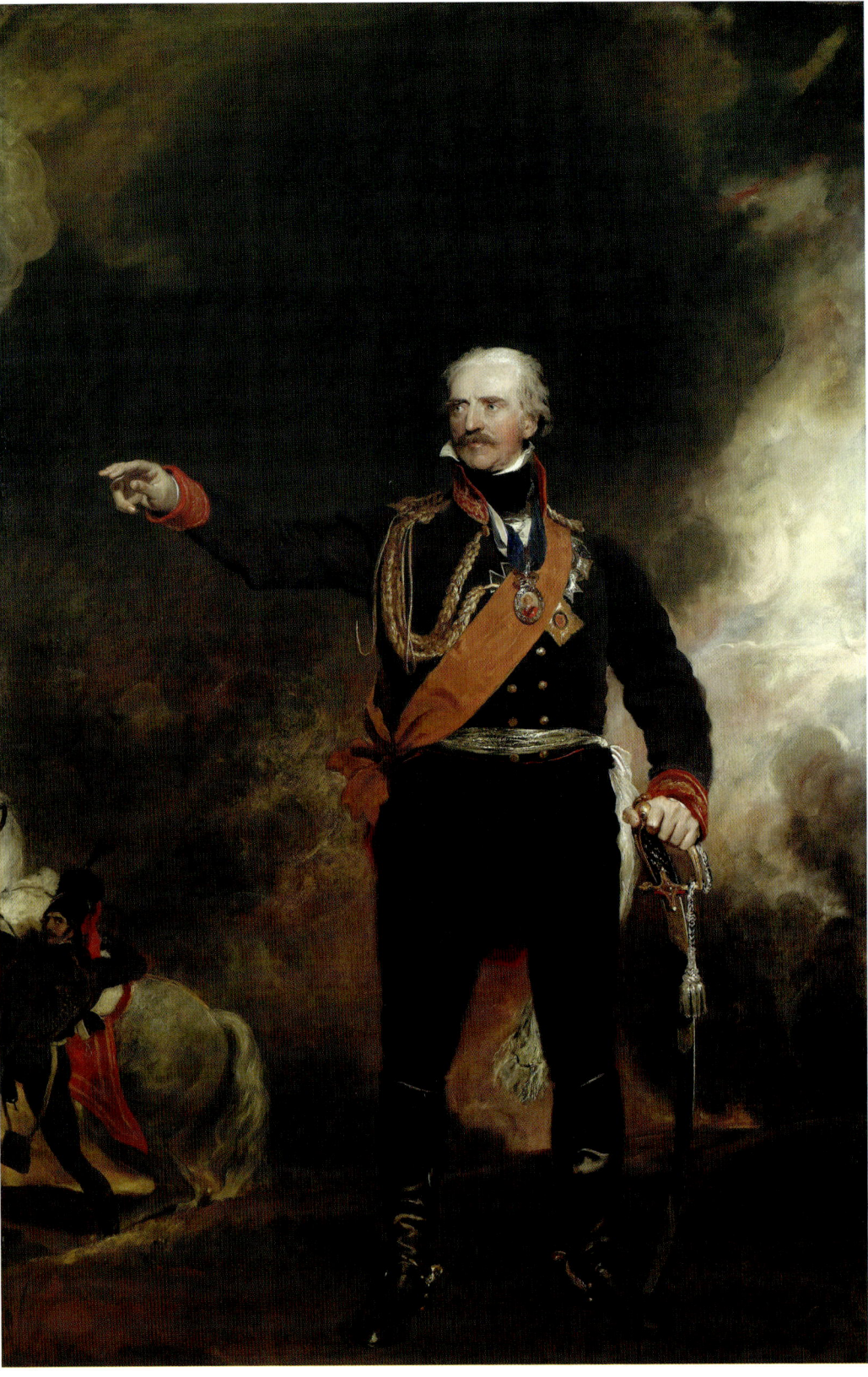

regent and to Lawrence in urgent prose: "If the *present opportunity is lost*, its strength and force from collecting the countenances as they *now are*, will be lost to you forever."[14] Whether or not it proved the actual instigation of the project, Barnard's letter is the first record of a massive undertaking that would consume the next half decade of Lawrence's career and transform his life: creating a record in individual portraits of every principal figure in the defeat of Napoleon.

In accord with the breathless entreaty of Lady Barnard, Lawrence set about fixing the facial likenesses and at least the portrait rudiments of every personage she recommended, for example the Prussian field marshal Gebhardt von Blücher (fig. 4.15). Lawrence's friend Charles Stewart, Castlereagh's brother-in-law and newly appointed British ambassador to the Austrian court, suggested to the artist in July 1816 that he come to Vienna to gather more impressions from the chief grandees among the assembled delegates to the Congress. Although Napoleon's return during the One Hundred Days put the plan into an extended suspension, Lawrence became yet another artist, though a previously reluctant continental traveler, displaced across Europe by the exigencies of the Restoration.[15]

*

In September 1818, when further diplomatic gatherings in Aix-la-Chapelle and Vienna presented a renewed opportunity, Stewart's strategy belatedly went into effect. By now secure within the circle of the prince regent, Lawrence was promised five hundred guineas for each full-length canvas and a thousand pounds in expenses (all conspicuously generous subsidies).[16] As Canova had been dispatched from Rome to travel across Europe in pursuit of papal property, Lawrence was dispatched in the opposite direction from London to Aix to Vienna in pursuit of likenesses on behalf of the prince regent, with Rome added in a late directive (Stewart had even had Russia in mind). Artist James Northcote, writing in wonder at Lawrence's "high employment" on the Continent, declared that there had been "nothing like it except in the instances of Rubens & Vandyke" and that "it wd. raise the credit of English Art abroad and make it more respected at Home."[17]

So much stock did Castlereagh put into the project that he had constructed for Lawrence a portable wooden three-room house and painting studio to be erected on the grounds of his own residences. In the event, the prefabricated structure, which also included his canvases and paints, failed to arrive in Aix before Lawrence had finished his labors there. The city magistrate had overcome that setback by supplying materials and a generous space in the hôtel-de-ville where he could paint: "*and it is certainly the best I ever had,*" Lawrence wrote to artist Joseph Farington (his italics).[18] With his initial efforts there, Lawrence developed a lasting template for representing these worthies: full-length representations in full ceremonial regalia, the commanders among them standing calmly against atmospheric but nonspecific backdrops of battle. To take his portrait of Emperor Alexander I (fig. 4.16), largely painted in Aix-la-Chapelle, Lawrence removes nearly all martial attributes from the Russian sovereign's surroundings, leaving the enveloping greatcoat and plumed hat to one side so as better to highlight the reportedly graceful figure that enhanced the czar's considerable popular celebrity. The uniform was, by the emperor's testimony, the one he wore in victory at the Battle of Leipzig, but Lawrence jettisoned the topographic details and maneuvering troops that had been customary for such portraits in the past. He put in their place subtly variable effects of flame and smoke merging into enveloping atmosphere. Perhaps nowhere did he deploy this device with more suggestive effect than in his later treatment, painted in Vienna, of Archduke Charles of Austria (fig. 4.17), leading allied field commander and younger brother of the emperor.

The artists who have been figuring most prominently in this book add up to a roll call of the indisputable greats of the period: David, Goya, Canova, Gros, Géricault, Ingres. But Lawrence? From shortly after his death in 1830 until relatively recently, Lawrence has been saddled with a reputation as a facile virtuoso and superficial flatterer of his largely aristocratic clientele. Even with some recent historical rehabilitation, few would place him in the company just listed. But our subject is above all change, and Lawrence's enlargement of the capacities of portraiture led to a pair of consummate Restoration canvases, indeed the works of art that may most lucidly and acutely figure that very subject.

✳

Canova's London visit in 1815 had proven as warm and honorific a tour as his stay in Paris had been abusive and punishing. Lawrence could count on the friendship he and Canova had formed on that occasion, marked by the sympathetic portrait he made of the Italian sculptor (fig. 4.18). But Canova was far from the only local support that Lawrence possessed when arriving in Rome in May 1819. As far back as 1805, he had painted this portrait (fig. 4.19), replete with classical allusions, of Elizabeth Foster, then mistress to the fifth Duke of Devonshire. He depicted her in the costume and setting of the Tiburtine Sybil, the ancient Roman prophetess who was credited with foretelling the coming of Christ. Her seat was at Tivoli, the hilltop settlement with its famous torrents and temple; the so-called Sybil's Temple can be glimpsed in the lower right corner of the portrait—her father, the Bishop Earl of Derry, had tried to buy it for removal to

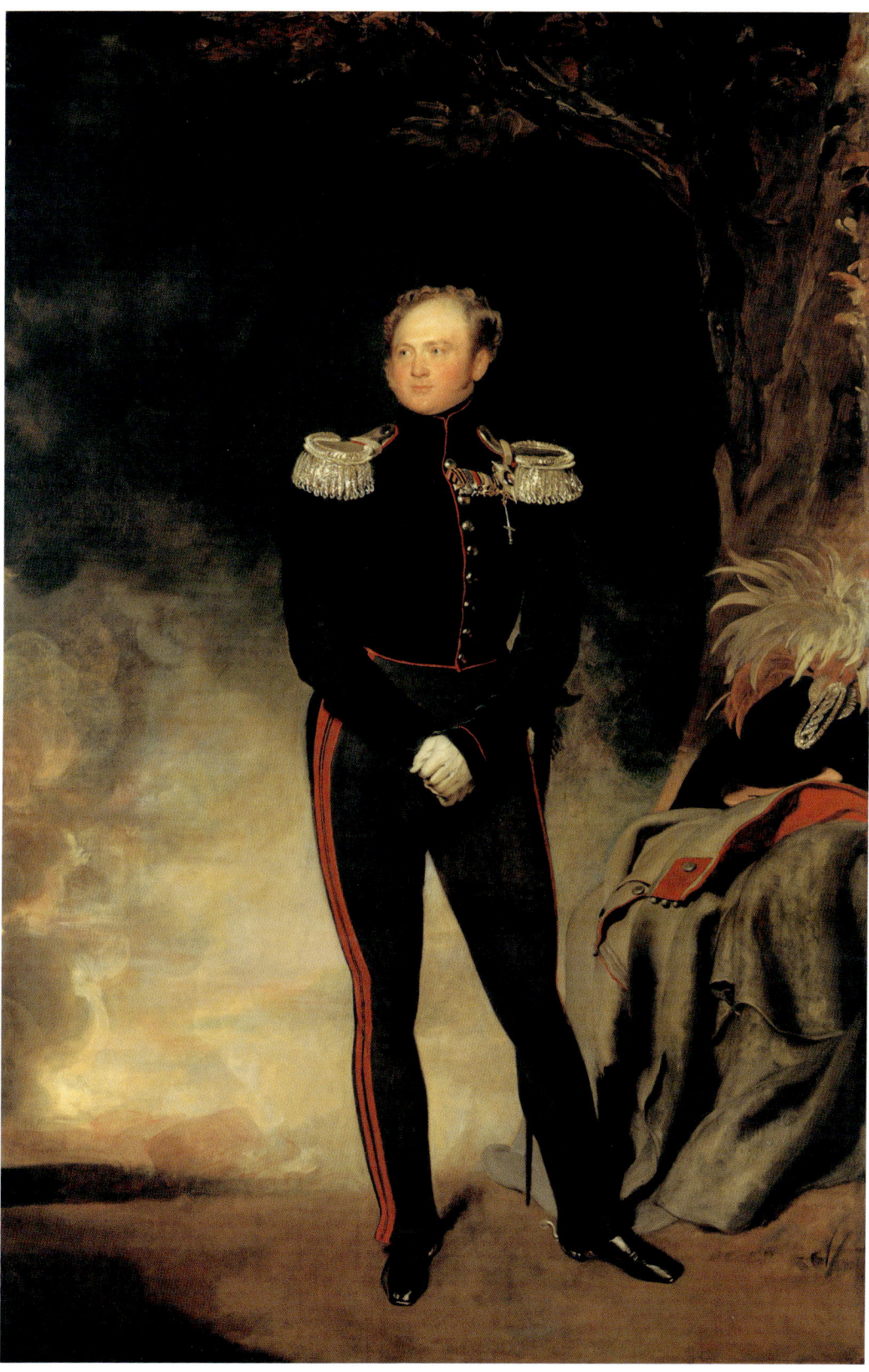

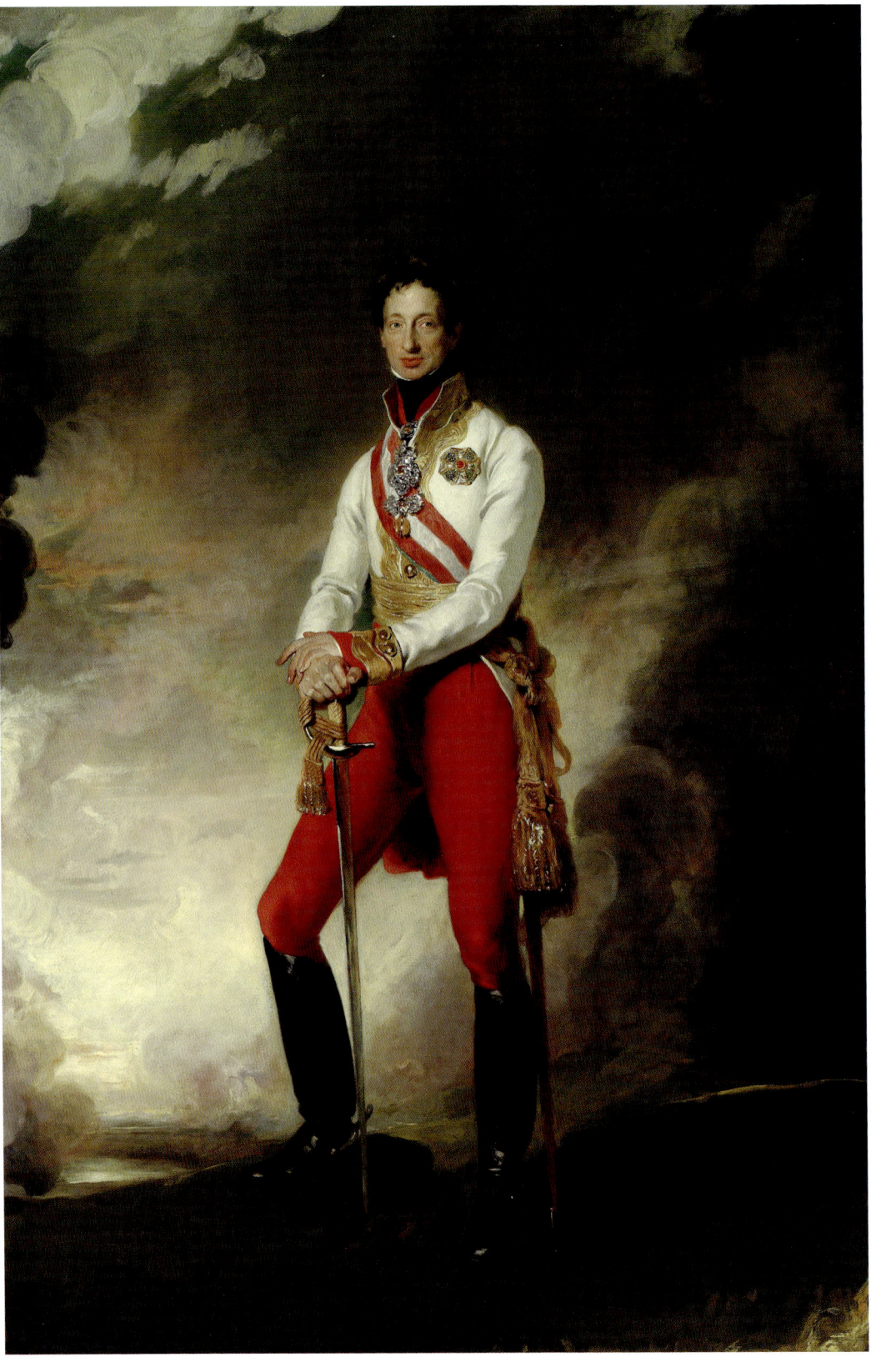

4.17. Thomas Lawrence, *Portrait of Archduke Charles of Austria*, 1819, oil on canvas, 106⅜ × 70⅝ in. (270.1 × 179.5 cm), The Royal Collection, Windsor Castle.

4.18. Thomas Lawrence, *Portrait of Antonio Canova*, 1815, oil on canvas, 35⅜ × 28⅜ in. (90 × 72 cm), Gypsotheca e Museo Antonio Canova, Possagno.

Ireland.[19] Foster had since become Duchess of Devonshire in her own right, second wife to the late duke, and the most prominent member of a significant expatriate English community in Rome. In the summer of 1819, she sat for Lawrence once again, yielding a remarkable likeness in chalk on paper (fig. 4.20). By the time of her sitting, she had become Cardinal Consalvi's closest companion—the two saw each other nearly every day, and she was the only other person permitted to enter his private garden hideaway. In that capacity, she knit English upper-crust fascination with papal pomp and splendor into the tight social fabric of the expatriate community. Both her stepson, the sixth duke, and the French writer Lamartine called her the uncrowned queen of Rome, dominant society hostess and patroness of learning.[20] Among other exploits, she organized archaeological excavations in the Forum and luxurious illustrated editions of Horace and Virgil in Italian translation.

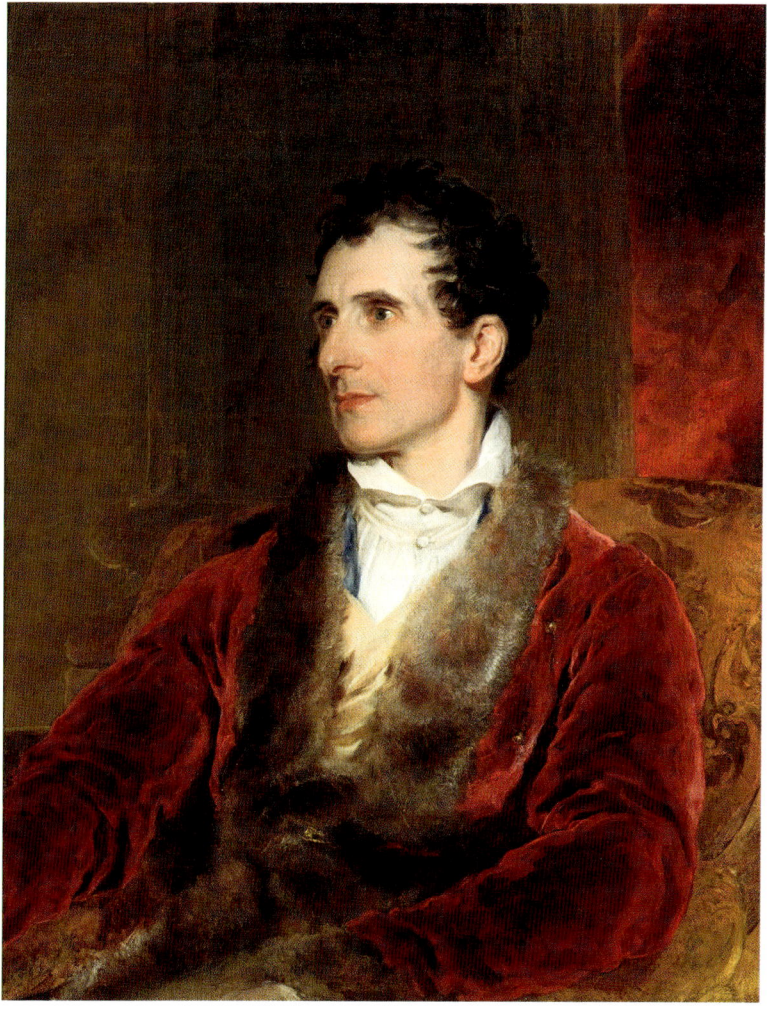

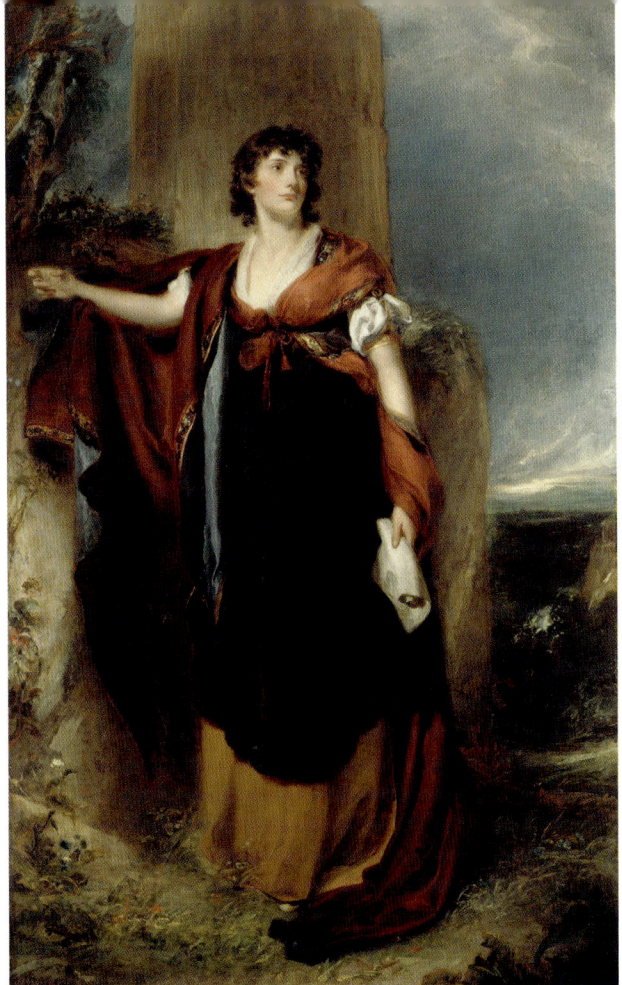

4.19. Thomas Lawrence, *Portrait of Lady Elizabeth Foster*, later Duchess of Devonshire, 1805, oil on canvas, 94½ × 58¼ in. (240 × 148 cm), National Gallery of Ireland, Dublin.

4.20. Thomas Lawrence, *Portrait of Elizabeth, Duchess of Devonshire*, 1819, pencil and chalk on paper, 14¾ × 10⅛ in. (37.3 × 25.7 cm), Timothy Clode Collection.

That the Duchess and Consalvi could be so publicly close owed something to the fact that the cardinal, though formally celibate, had never in fact been ordained as a priest. A statesman through and through, he leaned on a wealthy and influential ally like the duchess in his massive efforts to refurbish Rome as a destination for travelers and European expatriates. Some of these projects have made an appearance in the previous chapter in connection with the Roman studies of Géricault and Antoine Jean-Baptiste Thomas. The Piazza de Popolo, at the north entrance to the city, had been the particular focus of the cardinal's renovations, as he commissioned its newly balanced and embellished oval plan from the architect Giuseppe Valadier, augmented by the amphitheater and terraces leading to the gardens on the Pincian Hill above.[21] The cardinal had also set about reviving customs that had gone into obsolescence during the French occupation—or even earlier—in order to orchestrate a picturesque, folkloric experience for the increasingly numerous visitors. When Antoine Jean-Baptiste Thomas and his friend Géricault were recording cattle and horses careening through the streets around the Piazza del Popolo (which played such a prominent part in the previous

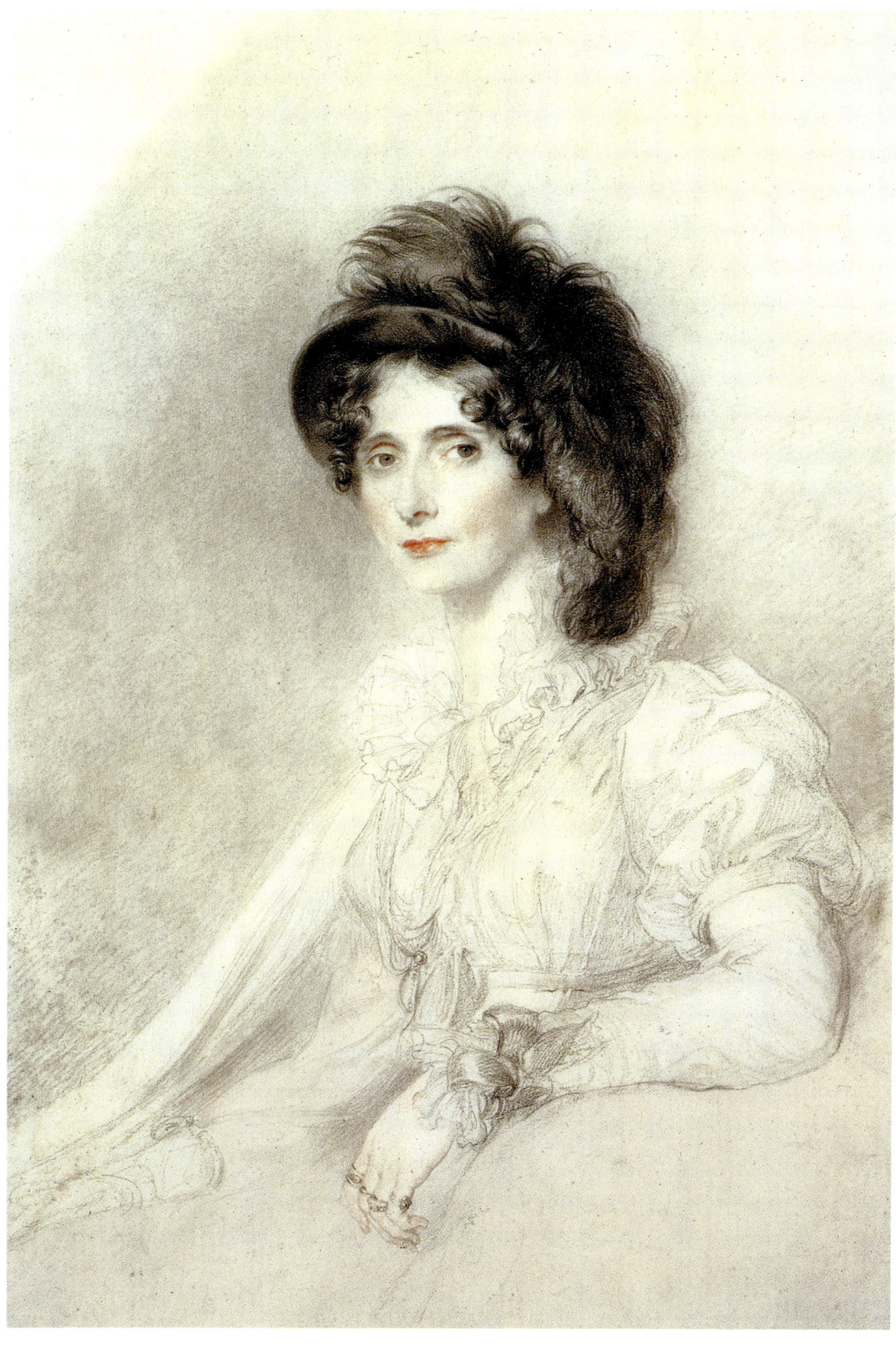

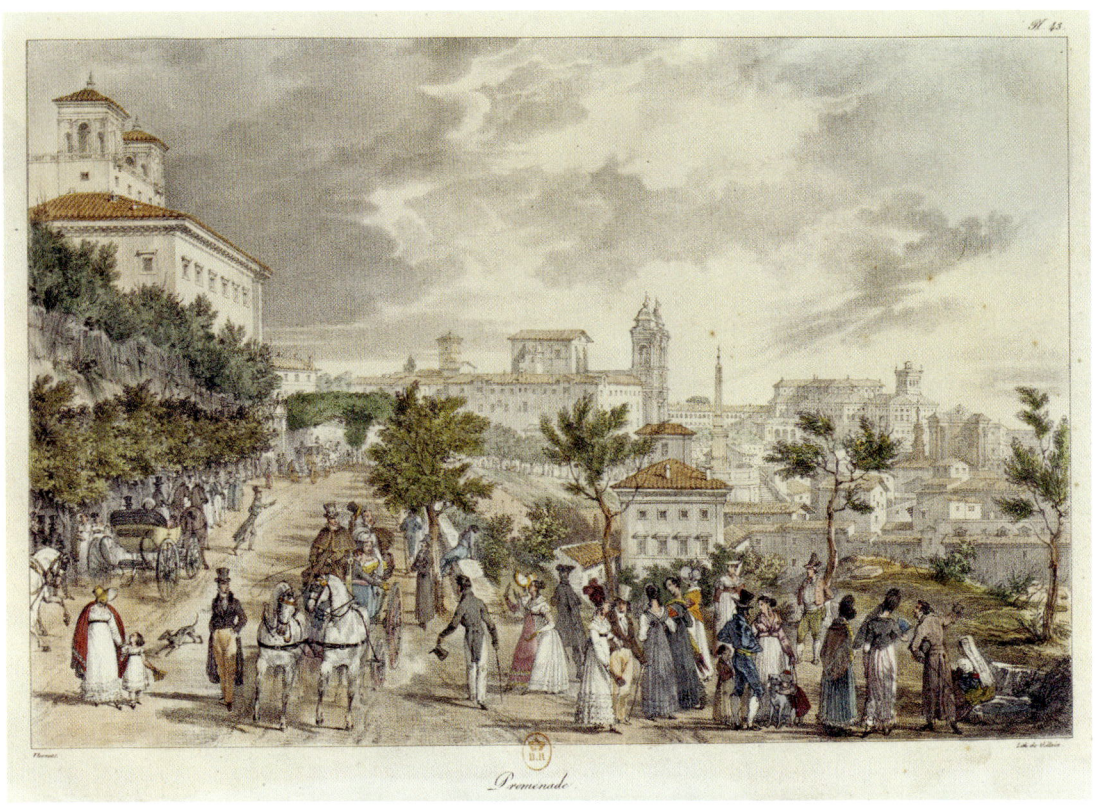

Pl. 45.

Promenade

4.21. Antoine Jean-Baptiste Thomas, "A Promenade," plate 43, 8⅛ × 12⅜ in. (20.6 × 31.4 cm), *Un an à Rome*, 1823.

chapter), it was against this newly refurbished and widely admired urban backdrop, the two artists taking full advantage of the aesthetically arresting interplay engineered by Consalvi between elegant urban order (fig. 4.21) and exciting popular energies.

In the print series that Thomas derived from his studies of 1816 to 1817, these orchestrated experiences of street life function as prologue to the overwhelming effects provided by high ceremony of Saint Peter's, from a close view of the pope at prayer to a wide prospect of the outdoor papal blessing (figs. 4.22–23). Lawrence's breathless descriptions of his life in the seat of Catholic Christendom capture the flavor of the voyeuristic cult that prevailed among the local English residents. He recounts one evening in a way that is difficult to condense: "I was yesterday St. Peter's Day," he wrote at the beginning of July to his confidant Farington, "as spectator of doubtless the most superb ceremony and spectacle ... that this world can exhibit; the celebration of high mass in St. Peter's. No words of mine have any power of conveying to you the magnificence and grandeur of it. By the care of the Cardinal [Consalvi], and the persons having direction of the ceremony, I was placed nearer to the Pope than any other stranger (with the exception of the Duke of Saxe Gotha, and some other persons of rank) in the seat that ranges on the side, and immediately behind

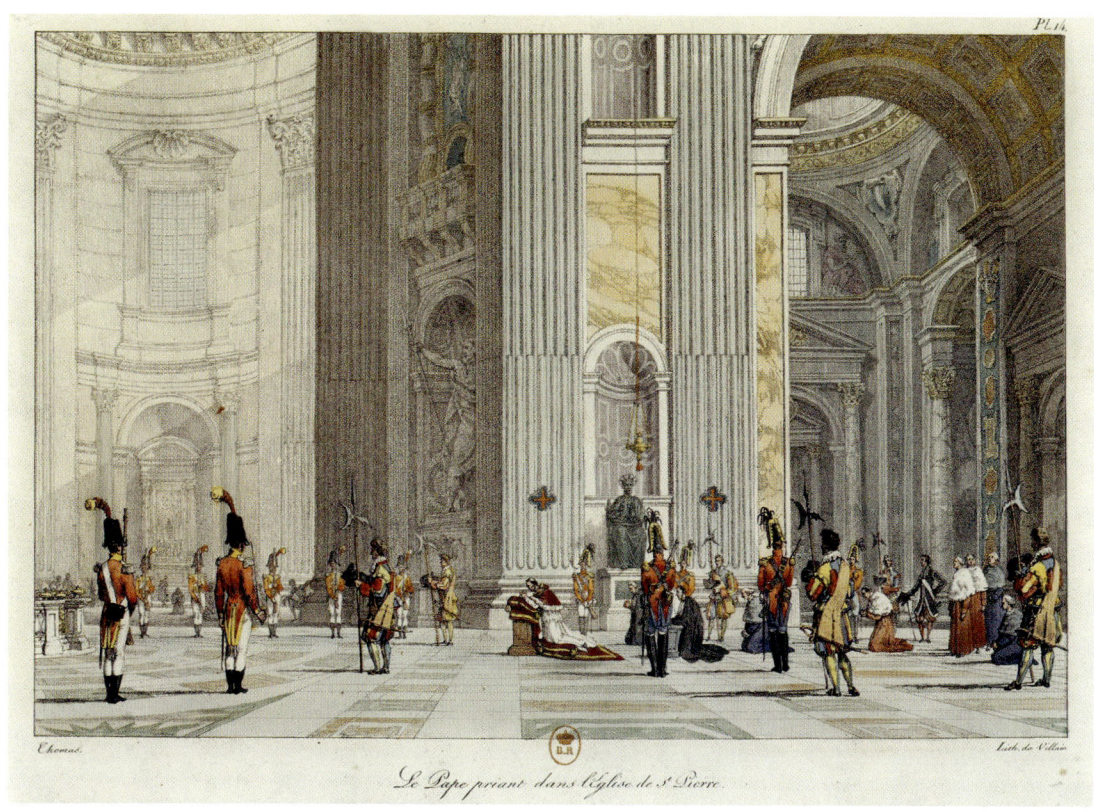

Le Pape priant dans l'Église de S.t Pierre.

4.22. Antoine Jean-Baptiste Thomas, "The Pope Praying in the Church of Saint Peter," plate 14, 7⅛ × 9⅞ in. (18.1 × 24.9 cm), *Un an à Rome*, 1823.

the Cardinals; so that I had an entirely convenient view of the whole ceremony. Titian never conceived anything more gorgeous, and at the same time solemn in dignity, than the accompaniments and dresses of the personages in this scene."[22]

But this was not the end of the day's events, as Lawrence then returns to the great basilica: "At three o'clock," he relates, "I dined with Lady Shaftesbury, and in the evening called on the Duchess of Devonshire, to go with her and her friends to vespers at St. Peter's.... We staid [*sic*], going frequently round that noble area, till the second illumination, and then drove to the house immediately opposite to the bridge and castle of St. Angelo, to see its display of fire-works, from the room and balcony which had been recently occupied by their Imperial Majesties [the Austrian Emperor and Empress] ... The night before, I had seen the fire-works from the same place, by the Cardinal Consalvi's direction. When the whole was over, I went to the French Ambassador's, Comte Blacas, which is always attended by the first society, and about one o'clock returned to the Quirinale Palace." Lately the Roman headquarters of Napoleon, the Quirinale in 1819 served as papal residence (Pius VII being sovereign of the entire territory beyond the Vatican). When Lawrence ended the evening at the palace, he was returning to the generous apartments supplied to

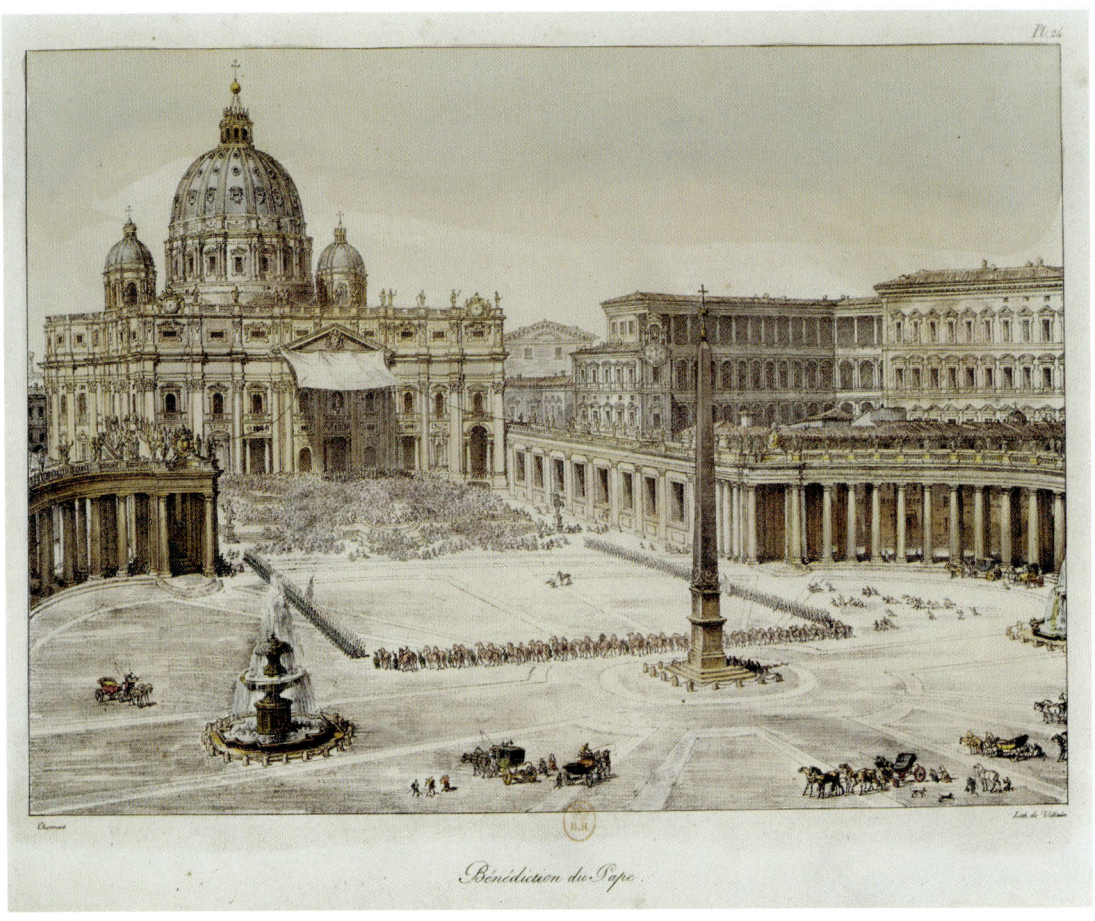

Bénédiction du Pape

4.23. Antoine Jean-Baptiste Thomas, "Blessing by the Pope," plate 24, 8¹/₁₆ × 11⅓ in. (20.5 × 28.7 cm), *Un an à Rome*, 1823.

4.24. Thomas Lawrence, *Portrait of Cardinal Ercole Consalvi*, 1819, oil on canvas, 106 × 69¼ in. (269.2 × 175.8 cm), The Royal Collection, Windsor Castle.

him by Consalvi and the pope. And it was there that he fashioned his assigned portraits of both.

The warmth of the Consalvi portrait (fig. 4.24) bespeaks Lawrence's own giddy insertion into a strangely crypto-Catholic way of life conducted by some of the highest English aristocracy. His fascination with the spectacle of Saint Peter's is writ large across his portrait of Consalvi, conspicuously in his rendering of its facade in mixed shadow and sun, the flare of evening illumination like the fireworks seen from the Castel Sant'Angelo opposite, the shadow serving to emphasize the force of the cardinal's brightly lit visage.[23] Before Lawrence left the city to return to London, the duchess begged him for a pencil version of the cardinal's portrait, which she afterward carried with her everywhere she went (fig. 4.25).[24] Also prominent among this set, as mentioned above, was the duchess's stepson, now the sixth Duke of Devonshire, making his residence in Rome and hesitating to marry. Their friend Consalvi's improvements to the fabric of the city, with the round of spectacles he encouraged, made Roman life more than congenial and continually diverting.

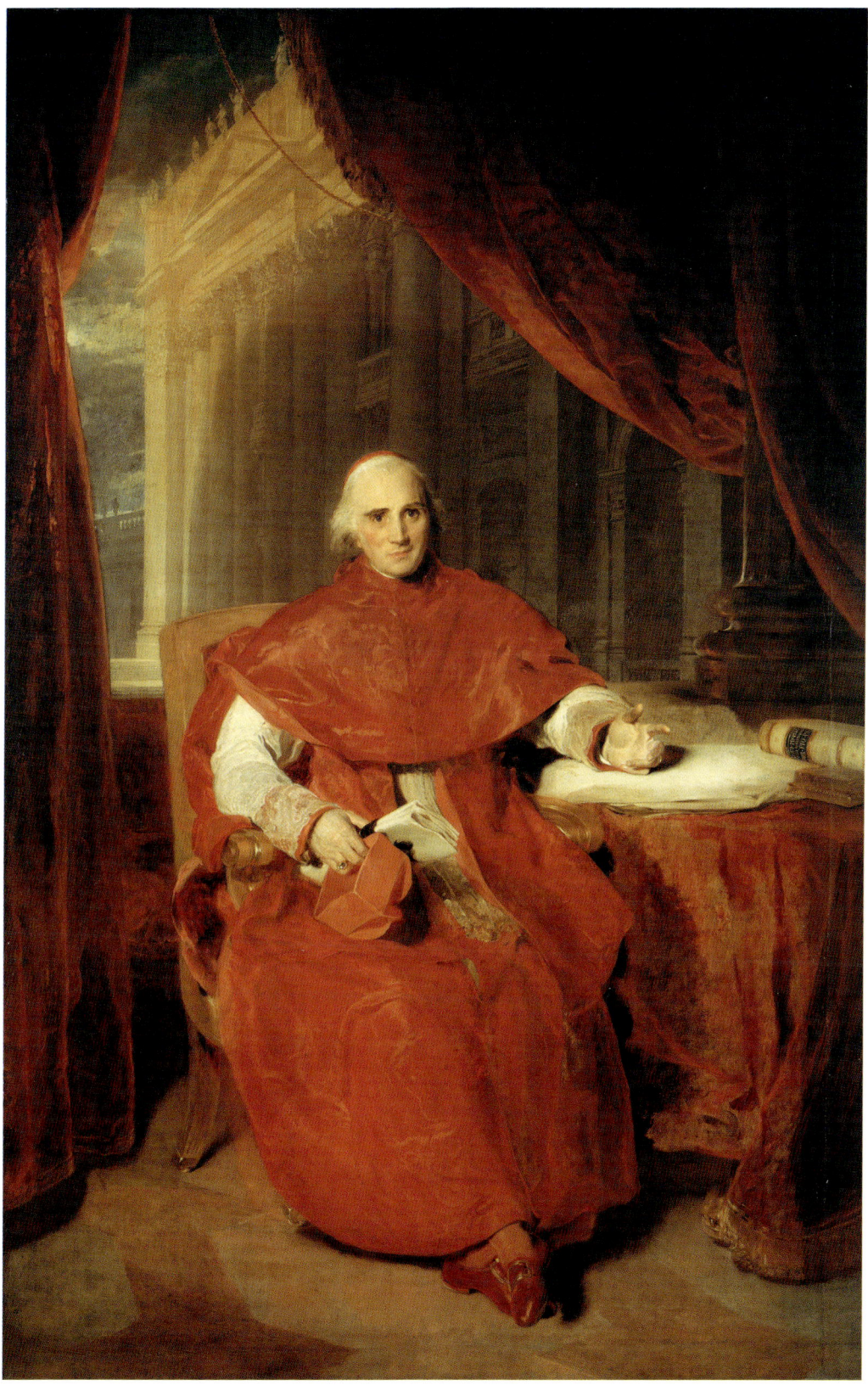

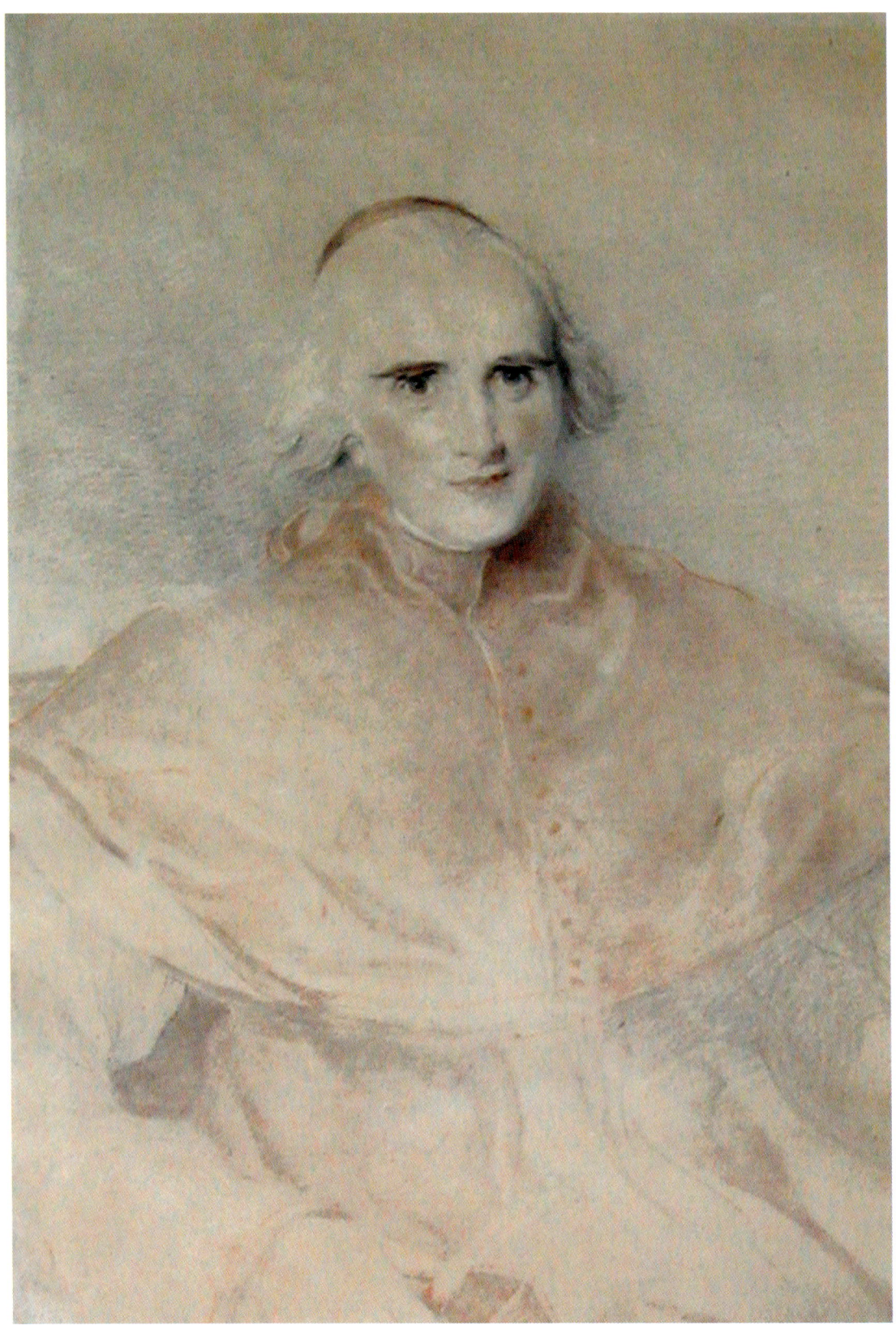

(facing page)

4.25. Thomas Lawrence, *Portrait of Cardinal Ercole Consalvi*, 1819, chalk on paper, 15⅜ × 10⅞ in. (39 × 27.5 cm), National Trust, Ickworth, Suffolk.

4.26. Jacques-Louis David, *Portrait of Pius VII*, 1805, oil on wood, 33⅞ × 28 in. (86 × 71 cm), Musée du Louvre, Paris.

4.27. Vincenzo Camuccini, *Portrait of Pius VII*, 1814–15, oil on canvas, 54 × 44¼ in. (137 × 112.5 cm), Kunsthistorisches Museum, Vienna.

Allowing for its privileged character, this phenomenon might be taken as a sign of benign ecumenical progress, old religious animosities softened by the displacements effected by the Restoration. But the cloud of apostasy also hung over this confessional rapprochement, darkened by the questions surrounding the duchess's title. One of her daughters wrote to her from London in 1818: "Though it may worry you I must tell you that all London is occupied with the strange story that you have written to the Prince Regent that the Duke is not the real heir, not the [first] Duchess's son; that being turned Catholic, you had confessed it to a priest."[25] Lawrence's deeper task in these portraits was simultaneously to celebrate this Anglo-Vatican entente (the prince regent had insisted on it) while finding plausible ways to represent Roman Catholic spiritual authority without giving himself or his painting over to it.

✳

In the same letter previously cited, written to Farington in July 1819,[26] Lawrence surveyed the chief precedents for his own papal portrait. His subject, he allows, had been "very successfully painted by David and by Camuccini [figs. 4.26–27], the two first painters of Paris and Rome. The reputation of the former you well know, and the latter is an able artist, and from his character and manners deservedly

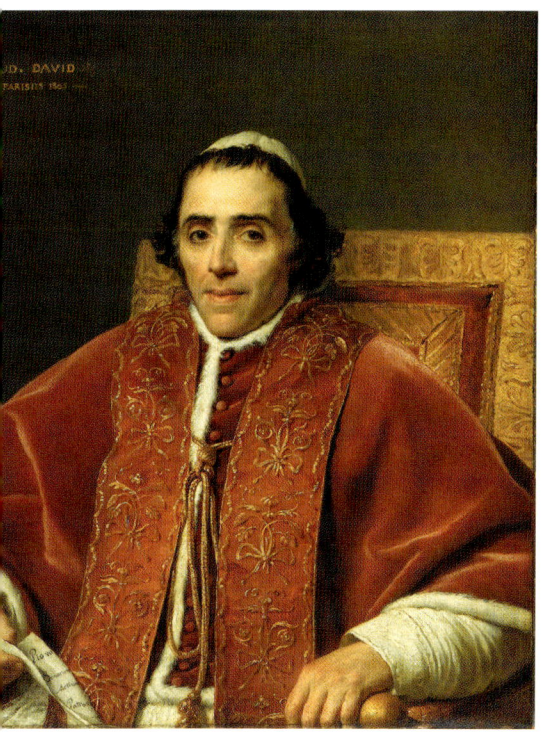

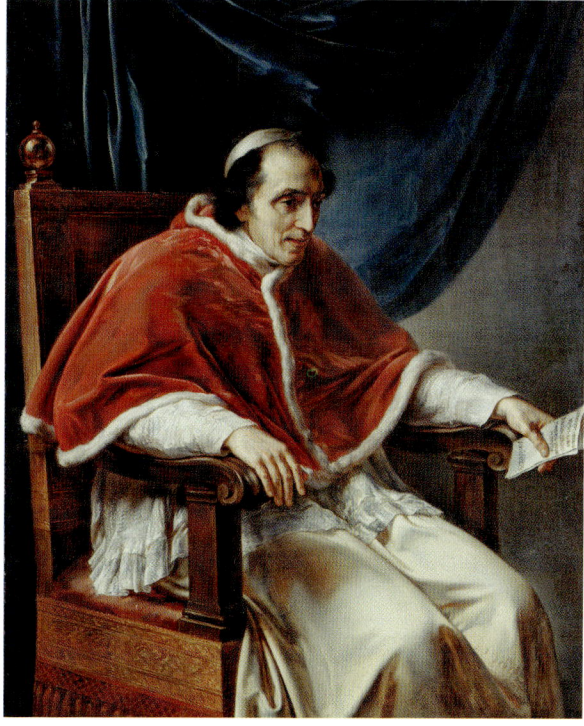

esteemed. His portrait of the Pope generally pleased; it was exceedingly well drawn. And with a very forcible effect; but he did not encounter the difficulties of its subject. He chose, if I may say so, its too obvious and quiescent character. His view of the face was nearly a profile, with eyes, and head, and frame bending down—an image of respectable decay."[27]

David's portrait of Pius VII, made on the occasion of Napoleon's self-coronation, would have been a commonplace point of reference. Camuccini, though hardly known today, was then deemed Rome's leading artist and had duly painted the portrait of Pius VII in 1815 to mark the pontiff's return from exile. Despite the politesse of Lawrence's phrasing, the final verdict is damning: Camuccini had failed to reconcile the pope's slight stature and stooped posture with the requisite aura of an authority that transcends physical considerations. In the hands of the Italian, those infirmities become no more than what one sees, occasions for sympathy perhaps, but not for the kind of admiring reverie that Lawrence had in mind for his own version (fig. 4.28), intended to trump both his French and Italian rivals: "I have painted him full in front," he writes, "with all but the eyes immediately directed to you, with every detail of his countenance (and it is one of many minute parts, but these animated with benevolence, and a sort of mild energy, that is the real character of his intellect and nature). The securing [of] this, with a good and true tone of color, has given me undisputed victory; and … has still more established the superiority of our English school."[28]

Lawrence had been knighted before setting off on his European journey, his sponsors thinking that the "Sir" before his name would smooth the way in dealing with his sitters and their courtiers: the English artist inserted his friend Canova's own warrant of nobility, the counterpart of his own, in the pontiff's grasp. On a similar note of triumph, Lawrence wrote to a female acquaintance in June 1819: "No picture that I have painted has been more popular with the friends of its subject, and the public, than my portrait of his Holiness; and, according to my scale of ability, I have executed my intention: having given him that expression of unaffected benevolence and worth, which lights up his countenance with a freshness and spirit, entirely free (except in the characteristic paleness of his complexion) from that appearance of illness and decay that he generally has, when enduring the fatigue of public functions."[29]

Nearly all characterizations of the pontiff mention his frail physique, making it a required attribute for any convincing portrait, but one that Lawrence claims to have overcome through sheer artistic alchemy (aided by the unnaturally dark hair that Pius VII retained into old age). But he did not rely only on his practiced way with a subject's face and hands to ensure the painting's success and to make

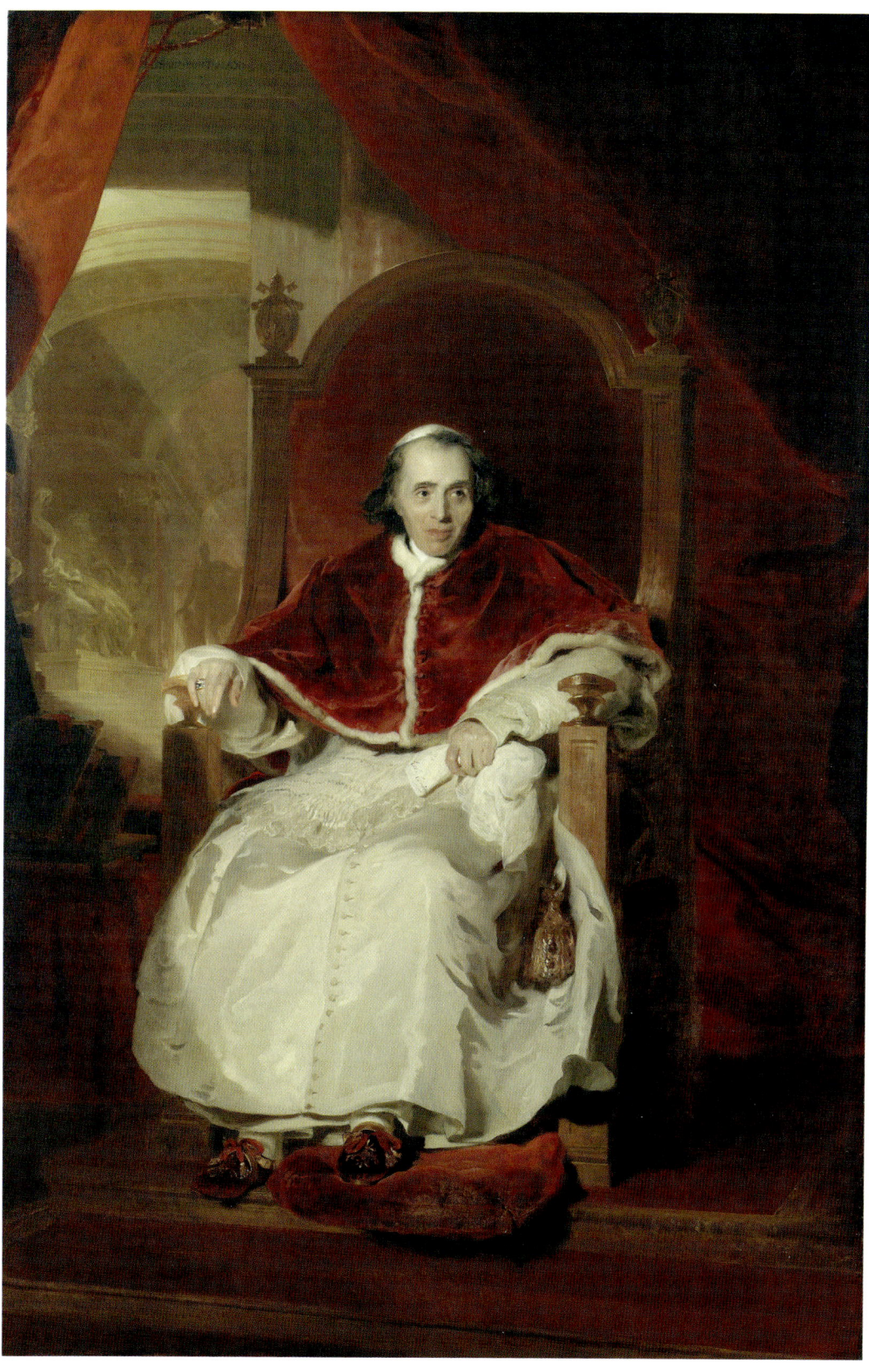

certain that it carried the right set of meanings back to his own sovereign. Lawrence had absorbed, whether he knew the anecdote or not, another piece of wisdom offered by Bernini (alongside the one discussed in the previous chapter) when he traveled to Paris in 1665 both to sculpt the portrait bust of the French king and to offer his designs for the renovation of the Louvre. In one recorded remark, Bernini subordinated the first of these tasks to the second under the common rubric of creating a likeness of the sovereign: the sculpted portrait, he said, can be no more than an exterior likeness, but "the grand schemes of the king" are the "portrait of his soul."[30] In Lawrence's portrait of Consalvi, the refurbished Saint Peter's served this function quite literally. One also sees on the table the thick bound plan issued by the cardinal in 1816, his *Motu Proprio*, devoted to the legal and administrative reform of the Papal States (which local resistances had essentially defeated);[31] another of the cardinal's great initiatives was the yet unfinished Braccio Nuovo of the Vatican Museum.

In his portrait of the titular sovereign of Rome, Lawrence placed this barrel-vaulted space adjacent to the right hand of the pope (fig. 4.28a), where the returned *Laocoön* and *Belvedere Apollo* appear beneath the dramatically shadowed ceiling. The backlit Apollo seems to sit on top of the pope's hand like a genie—the same hand that bears the Fisherman's Ring, remade for every new pope. The dynamic rising curve of the serpents enveloping Laocoön and his sons continues and dramatically animates the trajectory established by the white sleeve and ermine trim on his cape. Lawrence's portrait of Pius VII turned the most glamorous and charismatic objects of restoration into the pope's signal attributes, icons of power transfiguring the pontiff's mortal frailty—which would also have reminded the soon-to-be George IV of one piece of glory from the restoring of legitimate and monarchical Europe to which he had some public claim. Nonetheless, for all the goodwill generated by Canova and Consalvi among the English, there remained something perilous in an English artist crossing over to an inherent celebration of the papacy as restorative, given the historic strength of post-Reformation religious animosity. The heresy suspicions that dogged the Duchess of Devonshire could spread and indeed fall on the artist and the patron himself.

How then did Lawrence go about investing Pius VII with a metaphysical authority commensurable with his rank but independent of Catholic claims to God's own investiture in this individual human being? The answer might best be found in that contrast between the pope's slight frame and the magnitude of power conveyed by the totemic antiquities: Apollo subduing Python; the heroic musculature of Laocoön bested only by Poseidon's monsters, which Lawrence dramatized in one striking preparatory drawing (fig. 4.29). Lawrence makes their symbolized superhuman strength grow from

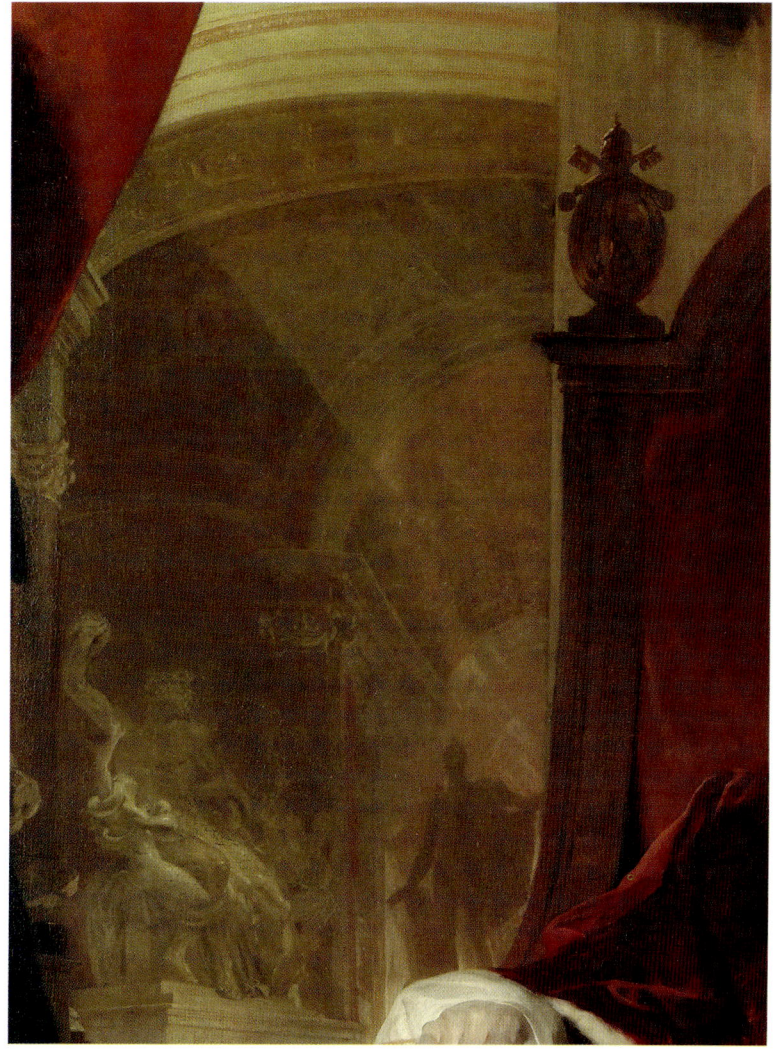

4.28a. Thomas Lawrence, *Portrait of Pius VII*, 1819 (detail), The Royal Collection, Windsor Castle.

the exemplary weakness of Pius VII as a humble, frail human being. The beams of sunlight that radiate down the length of the Braccio Nuovo—which is at this moment an imaginary realm—have their implied point of origin somewhere near the heart of the pontiff. Sir Walter Scott, who had witnessed the removal of the antiquities from Paris, remarked that French "attachment to these paintings and statues, or rather to the national glory which they conceive them to illustrate, is as excessive as if the Apollo and the Venus were still objects of actual adoration."[32] Lawrence shifts the location of metaphysical, not to say spiritual, meaning of his portrait away from the person and vestments of the office to this intermediate zone between exemplary human weakness and radiant mythologized strength. By virtue of its restoration, the ancient statuary recovers, as Scott implied, something of its original powers, bestowing pagan magic on their Christian

Sketch from the original Statue
in the Vatican for the background of
Portrait of Pius the 7th. T. Lawrence —

possessor, who summoned them back to Rome by deploying sources of strength nowhere evident in his mortal person.

Lawrence thereby finds a figure for the ambiguity of confessional identity that characterized his Roman milieu, as well as one for the coincidence in Rome of imposing classical inheritance and monumental religious sovereignty, harmonious by Church fiat but always in an unstable tension with one another. As such, his portrait of Pius VII, in concert with his instrument Consalvi, achieves a compact and cogent mastery of its own over some of the Restoration's most intractable ambiguities.

Chapter 5

The Laboratory of Brussels, 1816–19

The Apprentice Navez and
the Master David Redraw the
Language of Art

FOR ONE YOUNG FRENCH ARTIST in the studio of Jacques-Louis David, the departure of his master into Belgian exile was no exile for him. Ex-French would be the more accurate adjective, in that François-Joseph Navez, born in the fortress town of Charleroi, had been French only by virtue of Napoleon's annexation of present-day Belgium. With the creation of the United Kingdom of the Netherlands, Navez abruptly gained a new nationality and lost his old one, thereby forfeiting his eligibility for the Rome Prize competition in 1816 (which Géricault and Thomas were about to enter). He returned to settle in Brussels during January of that year, days before David and his wife arrived to set up house.[1]

Navez was eventually able to secure a private Belgian scholarship, setting out for Rome with commensurable support in the autumn of 1817. During the weeks preceding his departure, with the urgency of impending separation, he was able to complete three versions of his master's portrait. In the second and strongest of them (fig. 5.1), it would be difficult to say that David looks all of his sixty-nine years, despite the adroit gray highlights brushed into the coiffure. No prominent lines interrupt the smooth passages of flesh, and Navez has also taken care to mitigate if not disguise in shadow the protruding growth that David famously possessed on his left cheek, the viewer's attention further diverted by the flourishes of white that establish the wing of immaculate collar on the opposite side. The ribbon of the Napoleonic Legion of Honor appears all the more defiantly striking in its artful profile, while Navez signals his fealty with the inscribed Latin abbreviation for *discopulus*, disciple.

The polished composure of Navez's portrayal argues for David's formidable capacities in the present and his adaptability to his new and supportive surroundings. The period in Brussels in which David and Navez worked together amounted to about eighteen months, but in that span of time, the younger artist—then approaching the age of thirty—produced three further works of lasting significance. One is an accomplished portrait (fig. 5.2) of his friend and patron, Auguste-Donat de Hemptinne—professor of pharmacology and ambitious chemical entrepreneur—in the company of his young family.[2] The performance is assured, as Navez exhibits a command of detail in a self-consciously

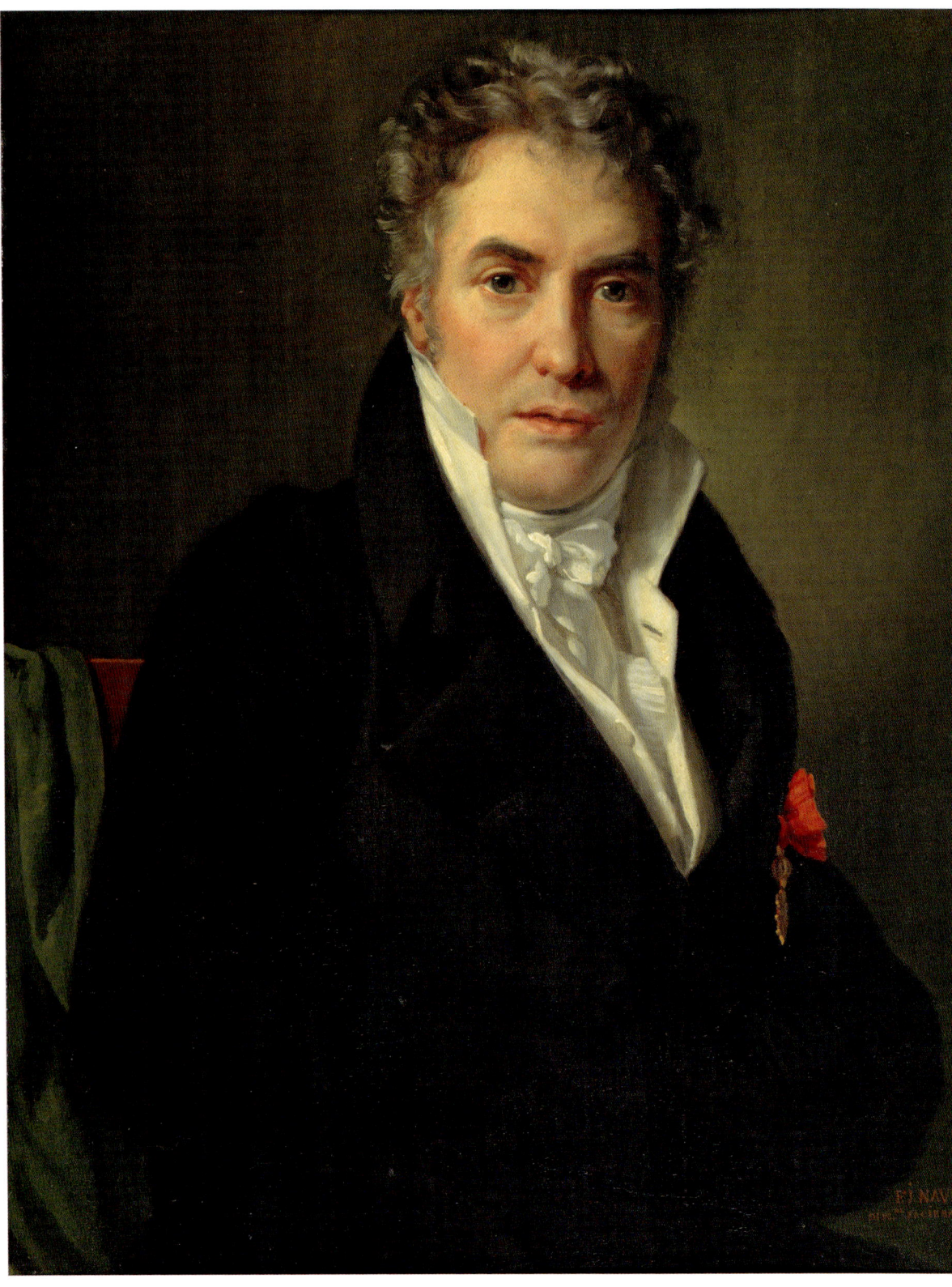

5.1. François-Joseph Navez, *Portrait of Jacques-Louis David*, 1817, oil on wood, 29⅜ × 23⅜ in. (74.5 × 59.5 cm), Royal Museums of Fine Arts of Belgium, Brussels.

5.2. François-Joseph Navez, *Portrait of Donat de Hemptinne and Family*, 1816, oil on canvas, 59 × 50 in. (150 × 127 cm), Royal Museums of Fine Arts of Belgium, Brussels.

Flemish manner (as in, for example, the scumbled light highlights on the sleeve of Mme de Hemptinne) married to an arresting disposition of the larger forms, which Navez chained to one another as if suspended from the light grip of the daughter on her father's hand.

The high technical quality and softened sympathy of Navez's group portrait links David to this world via his pupil, that is, to one pacified and open to scientific progress, commercial expansion, and general improvement (among other accomplishments, Hemptinne pioneered the concept of steam heat). But these exercises in companionable sympathy hardly prepare one for the younger artist's startlingly unusual presentation drawing on the subject of the *Lamentation over the Body of Christ* (fig. 5.3), likewise a commission from Hemptinne, this one presumably intended for domestic devotion (it

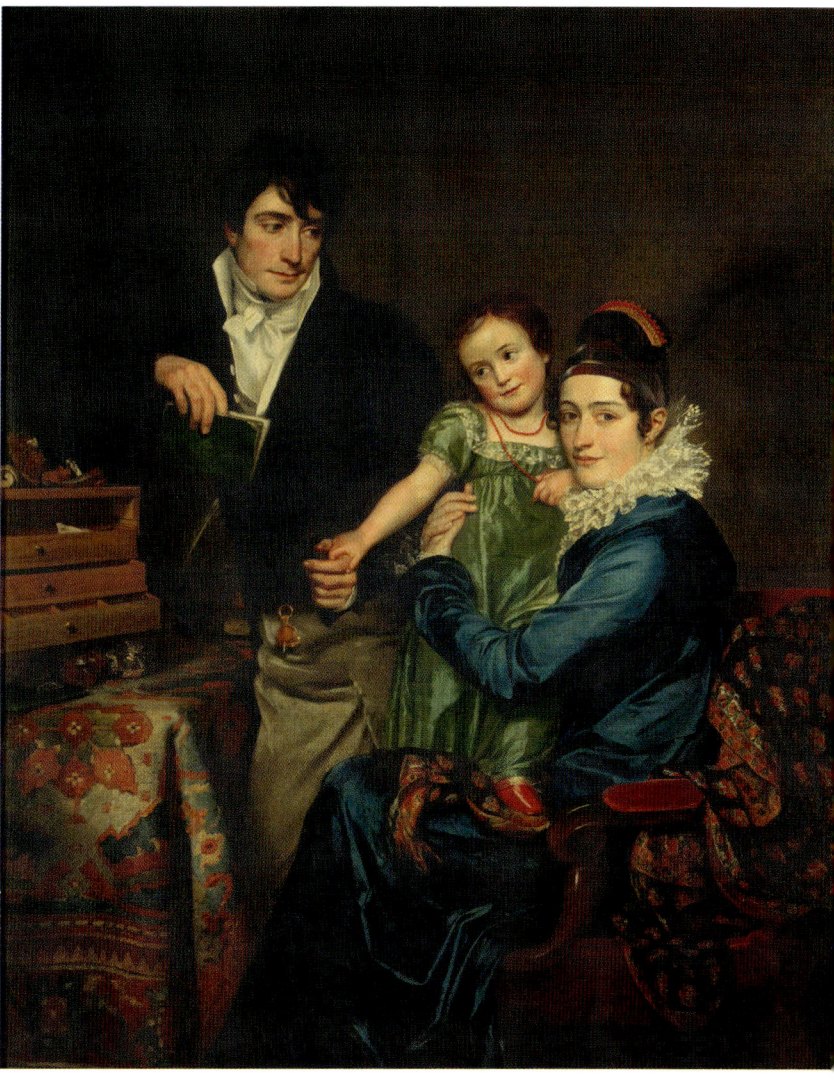

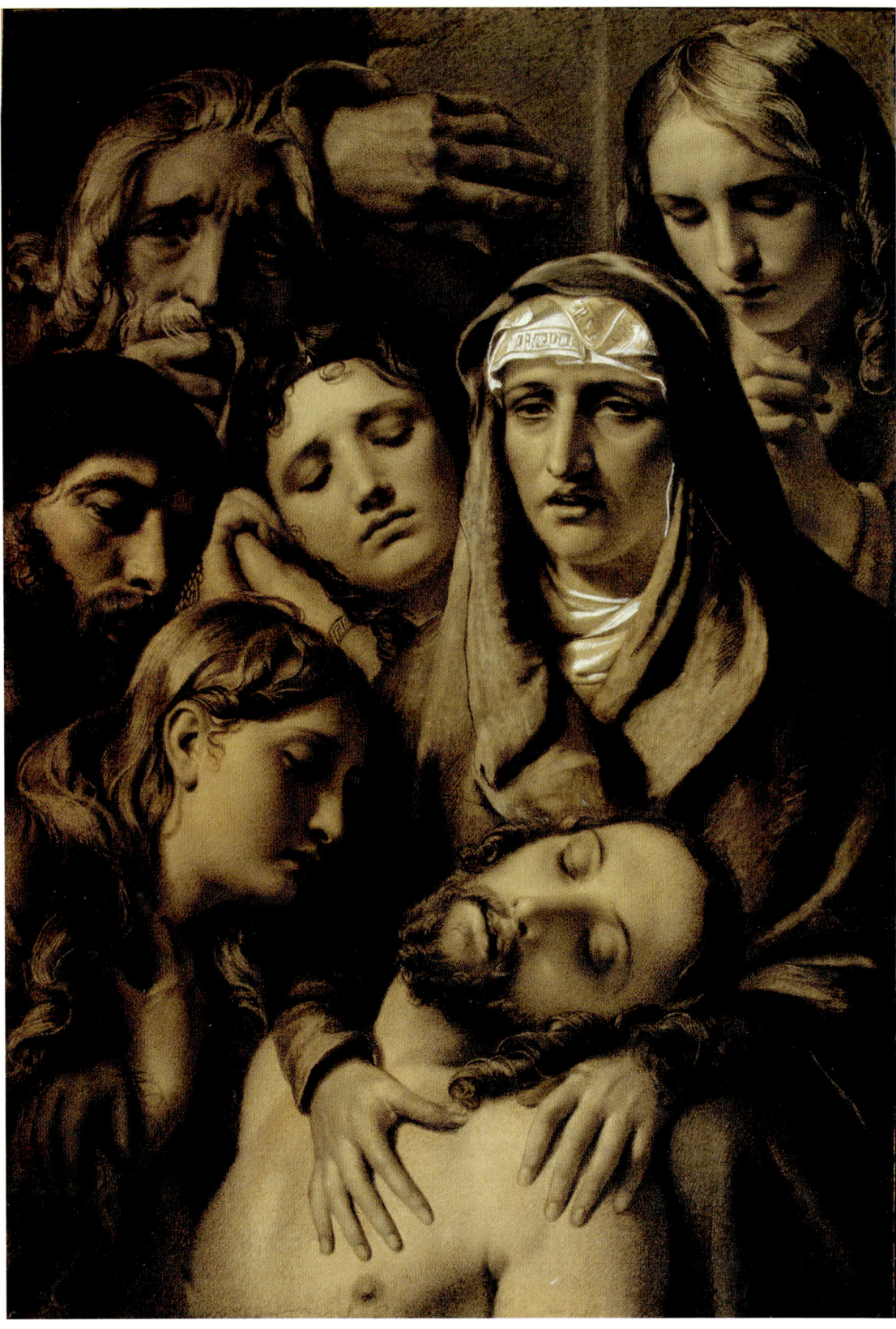

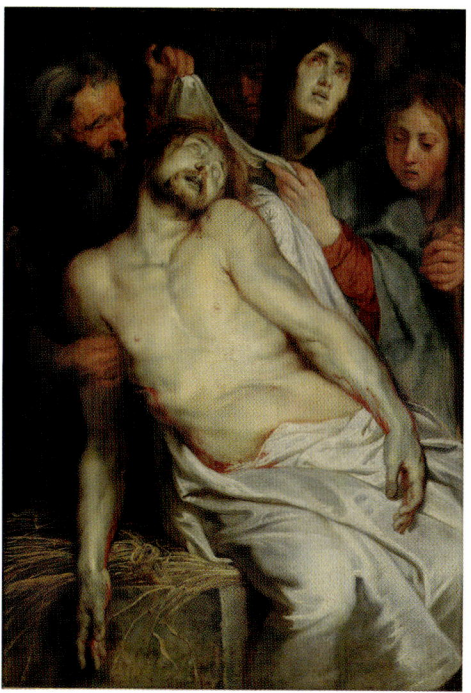

had remained in the family and largely unseen until entering the Louvre collection only a few years ago).[3]

Nothing in the previous work of Navez anticipates the radical syntax of this picture. It is finished in black and ocher chalk to nearly the highest possible refinement in tonal modeling. The contained white highlights at the forehead and throat of the Virgin scintillate with luminosity where no halo or other overt sign of divinity enters the picture. Its apparently lighter ground is in fact the top layer of the work, not its foundation: an opaque cladding of light ocher chalk laid over the black underneath. The entire surface is built up, more like a painting, to an extraordinarily thick and uniform degree across every square centimeter of its surface—and it is strikingly large for any work on paper, four feet in height, competing with painting not only by its material density but also by its size.

In sacrificing the extension of the bodies—indeed virtually all the ambient space—from the scene, Navez transforms inherited expectations for narrative tableaux in any medium. Gone are meaningful liaisons and directed gazes present in the close prototype with which Navez would have been intimately familiar: the central panel of the Michielsen altarpiece by Peter Paul Rubens in Antwerp Cathedral, nicknamed "Christ on the Straw" (fig. 5.4). The economy of Rubens's conception is striking in the lamentation genre, but does not anticipate the airless compression and suppression of legible narrative performed by Navez. The young Davidian essentially took the top part of

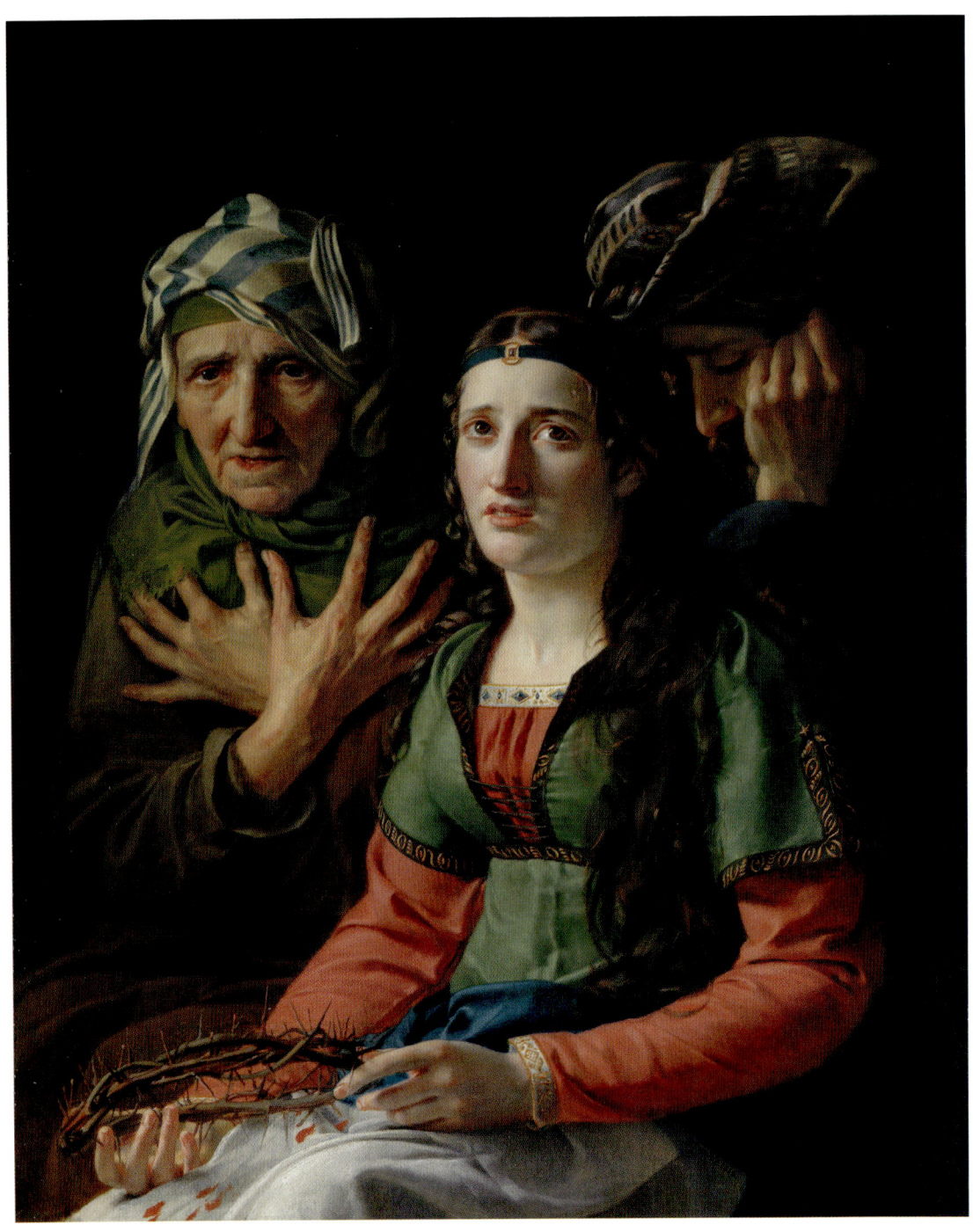

5.5. François-Joseph Navez,
Saint Veronica of Milan, 1817,
oil on canvas, 32¼ × 36¼ in.
(82 × 92 cm), Museum of Fine
Arts, Ghent.

Rubens's composition and stretched it to fill the entire upright format—even at the cost of pushing the body of Christ almost entirely out of view. The only connections between the actors lie in forced physical proximity, their visible bodies never more than partially seen, their gazes and attitudes swiveling without regard for one another. The extent of this compositional fragmentation is such that the presumed hand of the older male at the top dead center is so separate from the invisible body of the actor that it could conceivably belong to some other person reaching around the wall of the tomb. The left nipple of Christ, an un-elevating detail of the flesh, assumes outsized importance, belying its size, as it punctuates the bottom center of the composition.

At the same time, it is not as if Navez has abandoned compositional order for sheer accumulation of figural moments; the interlace of forms approaches elegance in its play with linkage and correspondence, but the expected devotional contemplation of Christ's body is hardly possible, as it seems already to be sinking out of view into Limbo. The concentrated emotion in each head invites separate consideration, and the thousand-yard stare of the Virgin assumes centrality, her gaze past the viewer focusing on an unknown earthly vision rather than elevating itself toward celestial consolation.

But what is Mary meant to be seeing? A pendant work by Navez offers a possible answer. In 1817, Navez produced a finely wrought oil on canvas—no larger than the paper *Lamentation*—likewise for his friend and patron Hemptinne (fig. 5.5). Its subject was *Saint Veronica of Milan* with her parents, so it counts as another kind of family portrait. The saint holding as an attribute the crown of thorns, still dripping with fresh blood, puts one instantly in mind of Veronica of the veil on the road to Calvary. But this is not she. This Veronica lived in a village near Milan during the late fifteenth century. Withdrawn and obsessively devoted to punishing menial tasks, she experienced a vision of the Virgin, who instructed her endlessly to contemplate the Passion of Christ. She obeyed this injunction to the point of ceasing all human communication, perpetually witnessing Christ's suffering in her own hallucinatory reality.[4] In Navez's painting, the saint's gaze is directed toward rather than beyond the viewer, who is thereby implicated in the perpetual moment of death, its redemption in the balance. Drops of blood find their way onto the lap of the saint (fig. 5.5a), either Christ's or her own, as she is said to have miraculously received the endlessly painful wounds of the Crown of Thorns, soon joined by stigmata in her palms.

The two works together could be taken as meditations on the perpetual present of Christ's sacrifice, regularly reenacted in the Eucharist, as betokened in the painting by spattered blood of trompe l'oeil vividness. In that light, psychological and formal detachment

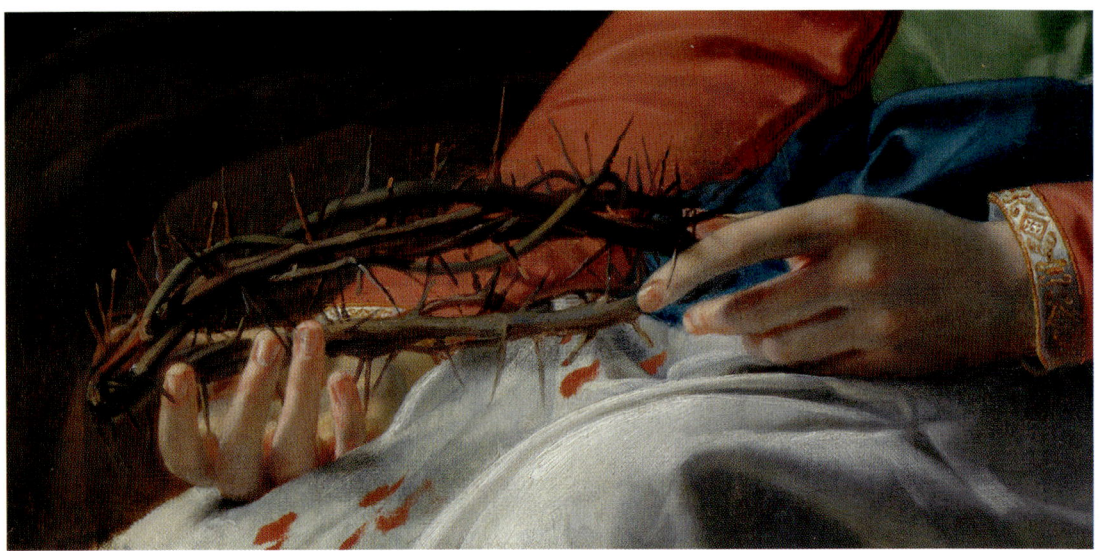

work together on a theological plane by removing the Passion from any particular, contingent place and time. The same model seems to have served Navez for both his Virgin and his Veronica, drawing the two saints together in shared contemplation of the son and savior's drawn-out death. The *Saint Veronica* shares the anomic logic of the drawing, likewise emphasizing the isolation of each bust-length personage from the others, rendering the expressions of each parent deeply ambiguous. It could be vicarious identification with their daughter's harrowing mental participation in Christ's sacrifice, as each withdraws into his or her own reverie. But it could also be asked if the parents are despairing over the loss of a child to what appears to have been some severe autistic or obsessive-compulsive mental condition, which the institution of the Church opportunistically transfigured into a beatific state.

The proximity of the two works in time suggests that he and his friend, the medical professor Hemptinne, at least entertained the second interpretation. The pervasive unreality of the *Lamentation* drawing, with its heightened vividness combined with a breakdown in normal artistic syntax, finds a form for disordered, hallucinatory vision, such as Saint Veronica might have inwardly experienced. With guiding ideologies in ruins, it may be the case that their imagination of sainthood reverts to a degree-zero of additive, detachable motifs, akin to a collapse of communicative syntax and personified in the *Saint Veronica* as the most abjectly alienated of possible Christian subjects. But a compensating empathy with her plight—and with alienated souls in general—rescues the work from clinical detachment or aesthetic negation, which would at any rate have been anachronisms in the period. Still less would Navez and Hemptinne have resembled some present-day neuroscientist popping up to "explain"—that is, explain away—a visionary work of art by somatic causes. The suffering of the unfortunate Veronica, however founded in earthly pathology, becomes altogether different if the suffering of Christ makes all the difference to your sense of the world. In the rendering of Navez, her sainthood does not place her in another world; that condition remains fully a part of the same unredeemed one that we all inhabit.

*

In forging such a drastically unconventional pictorial logic, how much was Navez collaborating with David? The pattern of their interaction in these years, the "disciple" inscription on the David portrait, suggest it would have been close. But signs of David's part in the conversation mostly postdate the departure of Navez for his extended Roman sojourn in the fall of 1817. One from the handful of David's drawings dated to 1817 (fig. 5.6), however, shares the logic of his pupil's *Lamentation* and *Saint Veronica*.

5.6. Jacques-Louis David, *Figure Group from the Painting of Léonidas at Thermopyles*, 1817, black chalk on paper, 5⅛ × 7⅝ in. (13 × 19.5 cm), private collection, Paris.

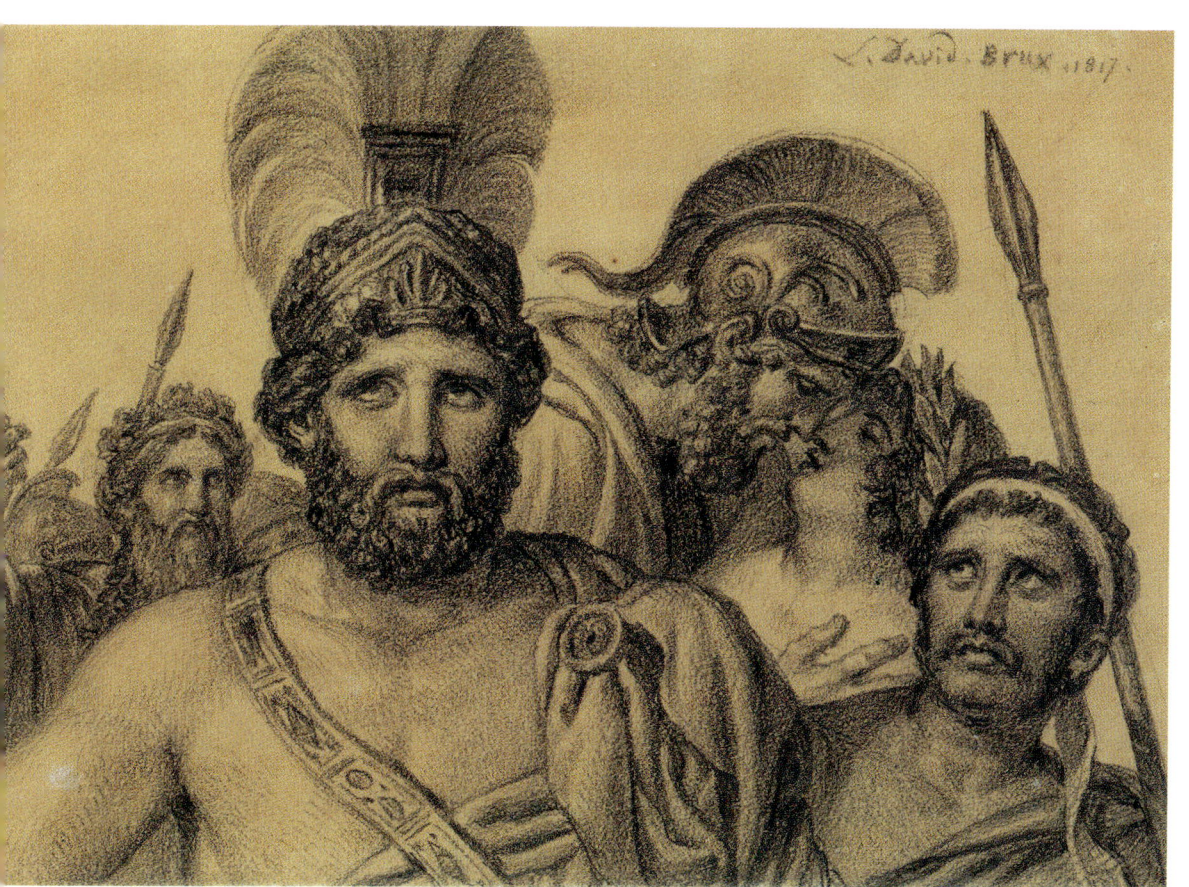

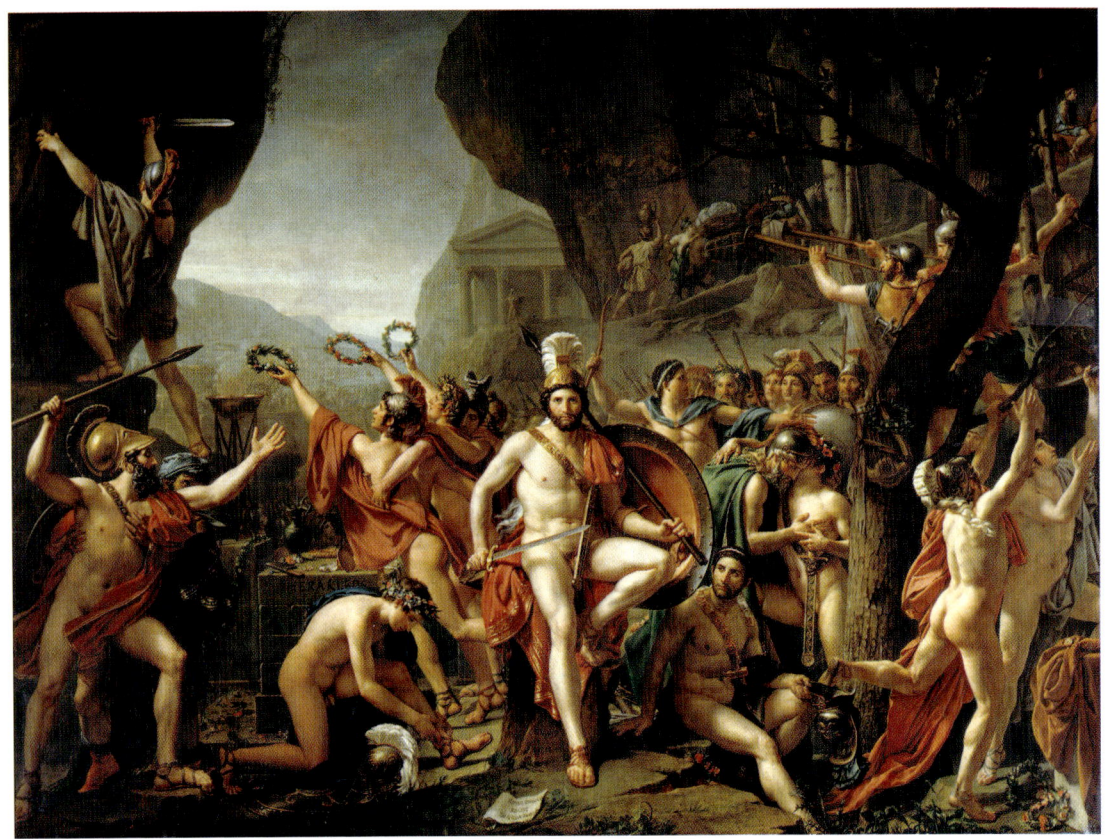

5.7. Jacques-Louis David, *Leonidas at Thermopylae*, 1814, oil on canvas, 155½ × 209 in. (395 × 531 cm), Musée du Louvre, Paris.

The obvious source of the drawing is David's own monumental canvas, *Leonidas at Thermopylae* (fig. 5.7), a work he had struggled over from 1801 until its belated completion in 1814, just as the French Empire collapsed. Tales from the studio tell of indecision, whole segments of the painting being removed and replaced, a swarm of studio apprentices doing much of the work.[5] He had been in no position to transport this huge work to Brussels, seeking to protect the canvas by sending it far from Paris. But one wonders whether he could have faced working again on that frustratingly immense scale. But, equally, he could not leave the themes of the painting behind. His recapitulation of the subject three years later becomes a constellation of just a few essential, bust-length motifs, the setting eliminated, spatial cues of only the most minimal kind remaining.[6] This drastic filtering, done from memory, casts the story of the steadfast Spartan three hundred warriors, killed to a man stopping the Persians at the Thermopylae pass, into a handful of fragments: the resigned gaze of the commander, the homosexual farewell between bearded veteran and his swooning ephebus, the ambivalent witnessing of the dark helot slave, and the skyward gesturing priest.

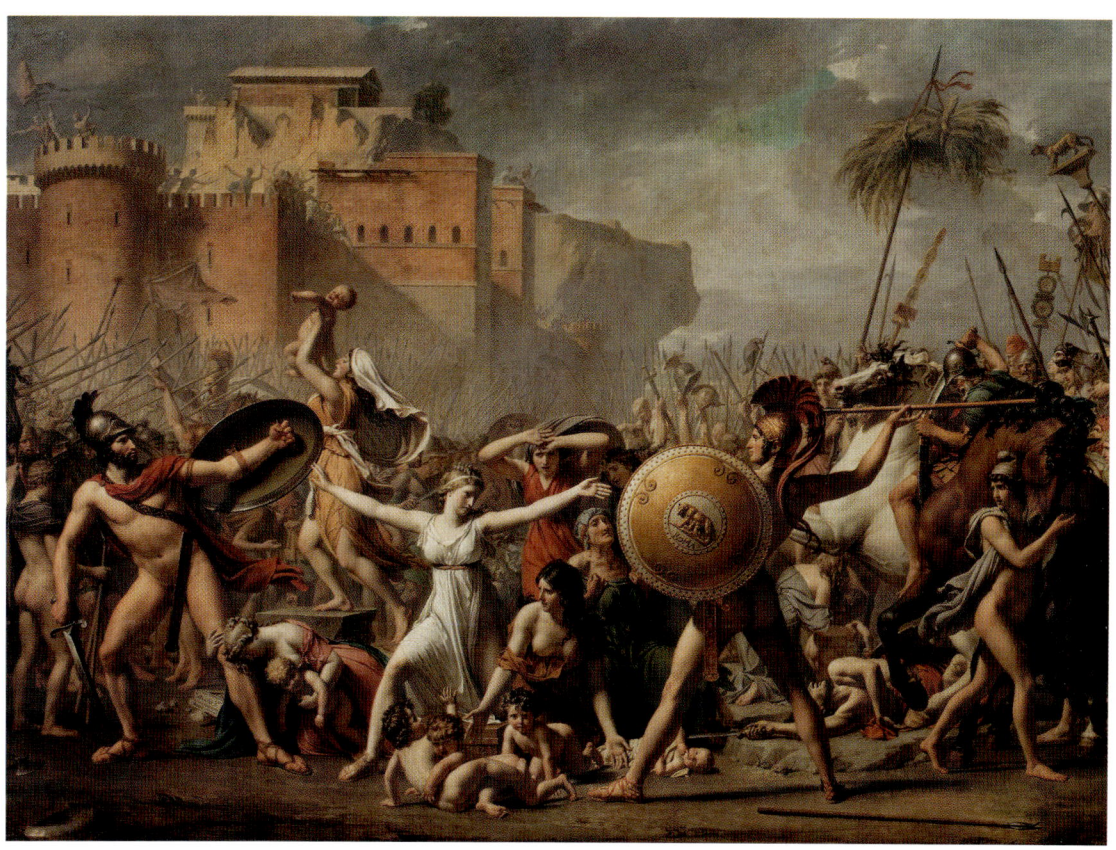

5.8. Jacques-Louis David, *Intervention of the Sabine Women*, 1799, oil on canvas, 151⅝ × 205½ in. (385 × 522 cm), Musée du Louvre, Paris.

This particular sheet might have been mainly a memory exercise, perhaps symptomatic of his isolation and reduced circumstances. Or it could represent David turning his back on a cumbersome, overweight rhetoric, so redolent of the imperial past, in favor of a more nimble, improvisatory mode of art altogether, one that he could command under his sole authorship. In support of the latter reading is the fact that the sheet is signed with a flourish, marked with place and date. In that the *Leonidas* had at its 1801 inception been intended as a companion to the *Intervention of the Sabine Women* (fig. 5.8), which David had triumphantly exhibited in 1799, it is telling that he recapitulated that pairing in Brussels. Sometime in 1818, his third year of exile, David distilled the *Sabine Women* into an even more reduced summation on paper (fig. 5.9), the bare trio of Hersilia, Sabine wife of Romulus, at the center as the pacifying force between her Roman husband at the right and the Sabine champion Tatius at the left.[7]

After these few, retrospective exercises, there followed a remarkable outpouring of drawings congruent with these exercises in revision and recollection but untethered to specific prototypes. Some three years after his temporary escape to Switzerland, during which he filled notebooks with arrangements of enigmatic figures (explored

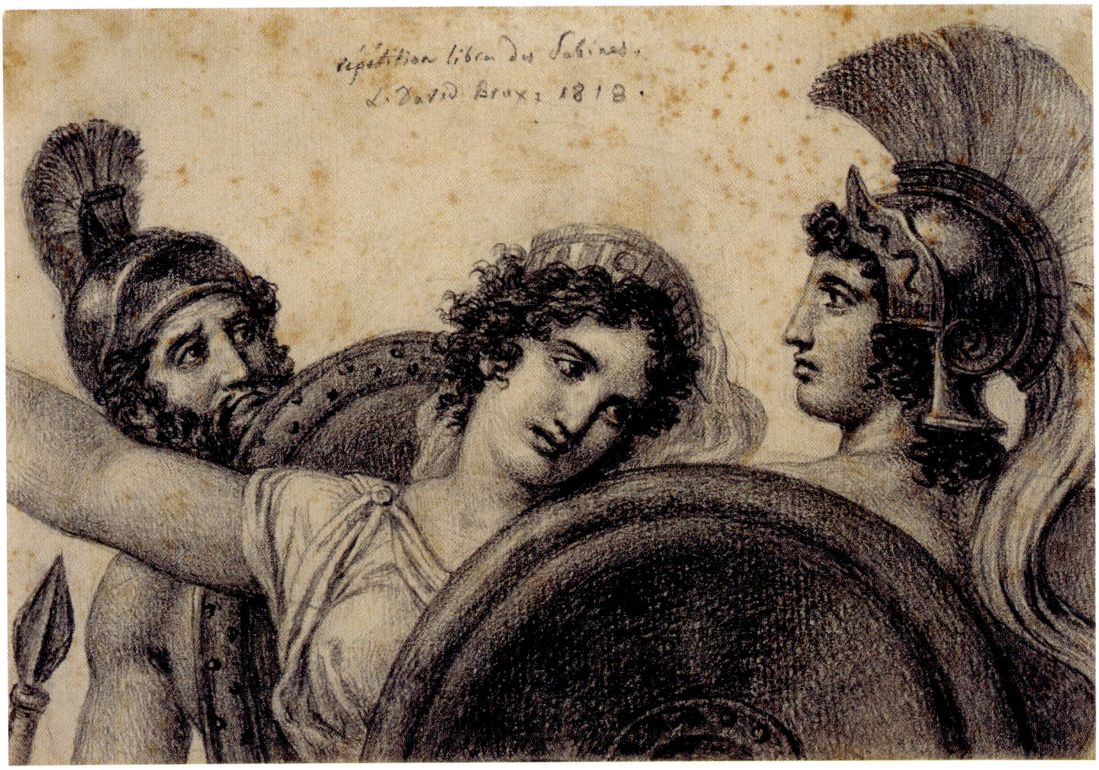

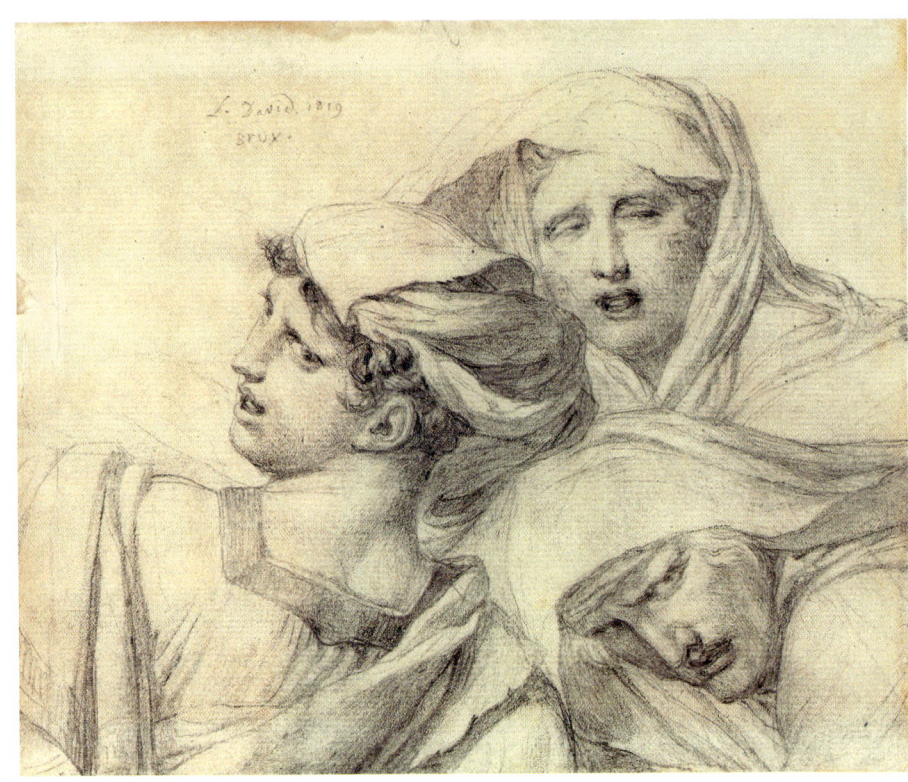

5.9. Jacques-Louis David, *Figure Group from the Painting of the Sabines*, 1818, black chalk on paper, Baltimore Museum of Art.

5.10. Jacques-Louis David, *Three Women Viewed at Bust Length*, 1819, black chalk on paper, 6½ × 7⅞ in. (16.5 × 20 cm), private collection, New York.

5.11. Jacques-Louis David, "The Prisoner," ca. 1816–22, black chalk on paper, 5¼ × 7¾ in. (13.3 × 19.6 cm), Cleveland Museum of Art.

in chapter 3), he returned to the same mode, now working up the same sort of compositions with greater definition and density of black crayon. As before, these include intractably puzzling combinations of dramatic figures in ancient or other historical costume—"caprices ... that come into my head," as David described them in a letter to another devoted Belgian pupil.[8] Any number of these sheets exemplifies the meaning of caprice as defined by the *Oxford English Dictionary*: "sudden change or turn of mind without apparent or adequate motive." Its French counterpart, *le Grand Robert*, offers the equivalent, more succinct "determination arbitraire."

In one apposite example (fig. 5.10), intricately intertwined scarves and wraps keep a trio of febrile female faces in continually restless circulation; each one emphatically expressive but in their combination ambiguous and fugitive. David accumulated scores of drawings in this vein from 1818 into the early 1820s, almost none of them intended as a study for any painted work. Some restrict themselves to a single figure. The post-1816 bust-length male figure, the face worked with exceptional vigor and enveloped in a Marat-like wrap, is rare in featuring any establishing details (fig. 5.11): the suspended chain and disconsolate expression have lent the personage its nickname: "The Prisoner." Others contain multiple figures, like the sheet known by convention as "A Scene of Mourning," inscribed with the date 1819

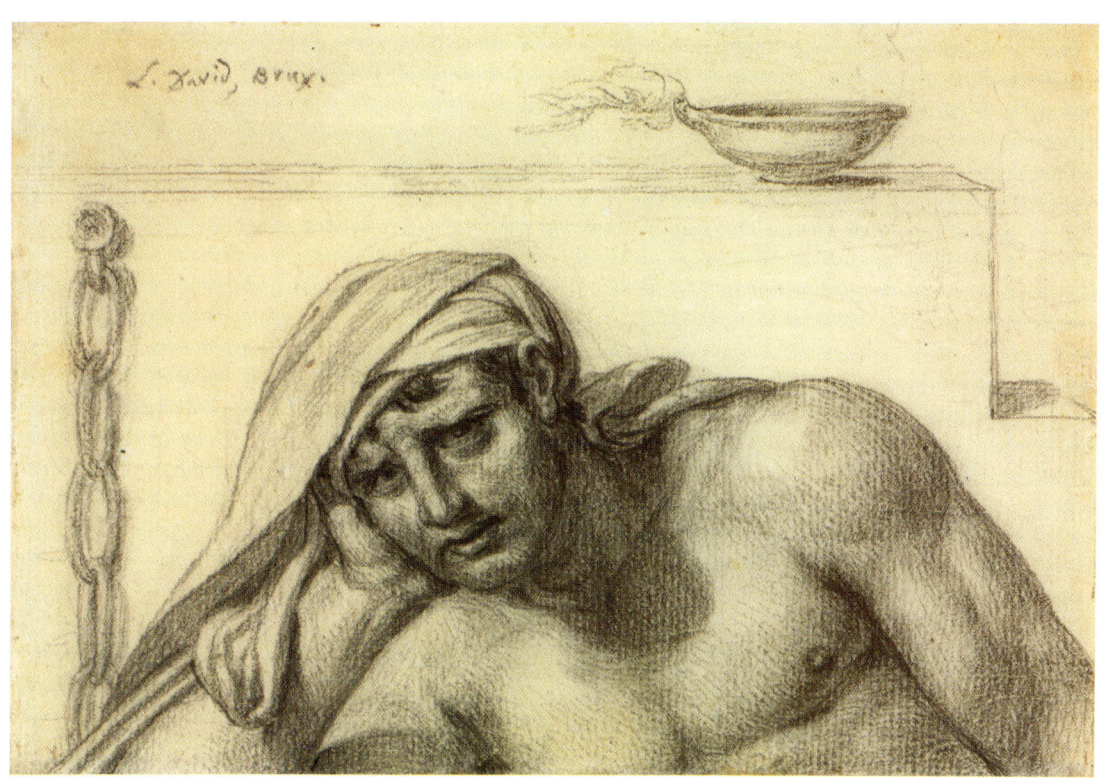

(fig. 5.12).[9] The tight compression of David's grouping exacerbates the paradoxical detachment of the figures from one another in narrative or emotional terms. That effect was one he intended to enlarge beyond the confines of any single sheet. In the same letter where he introduces the term "caprice," he also reveals that he did not intend to keep these drawings tucked away in an album or portfolio but instead wanted to frame them in eight groupings of four drawings each.[10] As each vignette on a single sheet distills some discrete complex of emotion, either among some compact group of characters or within a conflicted single figure, these matrices of drawings would have organized the basic data of narrative painting into abstract grids—as if to array all of these sketched possibilities as a simultaneous matrix of potential combinations—rather than pantomimes of fictional events. By this degree of separation of emotive units, David could have gone one better in that regard than the controlled detachment that Navez had achieved in his *Lamentation*. And, like the latter work, the overall size of David's projected array could have competed with the wall-holding capacity of a painting, while the large, heavy passages of dense crayon, similarly to Navez's heavy chalks, could have projected themselves over the requisite distance.[11]

5.12. Jacques-Louis David, *"A Scene of Mourning" (Composition with Five Figures)*, 1819, graphite and black chalk on laid paper, 5⅛ × 7⅞ in. (13 × 20 cm), Fine Arts Museums of San Francisco.

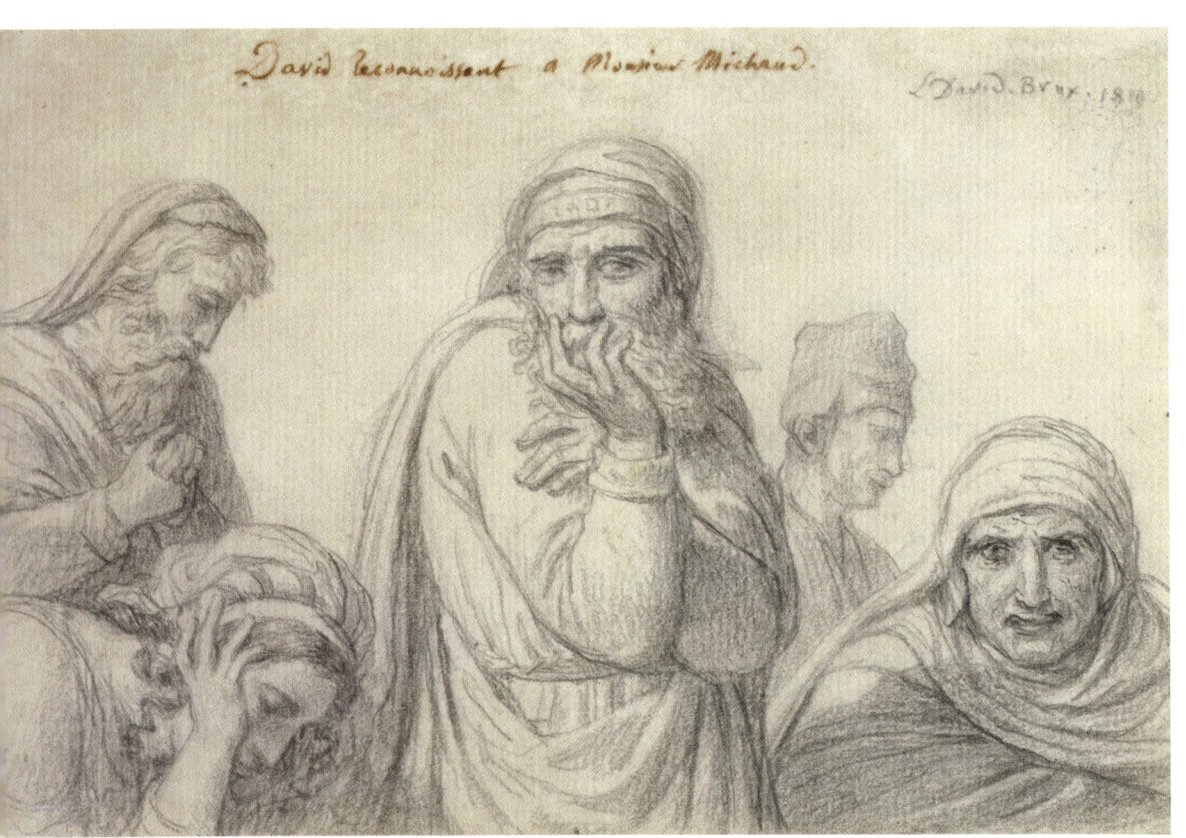

From 1815, David and Navez appear deliberately to have begun building not only a new foundation of combinable elements but also new, unconventional principles governing their selection and organization. For David especially, this meant a newly intensive immersion into dramatic poetry. The house in which David settled with his wife lay in the street directly behind the principal theater of the city, le Théâtre de la Monnaie (so named because it sat on the site of an old mint), the equivalent in Brussels to the Parisian Comédie Française. During their first years in Brussels, they endured the construction of a new, more elaborate and commodious theater than the one demolished in 1818. On the testimony of his family and friends, David could be seen in his regular chair at every performance, in both the old theater and the one that replaced it. Classical tragedy and lyric opera on the stage made for a nightly escape from his urban dwelling into a different world, one simpler but deeper in its outlines than the messy complexities of the contemporary life outside. His grandson relates that there was one chair (*fauteuil*) recognized by other patrons as his; any stranger unwittingly occupying it would be induced to move.[12] And on those evenings when the theater was dark, "he would sit after dinner at home in the large room that served as his salon and dining room; overlooked by his copies of *Napoleon Crossing the St. Bernard Pass* and the *Portrait of Napoleon in His Study*, he would conceive and execute drawings in black crayon."[13]

Certain of these sheets edge close to known tragic scenarios (fig. 5.13): the unconscious or dead young males in an 1819 example might call to mind the brothers of Antigone, daughter of Oedipus, for whom the frontally staring maiden, eyes glistening in delicately nuanced countenance, could easily stand. If that analogy is proffered, however, it is just as quickly withdrawn: as both of the young males here wear honorific laurels, when only one of Antigone's male siblings is honored, while the other dies disgraced. The question becomes: could the experiments of the drawings be translated to the settled format of oil on canvas? There can be no question that David's intensified interest in drawing followed from a lessening in his skill as a painter or his interest in the medium of oil on canvas. His contemporaneous portraits amply demonstrate the contrary, as they do an undiminished command over a range of effects as he documented the presence around himself of likewise exiled friends, family, and visitors. His 1817 portrayal (fig. 5.14) of the abbé Sièyes, old lion of Revolution, Consulate, and Empire, infuses his friend with a senatorial gravitas against the most austere backdrop.

As late as 1821, he could render the two daughters of Joseph Bonaparte, Zénaïde and Charlotte, nieces of the deposed emperor, with an

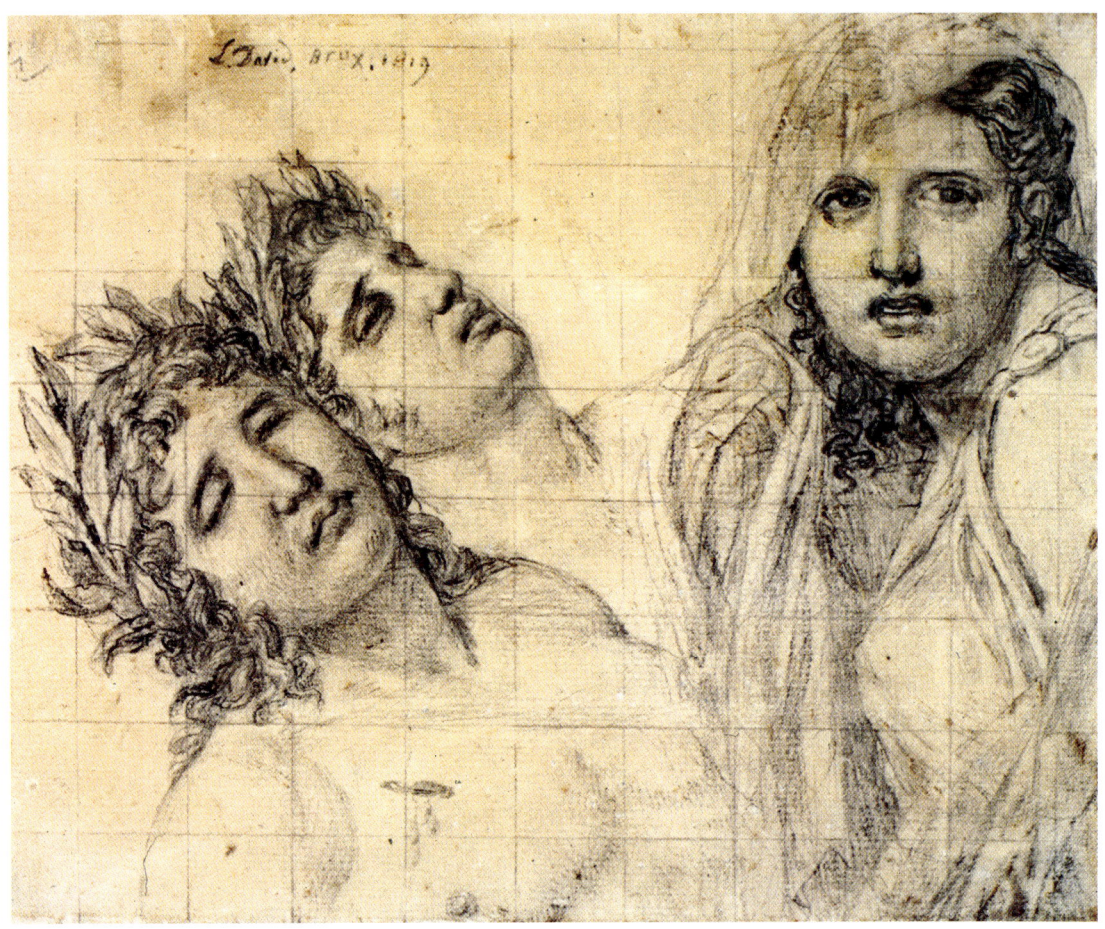

5.13. Jacques-Louis David, *Two Men in Laurel Wreaths Viewed at Bust Length with Veiled Woman*, 1819, black chalk on paper, Galerie Mazarini, Lyon.

unforced combination of seriousness and avuncular sympathy, as he placed them unapologetically against a crimson settee embroidered with the bees of the Empire (fig. 5.15). In the close and subtle joining of the sisters' heads, their hair entwined with delicate fabrics as they read a letter from their father in America, there appear lessons drawn from the experiments with such expressive juxtapositions and contrasts in the drawings. It was, nonetheless, as always, "history painting," the narration of significant actions by ennobled actors, that remained David's touchstone. His *Anger of Achilles* of 1819 (fig. 5.16), begun midway between these two exilic portraits, was only the third historical subject he had undertaken since his 1816 exile (illustrated here in its original frame). The logic of the scene more emphatically manifests key traits of the "caprices" on which David spent his non-theatrical evenings, but it bears a clear title and known characters of myth and literature—Achilles, Clytemnestra, her husband Agamemnon and daughter Iphigenia—principals from the cycles of the Trojan War and the house of Atreus.[14]

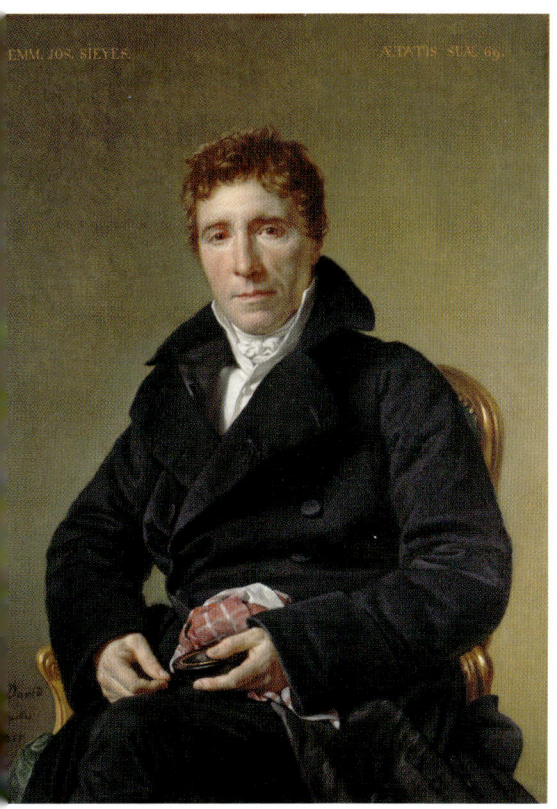

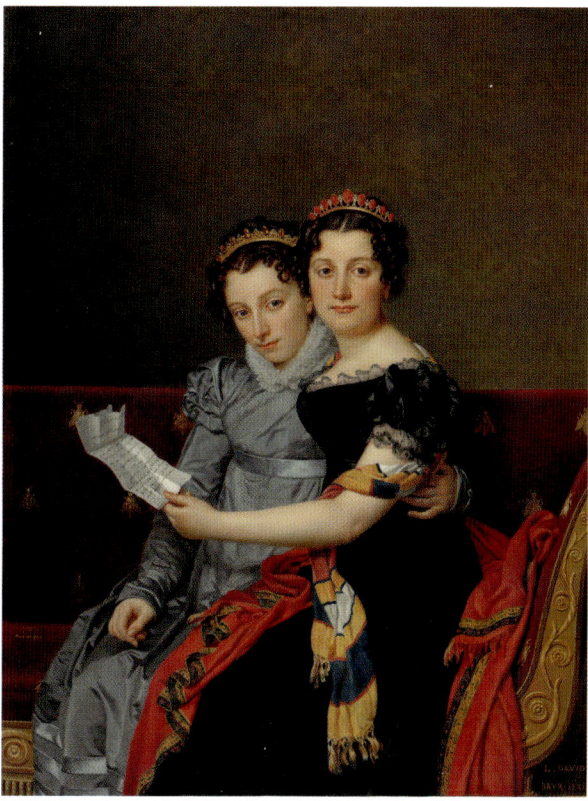

5.14. Jacques-Louis David, *Portrait of Emmanuel-Joseph Sièyes*, 1817, oil on canvas, 30¾ × 29⅛ in. (78 × 74 cm), Harvard Art Museums/Fogg Museum, Bequest of Grenville L. Winthrop.

5.15. Jacques-Louis David, *Portrait of the Sisters Zénaïde and Charlotte Bonaparte*, 1821, oil on canvas, 51 × 39⅝ in. (129.5 × 100.6 cm), Getty Center, Los Angeles.

David's packed, claustrophobia-inducing arrangement of just four truncated figures has puzzled observers over most of the two centuries since it was painted. But that puzzlement abates not only when the drawings come into consideration but also when the example of Navez is taken into account, the salience of which is underscored by the crowned head of Clytemnestra, its model being the same woman who provided Navez with the faces of Veronica and the Virgin.[15] The Greek commander sacrificing his daughter to appease Apollo, the god who had becalmed his fleet, is rarely adduced as an analogue to the divine sacrifice of Christ—in contrast to the Old Testament story of Yahweh commanding that Abraham sacrifice his beloved son Isaac. But the parallel is nonetheless patent, and David drew a correspondence between saintly imagination of Christ's martyrdom effected by his pupil and his own Clytemnestra, eyes brimming with tears, foreseeing her daughter's terrible death (the crime for which she will eventually murder her husband, then suffer fatal retribution in turn).

Every figure in the painting is doomed to untimely death, a mood that David deploys to overlay the Christian preoccupations of Navez with another, overriding theme of his own. When the painting appeared as part of a public charity in Brussels, David wrote to the burgomaster to express his own gratitude for the warmth with which

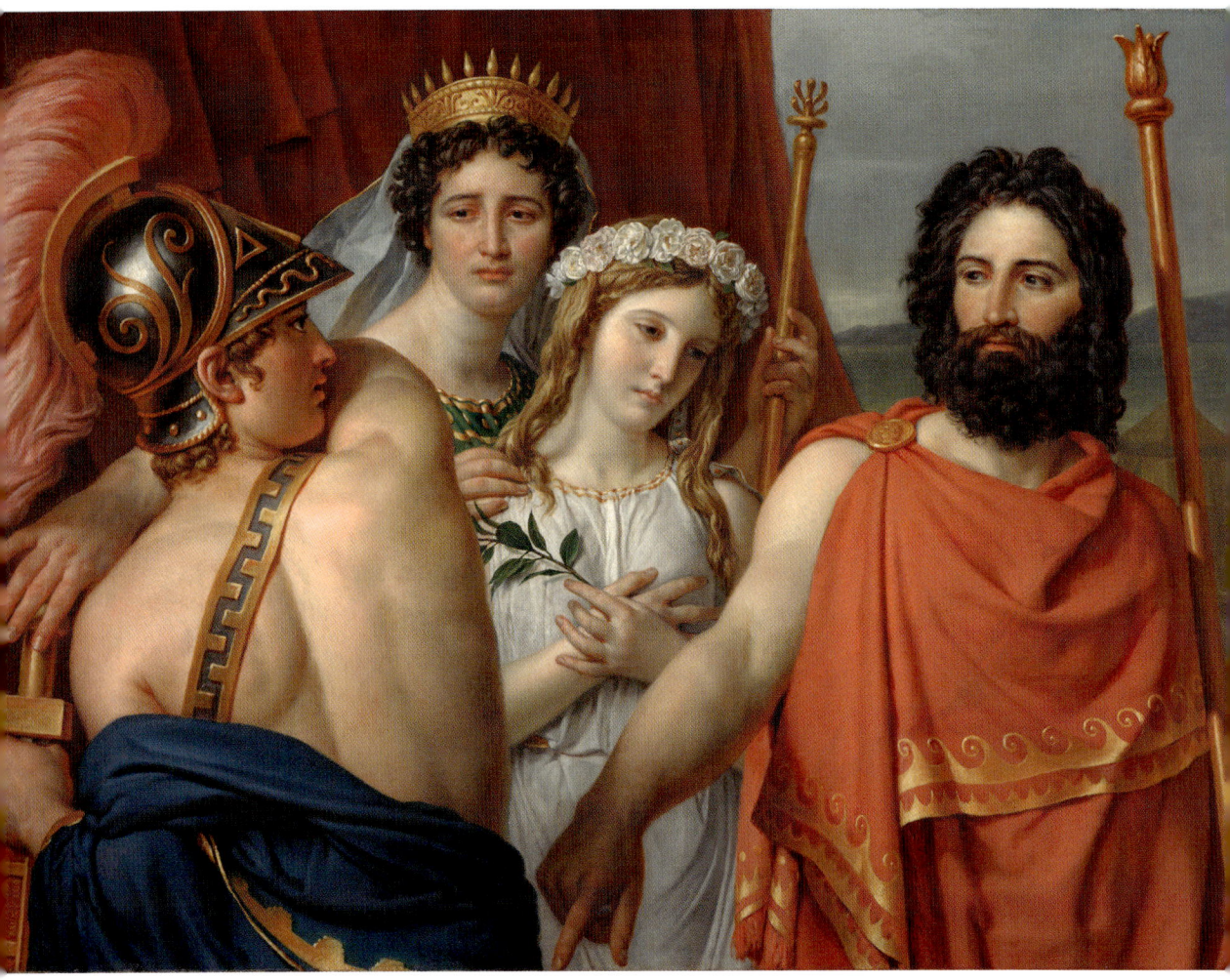

5.16. Jacques-Louis David, *The Anger of Achilles*, 1819, oil on canvas, 41⁷⁄₁₆ × 57⅟₁₆ in. (105.3 × 145 cm), Kimbell Museum, Fort Worth.

his philanthropy was being received: "These works," he wrote, "are the fruit of the tranquility of mind that I share with the fortunate inhabitants of this empire. What is more, to tell you the truth, I never pick up a brush without blessing the wise Sovereign who has procured them for me."[16] That sovereign would be King William I of the United Kingdom of the Netherlands, his realm a cobbled-together principality hastily declared a kingdom as a barrier to traditional French designs on the Netherlands. In the Dutch tradition of tolerance, William protected the exiled French in his domain and thus merited David's ceremonial expression of praise. But that straightforward reading might be complicated by the lines that come after: "Without pretending to learning," he concludes, "permit me to proclaim with Virgil: 'O Meliboeus, it is a god who has wrought for us this peace.'" (He rendered this in the Latin: *O Meliboe, Deus nobis haec otia fecit.*)[17]

David had enough learning to know that it was not Virgil the man who uttered these words, but rather it was one of his characters in the *Eclogues*, the first of his published poems, the quotation coming from *Eclogue I*. The shepherd Meliboeus invoked by David has fled the confiscation of his property, driving his starved flock ahead of him. His partner in the poem's dialogue, a shepherd named Tityrus, pronounces his grateful satisfaction in untroubled possession of a rural retreat and pastoral livelihood, but Meliboeus can foresee to no such peaceful future. It is true that Virgil himself, at the time he wrote this cycle of poems, had suffered the confiscation of his family's property in northern Italy, seized to reward veterans of Augustus's victory at Philippi—the same having happened, we learn as the poem proceeds, to the fugitive Meliboeus. When his guest inquires which god had procured Tityrus this enviable state, he replies that it was "the city they call Rome," the distant capital where he had sought and gained his freedom from slavery.

The puzzles in this short passage multiply: is this god to be identified with the actual Rome, the fondly remembered city where David had discovered his vision as an artist and the second home to which he had hoped to return on his exile from his native city? (The victorious royalists had closed that option to him, thus necessitating the second choice of nearby, French-speaking Brussels.) Or was it Paris, where he had joined in the exhilarating and cataclysmic revolution to make freedom a general human right and expectation? Or was it Brussels, which had granted him the freedom of his old age? And with which of the two partners in the dialogue would David, dispatched into exile by the restored French monarchy as a regicide Bonapartist, have most identified—the secure, grateful Tityrus or the dispossessed, aggrieved Meliboeus? When the latter declares, "We flee our country's borders … / Abandon home," leaving fields and crops in "the cruel hands" of foreign soldiers, the analogy fit precisely David's having abandoned Paris to the arrogant rule of British, Prussian, and Austrian troops propping up the ineffectual Louis XVIII.

It might be argued that the line from Virgil is no more than a fulsome commonplace, offered as flattery divorced from the complexities of its original poetic setting. But David's habitually deep and meditated approach to his classical sources makes one skeptical of such prosaic interpretation. A small epistolary flourish opens onto the quality and tenor of literary mediation that nourished his art in exile and turned back on exile as a dominant theme.

✳

Virgil's first *Eclogue* stands as one of the most profound reflections in the Western canon on the condition of exile in the wake of warfare and political revolution, especially as it bears on the making of art (exemplified in the piping of Tityrus's reed flute). David must have been meditating on the "lofty hills" around the abode of Virgil's shepherd since his own premature flight to the Swiss Alps in 1815. But what exactly does the sacrifice of Iphigenia have to do with such themes of displacement and exile? And why the dominance of Achilles, suspended in the action of drawing his sword?

The beginning of an answer to these questions lies in the dramatic poetry most proximate to the scene, made vivid to the artist by his theater-going habits. It had long been a device of the tragic dramatists to expand the role of Achilles in the story; Euripides, in order to assemble all his characters on the bleak shore of Aulis, has Agamemnon summon both Clytemnestra and their daughter from Mycenae on the pretext that Achilles has asked for her hand in marriage. Although Achilles knows nothing of this ruse to begin with, he swears his obligation to save Iphigenia from death once he learns of Agamemnon's deception. In Jean Racine's French homage to Euripides, *Iphigénie* of 1674, Achilles attempts to thwart the sacrifice, declaring to Agamemnon: "I know not Paris, Helen, Troy. I want / Your daughter, and I leave but at that price."[18]

Racine builds on the wedding motif from Euripides to erect a full-blown love triangle, with another potential victim vying for the love that Achilles has already sworn to Iphigenia. Thus the hero's speeches vowing to save his bride and denouncing the vainglory of Agamemnon are considerably sharpened over their counterparts in Euripides. The commander of the Greeks, coolly facing down the tirades of Achilles, replies: "I want less valor, more obedience. Flee. / I do not fear your ineffectual wrath, / And break all bonds attaching me to you." To which the enflamed Achilles retorts: "Then thank the only bond that holds me back. / I still respect the father of this child. / Perhaps, but for that name, the overlord / of kings would never brave me so again / But one word more. Listen, if you have ears / I will defend your daughter and my fame. / To reach the heart that you intend to pierce, / This is the path your blows will have to take."[19]

To rehearse this sequence of events is to locate the *Anger of Achilles* firmly within the world of Racine's tragedy.[20] David related in a letter that the tears of Clytemnestra are "suspended" by the hope that Achilles's threatening gesture arouses.[21] But if one were to ask where exactly does it correspond to the scenario of the tragedy, the answer would have to be: both everywhere and nowhere in particular. At its core must be the confrontation between Achilles and Agamemnon, but there is no such action described in the play, least of all the drawing of sword—a gesture of overt violence that would have violated the decorum of the tragic stage. Nor are the two women present as the deep animosity peaks between the Greek's commander and his fiercest warrior.

These departures from the decorum of tragedy and the coherence of inherited narratives link the *Anger of Achilles* to David's freely experimental drawings that preceded and followed it. And such liberties would have found affirmation in Racine's own process as a playwright. The preface to *Iphigénie* contains a long apology for his departures from Euripides in order to accommodate the sensibilities of a modern audience—along with a description of his mix-and-match approach to his various and sometimes contradictory sources. David would assume no less scope for himself and would preserve the thing that most distinguishes Racine's version of the story from all the others, that is, the deep motivation in love and pride for the eventual violence of Achilles's intervention.

"The anger of Achilles," as a phrase, sends one's mind well past the antiquity of Euripides to the founding moment of Western poetry, the opening lines of Homer's *Iliad*: "Sing, O goddess, the anger of Achilles son of Peleus, that brought countless ills upon the Achaeans. Many a brave soul did it send hurrying down to Hades, and many a hero did it yield a prey to dogs and vultures, for so were the counsels of Zeus fulfilled from the day on which the son of Atreus, king of men, and great Achilles, first fell out with one another."[22] Every action in the epic follows from this one.

5.17. William Blake, *Minerva Repressing the Fury of Achilles from The Iliad of Homer Engraved from the Compositions of John Flaxman, R.A., Sculptor*, 1805, line engraving, 10⅞ × 17⁹⁄₁₆ in. (27.6 × 44.6 cm), The Metropolitan Museum of Art, New York.

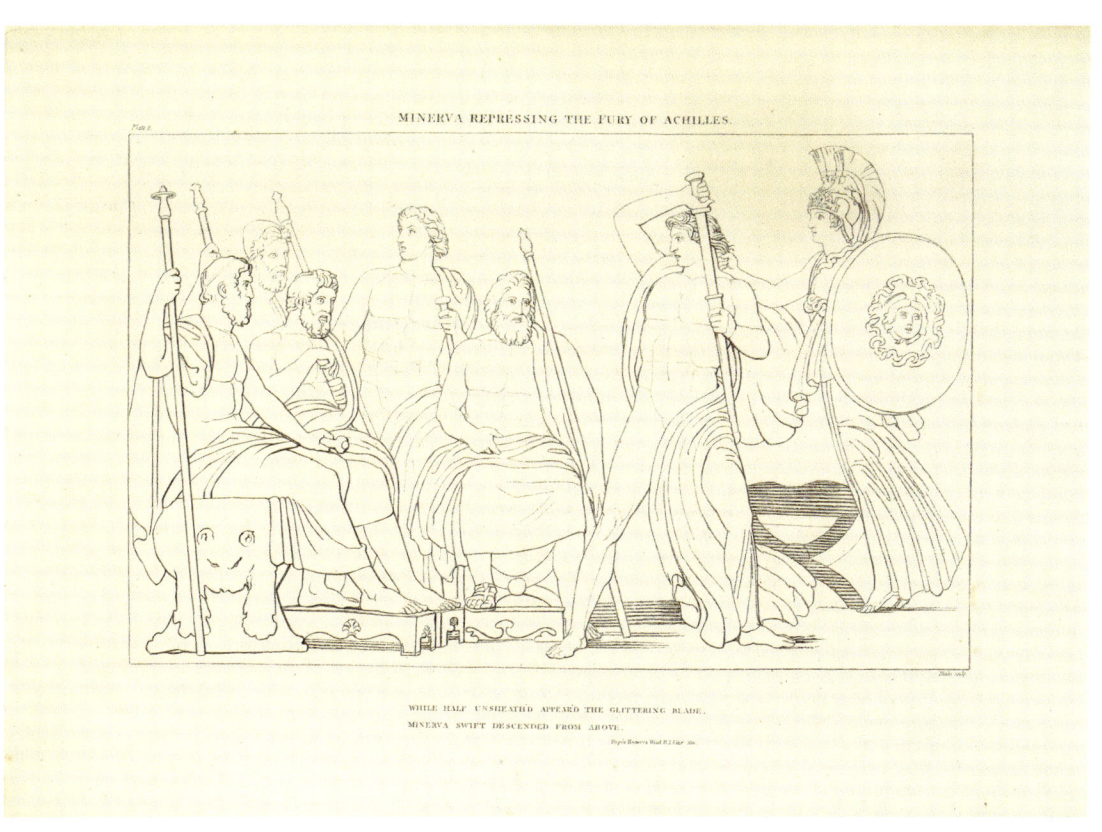

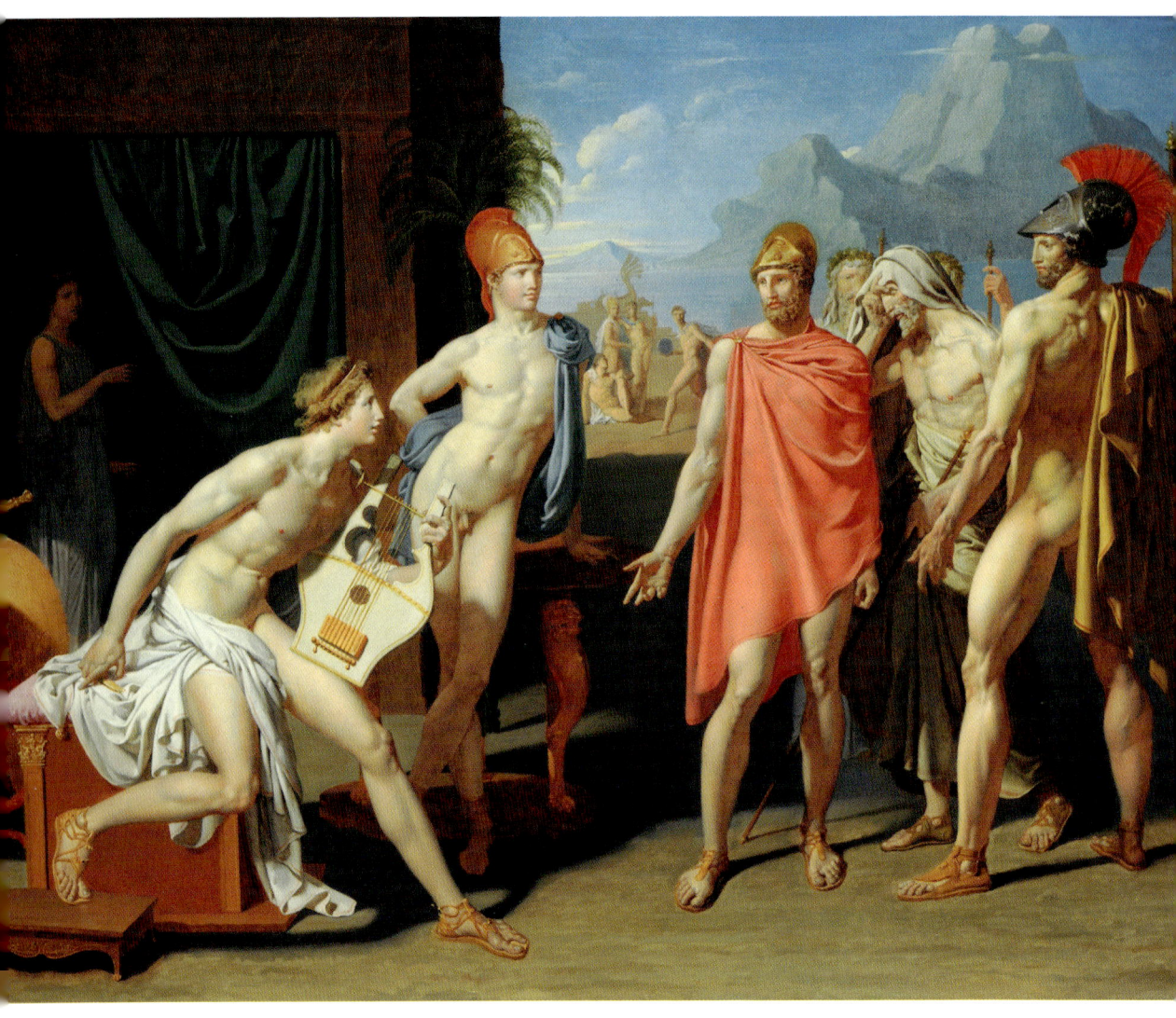

5.18. Jean-Auguste-Dominique Ingres, *The Ambassadors of Agamemnon Entreating Achilles,* 1801, oil on canvas, 44½ × 57½ in. (113 × 146 cm), Ecole nationale supérieure des Beaux-Arts, Paris.

The cause of the quarrel was Agamemnon being forced, by yet another divine curse, to yield up a female captive, and in her place, he demands as a substitute the captive Briseis already claimed by Achilles. In response, Achilles does indeed draw his sword. Only the physical intervention of Athena, who fears the ruin of the Greek cause, can stay the blow. The hero's arrested threat had been authoritatively imagined in the 1795 engraving after English artist John Flaxman's conception of the scene (fig. 5.17), one print from an enormously influential Homeric cycle. David imported the theme of the hero's rage from the opening verses of the *Iliad*, along with Flaxman's torsion in the reach for the sword that had come to serve as the reigning emblem for that rage—a move entirely in keeping with his recombinant approach to the motifs in his contemporaneous drawings and transforming his painting into a palimpsest of both provocations of the rage and hatred of Achilles toward his commander.

But neither the drawings nor the print after Flaxman contain within themselves a formula for translating their motifs up to the scale of a painting. It is the case that the size of the *Achilles* canvas, about three and a half by five feet, was not on the monumental dimensions on which he had been used to working. But David had not in fact given up his former monumentality. His actors are just as big as they always were, that is, life-sized; it is just that they are not revealed at full length (directly parallel to the compressed personages in the *Lamentation* of Navez). He had recently written to a student at work on a half-length figural piece, saying, "It is exceedingly difficult to put together a group of cropped figures without having drawn beforehand the entire figure in its movement."[23]

David added in the same note: "I forgot to tell you not to put too much background above your figures because that would make them look small." Both comments are apposite to Ingres's Grand-Prix-winning painting of 1801 (fig. 5.18). The pupil's *The Ambassadors of Agamemnon Entreating Achilles* depicts the hero singing at leisure in his tent with his companion Patroclus looking on, both withdrawn from battle over the Briseis affair, while the Greek commanders plead that he relent and so save the Greek army from annihilation. Ingres's figures, with their sinuous contours, indeed seem diminished. What is more, the subject centers on talk—and complicated colloquium at that—rather than on physical action. The silver-tongued Odysseus, shown at the center wrapped in his red cloak, can offer no more expressive charge than a worried look, awkward pose, and gesture of entreaty. Nowhere in evidence is Flaxman's tensely bottled force.

In 1818, Navez wrote to his patron Hemptinne from Rome: "The persecution of Ingres by M. David is too strong. Ingres is a talent and above all a man of taste like David himself," he asserts, before insisting on his resistance to imitating Ingres's style and palette.[24] It is plain from this and other letters of Navez that David has been hectoring him not to "ape" Ingres. And the strongest argument that David could have made in support of the young artist maintaining the idiom forged from their Brussels collaboration would have been the *Anger of Achilles* itself, as there is certainly no issue about the figures in the *Anger of Achilles* appearing too small. The background is minimal and pressed down on the rhythmic line of heads. The network of bonds in which Achilles is enmeshed manifests itself as a linking highway of flesh, beginning in the face and elongated neck of Clytemnestra and following an unbroken sequence of skin-to-skin transitions until halted at the gold medallion of authority that clasps the garment of Agamemnon. But the staying of the blow still must be generated from within the figure of Achilles, which is the likely motivation for the pronounced twisting of waist and neck, the sheer inflation of the torso, alongside the precise emphasis on the hovering fingertips over the hilt of the sword at the farthest left.

By the logic of Racine's narrative, Clytemnestra and Iphigenia cannot be there at all. Surveying all of David's theatrical caprices, one senses that he is moving to render the lineaments of dramatic conflict in terms of figural diagrams that simply leave the constraints of any temporal sequence behind—seeking the lineaments of a postnarrative history painting. So it is no wonder that the result in the *Anger of Achilles* has tended to appear so awkward and unmotivated to generations of dismissive observers with narrative in their bones. But what that predisposition had blocked from view is the tremendous compression in the picture's presentation of its theme, the whole of which partakes of the invisible, binding forces bearing down on Achilles. All of the hero's tirades protest loudly at his absence from home, the grief of his father, the undefended lands, his displacement from his true place and responsibilities by the self-interested vanity and arbitrary will of his master; he thus feels himself a warrior version of the dispossessed fugitive shepherd in Virgil's poem. The ornament emblazoning his sword belt and helmet derives from architecture and plant forms, the groundedness of home; while Agamemnon's costume carries the waves of the sea, a strip of which one sees behind his head and over which he means to carry the Greek army to a remote and alien battlefield. And there is, unmistakably, in the broad color scheme of the picture an emblazoned reminder of home for David. When the revolutionary Convention, early in 1794, decreed the *tricouleur* as the flag of the French Republic, it was David who recommended that the blue always appear on the left—which is just where he puts it in the three broad patches of blue, white, and red, thereby rendering the resolve of Achilles to resist a barbarous decree in the patriotically Republican colors of a French patriot.[25]

At this juncture, as one might expect, David was not the only art-ist reckoning with displacement and loss, nor were such undertakings a prerogative of advanced age. Navez and Géricault return in the final chapter, both of them devoting the years 1818 and 1819 to themes of outcasts and marooned survivors. For both, the emotional and social pathos of their subjects acquired extra urgency and symbolic weight from changes in the actual climate of Europe, strange weather beyond the capacity of contemporary science to comprehend, as if the earth itself shared the distress of humanity under the Restoration.

Chapter 6

Redemption in Rome and Paris, 1818–20

Ingres Revives the Codes of Chivalry while Géricault Recovers the Dispossessed

THE EVENTS BEHIND Thomas Lawrence creating his two Vatican portraits—one of the Pope Pius VII, the other of the Cardinal Consalvi, Vatican secretary of state and the effective ruler of Restoration Rome—occupied much of chapter 4. But one fact that remained unspoken in Lawrence's correspondence on the subject was just how perishingly hot it was while he worked on them in the summer of 1819. That fact comes to the fore in the letters of the much younger François-Joseph Navez, the Belgian pupil of Jacques-Louis David, who figured so importantly in the preceding chapter. In August 1819, he wrote to his patron, the scientist Auguste-Donat de Hemptinne, that he found himself on fire in more than one sense.[1] He had given himself over to his painting with such intensity that he "barely took the time to eat." The fervor of inspiration was accompanied by "the excessive heat we have endured for two months ... not a drop of rain for four and a half months." Everyone Navez knew had fled the city, fearing contagion as much as seeking cooler mountain retreats. But the young painter soldiered on, assuring his correspondent, a professor of pharmacology, that he owed his stamina to the excellent dietary regimen he followed (perhaps on his patron's advice): "I eat very little but only good roast meat when I do.... very little water, but two and a half bottles of wine per day."[2]

The drought and heat of the summer surely deepened his empathy and identification with the subject of *Hagar and Ishmael in the Desert*, the object of the energies fueled by this dietary regime (fig. 6.1). As recounted in Genesis, Hagar was the Egyptian servant in Abraham's household who bore the patriarch's first son, Ishmael. After his previously childless wife Sarah conceived Isaac, tensions built to the point where Hagar and Ishmael were expelled from the family into the neighboring desert with no more than a single bottle of water. In his first, half-length painted version of 1818 (fig. 6.2), Navez had discreetly revealed the spout of the clay canteen almost out of view in the lower right of the stately pyramid he made of mother and son. This rendition of the pair sufficiently impressed the Netherlandish ambassador on a visit to the studio in October of that year that he offered to buy it. Despite this accolade, Navez took the risk of refusing the ambassador's offer, promising him an improved, full-length canvas; he later

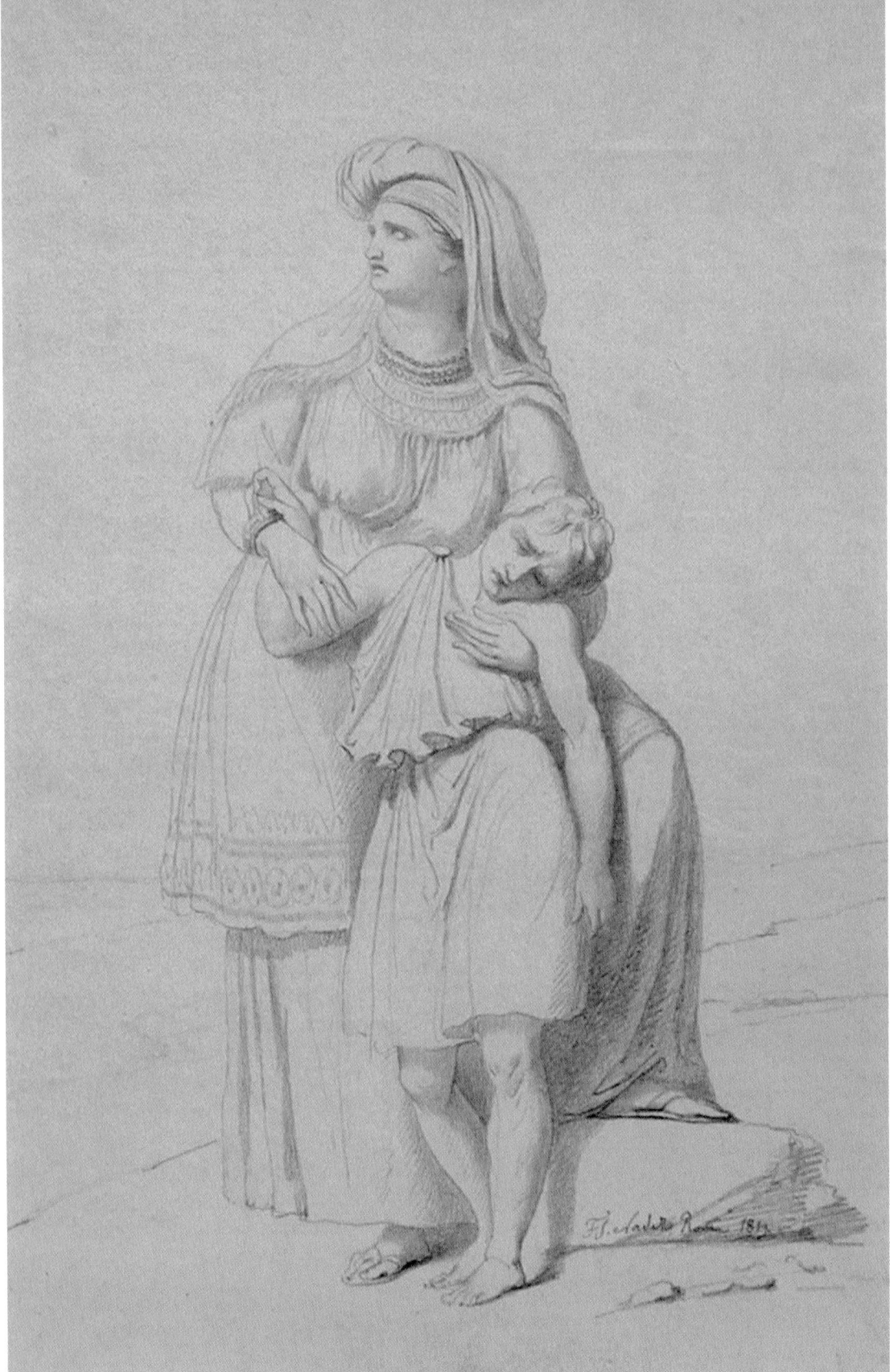

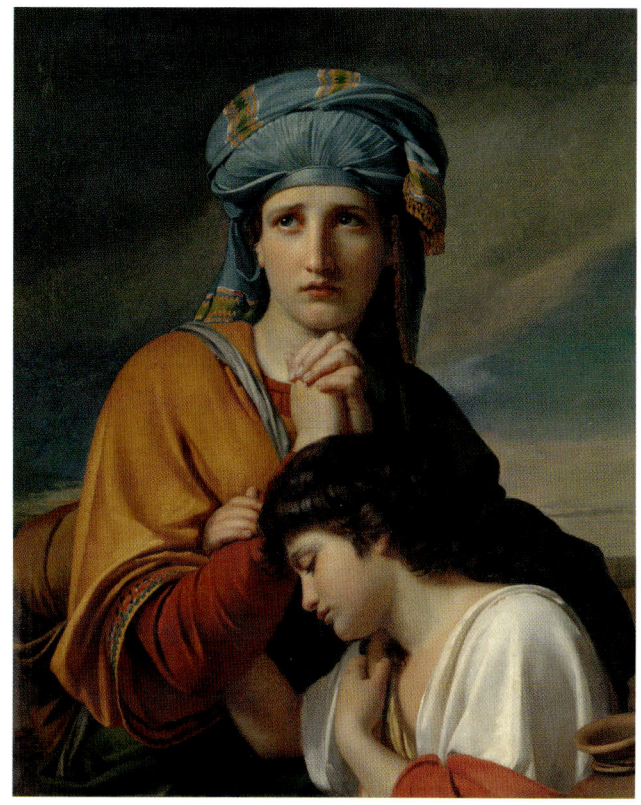

6.1. François-Joseph Navez, *Hagar and Ishmael in the Desert*, 1819, black chalk on paper, 17⅛ × 11⅜ in. (43.4 × 29 cm), Royal Museums of Fine Arts of Belgium, Brussels.

6.2. François-Joseph Navez, *Hagar and Ishmael in the Desert* (half-length) 1819, oil on canvas, 29¾ × 24½ in. (75.4 × 61.5 cm), Amsterdam Museum.

explained that he feared adverse comment from the artists who frequented the embassy.[3] It can only be surmised what aspect of the painting made him apprehensive about its reception, but the identity of the artists in question is clearer: It would have been the Germans going in and out of the Netherlandish legation whose opinion he dreaded. For the most part, these rivals belonged to a highly self-conscious brotherhood, which had become a fixture in Rome over the previous decade. Led by Johann Friedrich Overbeck, Peter von Cornelius, and Philipp Veit, they had called themselves the Lukasbund, after the patron saint of artists. But the group became generally known, on account of their ostentatious piety and primitivizing aesthetic doctrines, as the Nazarenes.

Although the presence of the Nazarenes well predated the restoration of Pius VII and Cardinal Consalvi, they acquired fresh prominence in its wake. Protestant members and followers responded to the renovations of the Church by converting to Catholicism en masse.[4] Just in advance of Navez arriving in Rome, the group had achieved a certain triumph by reviving true fresco as the medium for embellishing the villa of Prussia's consul general, a Jewish convert to Christianity named Jacob Salomon Bartholdy. Sited on the brow of the Pincian Hill, the Bartholdy palace was fully within the urban renovations around the Piazza del Popolo, the most concentrated such effort undertaken by the cardinal's administration. When Canova resumed in these same years his charge over the Vatican's Museo Chiaramonti of antiquities (honoring the family name of Pius VII), he included among the Italian painters assigned to decorate its lunettes the Nazarene Veit, who contributed *The Triumph of Religion* in 1817, like all the others prominently inscribing the name of the pope.[5]

For the Bartholdy decorations, also completed in 1817, the German group chose, perhaps as a theme apposite to the patron's personal history, to narrate the Old Testament life of Joseph. In the panel by Cornelius, *Joseph Makes Himself Known to His Brothers* (fig. 6.3), its overlapping planes, sharply delineated contours, and local color exemplify the quattrocento prototypes favored by the group. These they opposed to models from the High Renaissance or baroque periods, which they regarded as compromised by secular investments. None of this counted for much in the eyes of Navez. "The Germans here," he wrote to Hemptinne, "love to call attention to themselves; they affect to dress themselves in the manner of Raphael (fig. 6.4); they

6.3. Peter Cornelius, *Joseph Makes Himself Known to His Brothers*, 1816–17, fresco and tempera, 92⅞ × 114⅛ in. (236 × 290 cm), Nationalgalerie, Staatliche Museen, Berlin.

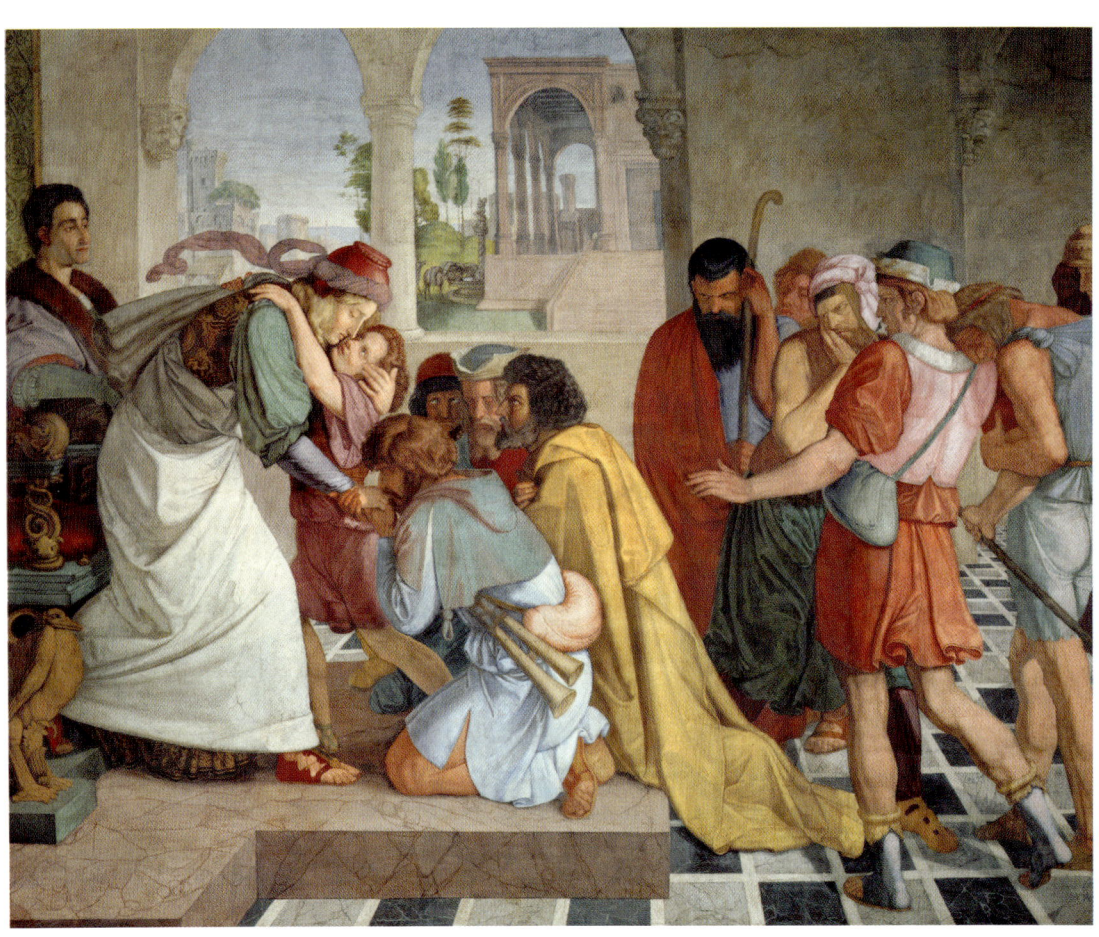

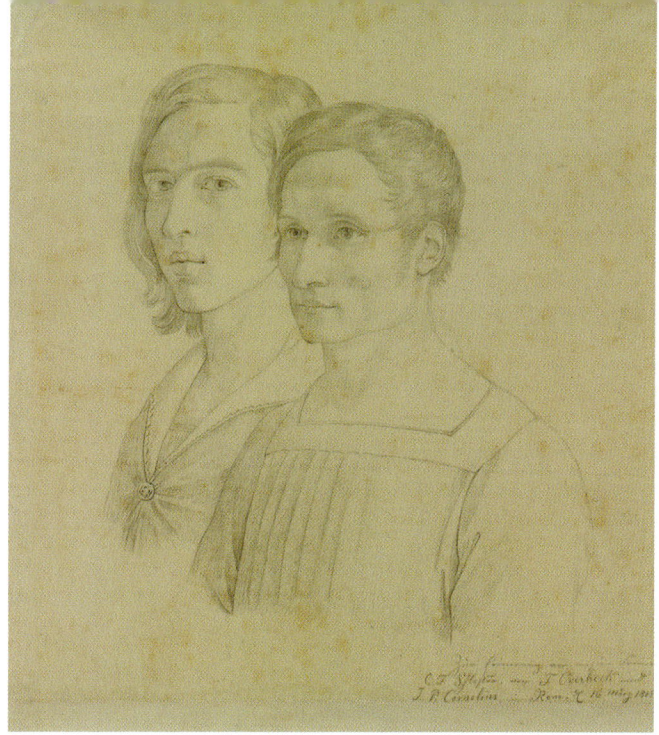

6.4. Peter Cornelius and Johann Friedrich Overbeck, *Mutual Double Portrait*, 1812, graphite on paper, private collection, Munich.

wear velvet toques, a belt with sword, a plume in their crowns. They seek out the most gothic pictures and declare that Raphael ruined painting. They are here universal objects of ridicule."[6]

In this passage Navez put his finger on the unresolved ambivalence of the German group toward Raphael—they dressed like him but also denounced his perceived preeminence out of pious determination to peel away the worldly sensuality that began, as they saw it, in the art of the High Renaissance. It is now commonplace to credit the Nazarenes as influencing any art of strongly linear and planar character made in this period, particularly if the subject is a religious one. Can one surmise, then, that Navez feared their judgment out of respect for their priority and their abilities, which he displaced by disdain for their mannerisms? The likely answer is no. If he declined to be represented by the half-length Hagar, this potentially impertinent reluctance could only have arisen out of desire to match the monumentality of the Bartholdy frescos with a definitive lesson in both Franco-Belgian artistic acumen and Franco-Belgian freedom from externally imposed dogma. He would have been highly conscious of the original mode that he and David had forged together in Brussels, with their own, superior emphasis on strongly delineated figures arrayed across a surface more than they are inserted into illusory depth. If one places his earlier *Hagar* next to David's contemporaneous *Anger of Achilles*, with its tearful countenance of Clytemnestra, the continuity between the two aggrieved mothers is patent. And the link becomes even stronger in the full-length version he went on to paint following his promise to the Netherlandish ambassador.

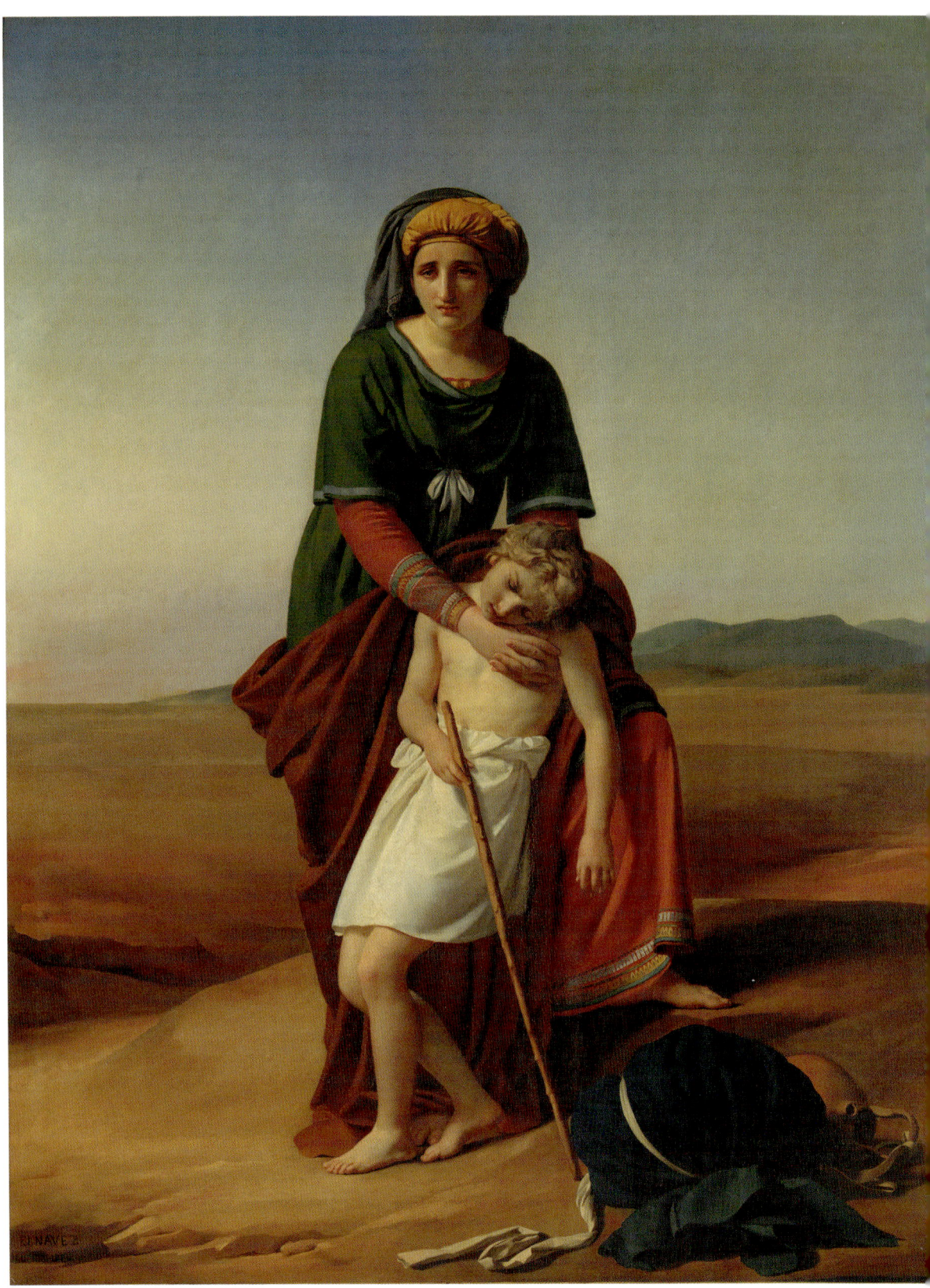

6.5. François-Joseph Navez,
Hagar and Ishmael in the Desert,
1820, oil on canvas, 87 × 67⅜ in.
(221 × 171 cm), Royal Museums
of Fine Arts of Belgium.

Navez's definitive canvas of *Hagar and Ishmael in the Desert* (fig. 6.5)—at seven feet in height, with generous space around a principal figure scaled somewhat over life size—possessed all the imposing presence required as a reply to Nazarene historicizing piety. The extra vertical scope allows the figure of Ishmael to exhibit the full measure of mortal suffering and physical breakdown implicit in the verses from Genesis. Prefiguring the intended sacrifice and divine rescue of his half brother Isaac, the life or death of the lolling, gray-faced Ishmael hangs in suspension. His virtual integration into the upright body of his mother draws a line between this moment and her later separating herself from the dying boy, placing him under a bush and moving away so as not to witness his expected death. Not even mooted is the angel who will, in scripture but not here, miraculously conjure a well into existence before their eyes. Navez offers in its place a full view of the hopelessly empty water container at the lower right. This stark silhouette, in concert with the desolate horizon, stamps this *Hagar and Ishmael in the Desert* with a morbidity solely redeemed by the dignity of the mother. As such it belongs fully in the archaizing register of Davidian tragedy as opposed to devotional uplift.

*

As Navez disparaged the Nazarene artists for their facile popularity, he cited the perceived unpopularity of J.A.D. Ingres as a mark of excellence. In another letter back to Brussels, he reported that Ingres's manner was "esteemed by so few people that I would die of hunger if ever I were to try it myself. It can be appreciated only by a small number of artists who possess some degree of refinement and sensibility above the vulgar."[7] Just how apart Ingres seemed from the international community of somewhat younger artists in Rome might be gauged by the self-presentation of his astonishing 1812 self-portrait (fig. 6.6), representing himself (in contrast to Nazarene group solidarity) working in diminutive, solitary isolation on a vast classical subject (*Romulus, Conqueror of Acron*) planned for Napoleon's occupation of the Quirinale Palace.

That improvised place of work lay inside the church of Trinità dei Monti, a French possession that had fallen into disrepair and out of liturgical use. It crowned the Spanish Steps adjoining the French Academy's Pincian hillside quarters in the Medici Villa (see fig. 3.15), and Ingres's home studio lay a short distance down the slope to the south. There he lived comfortably enough, on the testimony of this extraordinarily detailed and sympathetic domestic portrait (fig. 6.7) painted in 1818 by the young Grand Prix winner Jean Alaux: Madame Ingres in the foreground, her husband seated with his famous violin in the room that served as combined studio and showroom for the

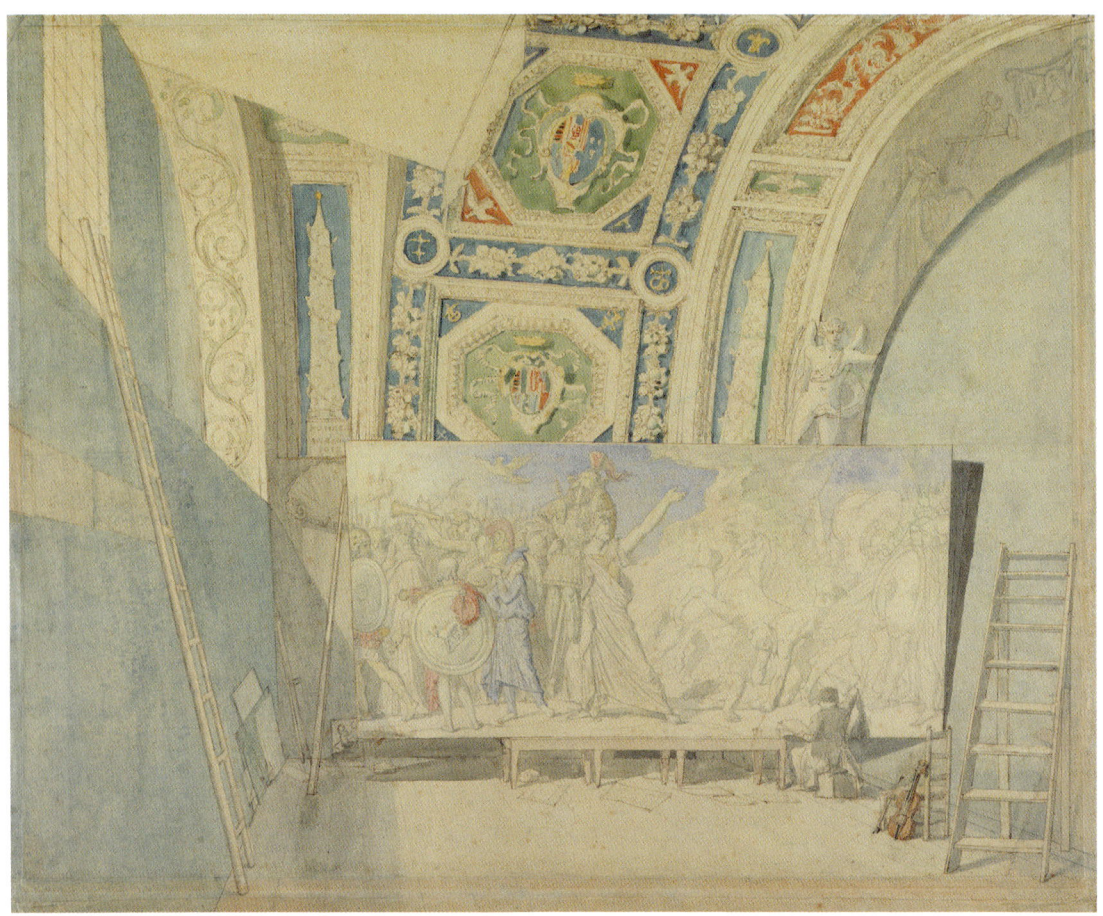

6.6. Jean-Auguste-Dominique Ingres, *Self-Portrait of the Artist at Work on His "Romulus Victor over Acron" in Santa Trinità dei Monti*, c. 1811, graphite, ink, and watercolor on paper, Musée Bonnat-Helleu, Bayonne.

private clients on whom he continued to depend.[8] But the sensitivities evident in the diminutive scale of his Trinità dei Monti self-portrait remained close to the surface. Géricault, during his stay in Rome the previous year, had visited Ingres in these rooms, committing a social error by taking a much greater interest in the drawings on view at the expense of the works on canvas.[9]

Far more than the mural-sized *Romulus* (unused in the end), the small *Pius VII in the Sistine Chapel* of 1814, discussed at length in chapter 1 as a private commission from a friend, would have matched Ingres's normal space and resources. That canvas testified to the artist's self-identification with the pre-Napoleonic established order, no doubt reinforced by his relative official neglect under the Empire. By 1818, however, he could present himself as spokesman for the restored French crown in its new role as patron of Italian culture. Although not the first artist to represent this scene, for Ingres to paint Leonardo dying in the arms of the French king François I—a tale told in Vasari's *Lives of the Artists*—carried significance that carried well beyond the annals of art history (fig. 6.8). As one of France's greatest rulers had

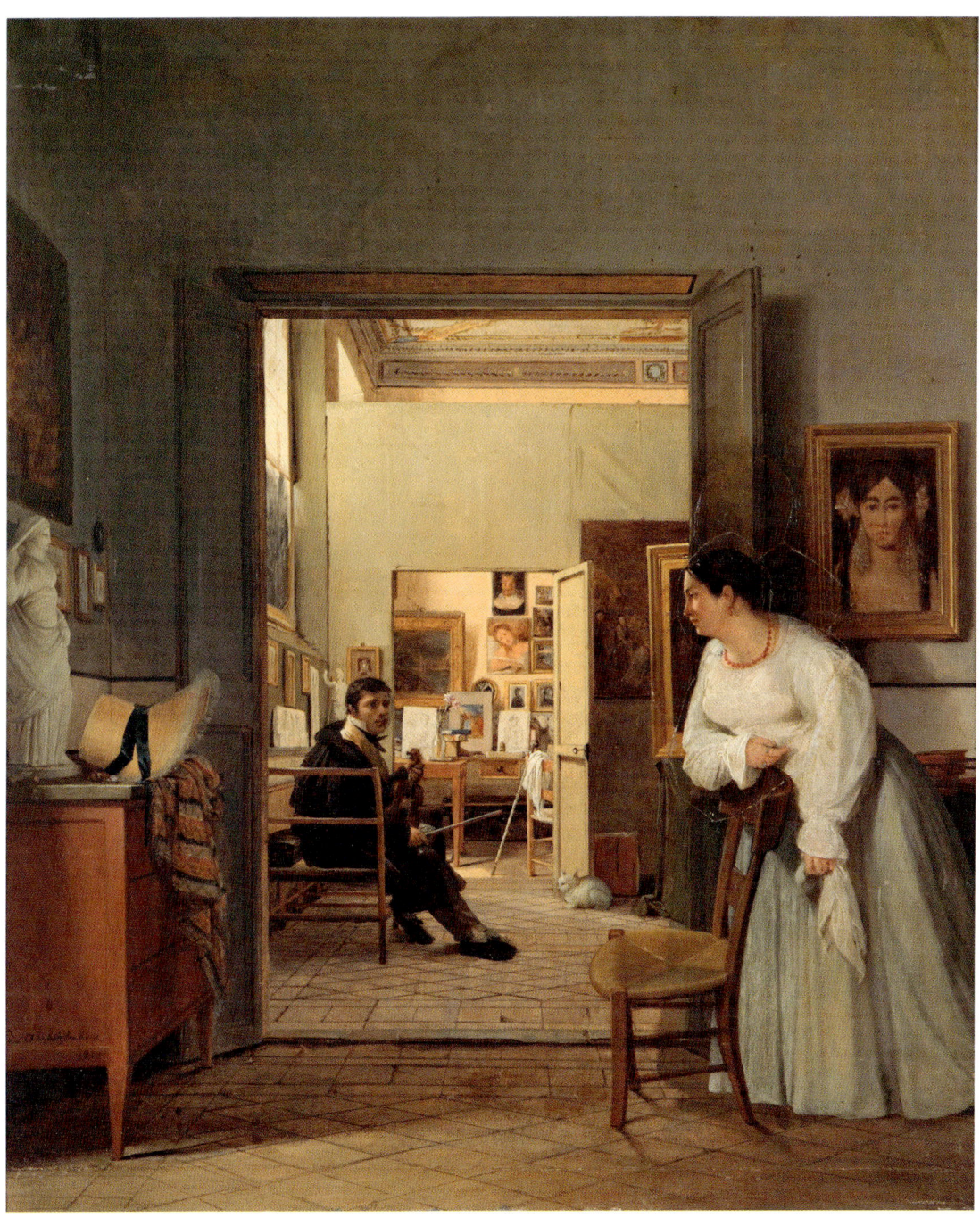

6.7. Jean Alaux, *The Roman Studio of Ingres in 1818*, 1818, oil on canvas, 21¾ × 18⅛ in. (55.4 × 46 cm), Musée Ingres, Montauban.

made a lowborn Italian artist his equal and friend, so France now lent its magnanimous support for the arts in order to support the cardinal Consalvi's initiatives, beginning with its possessions at the pinnacle of the Roman landscape. The comte de Blacas, French ambassador to the Holy See, commissioned Ingres's rendition of Leonardo embraced by the greatest Valois monarch at the same time that he undertook to support from his own funds the restoration and reconsecration of Trinità dei Monti, the church having become a diplomatic focus of French benevolence and contrition for past Napoleonic high-handedness. To this end, Blacas began to commission works of art to adorn the refurbished interior.[10] There had to have been a new and enormous sense of pride in Ingres—perhaps captured in the cheerfulness of Alaux's double portrait—on being commissioned in February 1817 to paint the church's high altarpiece, a vote of confidence that promised to remove him from professional isolation. The theme, in obvious tribute to the office of Pius VII, was to be *Christ Giving the Keys to St. Peter* (fig. 6.9).

Ingres cast his Trinità altarpiece directly from Raphael, specifically the 1516 tapestry cartoon depicting the charge to Saint Peter (fig. 6.10), that moment in the gospel of Matthew when Simon, alone among the disciples, can name Christ as "the son of the living God," rather than a reincarnated prophet of earlier times. Christ renames him Peter for the rock on which his church will stand, evoking in words—but not actually producing—the keys that will bind both on

6.8. Jean-Auguste-Dominique Ingres, *Death of Leonardo da Vinci in the Arms of François I*, 1818, oil on canvas, 15¾ × 19⅞ in. (40 × 50.5 cm), Musée du Petit Palais, Paris.

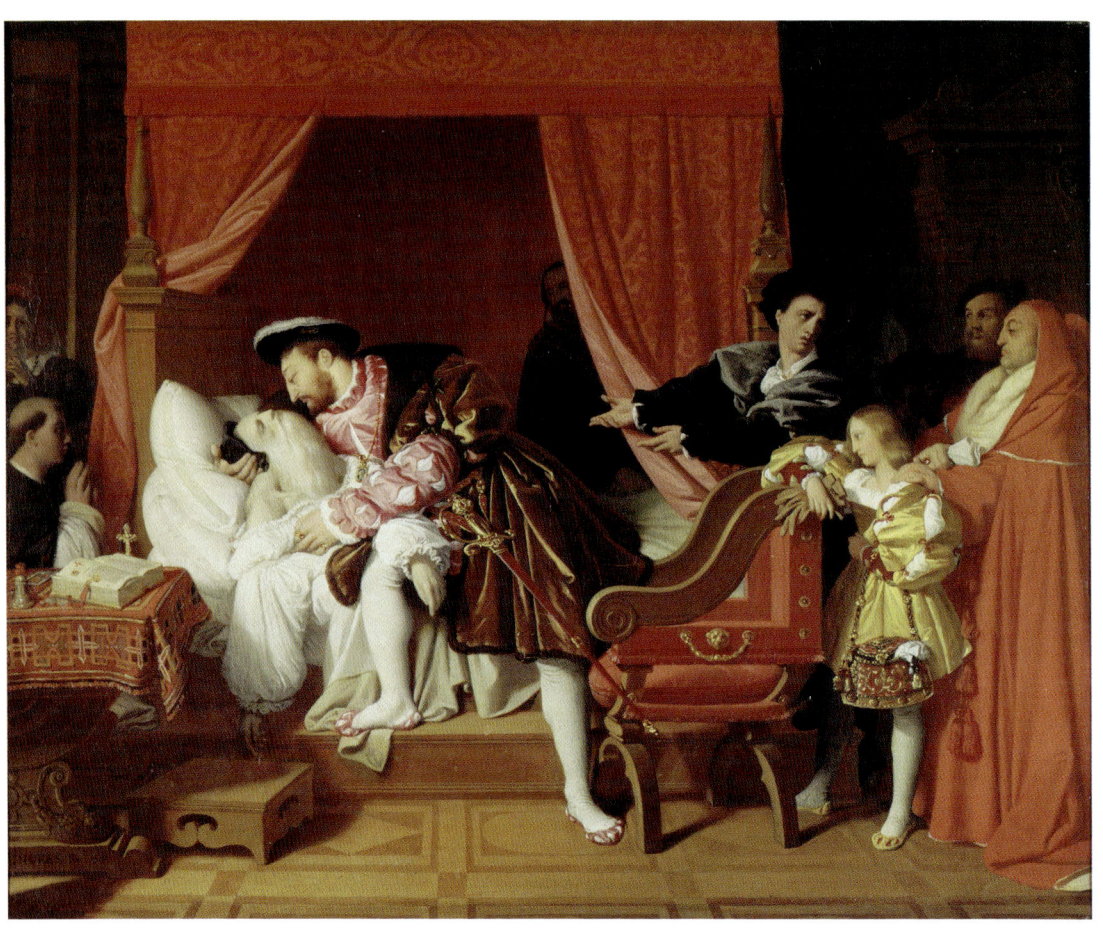

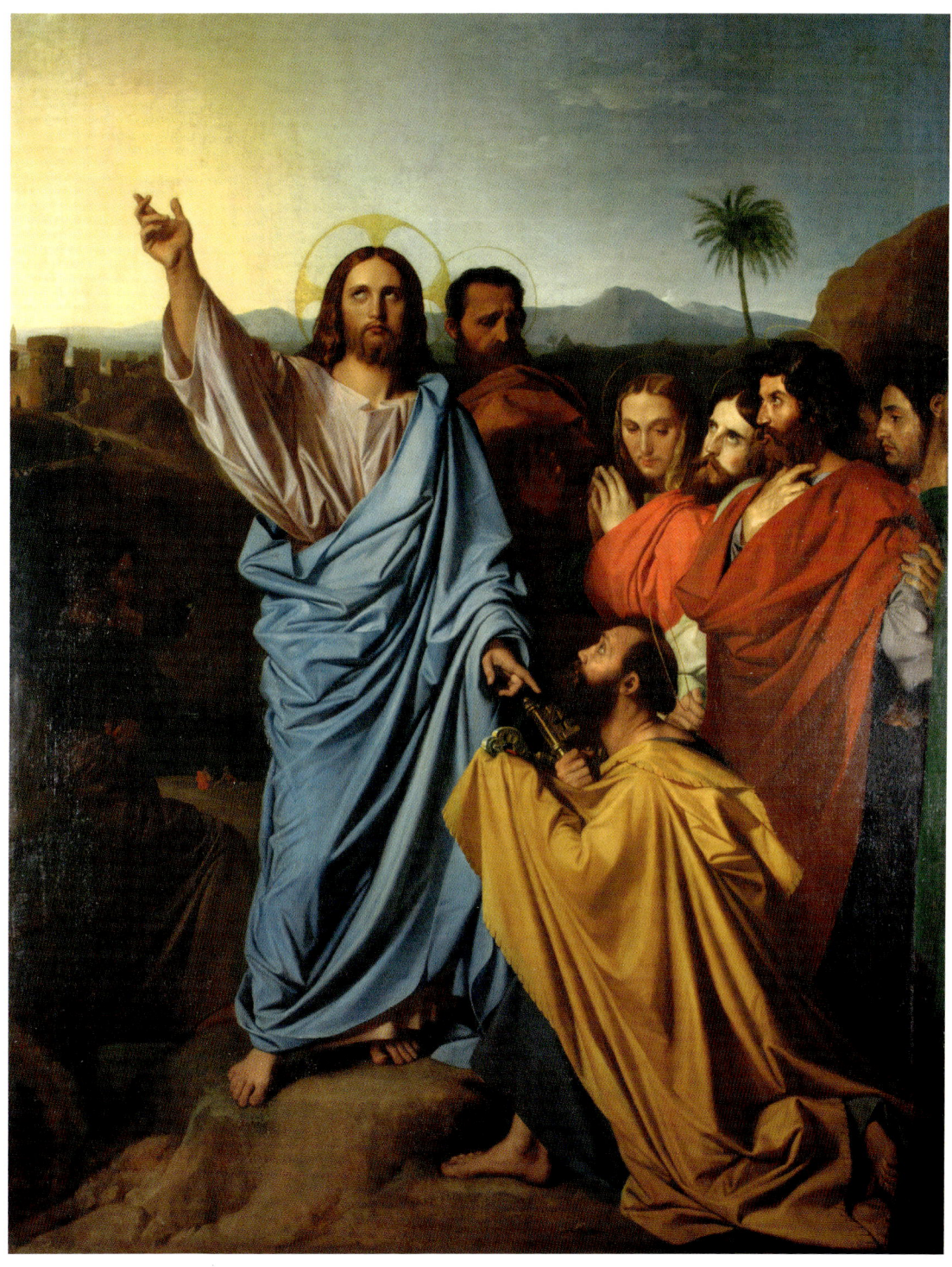

6.9. Jean-Auguste-Dominique Ingres, *Christ Giving the Keys to St. Peter*, 1820, Musée Ingres, Montauban.

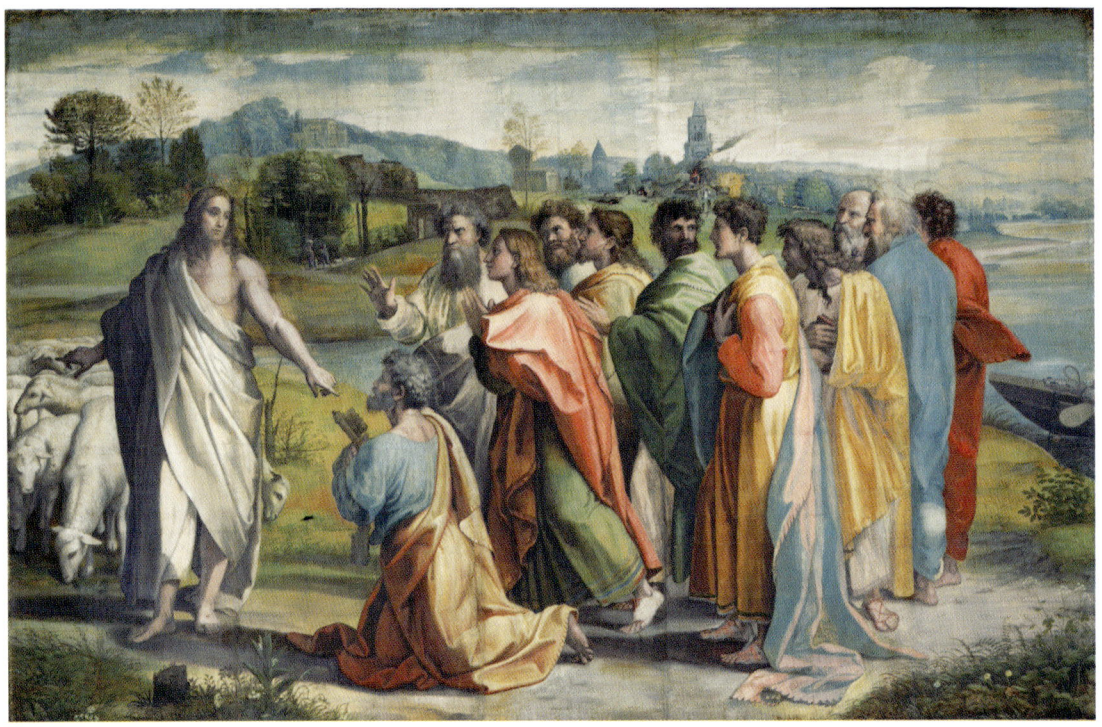

6.10. Raphael, *Cartoon for the Charge to St. Peter*, 1515–16, body-color over charcoal underdrawing on paper mounted on canvas, 135 × 209½ in. (343 × 532 cm), Victoria and Albert Museum, London.

6.11. Johann Friedrich Overbeck, *Easter Morning*, c. 1818, oil on canvas, 51⅝ × 40⅛ in. (131 × 102 cm), Museum Kunstpalast, Düsseldorf.

earth and in heaven. In light of its elevated patronage and destination, Ingres's *Christ Giving the Keys to St. Peter* can be grouped with other embellishments of Consalvi's new Rome, a shared endeavor of the victorious European powers.

Among those powers were the Prussian sponsors of the Nazarenes. And it has been easy ever since to discern a debt in Ingres's work to the frontal, linear simplifications already normative among those German artists. To be avoided, however, is the logical trap of asserting dependency in such a case when a shared point of departure is actually in evidence. To place *Christ Giving the Keys to St. Peter* next to Johann Friedrich Overbeck's *Easter Morning* (fig. 6.11), a contemporaneous example by the acknowledged Nazarene leader, is to highlight a common origin in Raphael. But which Raphael? Overbeck offers his homage to the young Raphael, channeling the perceived delicacy and sweetness of his provincial teacher Perugino. Ingres takes his template from the mature Raphael, artistic mainstay of Pope Leo X and, according to Nazarene sentiment, the worldly later master who ruined painting. In adapting the cognate scene from the Raphael's monumental tapestry cartoons of 1515–16, Ingres is adopting a mode of religious art consciously opposed to the one the German artists championed.

With the return of royal legitimacy as the European norm, it naturally followed that the painting of Christian subjects would regain

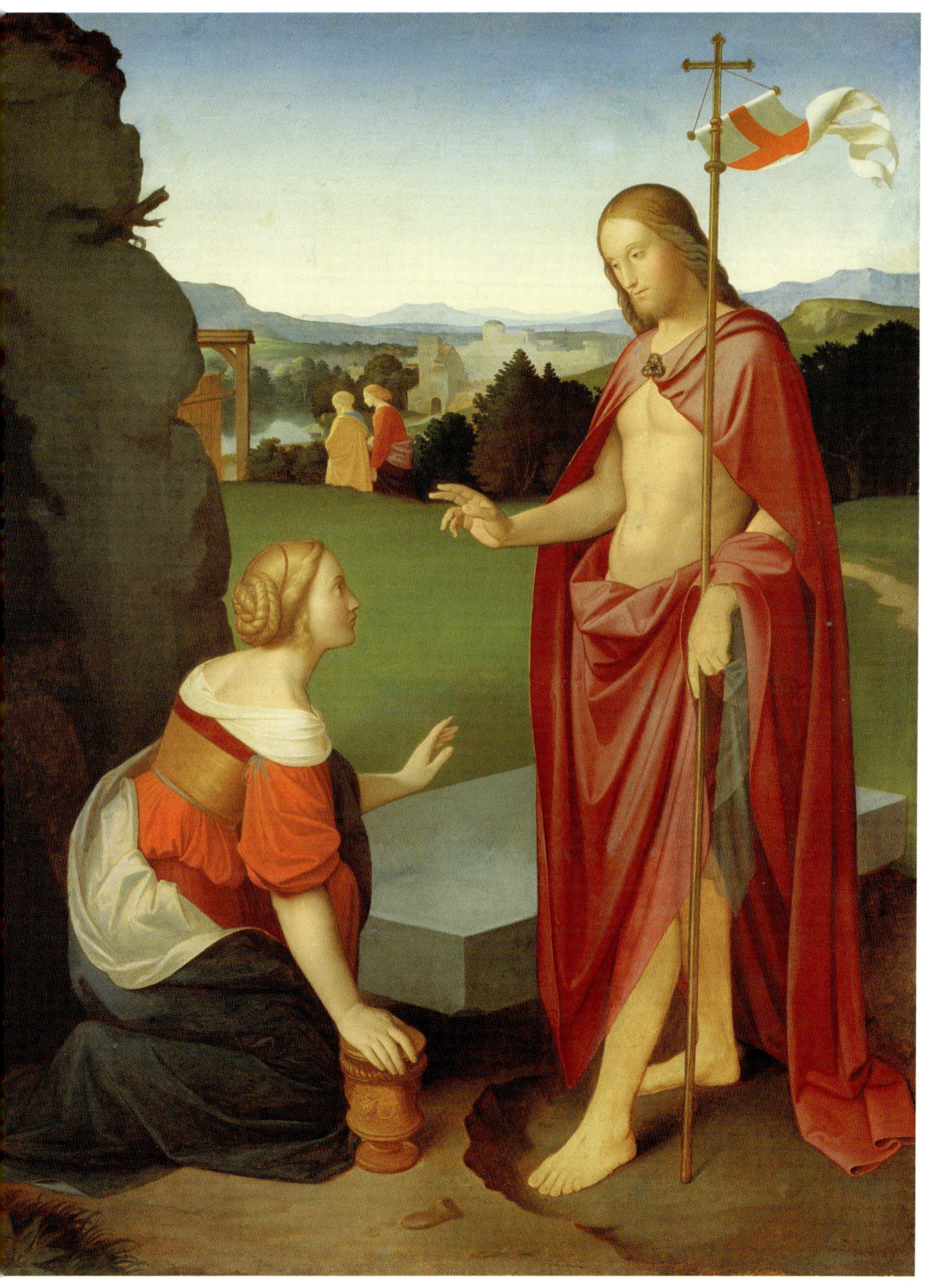

special importance. Authority again rested, nowhere more than in France, on renewed divine sanction of the throne. But in religion as in politics, a formal restoration could not with confidence reinstate the unquestioned norms overturned by the experience of revolution and empire. When Ingres's *Christ Giving the Keys to St. Peter* has been singled out for attention, it has typically been as a symptom of inauthenticity, of belief reduced to unconvincing ideology, as evident in its apparently stilted awkwardness, reduction of figures to pattern, and piling up of faces and draperies. Susan Siegfried, as part of her insightful exegesis of the painting in scriptural terms, notes the prevalence of a "modernist interpretation [that] would see formal disjunctions and discontinuities of this kind as ... symptoms of a larger breakdown of social coherence, religious beliefs, linguistic imperatives, or artistic traditions ... signs of breakdown or a falling away."[11]

It is certainly true that Ingres is brutal in his adaptation of his model in Raphael. The strange-looking apostle in profile, cut off by the right-hand edge, attests to the abrupt, almost violent transformation of his principal source. As he had been asked for a vertical altarpiece, some serious reconfiguring was of course required. But Ingres goes beyond mere issues of composition, enlisting the change of format to change the fundamental meaning of the event. In Raphael's version of the event, Christ does not touch the keys clutched in the hands of the earthbound Simon Peter and points earthward toward the grazing sheep, emphasizing pastoral responsibilities in this world. Ingres's Christ, as hieratic Pantocrator, signals with an exaggeratedly upward gaze his unearthly bond with the heavenly lordship he will exercise over the crouching mortal supplicant—Peter's visible extended foot in the lower right corner a sign of splayed near-prostration. Contact with the keys as sign of office seals Ingres's essentially feudal conception of Christ's lordship and the status of the church. Peter is being less bestowed with divine authority than he is accepting his place and obligations as the vassal of Christ. Mapped onto this set of coordinates, the apparent oddities of the composition do not signal the hollowing out of belief so much as its conforming to another, otherwise unseen order. In moving from a horizontal orientation, which emphasizes dialogue across the human company of disciples, Ingres deploys the new vertical arrangement in order to shift the coded significance of the work toward a firm hierarchy from low to high.

✳

In *Leonardo Dying in the Arms of François I*, Ingres reinforced a revived feudal mindset, embedding another lordly artistic figure in the velvets and silks of an archaizing, neo-Burgundian manner, thus evoking by color and style the splendid late flowering of chivalry. The pale

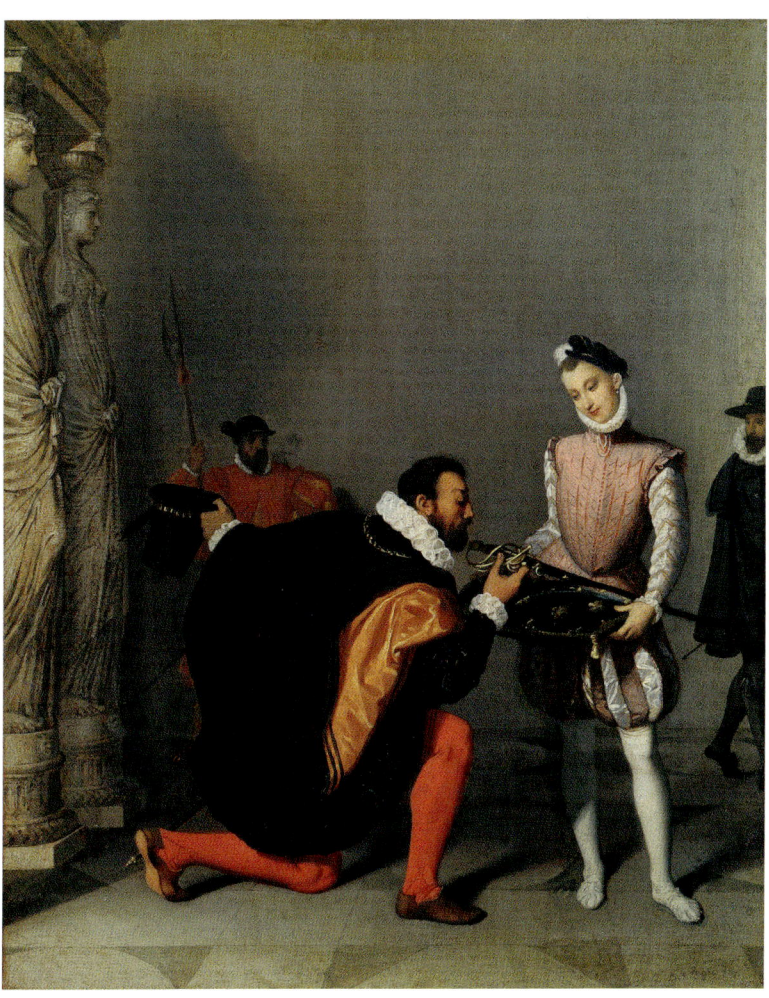

6.12. Jean-Auguste-Dominique Ingres, *Don Pedro de Toledo Kissing the Sword of Henri IV*, 1819, 17¹⁵⁄₁₆ × 14⅜ in. (45.5 × 36.5 cm), Pau, Musée national du château.

ghost of Leonardo barely makes an impression within the sumptuous array of courtly fabrics and heraldic tailoring that spreads itself across the relief-like tableau. The robes and profile of the cardinal on the extreme right seem cut from the *trecento* of Dante more than from the classicizing, sculptural idiom of the High Renaissance. Such affirmation of late feudalism is one in which emblems and heraldry, that is, works of art and artifice, constitute that order as much as the princes, nobles, and knights who bear them. Ingres's preoccupation with the chronicles of French history led him at the time of Napoleon's abdication in 1814 to a legend from the reign of Henri IV, which he repeated at this later juncture of 1819 (fig. 6.12). The Spanish ambassador, envoy of an adversary, is said to have encountered in the palace of the Louvre a page bearing the sword of the French monarch. This Don Pedro of Toledo is reported to have been so moved, despite the conspicuous fleurs-de-lis on the velvet cushion, that he knelt to kiss it. The ambassador's tribute, as Ingres grasped with approbation, celebrated a quasi-mystical system of rank and power that united Bourbon and Hapsburg dynasties—much as past and future antagonists among European rulers had set differences aside to defeat an upstart who could claim no noble ancestry.

What might appear as Ingres's stylistic mobility or eclecticism acquires consistency as parallel affirmations of feudal order, each properly treated according to the decorum of its genre and occasion. As if to seal this pact, he painted for Blacas in 1819 a virtual manifesto of chivalric romance as a contemporary theme (fig. 6.13). The northern Italian poet Ludovico Ariosto first published his epic of chivalry, *Orlando Furioso*, in the same year of 1516 that Raphael completed the Vatican tapestry cartoons. It was thus an artifact of the High Renaissance, composed in the circle of the d'Este dynasty of Ferrara, prominent sponsors of classical learning, though the tale is laid in the time of Charlemagne. Ariosto's paladins maneuver—among countless other intrigues—against invading armies of Africans and Saracens while contending with one another over the affection of the Asian princess Angelica. Already at the time of its writing in the early sixteenth century, this Italian epic looked back on a feudal past long superseded by

6.13. Jean-Auguste-Dominique Ingres, *Roger Freeing Angelica*, 1819, oil on canvas, 57⅞ × 74¾ in. (147 × 190 cm), Musée du Louvre, Paris.

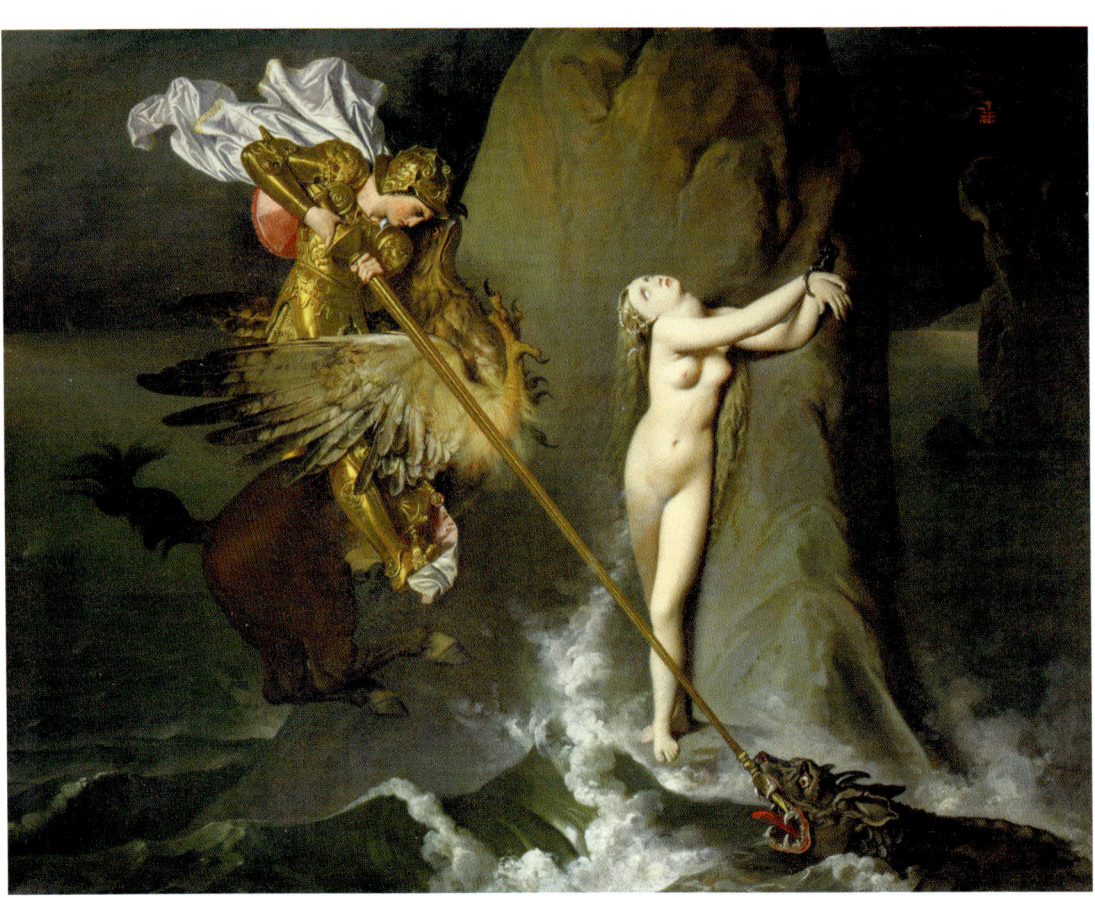

modern trade, urbanism, and armaments, making all the more necessary the perpetuation of existing orders of rank and rule in the realm of the imagination. The poet acknowledges this belatedness in the wit and playful exaggeration with which he recounted the magical events of his epic, a pleasing play of irony that permitted a sophisticated readership to identify with its fantastic personages and outlandish storylines.

If Ariosto had been thus belated, Ingres might have asked, what was a little more belatedness? Three hundred years later, Ingres discerned a parallel opportunity to revive the poet's imagery on behalf of the Restoration elite. The path of Roger (Ruggiero in the poem) leads from Africa, a Saracen lineage, and the tutelage of a sorcerer to eventual Christian conversion and marriage to the warrior princess Bradamante. Along the way, he replicates the feats of Perseus and Saint George, rescuing Angelica from misadventure by slaying the water-dwelling orc from the back of an enchanted flying hippogriff. Ingres could not have been in the least blind to the whiff of absurdity that attended his subject; indeed, he plays it up by extending Roger's lance to improbable length, diminishing the orc to dog-like proportions, and reducing the formidable Angelica to melodramatically languishing victimhood. These aspects are accessory to his chief concern, which was to construct his picture in a fully heraldic mode, his knight more an accumulation of appliqué devices: gilded armor, shield, embroidered silk with the claws, jaws, and feathers of a rampant beast flattened as on a coat of arms. The predictable ridicule that such works attracted from the critics in Paris, who jeered at Ingres's "Gothicizing" archaisms, could not deter him from his mission.

✳

Ingres may have struck his contemporaries as a loner, even an eccentric one, but his attraction to feudal themes across the boundaries of conventional categories of subject matter put him in the artistic if not the social company of Sir Thomas Lawrence.[12] Each one of Lawrence's contemporaneous portraits, ultimately to be installed in the Waterloo Chamber at Windsor Castle (fig. 6.14), carried the subject's characteristic livery, his uniform and decorations as distinctive heraldry, signs of their wearer's place in a system. There would be no center, no dominant human authority apart from the positioning of these separate, insignia-laden bodies in a glittering constellation. This ultimate statement of Restoration legitimacy functions as an allegory composed from discrete emblems, none of which can individually sum up the whole.

Even the tokens of the restored Rome that adorn Lawrence's portraits of Pius VII and Cardinal Consalvi (inventoried in chapter 4)

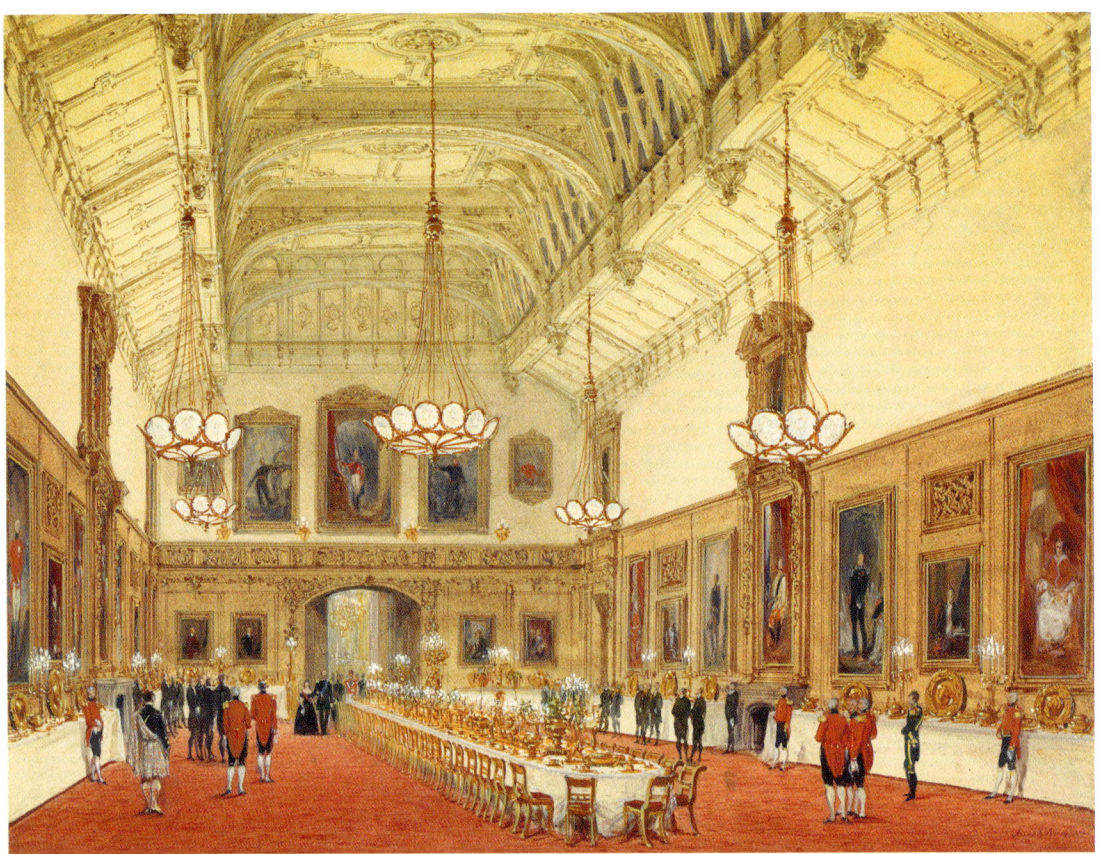

6.14. Joseph Nash, *Windsor Castle: The Waterloo Chamber, 5 June 1844*, 1844, watercolor and body color over pencil, 11⅛ × 14½ in. (28.2 × 36.8 cm), Royal Collection Trust.

resolve themselves as signs of position in this feudal zodiac. While Ingres was the idiosyncratic author of his own expression of this order, Lawrence had it provided for him, courtesy of his patron the prince regent of Britain. With the knighthood he received in order to speed him on his way, he assumed a minor position in the system he was charged with rendering in visual form. He had no need for further supplication; the comte de Blacas was for him a social acquaintance, not a distant fount of precious patronage. And one does not read Lawrence complaining about the heat wave of 1819, perhaps because he had ways to compensate that were unavailable to a Navez or an Ingres. In late May, he described in a letter to Joseph Farington the end of an exciting day and evening of amusements (a scene also recorded by J.M.W. Turner in the same year [fig. 6.15]):

> the night coming on with singular beauty, I went with Prince Metternich and his daughter in their chariot, to the Coliseum. The moon was in her fullest splendor—the air as soft and balmy as Shakespeare's

[he quotes] "Like the sweet south
That breathes upon a bank of violets,
Stealing and giving odour."[13]

The seeming ease of Lawrence's painting technique, along with a manner to charm a prince and princess, made him perhaps the only artist in Europe with the gifts to bring this off, that is, to create a romance of the code itself as the ultimate ground of legitimacy. From their respective positions of insider and outsider, Lawrence and Ingres most decisively grasped this imperative and fashioned what can be counted as the consummate art of Restoration, at least from the perspective of its satisfied beneficiaries. But the years between 1815 and 1819 brought widespread suffering to a vastly greater number. Their artist would be Théodore Géricault.

✳

6.15. Joseph Mallord William Turner, *The Colosseum by Moonlight*, 1819, graphite, body color, and watercolor on paper, 9⅛ × 14½ in. (23.2 × 36.9 cm), Tate Gallery, London.

The place to begin would be a canvas (fig. 6.16) that Géricault fashioned just before his journey to Rome in the autumn of 1816. Its title is *Scene of Deluge*, the work belonging to a recent lineage of such subjects that likewise suspended themselves between mythic floods and generic scenes of disaster and mortal distress—all of them tracing

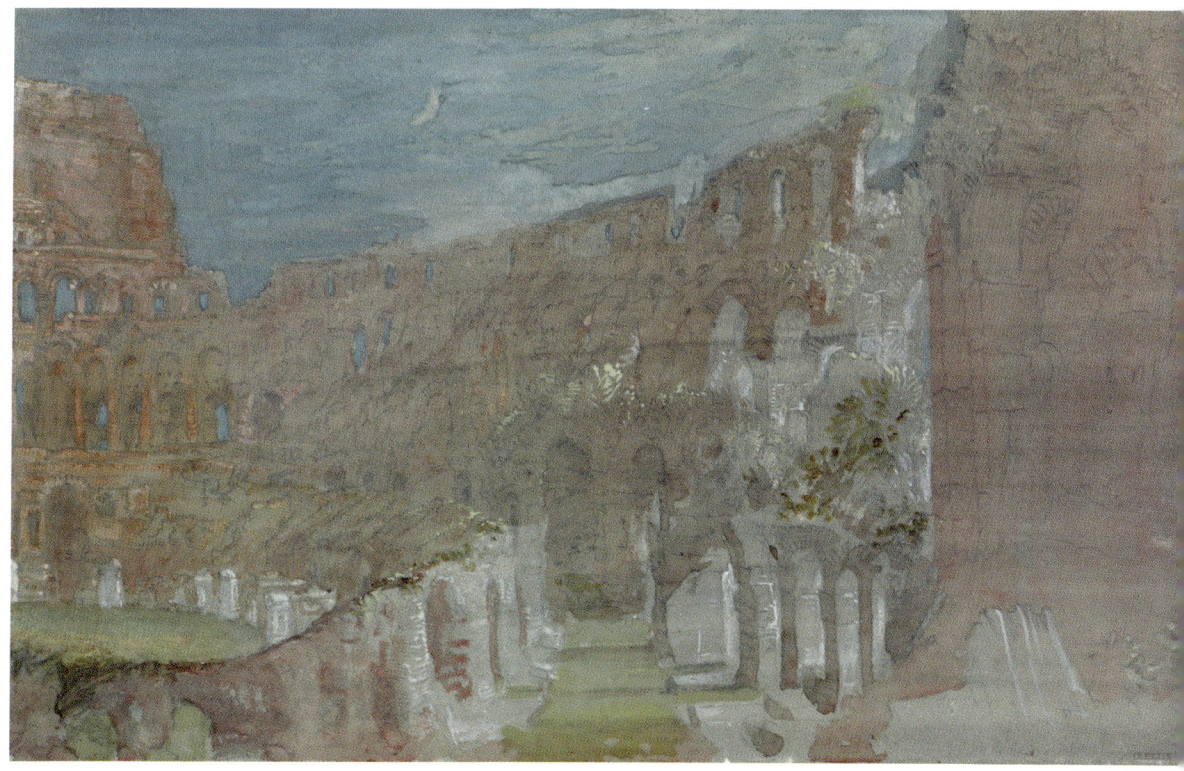

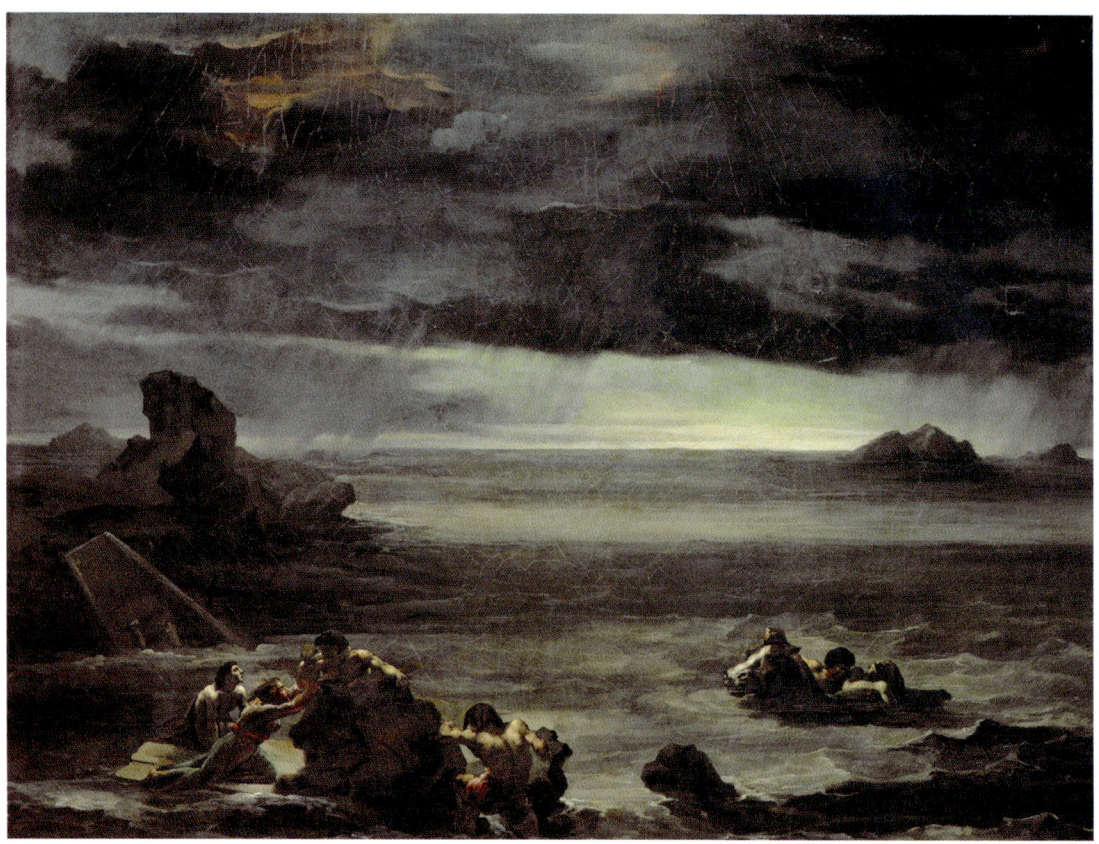

6.16. Théodore Géricault, *Scene of Deluge*, 1815–16, oil on canvas, 38¼ × 51¼ in. (97 × 130 cm), Musée du Louvre, Paris.

their prototype to Nicolas Poussin's venerated *Winter* of 1660. What distinguishes Géricault's medium-sized picture is the fact that it had recently been a different painting altogether. Underneath the murk of swampy greens, grays, and browns is a copy of the vibrantly colored *Battle of the Pyramids* by Antoine-Jean Gros (fig. 6.17).[14] There could hardly be a more dramatic act of effacing Napoleonic glory, leaving no hopeful prospects for the future, only morbid discards and remnants. What remains in Géricault's drowned world? An almost submerged horse and rider, trying in vain to save his family, harks directly back to his great cavalry subjects of 1812 and 1814, while in the lower left his only other survivors cling to the planks of a raft striking jagged rocks, dwarfed and adrift in an immensity of devastation.

On the eve of his yearlong Roman sojourn, this exercise anticipates the torrent of inspired fragments of a possible art observed in chapter 4. As noted there, persuasive translation of these fragments into painted form had eluded him, but he began in 1818, once he had reestablished himself in a Paris studio, taking deliveries of several large lengths of canvas. His goal, prompted by no known commission or destination, was to complete a monumental series of three landscapes.[15] While his small *Deluge* assumed a place in a venerable

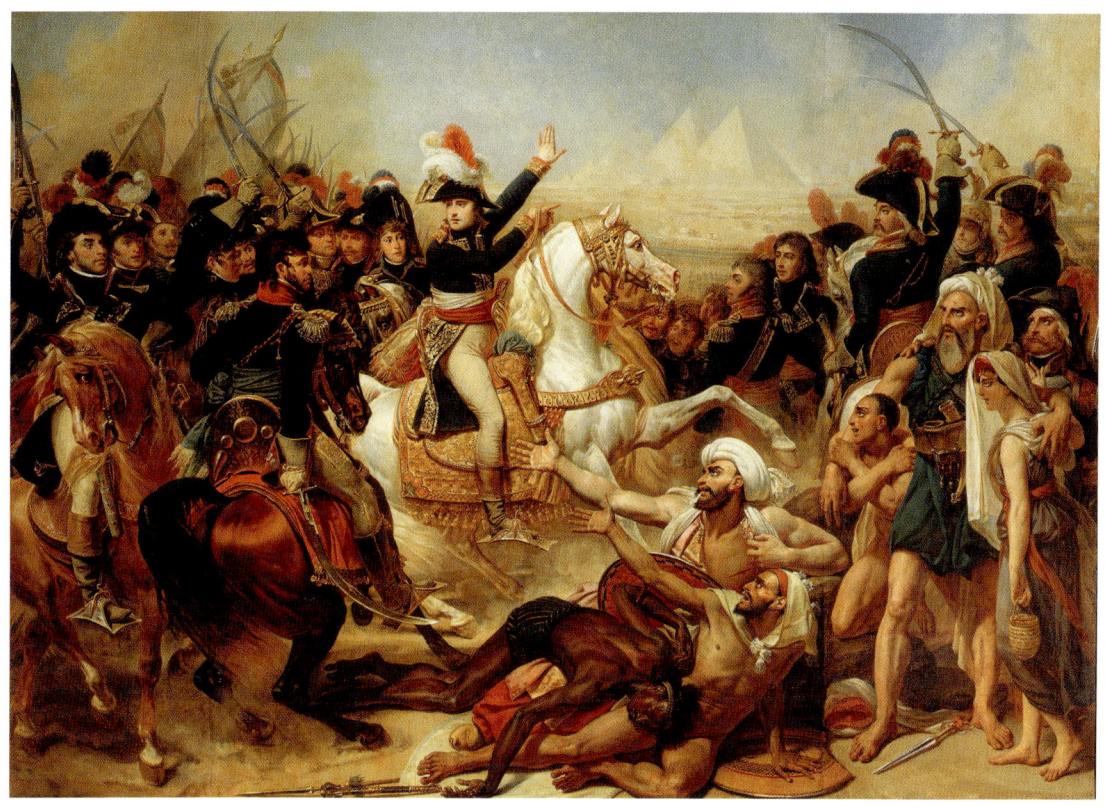

6.17. Antoine-Jean Gros, *Bonaparte Haranguing the Army before the Battle of the Pyramids, July 21 1798*, 1810, oil on canvas, 153⅛ × 198⅞ in. (389 × 505 cm), Châteaux de Versailles et de Trianon, Versailles.

tradition of allegories on the fragility of life and the ultimate vanity of human endeavor, Géricault's return to the theme on an enormously larger scale betokened experiences he could not have foreseen two years before, changes in the actual weather that made the Restoration appear as much a cosmic calamity as a political turn of events.

✳

As Géricault made his way across the Alps to Italy in the autumn of 1816, he traveled in the wake of widespread crop failures, harvests ruined by persistently frigid temperatures and soaking rains. What he could not have known, nor was the science of the time equipped to explain, was that these baleful events stemmed from the volcanic eruption of Mount Tambora in the Indonesian archipelago on April 10, 1815. After a year of high-altitude ash being carried north and west, reduction in solar radiation began unleashing a litany of meteorological and human disasters. As he returned to Paris roughly a year later, a second wave of crop failures had prolonged and compounded the devastation.[16] When David made his brief escape to the Alps in the summer of 1815, as recounted in chapter 3, the eruption of Tambora, locally catastrophic, had yet to make itself felt across the world.

When Lawrence made his way to Vienna and then to Rome, its effects had largely dissipated. But Géricault could not have escaped the volcano's repercussions on either his outbound or return journeys.

While he left no personal account of either passage, there are other records left by travelers over the same regions in the same years. The summer of 1817 in particular attracted English travelers eager to see the Continent after so many years of Napoleonic blockade. One was the Liverpool pastor Thomas Raffles, a sanctimonious reactionary keen to witness the happy effects on the Continent of the tyrant's overthrow (and, oddly enough, brother of Joseph Raffles, the British regional governor who was among the earliest eyewitnesses to Tambora's destructiveness). In his published travel diary, Raffles does his best, but certain encounters confound his optimism. On their initial passage from Paris to Dijon, he relates: "Indeed, we could not but notice the almost total absence of life and activity in the several places through which we had passed, as affording by no means a favorable indication of the improved state of things in the provinces. There was an air of gloom and desertion pervading them. No one was seen in the streets—they looked as if deserted by their population.... The roads have been as much deserted as the towns."[17] Crossing the mountains of the Jura, Raffles finds his admiration of the scenery disturbed by "the great increase in beggars ... chiefly children, and their numbers and their importunity were truly astonishing. At the very slow rate at which we traveled, they were frequently enabled to follow us for a considerable distance, and this they did, entreating in the most piteous accents." Exemplifying Christian charity, he is momentarily relieved "when a little level road allowed us to go on at a quick rate, and thus lose, for a while, the distressing din."[18]

Louis Simond provides another 1817 travelogue along much the same route. A French-born cosmopolitan who spent much of his life in New York, Simond offers more disabused descriptions, beginning with the riots over dearth and bread prices as close to Paris as Sens, an outcome of the failed harvest of the previous year. Beggars likewise impede his carriage, one woman, when [mistakenly] reassured that a successful harvest was imminent, "answered in a tone of despair, *but in the meantime we must die!*"[19] In one Jura village, "all means of subsistence having failed at once," the inhabitants implore Simond for advice about immigrating to the United States.[20] In Switzerland, he witnesses the confiscation of sixteen bags of oats from a smuggler, the formerly free trade between cantons having been blocked in order to protect existing stocks.[21] In the duchy of Baden, he found that "beggars swarm almost as much as in France." And at the Swiss town of Wattwyl, "we understand that many distressed people are dead, if not absolutely of hunger, yet of the consequences. After supporting for some time a miserable existence, on scarcely anything but boiled

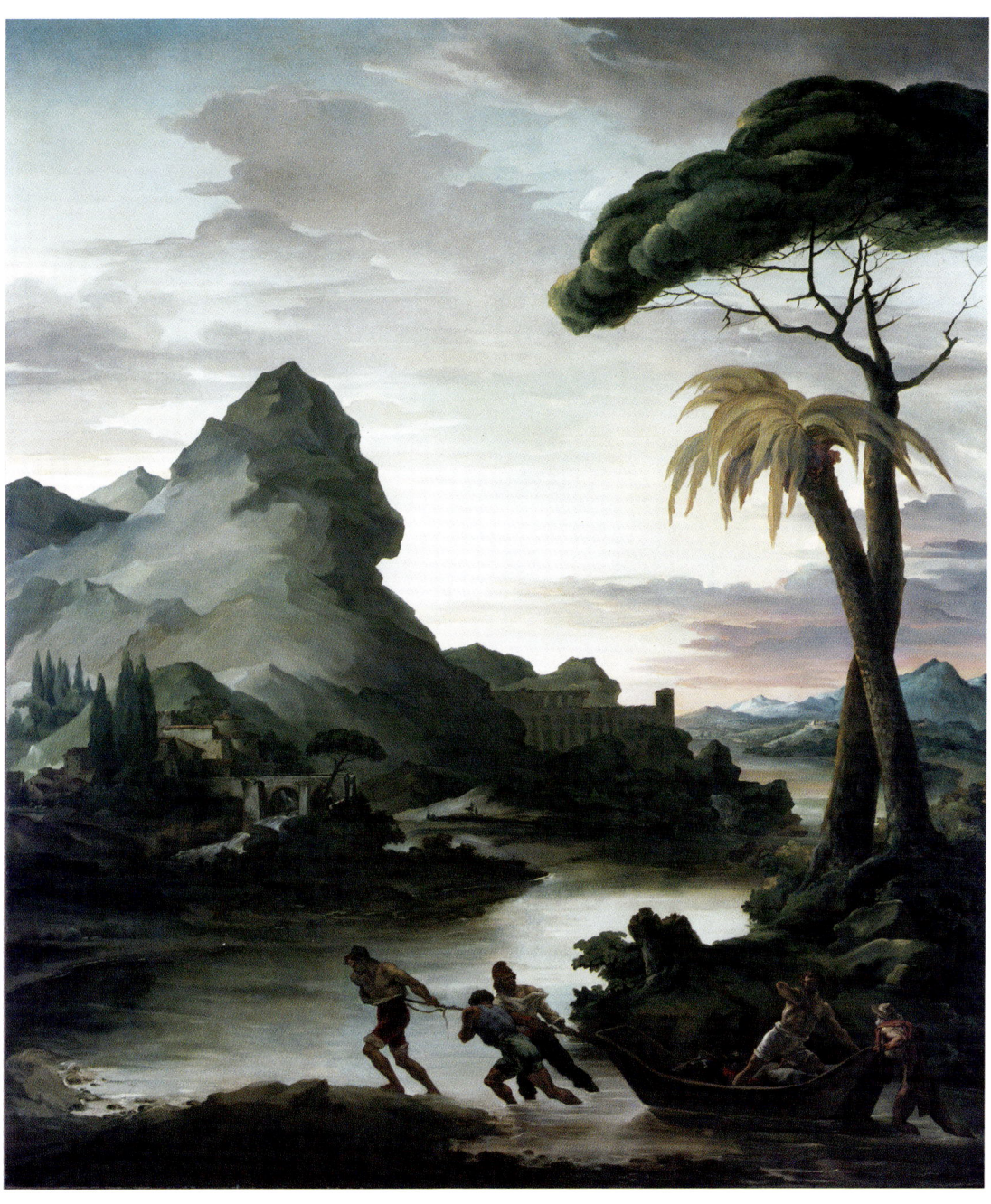

6.18. Théodore Géricault, *Morning: Landscape with Fishermen*, 1818, 98¼ × 85⅝ in. (249.5 × 217.5 cm), Neue Pinakothek, Bayerische Staatsgemäldesammlungen, Munich.

nettles and other herbs ... their extremities swelled, and they perished in a few days."[22]

In the nonspecific, vaguely ancient world that Géricault creates in his three monumental landscapes, these travelers' motifs of destitution, pleading for relief, and fantasies of escape find their place. Keyed to the traditional rubric of the times of day, *Morning*, *Noon*, and *Evening* (but absent *Night*), the paintings reject any trace of the pastoral

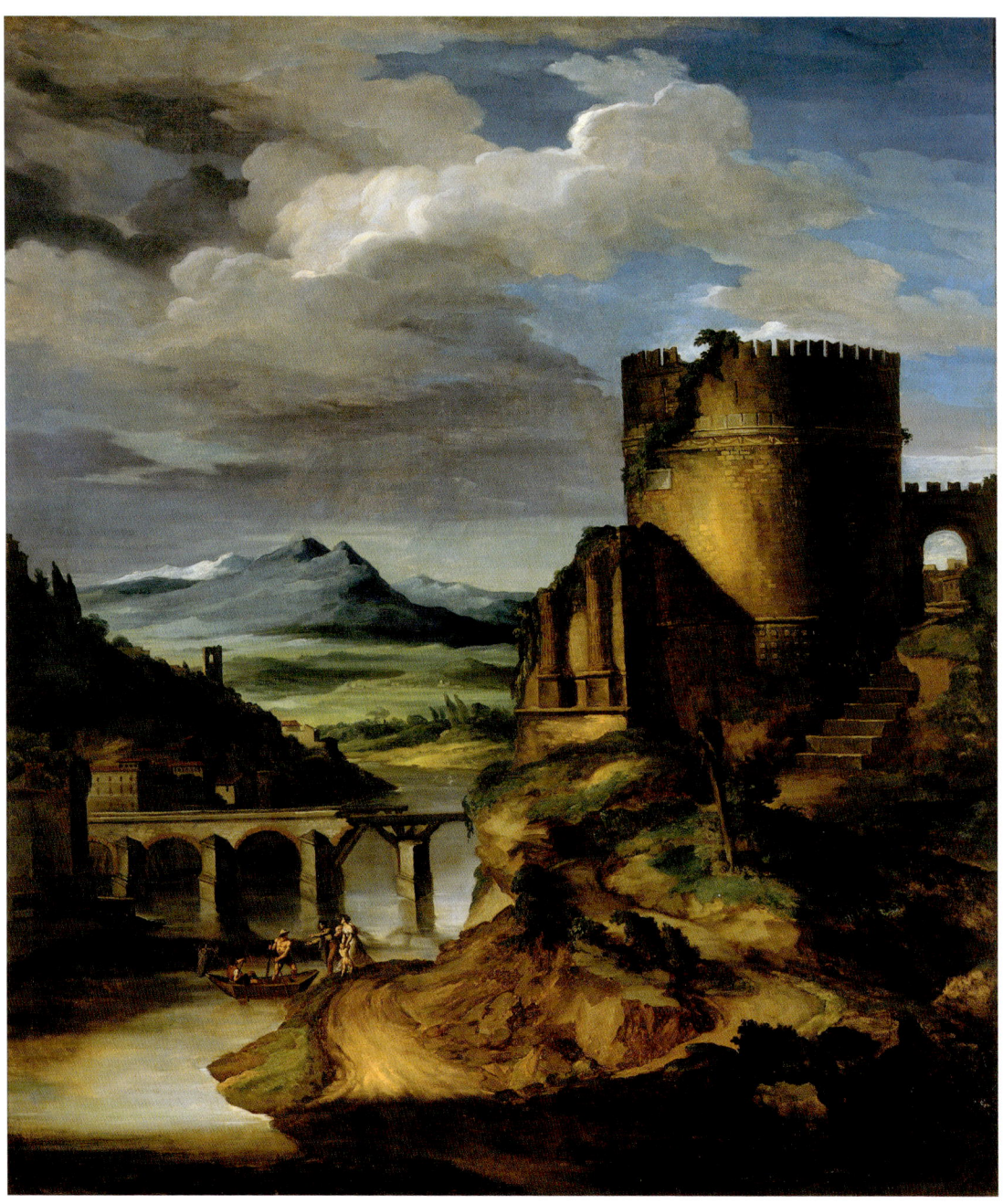

6.19. Théodore Géricault, *Noon: Landscape with Roman Tomb*, 1818, oil on canvas, 98⅜ × 86⅝ in. (250 × 220 cm), Musée du Petit Palais, Paris.

delectation customary in such exercises (figs. 6.18–20). Their gigantic size, some eight feet in height, already confound the domestic connotations of the genre. The world they create thus asserts itself as historically important, but one best characterized as the stilled, morbid aftermath of a deluge where scattered survivors cling to life. As floodwaters drain away, left behind is the muck and a ruined, depopulated world, viewed in a sickly green light redolent of contagion, even with

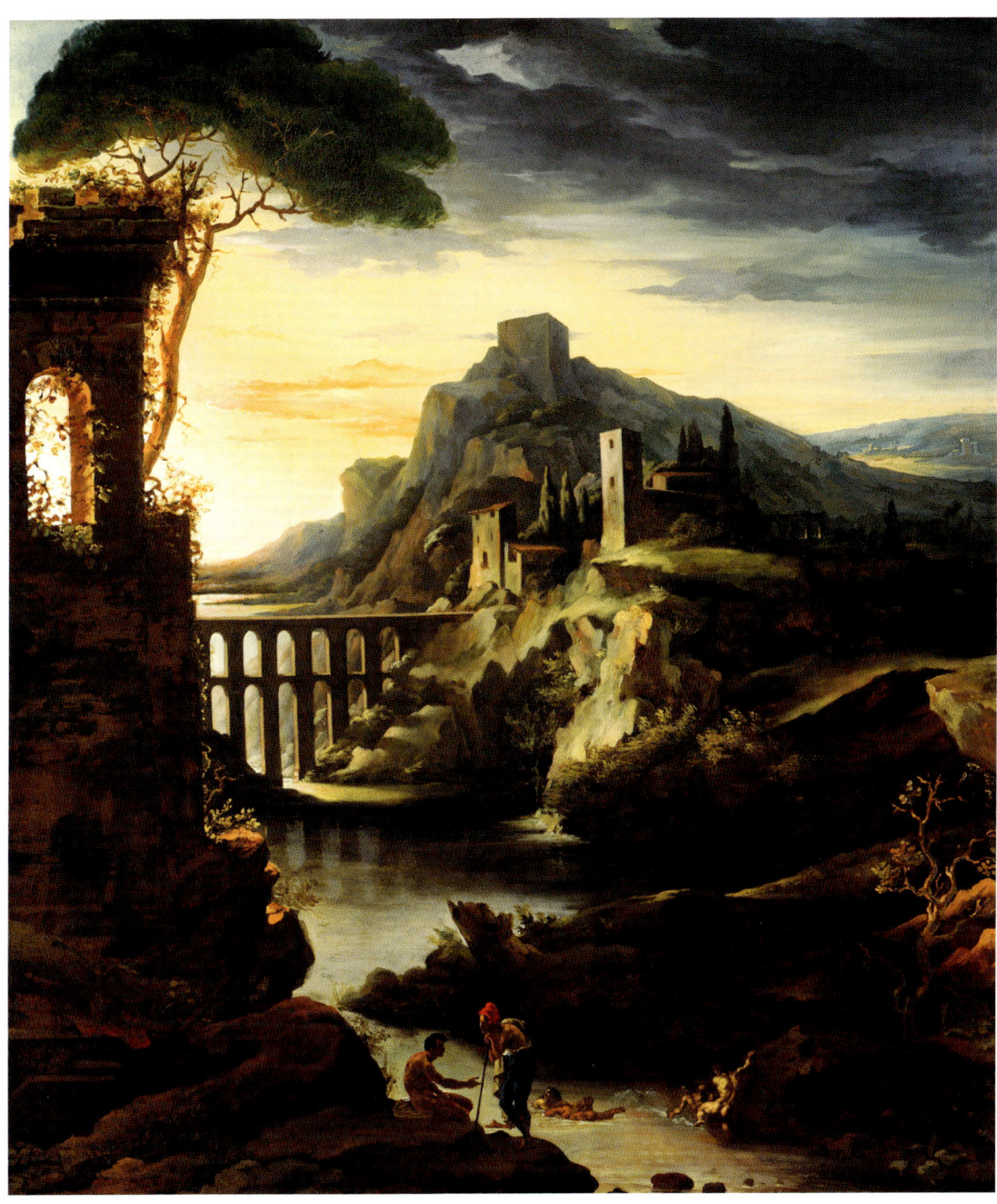

6.20. Théodore Géricault, *Evening: Landscape with an Aqueduct*, 1818, oil on canvas, 98½ × 86½ in. (250.2 × 219.7 cm), Metropolitan Museum of Art, New York.

the sun at its height. In *Morning* (fig. 6.18), five men unaccountably strain to move a small boat out of the shallows. At his bleak *Noon* (fig. 6.19), the broken bridge forces a desperate family of means to plead with an indifferent boatman for passage to some hoped-for refuge. In the backlit figure group occupying the shadowed foreground of *Evening* (fig. 6.20), an outwardly robust naked male makes a pathetic entreaty toward an aged, barefoot vagabond, the younger man's gesture extending to a group of his fellows ambiguously disporting themselves in the water beyond, one group possibly warding the other away from the steep bank.

Géricault deployed the lessons of his Roman sojourn, but the nudity of the figures in *Morning* and *Evening* slips from the Michelangelesque into signs of dispossession and raw exposure to the elements. No evidence survives of any commission or exhibition of the works during the artist's lifetime, making them in all likelihood a lonely, compulsive effort to reconcile the traumatized, post-Tambora condition of rural Europe with the generalizing demands of major art. All else, even when propelled by meticulous scholarship, remains conjectural.[23] But self-evident is an overpowering need on his part to channel his recent experience into expressive forms of commensurable scale and power. His nomadic existence in Rome had restricted his experiments to small-scale exercises; once back in a Montmartre studio, however, he regained free rein to project loss, pain, and discord onto nearly the largest possible scale for, it appears, his own satisfaction (or dissatisfaction) alone.

✳

While these monumental canvases gained Géricault no renewed purchase on the art world of Paris, the time and energy they demanded laid the ground for his turning to the other mortal catastrophe that had been in the news during the nonsummer of 1816. His small *Deluge* of that year had included, in the bare life that remains after storm and flood, a ramshackle raft with clinging castaways as an emblem of vain, dashed hope. In his preparations for the journey to Rome, was he already aware of the foundering of the French frigate *Medusa* on its voyage to Senegal, which occurred on July 2? Of the four hundred on board, only 250 had been accommodated in the ship's lifeboats. The rest were loaded onto a makeshift raft lashed together from planks, spars, and lines taken from the wreckage; of those 150, only fifteen survived. The discovery of the bare complement of survivors by the rescue ship *Argus* came after episodes of mutiny, madness, murder, and cannibalism that touched the horrific extremes of human depravity and pain.

All this became public knowledge by September 13, when a coruscating report by the surviving engineer on board, Alexandre Corréard, had been leaked to the opposition press. But Géricault was then days away from embarking on his Italian journey, and no inkling of interest or knowledge of the *Medusa* survivors' ordeal is evident before he undertakes a vast new canvas on the theme in 1818, only commencing in earnest after completing the three dystopic *Times of Day*.

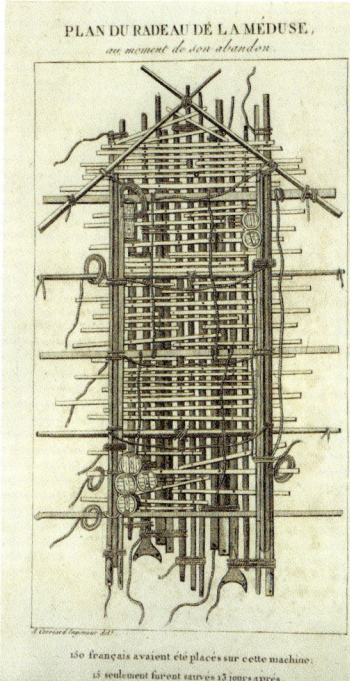
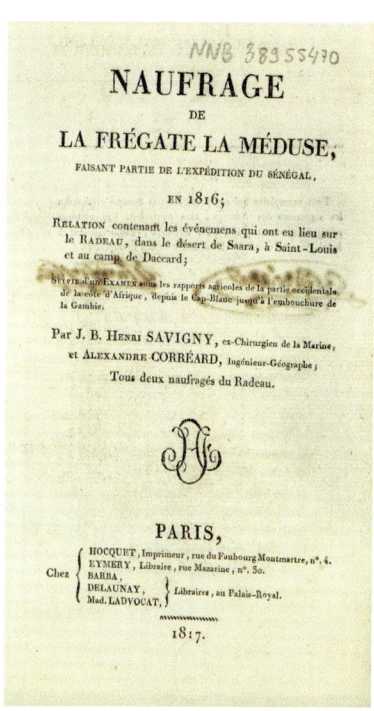

6.21. J. B. Henri Savigny and Alexandre Corréard, *Naufrage de la Frigate La Méduse*, 1817, frontispiece and title page, Bibiothèque nationale de France, Paris.

The horrific story of the raft's occupants has become one of the inescapable narratives of modern art history, so familiar it requires little further rehearsal. For present purposes, its central significance would seem to lie in its status as quintessential allegory of the Restoration. The incompetent admiral responsible for the frigate running aground had been an aristocrat recently returned to France in the retinue of Louis XVIII, then appointed to this command as talented and experienced officers tainted by Bonapartism were shunted aside. It required next to no metaphorical imagination to view the flagship *Medusa* as the ship of state adrift and in peril; indeed, it had in a very real sense been a ship of state, carrying as it did the new governor of Senegal, a colony awarded France at the Congress of Vienna, along with much of his personnel and infrastructure of rule. The abolitionist Corréard well knew that a surreptitious part of the governor's mission was to restart the slave trade. By 1817, a hasty court-martial of the admiral had put the scandal officially to rest, but Corréard with the expedition surgeon Jean-Baptiste-Henri Savigny would not let the matter rest, publishing a book that described and documented their ordeal in greater detail than the leaked report, seeking to keep alive public awareness of its political causes and unresolved ramifications (fig. 6.21).[24] Géricault took much of his material from this source, which included the precise plan of the raft as its frontispiece. And he sought out its authors for firsthand elaboration. As he began studies for the project, he drew one distressed nude male with a military

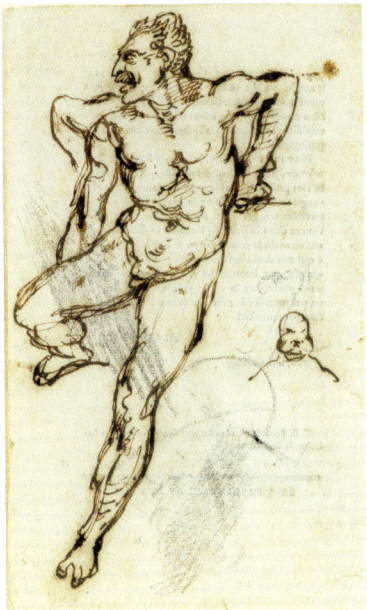
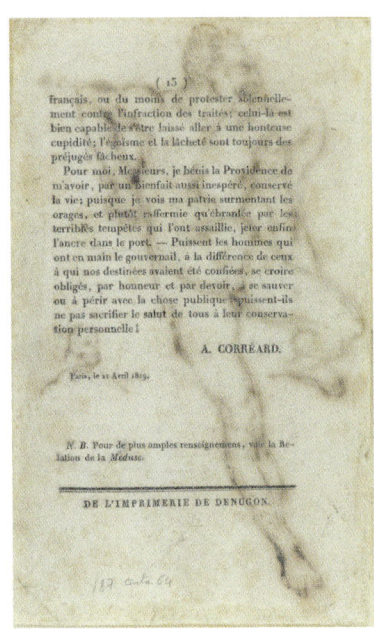

6.22. Théodore Géricault, study for *The Raft of the Medusa* on a page from Savigny and Corréard, *Naufrage de la Frigate La Méduse*, c. 1817, 7⅞ in. (20 cm) h, Musée des Beaux-Arts, Rouen.

mustache directly on the back of one page from their book, its type visibly bleeding through from the other side (fig. 6.22).

While his commitment was topical, documentary in its way, Géricault's project had been long in the making. The trackless expanse of ocean that had trapped the dwindling band of *Medusa* survivors made actual his catastrophic imaginings in the *Deluge*, which established the theme of overwhelming disaster and the terrifying fates of its survivors. The visceral immediacy of battle with ax and knife, of dismemberment and cannibalism (fig. 6.23), readily mapped themselves onto the scenes of butchery and beheading by which he had been so captivated in Rome. In the *Times of Day* landscapes of 1818, he built this theme up and out into a world smothered with despair, punctuated here and there by vestigial vignettes of derelict humanity. The following year, he would restore a revitalized but stripped humanity to the center of his vision in the vast, storied canvas (fig. 6.24) he sent to the Salon of 1819.[25]

For Géricault, as much as for Ingres and Lawrence, the Restoration demanded consolidation on the level of art, but his consolidation refuses the neofeudal symbolic code that Ingres and Lawrence put in place of its nonexistent hero; for Géricault, once the proud wearer of the king's uniform, feudal symbols represented a standing insult to humanity. This he made abundantly clear by a lithograph of 1818 (fig. 6.25) in which a crippled veteran of Napoleon's wars finds himself barred from the Louvre by a mercenary Swiss guard in immaculate kit and uniform. The veteran's tiny combat medal avails him

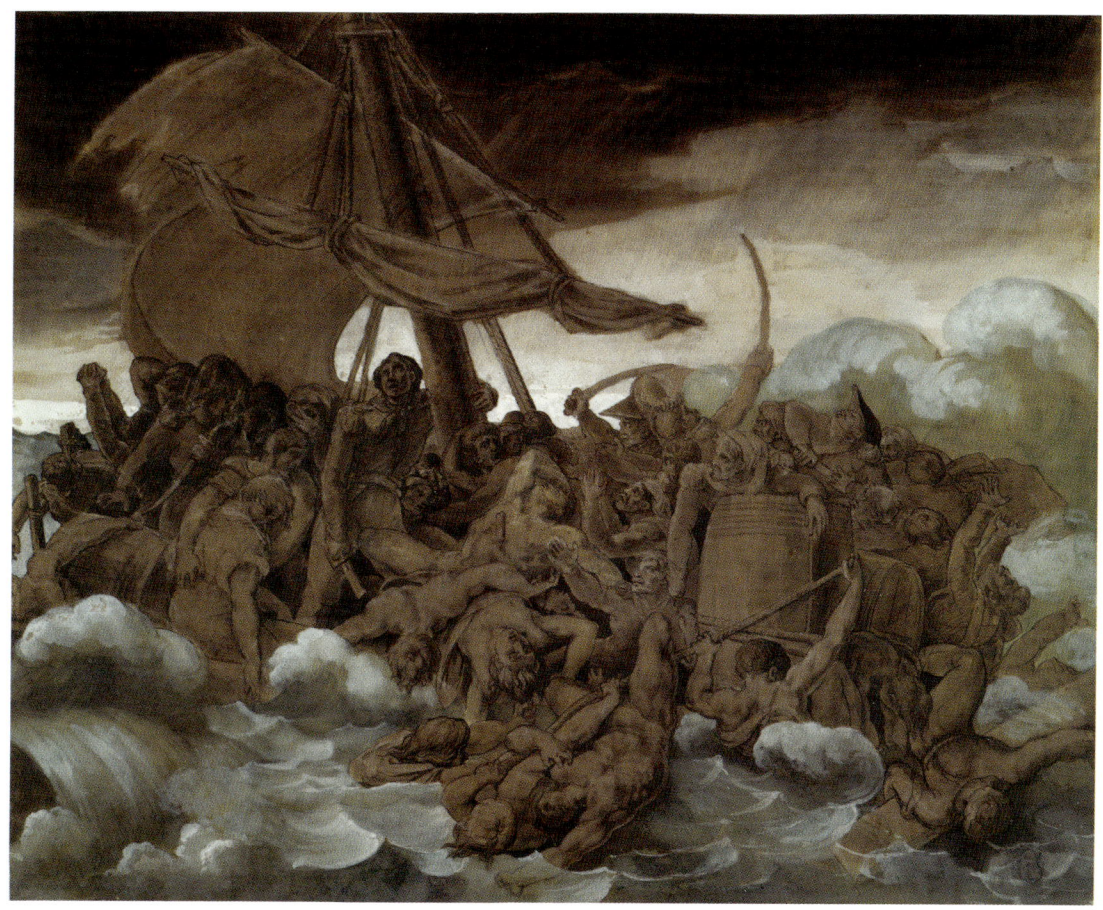

6.23. Théodore Géricault, *Mutiny on the Raft of the Medusa*, 1818–19, black chalk, black crayon, white chalk, brown and blue-green watercolor, and white gouache on brown laid paper, 15 15/16 × 20 1/16 in. (40.5 × 51 cm), Harvard Art Museums/Fogg Museum, Bequest of Grenville L. Winthrop, Cambridge, MA.

(following spread)
6.24. Théodore Géricault, *The Raft of the Medusa*, 1819, oil on canvas, 193 1/4 x 281 7/8 in. (491 × 716 cm), Musée du Louvre, Paris.

nothing and recedes into insignificance compared to the amputated leg, his nonsymbolic mark of intrinsic merit. The raft survivors are likewise so marked as Géricault's confreres. The trappings of rank and order survive among them only as one soiled and discarded remnant of uniform clinging to the edge of the listing, disintegrating platform (fig. 6.24a). Their experience of Restoration had meant only dispersal, disintegration, and desperation: a continuation of warfare's violence by other means. All that is left is the barest, pathetically triumphant solidarity of dispossessed and abandoned souls.

Géricault had not wasted his exposure to the classical monuments in Rome, the artistic models of the kind that Canova and Consalvi had restored to their former pride of place. Amid the virtuoso displays of male anatomy with which he invests the classless stalwarts of the raft, he used his acquired command of the ideal figure to bestow heroic status on a singular redeeming figure, the African sailor, the most dispossessed of them all, whose agile grace signals the distant rescue ship from the pinnacle of the pyramidal cluster of bodies. The Europeans

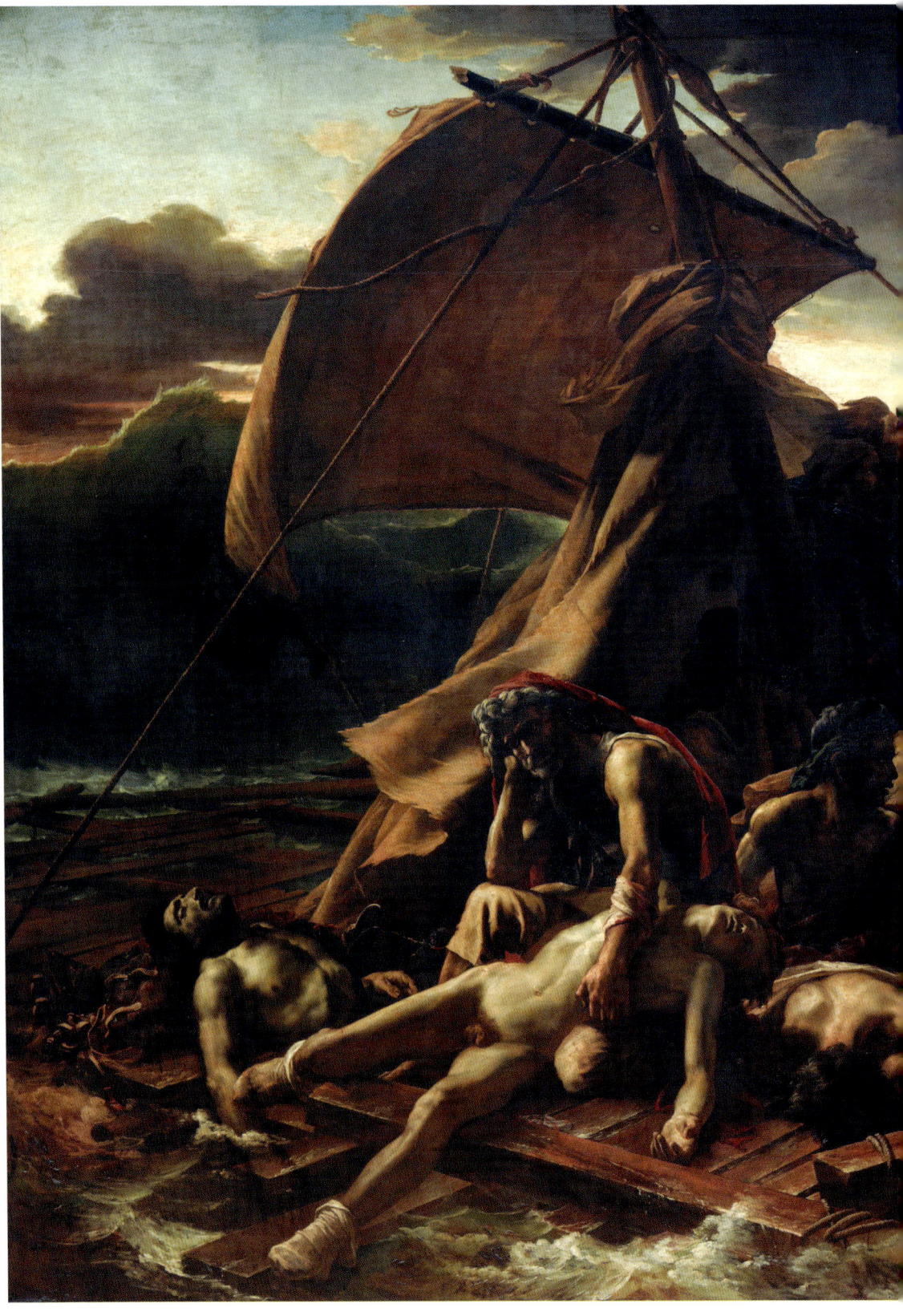

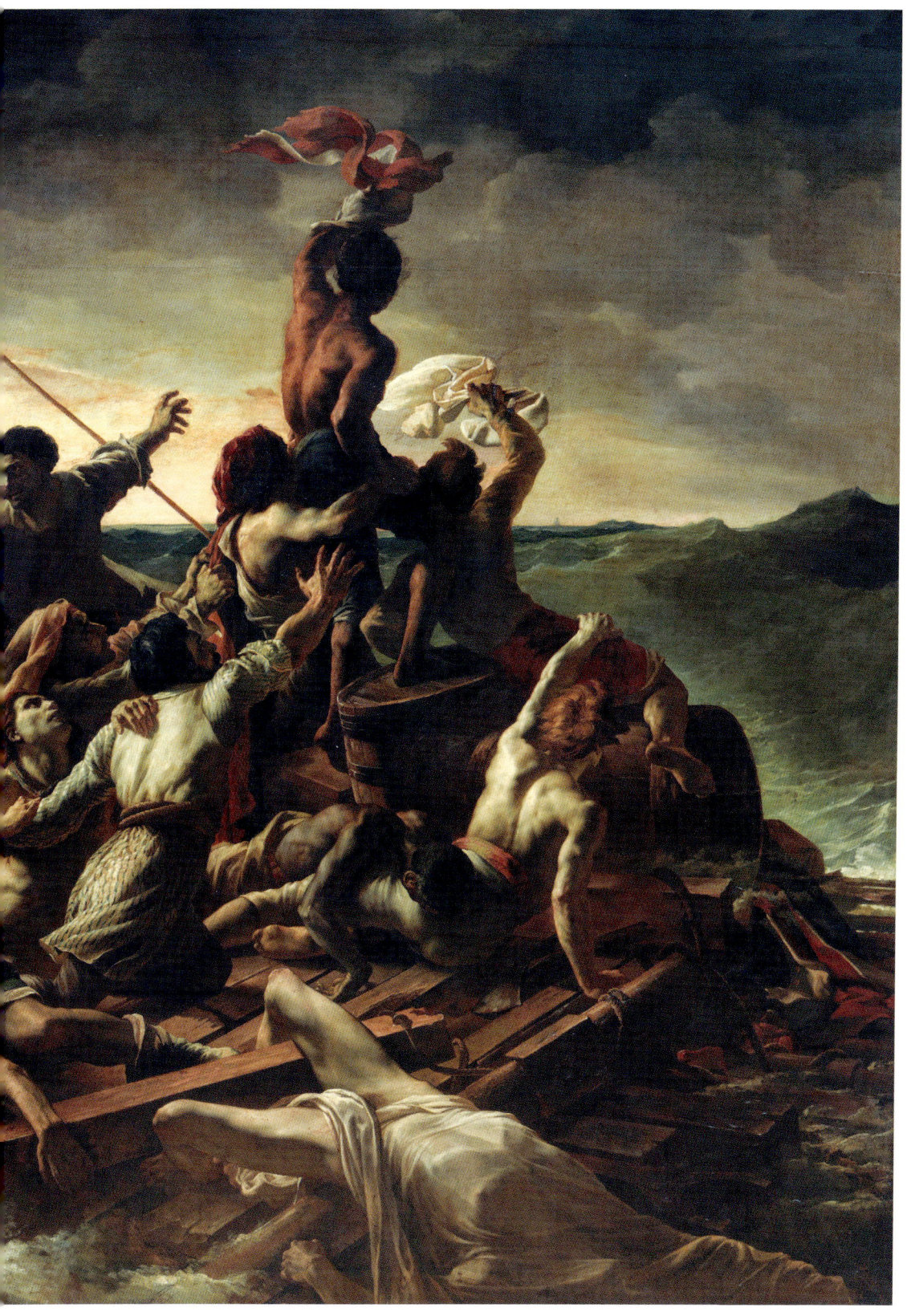

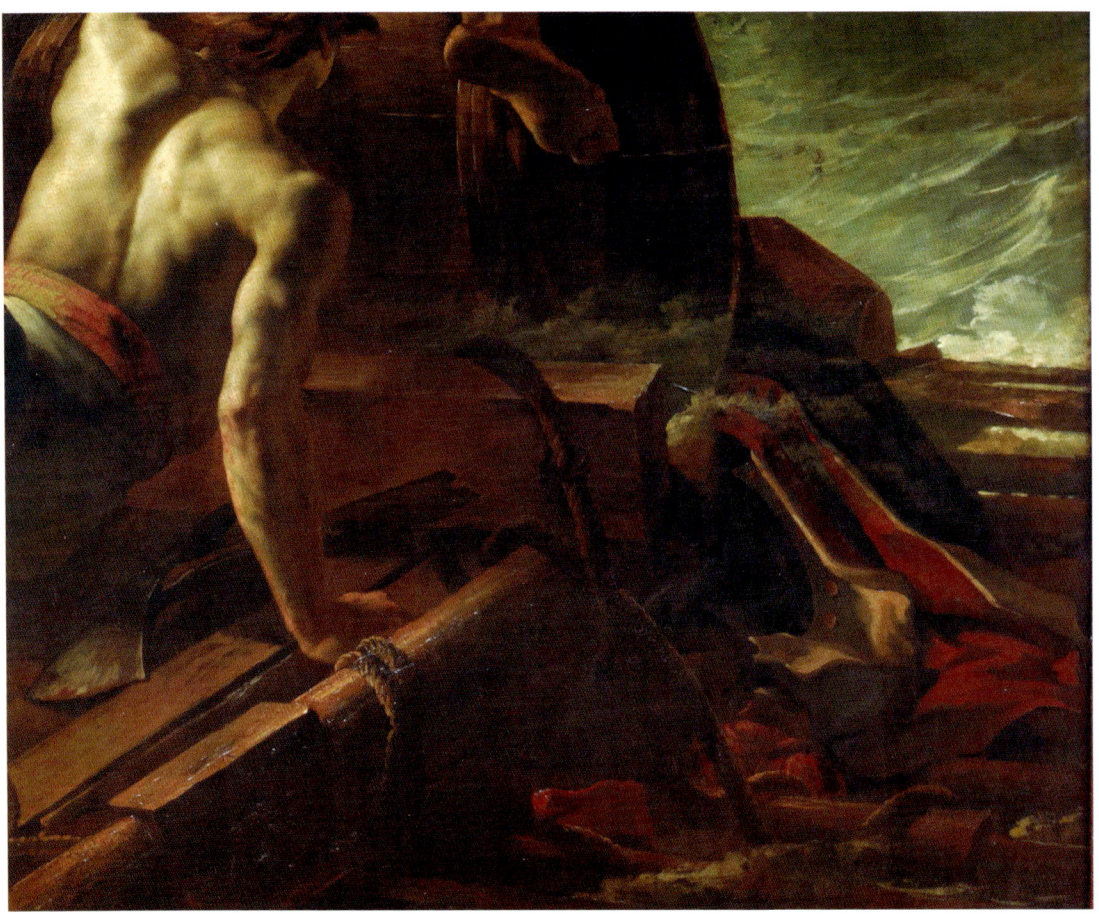

6.24A. Théodore Géricault, *The Raft of the Medusa*, 1819 (detail).

below him extend their arms to support his precarious perch on the tipping barrel, but seem at the same time to be reaching out to touch a holy figure.

The consequent unity of the main group extends to the compelling coherence of the entire composition, which makes its own declaration about the primacy of unmediated human solidarity. But that achievement pressed Géricault's technical abilities past their limitations. In seeking to intensify the dark passages out of which his straining figures emerge—thus rendering the light on the horizon even more salvific—he mixed far too much black bitumen into his medium. The result has been a growing opacity without nuance and the pervasive cracking over much of the work's semiruined surface. A great loss to be sure, but forgoing chapters contain the signal lesson that culminating and consummate work in this period need not announce itself as such; it can and most often does assume the appearance of the provisional or fragmentary.

Such is the case with the cloud of studies and propositions that form the whole of Géricault's project around the *Raft of the Medusa*.

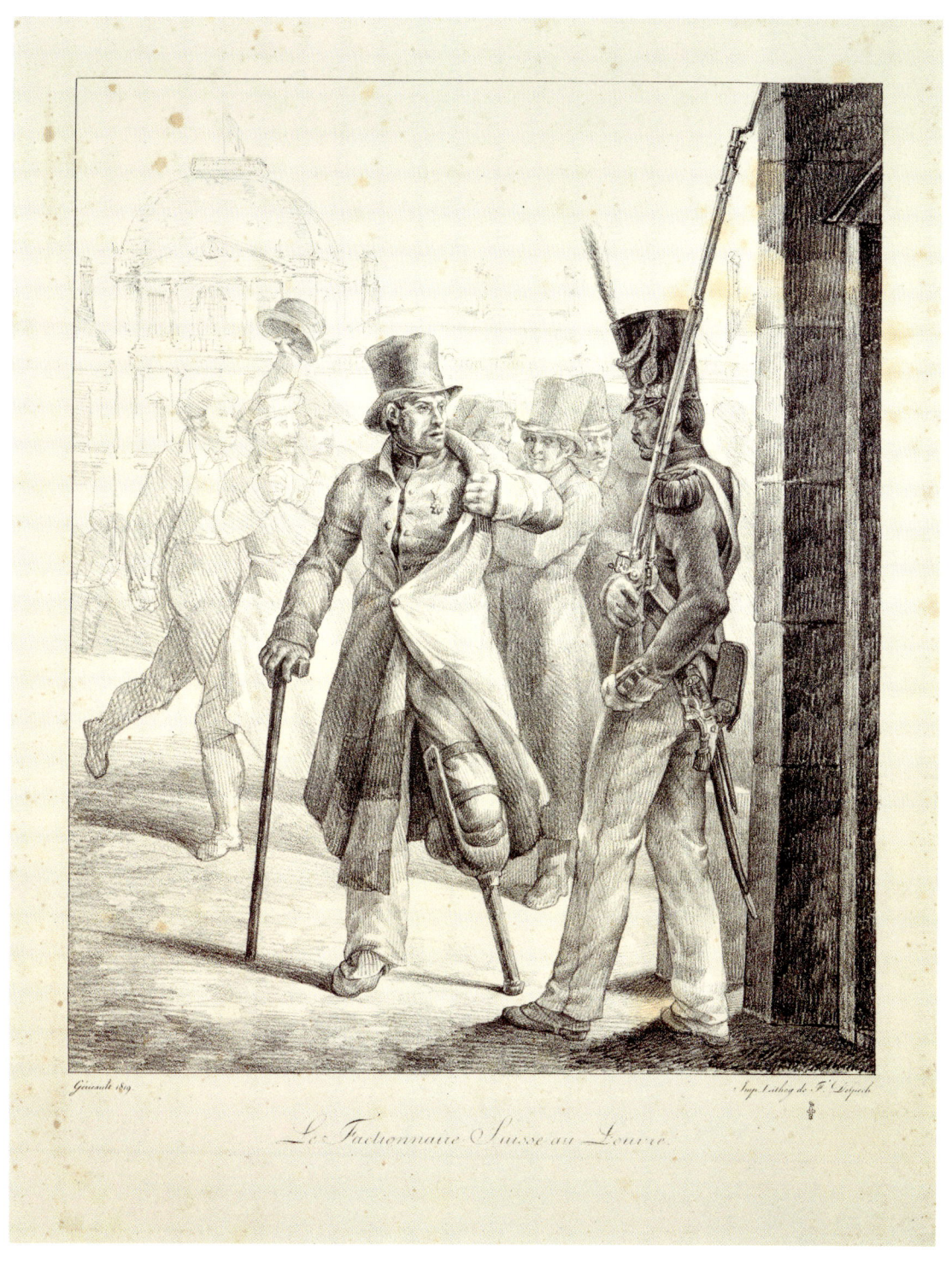

Le Factionnaire Suisse au Louvre

6.25. Théodore Géricault,
The Swiss Guard at the Louvre,
1819, lithograph, 22 × 15⅞ in.
(56 × 40.3 cm), Musée Condé,
Chantilly.

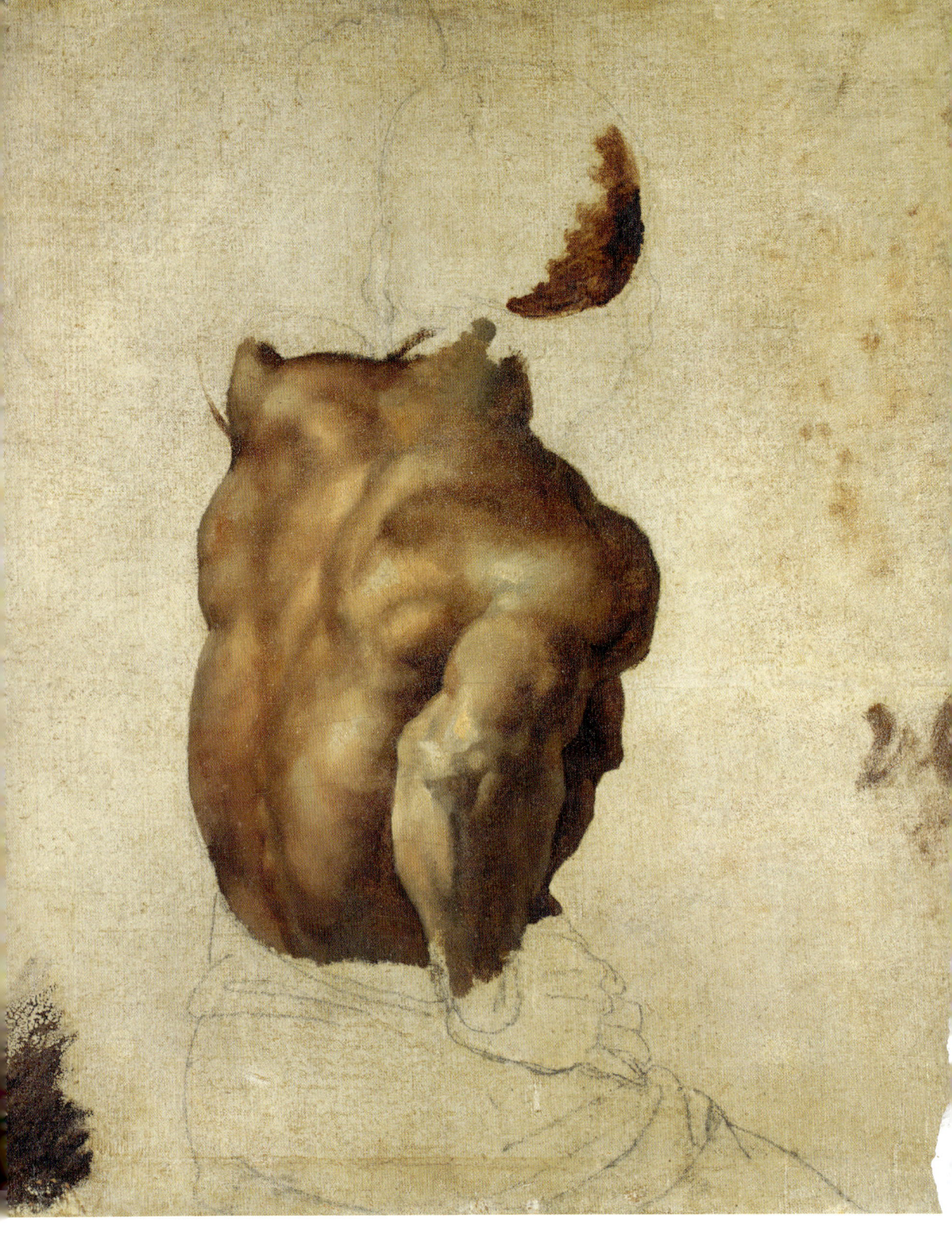

6.26. Théodore Géricault, *African Signaling*, study for *Raft of the Medusa*, 1819, oil on canvas, Musée de Montauban.

Nowhere in his body of work is technical and anatomical mastery so consummately in evidence as in the oil study (fig. 6.26) for the African figure's torso, in its way a standing reproach to the vanity bound up in pretensions to completion or synthesis. Yet synthesize it does, despite the paint being applied with near-microscopic thinness. From that merest membrane of pigment emerges the startling volume of the drastically foreshortened elbow thrusting into virtual space, angular bone and cartilage as palpable as painting can deliver. Pigment seems transmuted into sculpture, and not necessarily sculpture in the abstract: the isolated torso and arm might be for all the world a damaged, hollow ancient bronze, divested of attributes but as eloquent as the great *Belvedere Torso* in stone.

The universality so often claimed for the classical nude is in this modest canvas won by Géricault from the person of the survivor most marked and thereby relegated to insignificance in European eyes. His African model, known to artists by the single name of Joseph, had first made his name as an acrobatic performer, and it shows: in him were embodied the grace, agility, and toned harmonious musculature central to the *beau idéal* of masculine form.[26] The African's feat, as represented on the gargantuan canvas, was to have caught the attention of the ship, but the bare, unadorned silhouette of Géricault's small study enlarges that triumph, making of it a victory over the invidious distinctions of rank that disfigure their bearers: the Restoration unrestored.

Acknowledgments

THREE GREAT SCHOLARLY INSTITUTIONS immeasurably aided the writing of this book. Central to the undertaking was the Center for Advanced Study in the Visual Arts at the National Gallery of Art, Washington. Under its auspices, in spring 2015 I delivered the six A. W. Mellon Lectures in the Fine Arts that were the volume's foundation. For that hugely gratifying opportunity and trust, I am greatly in the debt of the Center's dean, Elizabeth Cropper, and the gallery director, Earl A. Powell III. Therese O'Malley, Peter Lukehart, Faya Causey, and Hayley Plack, among many others, made my stay at CASVA as warm and stimulating as I could have imagined. The generous interest shown by my colleagues among the fellows of the Center and the audiences who so faithfully attended the talks carried me through the subsequent months of revision and rethinking.

It was my great good fortune to have been the first Holly Fellow at the Clark Art Institute during the previous fall when I was preparing the lectures. In every respect, the library of the Clark—its scope, ease of use, and magnificent staff—offers an unsurpassed resource for an art historian immersed in a project like this one. Michael Holly herself, with Marc Gotlieb, Deborah Fehr, and a wonderful class of Clark Fellows all encouraged and enlivened the task of writing. When it came time to re-assess the lectures, I could not have found myself in a better situation than the American Academy in Rome. I enjoyed its James S. Ackerman residency in the fall of 2016, made possible by Director Kimberly Bowes and Mellon Professor Lindsay Harris, to whom I am greatly indebted. Gianpolo Battaglia made all practical problems go away. As so much of *Restoration*, whatever the nationality of the artist in question, is set in the streets, piazze, churches, and palazzi of Rome, the preparation of the book manuscript was inspirited by those surroundings and enriched there by unanticipated discoveries.

Along the converging paths marked David, Géricault, Lawrence, and Ingres, I have been able to join remarkable companions of humbling expertise and acumen: among them Mark Ledbury, Régis Michel, Richard Rand, Philippe Bordes, Alex Potts, Bruno Chénique, Darcy Grimaldo Grigsby, Cassandra Albinson, Mark Hallett, and Susan Siegfried. Students in my seminars at the Institute of Fine Arts have kept these past events alive in the present, with special recognition due Lauren Cannady, William S. Smith, Andrea Bell, Elyse Nelson, Daniella Berman, Alyse Muller, Jason Vrooman, and Marina Kliger. Production of this book was close to ideal thanks to the attention of Michelle Komie, Terri O'Prey, Dawn Hall, Sara Sanders-Buell, and Steven Sears.

The life-adventures in Paris, London, Rome, and Madrid that lie behind these chapters belong to my family—Catherine, Hannah, Emily, Juliet, and Sadie—as much as to me, and their presence sustained as always the research and the writing that followed. All the acknowledgments pages in the world could not convey my gratitude.

Notes

Chapter 1
Moscow Burns/The Pope Comes Home

1 On Lord Douglas as a collector and patron, see A. A. Tait, "The Duke of Hamilton's Palace," *Burlington Magazine* (July 1983): 394–402.

2 On the temporal progress of the work, see the letter of David's student, Jean Suau, cited in Paul Mesplé, "David et ses elèves Toulousains," *Archives de l'art français*, new series, 24 (1969): 100.

3 For such a hearsay report, see Frank Booth Goodrich, *The Court of Napoleon; or, Society under the First Empire: With Portraits of Its Beauties, Wits, and Heroines* (New York: Lippincott, 1875), 301.

4 Quoted in Tait, "Duke of Hamilton's Palace," 401.

5 See Jean Tulard, *Napoléon: Le pouvoir, la nation, la légende* (Paris: Le Livre de Poche, 1997), 137–38.

6 See Tulard, *Napoléon*, 138.

7 The literature on the drawing is undeveloped; for a perceptive, succinct characterization, see David O'Brien, *After the Revolution: Antoine-Jean Gros, Painting and Propaganda under Napoleon* (University Park: Pennsylvania State University Press, 2006), 186. O'Brien's is the indispensable synthetic work on the artist.

8 J. B. Delestre, *Gros et ses ouvrages; ou, Mémoires historiques sur la vie et les travaux de ce célèbre artiste* (Paris, 1845), 233.

9 On the large contributions made by Anne-Louis Girodet and François Gérard to the execution of the Brutus, see Thomas Crow, *Emulation: David, Drouais, and Girodet in the Art of Revolutionary France* (New Haven, CT: Yale University Press, 2006), 109–10.

10 On Gros's self-torment over this issue, see Crow, *Emulation*, 205–6.

11 For the best summary of scholarship on the painting, see Colin T. Eisler, *Paintings from the Samuel H. Kress Collection: European Schools Excluding Italian* (Oxford: Phaidon Press for the Samuel H. Kress Foundation, 1977), 366–73.

12 See Daniel Ternois, *Lettres d'Ingres à Marcotte d'Argenteuil: Dictionnaire* (Nogent-le-Roi: Librairies des Arts et Métiers, 2001), 21.

13 See Lorenz Eitner, *French Paintings of the Nineteenth Century*, part 1 (Washington, DC: National Gallery of Art, 2000), 290–91.

14 J.A.D. Ingres to Charles Marcotte d'Argenteuil (May 26, 1814), in Ternois, *Lettres d'Ingres à Marcotte d'Argenteuil*, 59.

15 Quoted in Henri Lapauze, *Ingres: Sa Vie & Son Oeuvre (1780–1867), d'après des documents inédits* (Paris, 1911), 142.

16 Stendhal, *Rome, Naples et Florence* (Paris, 1826), 572.

Chapter 2
At the Service of Kings, Madrid and Paris, 1814

1 For a summary, see Manuela B. Mena Marqués, ed., *Goya en tiempos de Guerra* (Madrid: Museo Nacional del Prado, 2008), 357–60.

2 On the evolving position and role of the Mamelukes, see Darcy Grimaldo Grigsby, *Extremities: Painting Empire in Post-Revolutionary France* (New Haven, CT: Yale University Press, 2002), 155–62.

3 See Janice Tomlinson, *Goya in the Twilight of Enlightenment* (New Haven, CT: Yale University Press, 1992), 132–33; also Pierre Gassier, *Goya: A Witness of His Times* (Secaucus, NJ: Chartwell, 1983), 226–33.

4 See Chenique, *Géricault: La Folie d'un monde* (Lyon: Musée des Beaux-Arts, 2006), 77.

5 For documents concerning Géricault's cavalry service and the Salon of 1814, see Germain Bazin, *Théodore Géricault: Étude critique, documents, et catalogue raisonné*, vol. 1 (Paris: La Bibliothèque des Arts, 1987), 32–36.

6 See Sylvain Laveissière and Régis Michel, *Géricault* (Paris: Réunion des Musées Nationaux, 1991), 342.

7 For an invaluable reconstruction of the album pages in their original order, see Pierre Rosenberg and Louis-Antoine Prat, *Jacques-Louis David, 1748–1825: Catalogue raisonné des dessins*, vol. 2 (Milan: Leonardo Arte, 2002), 778ff.

8 See A. Th[ibaudeau], *Vie de David, Premier Peintre de Napoléon* (Brussels, 1826), note 21, 110–11. The sheet is

dated 1813 on its recto; see Th[ibaudeau], *Vie de David*, I: 302–3; David would give this sheet to the devoted former pupil Antoine-Jean Gros in 1820.

9 Pliny, *The Natural History*, 36: 48–51.

10 Paul Fréart de Chantelou, *Journal de Voyage du Cavalier Bernin en France*, ed. Jean Paul Guibbert (Paris: Pandora Editions, 1981), June 27, 1665, 45–46. For insight into the significance of this episode, see Rudolf Preimesberger, "Bernini Portraits, Stolen and Non-stolen, in Chantelou's *Journal* and the Bernini *Vite*," in *Bernini's Biographies: Critical Essays*, ed. Maarten Delbeke, Evonne Levy, and Steven F. Ostrow (University Park: Pennsylvania State University Press, 2006), 201–10.

11 The story comes from Etienne Jean Delécluze, *Louis David: Son école et son temps* (Paris, 1855), 232.

12 On the painting, see Paul Spencer-Longurst, "Appelles Painting Campaspe by Jacques-Louis David: Art, Politics, and Honour," *Apollo* 135 (March 1992): 157–62; Philippe Bordes, *Jacques-Louis David: Empire to Exile* (New Haven, CT: Yale University Press, 2005), 225–30.

Chapter 3
Waterloo Sunset, 1815–17

1 For this sequence of events, see Chenique, "Géricault: Une vie," in Laveissière and Michel, *Géricault*, 273–74.

2 Jacques-Louis David to comte Decazes, ministre de la Police Générale, August 14, 1815, cited in Elisabeth Agius-d'Yvoire, "Chronologie," in *Jacques-Louis David, 1748–1825*, ed. Arlette Sérullaz et al. (Paris: Réunion des Musées Nationaux, 1981), 621.

3 See Jules David, *Le Peintre Louis David, 1748–1815: Souvenirs et documents inédits* (Paris: V. Havard, 1880–82), I: 520–21.

4 See Rosenberg and Prat, *Jacques-Louis David, 1748–1825*, 2: 1155–58.

5 David, *Le Peintre Louis David*, 520–21.

6 David, *Le Peintre Louis David*, 527–28.

7 David, *Le Peintre Louis David*, 530.

8 See Daniel Wildenstein and Guy Wildenstein, *Documents complémentaires au catalogue de l'oeuvre de Jacques-Louis David* (Paris: Fondation Wildenstein, 1973), 203–4.

9 David, mémoire addressed to le comte Mercy d'Argenteau, Gouverneur de Bruxelles, in Wildenstein and

Wildenstein, *Documents complémentaires*, 205, where, speaking of his adopted country, he cites "l'excellent esprit de son souverain" and "la sagesse et la modération du Chef de l'Etat."

10 See Laveissière and Michel, *Géricault*, 60–65, 275.

11 Laveissière and Michel, *Géricault*, 275–76.

12 For an account, see Crow, *Emulation*, 47–81, 128–55.

13 See Giovanna Capiletti, "Antoine Jean-Jaen-Baptiste Thomas (Parigi, 1791–1834): Biografia e primo catalogo delle opera," in *Antoine Jean-Baptiste Thomas e il popolo di Roma, 1817–1818*, ed. Angela Maria D'Amelio and Simonetta Tozzi (Rome: Campisano Editore, 2016), 19.

14 See Susan Vandiver Nicassio, *Imperial City: Rome under Napoleon* (Chicago: University of Chicago Press, 2009), 96–98.

15 Antoine-Jean-Baptiste Thomas, *Un an à Rome et dans ses environs: Recueil de dessins lithographiés, représentant les costumes, les usages et les cérémonies civiles et religieuses des états romains, et généralement tout ce qu'on y voit de remarquable pendant le cours d'une année* (Paris: Firmin Didot, 1823).

16 Charlotte Anne Eaton, *Rome, in the Nineteenth Century* (Edinburgh: Printed by James Ballantyne, for Archibald Constable, 1820), 3: 240.

17 He obviously thought that wide interval between ax and scaffold so important he erased a figure to the left of the main group.

18 Eaton, *Rome, in the Nineteenth Century*, 3: 240.

19 Eaton, *Rome, in the Nineteenth Century*, 3: 236–37.

Chapter 4
The Religion of Ancient Art from London to Paris to Rome, 1815–19

1 The literature on Consalvi, given his large historical importance, is surprisingly thin. The best modern synthesis is John Martin Robinson, *Cardinal Consalvi, 1757–1824* (London: Bodley Head, 1987).

2 Quoted in Robinson, *Cardinal Consalvi*, 122–23.

3 For a good summary of these circumstances, see Christopher M. S. Johns, *Antonio Canova and the Politics of Patronage in Revolutionary and Napoleonic Europe* (Berkeley: University of California Press, 1998), 171–74; see also the well-documented account of Katherine Eustace, "'Questa Scabrosa Missione': Canova in Paris and London," in *Canova: Ideal Heads*, ed. Katherine Eustace (Oxford: Ashmolean Museum,

1997), 9–15; on German actions and attitudes, see Bénédicte Savoy, "'Une naufrage de toute un époque': Regards allemands sur les restitutions de 1814–1815," in *Dominique-Vivant Denon: L'Oeil de Napoléon*, ed. Pierre Rosenberg (Paris: Réunion des Musées Nationaux, 1999), 258–67.

4 See Isabelle Leroy-Jay Lemaistre, "Le Musée du Louvre," in *Napoléon et le Louvre*, ed. Sylvain Laveissière (Paris: Réunion des Musées Nationaux, 2002), 175–97.

5 On the nuptial consecration of the museum, see Anne Dion-Tenenbaum, "Le marriage de Napoléon I et de Marie-Louis," in Laveissiére, *Napoléon et le Louvre*, 95–106.

6 On Zix, see Régis Spiegel, "Benjamin Zix, ami et collaborateur de Vivant Denon," in Rosenberg, *L'Oeil de Napoléon*, 272.

7 See Peter Zamoyski, *Rites of Peace: The Fall of Napoleon and the Congress of Vienna* (New York: Harper Perennial, 2008), 514.

8 A. Robertson, *Letters and Papers of Andrew Robertson, A.M.*, ed. E. Robertson (London, 1895), September 21, 1815, 244; see also Lawrence's similar sentiments in a letter written to Joseph Farington, January 11, 1814, months before Napoleon's first abdication. Archives of the Royal Academy of Art, London, LAW/2/56.

9 Quoted in Robinson, *Cardinal Consalvi*, 121.

10 Richard Reinagle to Dawson Turner, November 23, 1815; Dawson Turner Papers, Trinity College, Cambridge, quoted in Eustace, *Canova: Ideal Heads*, 19.

11 Thomas Phillips to Dawson Turner, November 10, 1815; Dawson Turner Papers, Trinity College, Cambridge, quoted in Eustace, *Canova: Ideal Heads*, 19.

12 Robertson, *Letters and Papers*, September 24, 1815, 251.

13 Consalvi also visited London after Napoleon's abdication, in full cardinal's regalia despite the legal ban on Roman Catholic ecclesiastical dress, in order to make a maximal "coup d'éclat"; see Robinson, *Cardinal Consalvi*, 102–9.

14 A. Aspinall, ed., *The Letters of King George IV, 1812–1830* (Cambridge: Cambridge University Press, 1938), 1: 439.

15 Stewart had needed to cajole Lawrence into crossing the channel in order to see the Napoleonic collections before their partial dispersal. He wrote from Vienna early in January 1819 with a rare note of melancholy (to J. J. Angerstein, January 3, 1819) in D. E. Williams, *The Life and Correspondence of Sir Thomas Lawrence* (London: Henry Colburn and Richard Bentley, 1831), 2: 129:

"To visit Rome has been one of those daydreams that I have frequently indulged in; and the circumstances under which I may now gratify that wish, are, perhaps, the most favorable that could have been imagined, unless I had procured an ample fortune and proceeded thither at my entire leisure. Yet I will own, that, either from my unfitness for such enterprise in travelling, or from the proposition not forming part of the original plan, and therefore being unprovided for, in my professional arrangements at home, in which indeed this journey to Vienna was not in my contemplation— from these and many home-feelings, I have certainly had less pleasure in the anticipation of this extended close of my mission, than perhaps it is grateful in me to feel."

16 Williams, *Life and Correspondence of Sir Thomas Lawrence*, 2: 129.

17 James Northcote, quoted in Olivar Millar, *The Later Georgian Pictures in the Collection of Her Majesty the Queen* (London: Phaidon, 1969) 1: xxxiv; Millar provides an excellent, succinct summary (xxxiv–xxxv) of the entire venture.

18 Thomas Lawrence to Joseph Farington (November 5, 1818), in Williams, *Life and Correspondence of Sir Thomas Lawrence*, 2: 109–10. In the satisfied tone he maintained throughout his journey, Lawrence wrote: "The building itself is of vast size, and the length and height of the gallery and the portions of it reserved for me, are in proportion to it. It has three large windows, one north, and though it is of great depth, from an excellent German stove, it is of the most temperate heat throughout."

19 Lawrence may have been providing some symbolic compensation for the recent death of the subject's father, resident in Italy, where he had dissipated the family fortune on palaces and works of art. When his body was returned to the Suffolk family seat of Ickworth, owing to sailors' superstitions about carrying corpses, it came in a box labeled "antique statuary"; see Caroline Chapman and Jane Dormer, *Elizabeth and Georgiana: The Duke of Devonshire and His Two Duchesses* (London: John Murray, 2002), 143, 162.

20 See Robinson, *Cardinal Consalvi*, 144–45.

21 Robinson, *Cardinal Consalvi*, 147–51.

22 Lawrence to Farington (July 2, 1819), Archive of the Royal Academy of Art, London, LAW/3/52; partially transcribed in Williams, *Life and Correspondence of Sir Thomas Lawrence*, 2: 196.

23 Physical investigation of the painting is needed in order to account for the obvious enlargement of the canvas to match the dimensions of the Pius VII portrait, whether this was done in Rome or later as preparation for their installation in Windsor Castle.

24 On Elizabeth Foster, Duchess of Devonshire, in Rome, the most complete account is Chapman and Dormer, *Elizabeth and Georgiana*, 224–61; see also Dorothy Margaret Stuart, *Dearest Bess: The Life and Times of Lady Elizabeth Foster afterwards Duchess of Devonshire from Her Unpublished Journals and Correspondence* (London: Methuen, 1955), 199–245.

25 Caro George to Elizabeth Foster, March 1818, quoted in Stuart, *Dearest Bess*, 224.

26 Lawrence to Farington (July 2, 1819), transcribed in Williams, *Life and Correspondence of Sir Thomas Lawrence*, 2: 194.

27 Lawrence to Farington (July 2, 1819), transcribed in Williams, *Life and Correspondence of Sir Thomas Lawrence*, 2: 194.

28 Williams, *Life and Correspondence of Sir Thomas Lawrence*, 2: 196; Farington, in his diary entry for December 21, 1819, notes the reports of a returning traveler from Rome, which suggest that Lawrence took care to secure positive public response: "He had completed the whole lengths of the Pope and Cardinal Gonsalves [Consalvi], both sitting figures and finely painted—with these he also had his portraits of the Emperor of Russia and Austria and others and they were placed for inspection in a room as in a gallery." Kathryn Cave, ed., *The Diary of Joseph Farington* (New Haven, CT: Yale University Press, 1984), 15: 5439.

29 Lawrence to unidentified female recipient (June 26, 1819), reproduced in Williams, *Life and Correspondence of Sir Thomas Lawrence*, 2: 186.

30 See Rudolf Preimesberger, "Bernini Portraits, Stolen and Nonstolen, in Chantelou's *Journal* and the Bernini *Vite*," in Delbeke et al., *Bernini's Biographies*, 201–4.

31 See Robinson, *Cardinal Consalvi*, 128–37.

32 Sir Walter Scott, *Paul's Letters to His Kinfolk* (Edinburgh, 1916), 329.

Chapter 5
The Laboratory of Brussels, 1816–19

1 The best source on Navez is Denis Coekelberghs, *François-Joseph Navez: La nostalgie de l'Italie* (Brussels: Snoeck-Ducaju and Zoon, 1999); see also M. L. Alvin, *Fr. J. Navez: Sa vie, ses oeuvres et sa correspondance* (Brussels, 1870).

2 See Coekelberghs, *François-Joseph Navez*, 27–29.

3 See Arlette Sérullaz, *Gérard, Girodet, Gros: David's Studio* (Paris: Musée du Louvre, 2005), 86.

4 See Coekelberghs, *François-Joseph Navez*, 29–30.

5 See the correspondence of the David pupil of the era, Pierre-Théodore Suau, quoted in Paul Mesplé, "David et ses élèves toulousiains," *Archives de l'Art Français*, new series, 24 (1969): 101–2: on July 28, 1813, Suau writes: "Si je ne me trompe, le tableau sera de M. David et compagnie."

6 See Bordes, *Jacques-Louis David: Empire to Exile*, 239–41.

7 See Bordes, *Jacques-Louis David: Empire to Exile*, 242–43.

8 Jacques-Louis David to Joseph-Denos Odevaere, January 21, 1818, inv. no. 2003-A. 1234, fol. IV, Fondation Costodia, Paris; I owe this reference to the research of Mark Ledbury.

9 For a summary of the inconclusive attempts to discover some conventional logic to the assembly of figures, see Bordes, *Jacques-Louis David: Empire to Exile*, 276.

10 David to Odevaere, fol. IV: "J'ai fait depuis votre depart trente deux dessins répartis en huit cadres contenant chacun quatre dessins; ce sont des croquis, des caprices, j'ai commencé d'abord sans pretention, je jetois sur le papier les folies qui me passoient par la tête."

11 Eyewitness descriptions of David's actual drawing practice at this moment have not yet come to light, but the letters of Joseph Suau from the years immediately preceding David's exile are suggestive. As Mesplé ("David et ses élèves toulousiains," 95–96) presents their observations:

"Il n'y a pas à proprement parler de manière dominante, les élèves dessinent indifféremment sur du papier de couleur ou blanc; celui-ci est cependant plus généralement en usage; nous massons avec du crayon notre figure au fur et à mesure, mais solidement: l'on ne se sert presque pas de tortillons. M. David aime que le dessin soit gras et moelleux, il n'aime pas les petits détails" (October 7, 1810).

"M. David préfère que l'on fasse noir que blafard, il dit que si l'on fait froid étant jeune, on fera comme glace dans un âge plus avancé" (May 21, 1811). En peinture: "Il ne veut pas que l'on adoucisse; les blaireaux sont bannis de l'atelier à perpétuité" (April 28, 1811).

"M. David ne veut pas que l'on fasse des dessins finis d'après l'antique sur des grandes feuilles, il veut que l'on se serve de livres de croquis, par ce moyen, dit-il on étudie sans se fatiguer; aujourd'hui on dessine une tête, demain, une rotule, une jambe, etc., c'est de cette manière que l'on doit étudier l'antique" (December 1, 1811).

12 See David, *Le Peintre Louis David*, 1: 565–66: "Quant à David, il passait, comme à Paris, Presque toutes les soirées au theater. Sa place, à la salle de la monnaie, était bien connue des habitués qui avaient soin de la lui conserver si quelque étranger se disposait à l'occuper. Il trouvait dans cette distraction un souvenir de Paris, car les artistes des Français ou des Bouffons, comme Talma et Mme Catalani, venait souvent donner des representations à Bruxelles. Il savourait alors des operas italiens dont il toujours enthousiaste. Car son amour pour la musique ne l'avait pas abandonné; et, souvent au foyer du theater, il parlait encore du goût qu'il avait pour cet art, dans lequel, s'il avait cultivé, il se serait, disait-il avec regret, plus distingué que dans celui de la peinture."

13 David, *Le Peintre Louis David*, 1: 566: "Les jours où le theater était fermé il restait, dans la grande pièce qui servait de salon et salle à manger, décorée du *Mont Sait-Bernard* et du *Portrait du Napoléon dans sa* cabinet, à composer et à éxécuter des dessins à crayon noir."

14 David provided explicit instructions that his description of the subject be displayed adjacent to the canvas when it was exhibited in late July 1819: "le peintre a choisi l'instant ou Achille s'oppose à Agamemnon au moment qu'il conduit sa fille Iphigénie pour être immoleée. Cette fureur d'Achille suspend les larmes de Clytemnestre, et lui fait entrevoir une lueur d'espérence en faveur de sa fille." Letter dated July 24, 1819, offered for sale by Bonhams and Butterfields, San Francisco, November 2005.

15 See Coekelberghs, *François-Joseph Navez*, 30.

16 J. L. David to "monsieur le Bourgmestre," July 3, 1819, Brussels (cited in David, *Le Peintre Louis David*, 1: 555–56): "Ces ouvrages sont le fruit de la tranquilité d'esprit que je partage avec les heureux habitants de cet empire, et, pour vous dire toute la vérité, je vous avouerai que je ne prends jamais le pinceau sans bénir le sage Souverain qui me la procure."

17 David, *Le Peintre Louis David*, 1: 555–56: "Et sans faire le savant, qu'il me soit permis de m'écrier avec Virgile."

18 Jean Racine, *Iphigénie* (1674), 4.6, in Racine, *Iphigenia/ Phaedra/Athaliah*, trans. John Caincross (Harmondsworth: Penguin, 1970).

19 Racine, *Iphigénie* (1674), 4.6, in Racine, *Iphigenia/ Phaedra/Athaliah*.

20 The link to Racine has been made by Dorothy Johnson, *Jacques-Louis David: Art in Metamorphosis* (Princeton, NJ: Princeton University Press, 1993), 258–60.

21 See note 14 this chapter.

22 Modified trans. Samuel Butler (1898), http://classics .mit.edu/Homer/iliad.1.i.html.

23 J. L. David to Navez, March 22, 1818, cited in David, *Le Peintre Louis David*, 1: 555: "Il est bien difficile de mettre ensemble des figures coupées sans faire auparavant un ensemble complet de movement general de la figure."

24 "La persecution de M. David contre Ingres est trop forte. Ingres est un talent et surtout un homme de gout comme M. David lui-même. Quant à l'imiter, je n'y ai jamais pensé." Quoted in Alvin, *Fr. J. Navez*, 146–47.

25 Decree of French National Convention, 27 Pluviose year II (February 15, 1794).

Chapter 6
Redemption in Rome and Paris, 1818–20

1 Navez, letter of August 12, 1819, in Alvin, *Fr. J. Navez*, 116–17: "Ce qui est surtout incommode, c'est la chaleur excessive que nous avons depuis près de deux mois … Pas une goutte de pluie depuis quatre mois et demi."

2 Navez, letter of August 12, 1819, in Alvin, *Fr. J. Navez*, 117: "Je me fie à ma bonne étoile et ma bonne santé, et surtout au regime excellent que j'observe: peu d'eau, deux bouteilles et demie de vin par jour; je mange peu, mais toujours de bonne viande rotie."

3 Navez, letter of October 20, 1819, in Alvin, *Fr. J. Navez*, 118–19: "Notre ministre et sa famille sont venus nous voir; ils ont paru enchantés de nos travaux, entre autres d'une Agar que j'ai faite. Le minister voulait l'avoir; mais, comme je n'en suis pas complètement satisfait, et que je n'ai pas voulu m'exposer aux critiques des Allemands qui fréquentent la legation, et meme de nos compatriots, je lui a proposé de le faire en grand."

4 See Keith Andrews, *The Nazarenes: A Brotherhood of German Painters in Rome* (New York: Hacker, 1988), 29.

5 See Robinson, *Cardinal Consalvi*, 155.

6 Navez, letter of January 4, 1818, quoted in Denis Coekelberghs, *Les peintres belges a Rome de 1700 a 1830* (Brussels: l'Insitut historique belge de Rome, 1976), 259: "Les Allemands ici aiment à se faire remarquer: ils affectent de s'habiller comme Raphaël; ils portent la toque de velours, une ceinture, une épée, une plume sur la tête. Ils cherchent les tableaux les plus gothiques et disent que Raphaël a gaté la peinture. Ils sont ici la risée de tout le monde."

7 Navez, letter of April 1818 to Donat de Hemptinne, quoted in Alvin, *Fr. J. Navez* 146–47: "Je ne parlerai plus de M. Ingres à M. David; je suis loin de vouloir suivre sa manière, car elle est goûtée de si peu de monde que je crèverais de faim si j'en tâtais. Elle ne peut ête appréciée que par un petit nombre d'artistes qui ont

un degré de delicatessen et de sentiment au-dessus du vulgaire."

8 On Ingres's studios and pattern of residence in this period, see Christian Omodeo, "Rome, 1806–1820: Ingres et le monde des arts," in *Ingres, un homme à part?: Entre carrière et mythe, la fabrique du personage*, ed. Claire Barbillon et al. (Paris: École du Louvre, 2009), 256–69.

9 See Bruno Chenique, "Géricault: Une Vie," in Régis Michel and Sylvain Laveissière, *Géricault* (Paris: Réunion des Musées Nationaux, 1991), 278.

10 See Susan Siegfried, *Ingres: Painting Reimagined* (New Haven, CT: Yale University Press, 2009), 298–301.

11 Siegfried, *Ingres*, 303.

12 At the time of their making, the portraits were intended to be displayed in Carlton House on Pall Mall, the prince regent's London residence; see Millar, *Later Georgian Pictures*, xxxv.

13 Thomas Lawrence, letter of May 19, 1819, quoted in Williams, *Life and Correspondence of Sir Thomas Lawrence*, 2: 163.

14 See the astute discussion of the painting's genesis in Grigsby, *Extremities*, 162–63.

15 For the most thorough study of these paintings, see Gary Tinterow, "Géricault's Heroic Landscapes: The Times of Day," *Metropolitan Museum of Art Bulletin* (Winter 1990–91).

16 See Patrick Webb, "Emergency Relief during Europe's Famine of 1817: Anticipated Responses to Today's Humanitarian Disasters," Tufts Nutrition Discussion Paper no. 14 (September 2002): http://nutrition.tufts.edu/sites/default/files/fpan/wp14-relief_1817.pdf, accessed December 2016.

17 Thomas Raffles, *Letters during a Tour through Some Parts of France, Savoy, Switzerland, Germany, and the Netherlands in the Summer of 1817* (Liverpool, 1818), 147–48.

18 Raffles, *Letters*, 160.

19 Louis Simond, *Switzerland; or, A journal of a tour and residence in that country in the years 1817, 1818, and 1819: Followed by an historical sketch of the manners and customs of ancient and modern Helvetia* (Boston: Wells and Lilly, 1822), 1: 7–9.

20 Simond, *Switzerland; or, A journal*, 22.

21 Simond, 52.

22 Simond, 70, 93.

23 See Tinterow, "Géricault's Heroic Landscapes."

24 Henri Savigny and Alexandre Corréard, *Naugrage de la frigate la Méduse faisant partie de l'expédition du Sénégal en 1816 ...* (Paris, November 1817); see Bazin, *Theodore Géricault*, 6: 77–91.

25 The literature on the *Raft of the Medusa* is too abundant to be summarized here. For the author's more extended discussion of the painting, with further references, see Crow, *Emulation*, 279–99.

26 To be explored by Grigsby in her forthcoming *Creole Looking: Portraying France's Foreign Relations in the Nineteenth Century*.

Index

Note: Page numbers in italic type indicate illustrations.

Photography and Copyright Credits

Permission to reproduce illustrations is provided by the owners and sources as listed in the captions. Additional copyright notices and photography credits are as follows. Numbers refer to figure numbers.

Museum purchase, Achenbach Foundation for Graphic Arts purchase, 1974.2.11: 5.12
© Agence La Belle Vie / Réunion des Musées Métropolitains Rouen Normandie: 6.22
Alamy Stock Photo: 3.9
Album / Art Resource, NY: 4.7
Amsterdam Museum: 6.2
Archive Timothy McCarthy / Art Resource, NY: 4.4
© Bayonne, musée Bonnat-Helleu / cliché: A. Vaquero: 6.6
© Beaux-Arts de Paris, Dist. RMN-Grand Palais / Art Resource, NY: 3.16, 3.36, 5.18
© Besançon, musée des beaux-arts et d'archéologie–Photo Pierre GUENAT: 1.9
Bibliothèque nationale de France, département Estampes et photographie, RESERVE QB-370 (50)-FT 4: 4.8
Bibliothèque nationale de France, département Estampes et photographie, RESERVE FOL-QB-201 (158): 4.14
Bibliothèque nationale de France, département Réserve des livres rares, RESAC K-845: 3.32, 3.37, 3.38, 3.48, 3.50, 4.21, 4.22, 4.23
Bibliothèque nationale de France, Philosophie Histoire Sc. Homme, 2003-52587: 6.21
bpk Bildagentur / Alte Nationalgalerie / Klaus Goeken / Art Resource, NY: 3.11, 6.3
bpk Bildagentur / Goethe House and Museum / Art Resource, NY: 3.10
© British Library Board. All Rights Reserved/Bridgeman Images: 1.3
©The Trustees of the British Museum: 4.29
Photo: Brooklyn Museum, 43.81_PS6.jpg: 2.14
Brown Digital Repository. Brown University Library: 2.7
© Christie's Images / Bridgeman Images: 1.2, 4.20
© Cleveland Museum of Art: 5.11
© Colección Fundación Ibercaja. Museo Goya: 2.6
© Fitzwilliam Museum, Cambridge / Art Resource, NY. Photo by Michael Jones: 3.43
Digital image courtesy of the Getty's Open Content Program: 2.18, 5.15
Photography by Erik Gould, courtesy of the Museum of Art, Rhode Island School of Design, Providence: 3.13
Photo: © Blauel Gnamm—ARTOTHEK: 6.18
Gypsotheca e Museo Antonio Canova, Possagno: 4.13, 4.18
Photo: Imaging Department © President and Fellows of Harvard College: 3.39, 5.14, 6.23
KHM-Museumsverband: 4.27
Kimbell Museum, Fort Worth: 5.16
Photograph by Renate Kühling: 4.2
© 2017 Kunsthaus Zürich: 3.33, 3.34, 3.35
© C. Lancien, C. Loisel / Réunion des Musées Métropolitains Rouen Normandie: 3.17
Erich Lessing / Art Resource, NY: 1.6, 1.8, 2.24, 3.15, 6.16
© www.lukasweb.be—Art in Flanders vzw, photo Hugo Maertens: 5.4, 5.5, 5.5a
© Her Majesty Queen Elizabeth II 2017: 4.15, 4.16, 4.17, 4.24, 4.28, 4.28a, 6.14
© Madrid, Museo Nacional del Prado: 2.2, 2.4, 2.5, 2.8, 2.9
© The Metropolitan Museum of Art: 2.3, 6.20
© The Metropolitan Museum of Art. Image source: Art Resource, NY: 5.17
© Montauban, musée Ingres, Cliché Guy Roumagnac, photographe: 6.7

© Montauban, musée Ingres, Cliché Marc Jeanneteau, photographe: 4.1, 6.9, 6.26
Musée des Beaux-Arts de Chambéry: 3.18
© Musée du Louvre, Dist. RMN-Grand Palais / Angèle Dequier / Art Resource, NY: 5.8
© Musée du Louvre, Dist. RMN-Grand Palais / Laurent Chastel / Art Resource, NY: 2.21
© Museum Kunstpalast—H. Maertens—ARTOTHEK: 6.11
© National Gallery, London / Art Resource, NY: 3.12, 6.13
Courtesy National Gallery of Art, Washington: 1.7
Courtesy of the Board of Trustees, National Gallery of Art, Washington: 1.1, 1.7
Photograph courtesy of the National Gallery of Ireland: 4.19
© National Trust: 4.25
Photo: © Nationalmuseum: 3.44
Pierpont Morgan Library Department of Drawings and Prints, New York: 2.19
Portland Art Museum, Gift of James D. Burke in honor of Walker Cahall, 2015.19.1: 3.14
© RMN-Grand Palais / Art Resource, NY: 2.23, 3.42
© RMN-Grand Palais / Art Resource, NY. Photo by Agence Bulloz: 6.19
© RMN-Grand Palais / Art Resource, NY. Photo by Daniel Arnaudet: 6.12
© RMN-Grand Palais / Art Resource, NY. Photo by Daniel Arnaudet / Jean Schormans: 6.17
© RMN-Grand Palais / Art Resource, NY. Photo by Michèle Bellot: 1.4, 2.16, 3.41, 3.41a
© RMN-Grand Palais / Art Resource, NY. Photo by Jean-Gilles Berizzi: 4.5
© RMN-Grand Palais / Art Resource, NY. Photo by Philipp Bernard: 3.49
© RMN-Grand Palais / Art Resource, NY. Photo by Gérard Blot: 2.15, 2.20, 4.3, 4.9, 4.10, 4.12
© RMN-Grand Palais / Art Resource, NY. Photo by Gérard Blot / Christian Jean: 1.5
© RMN-Grand Palais / Art Resource, NY. Photo by Christophe Fouin: 2.10
© RMN-Grand Palais / Art Resource, NY. Photo by Jacques L'Hoir / Jean Popovitch: 6.8
© RMN-Grand Palais / Art Resource, NY. Photo by Thierry Le Mage: 4.11, 5.3
© RMN-Grand Palais / Art Resource, NY. Photo by Hervé Lewandowski: 2.13
© RMN-Grand Palais / Art Resource, NY. Photo by René-Gabriel Ojéda: 5.7
© RMN-Grand Palais / Art Resource, NY. Photo by Franck Raux: 3.2, 4.26
© RMN-Grand Palais / Art Resource, NY. Photo by Michel Urtado: 3.51, 6.24, 6.24a, 6.25
© Roma—Sovrintendenza Capitolina ai Beni Culturali—Museo di Roma: 3.19, 3.20, 3.21, 3.22, 3.23, 3.24, 3.25, 3.26, 3.27, 3.28, 3.29, 3.30, 3.31, 3.40, 3.45, 3.46, 3.47
© The Royal Collection, HM The Queen / Victoria and Albert Museum, London: 6.10
© Royal Museums of Fine Arts of Belgium, Brussels: 6.1
© Royal Museums of Fine Arts of Belgium, Brussels / photo: J. Geleyns - Ro scan: 5.1, 5.2, 6.5
© Scala / Art Resource, NY: 2.12, 4.6
Schloß Schönbrunn Kultur- u. Betriebsges.m.b.H. / Fotograf: Fritz Simak / Sammlung Bundesmobilienverwaltung: 2.1
© Sterling and Francine Clark Art Institute, Williamstown, Massachusetts, USA / Bridgeman Images: 3.1
Photo: ©Tate, London 2017: 6.15

The A. W. Mellon Lectures in the Fine Arts 1952–2018

1952 Jacques Maritain, *Creative Intuition in Art and Poetry*

1953 Sir Kenneth Clark, *The Nude: A Study of Ideal Art* (published as *The Nude: A Study in Ideal Form*, 1956)

1954 Sir Herbert Read, *The Art of Sculpture* (published 1956)

1955 Etienne Gilson, *Art and Reality* (published as *Painting and Reality*, 1957)

1956 E. H. Gombrich, *The Visible World and the Language of Art* (published as *Art and Illusion: A Study in the Psychology of Pictorial Representation*, 1960)

1957 Sigfried Giedion, *Constancy and Change in Art and Architecture* (published as *The Eternal Present: A Contribution on Constancy and Change*, 1962–1964)

1958 Sir Anthony Blunt, *Nicolas Poussin and French Classicism* (published as *Nicolas Poussin*, 1967)

1959 Naum Gabo, *A Sculptor's View of the Fine Arts* (published as *Of Divers Arts*, 1962)

1960 Wilmarth Sheldon Lewis, *Horace Walpole* (published 1960)

1961 André Grabar, *Christian Iconography and the Christian Religion in Antiquity* (published as *Christian Iconography: A Study of Its Origins*, 1968)

1962 Kathleen Raine, *William Blake and Traditional Mythology* (published as *Blake and Tradition*, 1968)

1963 Sir John Pope-Hennessy, *Artist and Individual: Some Aspects of the Renaissance Portrait* (published as *The Portrait in the Renaissance*, 1966)

1964 Jakob Rosenberg, *On Quality in Art: Criteria of Excellence, Past and Present* (published 1967)

1965 Sir Isaiah Berlin, *Sources of Romantic Thought* (published as *The Roots of Romanticism*, 1999)

1966 Lord David Cecil, *Dreamer or Visionary: A Study of English Romantic Painting* (published as *Visionary and Dreamer: Two Poetic Painters, Samuel Palmer and Edward Burne-Jones*, 1969)

1967 Mario Praz, *On the Parallel of Literature and the Visual Arts* (published as *Mnemosyne: The Parallel between Literature and the Visual Arts*, 1970)

1968 Stephen Spender, *Imaginative Literature and Painting*

1969 Jacob Bronowski, *Art as a Mode of Knowledge* (published as *The Visionary Eye: Essays in the Arts, Literature, and Science*, 1978)

1970 Sir Nikolaus Pevsner, *Some Aspects of Nineteenth-Century Architecture* (published as *A History of Building Types*, 1976)

1971 T. S. R. Boase, *Vasari: The Man and the Book* (published as *Giorgio Vasari: The Man and the Book*, 1979)

1972 Ludwig H. Heydenreich, *Leonardo da Vinci*

1973 Jacques Barzun, *The Use and Abuse of Art* (published 1974)

1974 H. W. Janson, *Nineteenth-Century Sculpture Reconsidered* (published as *The Rise and Fall of the Public Monument*)

1975 H. C. Robbins Landon, *Music in Europe in the Year 1776*

1976 Peter von Blanckenhagen, *Aspects of Classical Art*

1977 André Chastel, *The Sack of Rome: 1527* (published 1982)

1978 Joseph W. Alsop, *The History of Art Collecting* (published as *The Rare Art Traditions: The History of Art Collecting and Its Linked Phenomena Wherever These Have Appeared*, 1982)

1979 John Rewald, *Cézanne and America* (published as *Cézanne and America: Dealers, Collectors, Artists, and Critics, 1891–1921*, 1989)

1980 Peter Kidson, *Principles of Design in Ancient and Medieval Architecture*

1981 John Harris, *Palladian Architecture in England, 1615–1760*

1982 Leo Steinberg, *The Burden of Michelangelo's Painting*

1983 Vincent Scully, *The Shape of France* (published as *Architecture: The Natural and the Manmade*)

1984 Richard Wollheim, *Painting as an Art* (published 1987)

1985 James S. Ackerman, *The Villa in History* (published as *The Villa: Form and Ideology of Country Houses*, 1990)

1986 Lukas Foss, *Confessions of a Twentieth-Century Composer*

1987 Jaroslav Pelikan, *Imago Dei: The Byzantine Apologia for Icons* (published 1990)

1988 John Shearman, *Art and the Spectator in the Italian Renaissance* (published as *Only Connect: Art and the Spectator in the Italian Renaissance*, 1992)

1989 Oleg Grabar, *Intermediary Demons: Toward a Theory of Ornament* (published as *The Mediation of Ornament*, 1992)

1990 Jennifer Montagu, *Gold, Silver, and Bronze: Metal Sculpture of the Roman Baroque* (published 1996)

1991 Willibald Sauerländer, *Changing Faces: Art and Physiognomy through the Ages*

1992 Anthony Hecht, *The Laws of the Poetic Art* (published as *On the Laws of the Poetic Art*, 1995)

1993 John Boardman, *The Diffusion of Classical Art in Antiquity* (published 1994)

1994 Jonathan Brown, *Kings and Connoisseurs: Collecting Art in Seventeenth-Century Europe* (published 1995)

1995 Arthur C. Danto, *Contemporary Art and the Pale of History* (published as *After the End of Art: Contemporary Art and the Pale of History*, 1997)

1996 Pierre M. Rosenberg, *From Drawing to Painting: Poussin, Watteau, Fragonard, David, Ingres* (published as *From Drawing to Painting: Poussin, Watteau, Fragonard, David, and Ingres*, 2000)

1997 John Golding, *Paths to the Absolute* (published as *Paths to the Absolute: Mondrian, Malevich, Kandinsky, Pollock, Newman, Rothko, and Still*, 2000)

1998 Lothar Ledderose, *Ten Thousand Things: Module and Mass Production in Chinese Art* (published 2000)

1999 Carlo Bertelli, *Transitions*

2000 Marc Fumaroli, *The Quarrel between the Ancients and the Moderns in the Arts, 1600–1715*

2001 Salvatore Settis, *Giorgione and Caravaggio: Art as Revolution*

2002 Michael Fried, *The Moment of Caravaggio* (published 2010)

2003 Kirk Varnedoe, *Pictures of Nothing: Abstract Art since Pollock* (published 2006)

2004 Irving Lavin, *More than Meets the Eye*

2005 Irene J. Winter, *"Great Work": Terms of Aesthetic Experience in Ancient Mesopotamia*

2006 Simon Schama, *Really Old Masters: Age, Infirmity, and Reinvention*

2007 Helen Vendler, *Last Looks, Last Books: The Binocular Poetry of Death* (published as *Last Looks, Last Books: Stevens, Plath, Lowell, Bishop, Merrill*, 2010)

2008 Joseph Leo Koerner, *Bosch and Bruegel: Parallel Worlds* (published as *Bosch and Bruegel: From Enemy Painting to Everyday Life*, 2016)

2009 T. J. Clark, *Picasso and Truth* (published as *Picasso and Truth: From Cubism to Guernica*, 2013)

2010 Mary Miller, *Art and Representation in the Ancient New World*

2011 Mary Beard, *The Twelve Caesars: Images of Power from Ancient Rome to Salvador Dalí*

2012 Craig Clunas, *Chinese Painting and Its Audiences* (published 2017)

2013 Barry Bergdoll, *Out of Site in Plain View: A History of Exhibiting Architecture since 1750*

2014 Anthony Grafton, *Past Belief: Visions of Early Christianity in Renaissance and Reformation Europe*

2015 Thomas Crow, *Restoration as Event and Idea: Art in Europe, 1814–1820* (published as *Restoration: The Fall of Napoleon in the Course of European Art, 1812–1820*, 2018)

2016 Vidya Dehejia, *The Thief Who Stole My Heart: The Material Life of Chola Bronzes in South India, c. 855–1280*

2017 Alexander Nemerov, *The Forest: America in the 1830s*

2018 Hal Foster, *Positive Barbarism: Brutal Aesthetics in the Postwar Period*